AF348620

In My Nature

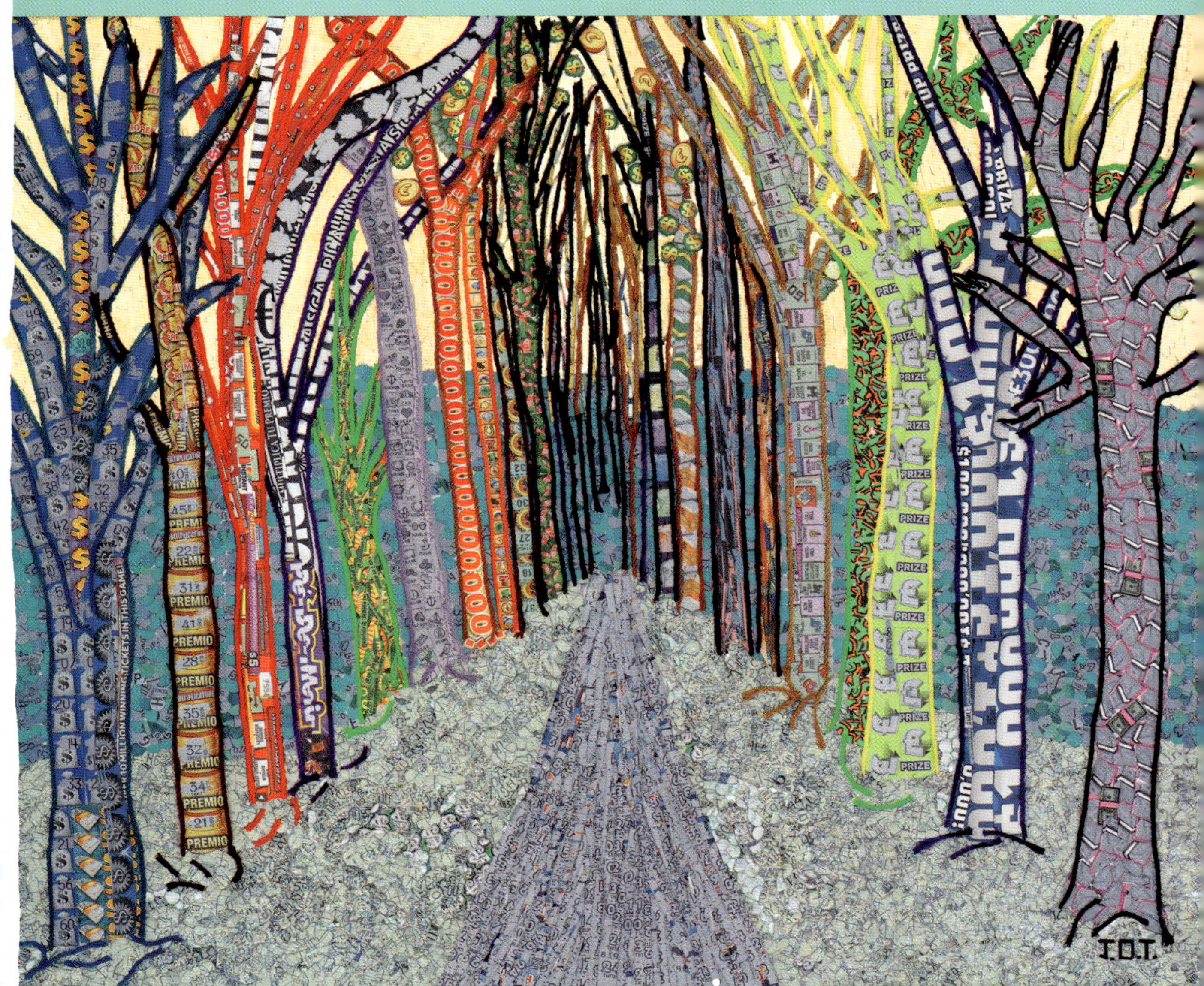

HERBERT PRESS

Bloomsbury Publishing Plc

50 Bedford Square, London, WC1B 3DP, UK

29 Earlsfort Terrace, Dublin 2, Ireland

Bloomsbury, Herbert Press and the Herbert Press logo are trademarks of Bloomsbury Publishing PLC

First published in Great Britain in 2025

A catalogue record for this book is available from the British Library.

Library of Congress Cataloguing-in-data has been applied for.

ISBN: 9781789942200; eBook: 9781789942217

2 4 6 8 10 9 7 5 3 1

Design by Jeremy Goldie Graphic Design

Printed and bound in China by RR Donnelley Asia Printing Solutions Limited

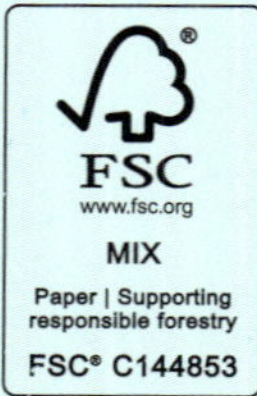

To find out more about our authors and books, visit www.bloomsbury.com and sign up for our newsletters

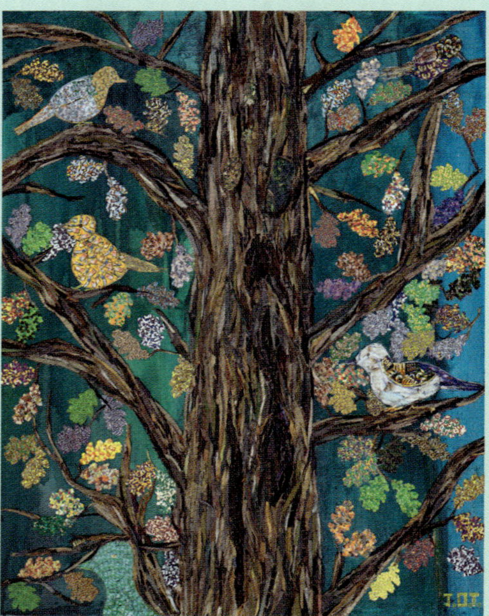

Page 1 image: *James photographed an avenue of trees at Thorp Perrow Arboretum near Bedale, North Yorkshire, where he had once volunteered with the gardening team. Using a selection of colourful scratchcards, he has created* Woodland Magic, *which invites you to take a quiet walk along a magical path and let your imagination take you where it will.*

Page 2 image: *Árbol de la Vida (Tree of Life) (See page 143).*

Page 3 image: *Durham Cathedral is collaged entirely from scratchcards, with glitter varnish used in the sky.*

Image credits: *All images are copyright James Owen Thomas unless otherwise stated.*

EDITOR'S NOTE: One of the aims of this book in detailing different stages of James' life is to give encouragement to other parents of children with autism.

We hope that readers will understand the use of the various 'voices' in the book and that this will aid their appreciation of the different aspects of James' life and work.

In My Nature

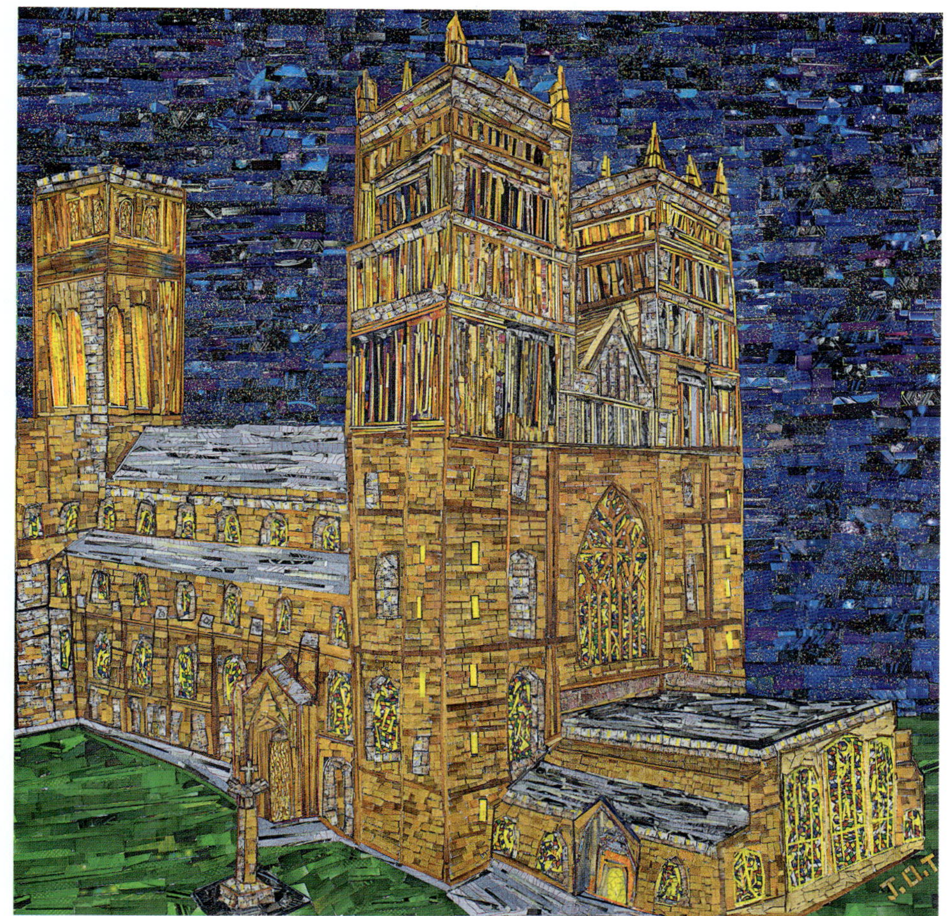

Sustainable Art and Autism

James Owen Thomas

HERBERT PRESS

LONDON · OXFORD · NEW YORK · NEW DELHI · SYDNEY

CONTENTS

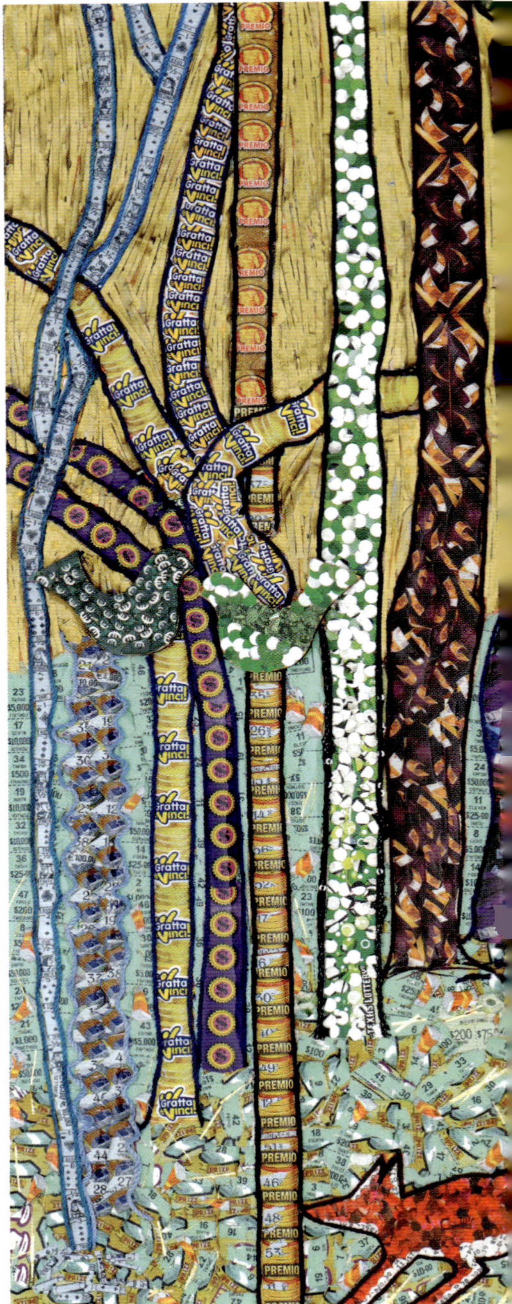

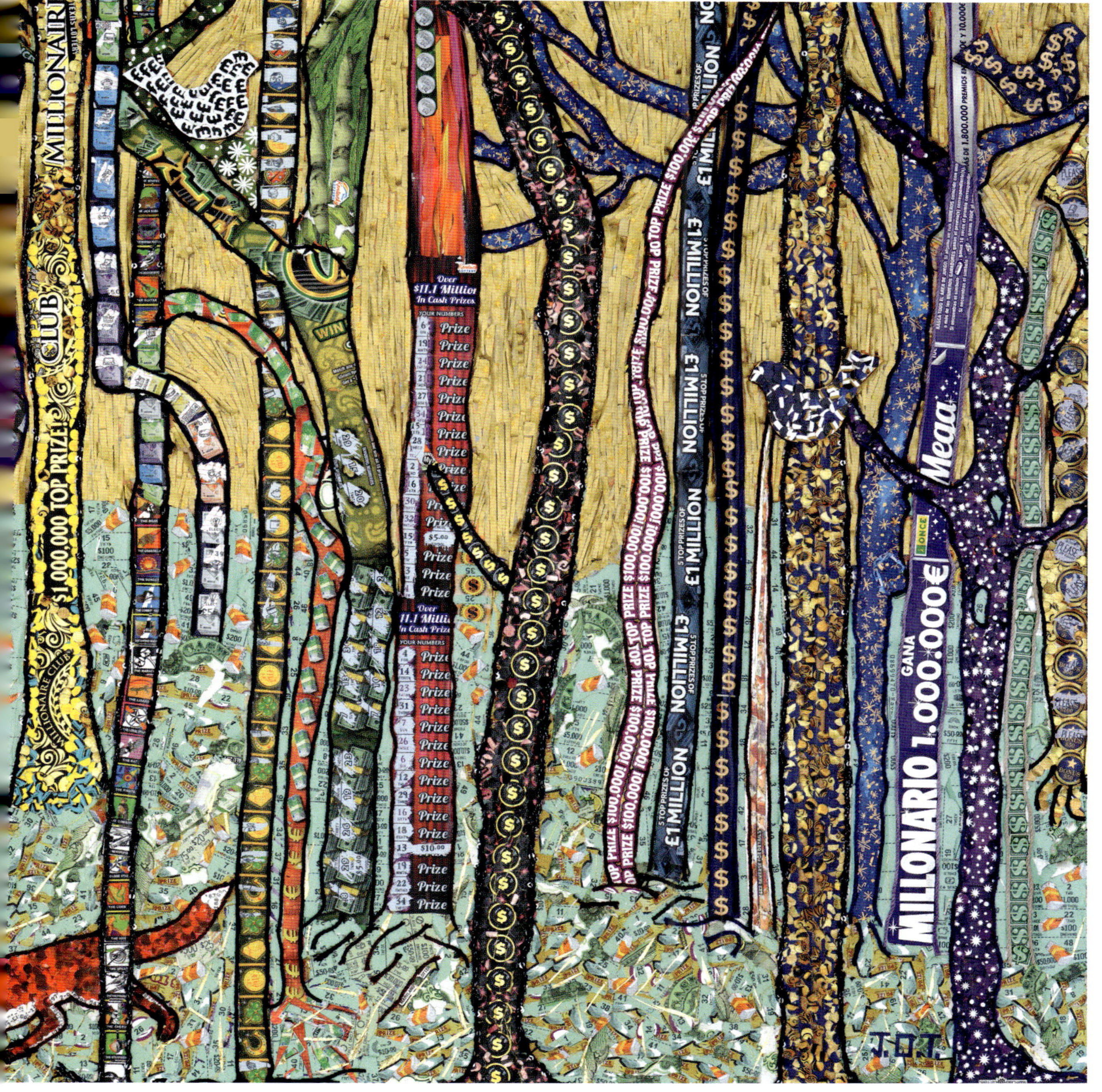

Reconnecting with Nature is one of James' best-known and loved scratchcard collages, using many of the techniques explained in the book, including bank notes for the woodland floor, various symbols and motifs applied to particular trees, gold strips for the sky, black threads for definition, and a fleeting fox depicted with hole-punched shades of red and white.

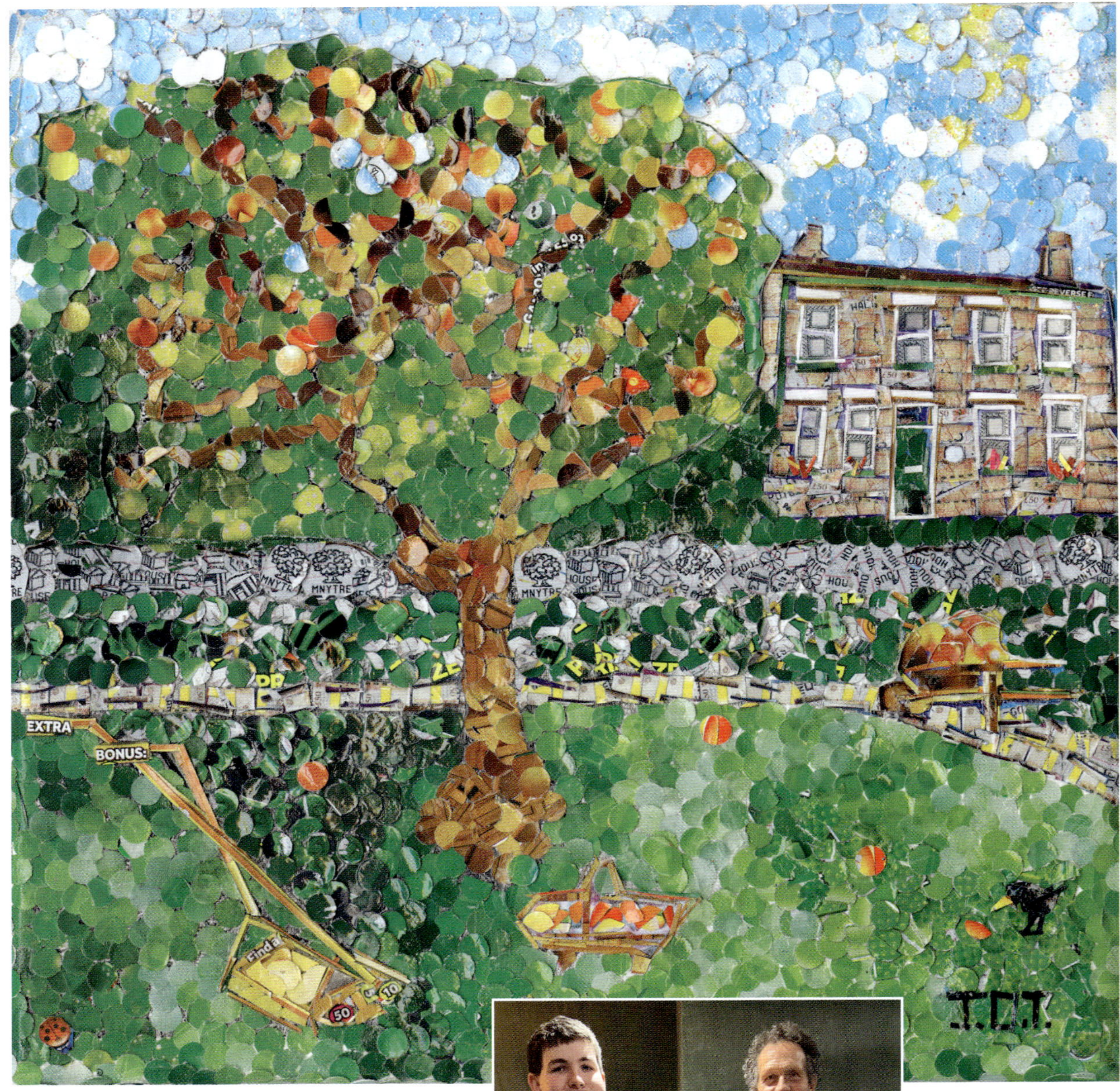

▲ *The artwork presented to Monty Don.*

▶ *Monty Don with James Owen Thomas at the Harrogate Convention Centre, 2022.*

first saw James' work via a short film that we made for *Gardeners' World*. The nature of the programme is that we focused on the horticultural side of James' artwork and the inspiration behind it but from what I could see on the screen there was something very special being created. Yes, he was a young man that was neurodiverse and yes, the short film was heartwarming and unusual but much more importantly it was apparent to me that he was an artist and a very good one.

That his artwork is composed of the detritus and waste that most of us create and abandon – all too often carelessly as litter – adds a layer of fascination and complexity that enriches his work and our appreciation of it. But it does not define it, let alone somehow make it more worthy – God forbid.

James' work is worthy and enriching because it is good art. Clearly this is open to interpretation and opinion, but I am very happy to stand up and be counted on this. Some of this is because he is a fine artist and some because his view of the world is idiosyncratic and formed from experiences that most of us do not share, or at least not in the same way. But the result is something that all of us can recognise, draw upon and be enriched by.

When I saw that film on *Gardeners' World* I said on camera that I liked his work, James contacted me and we met when I was giving a talk at Harrogate and James gave me a much-treasured picture. He said then that there was talk of a book and now here it is – looking wonderful and giving an opportunity for many more people to see much more of his work.

But James is young. He is only beginning. Really good art enlarges our world but it can only come from a life devoted to creation with an intensity that few of us can comprehend, let alone produce. James is blessed with the gift of that devotion and as long as he transforms his world through his unique vision into work that we can share then this strange, difficult world is made better for all of us.

Monty Don

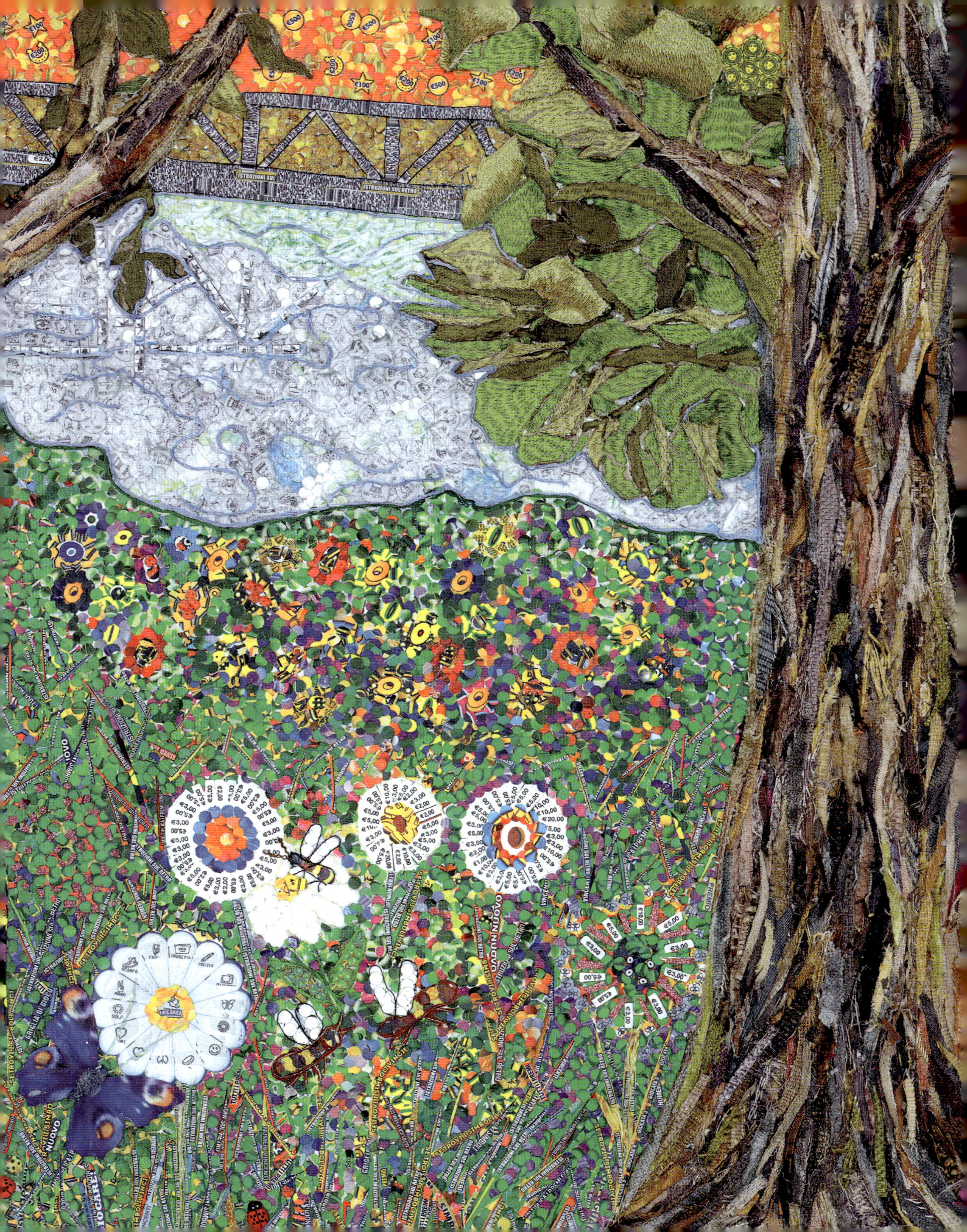

INTRODUCTION

I felt pleased to have been contacted by Bloomsbury Publishing's craft team at Herbert Press after my appearance on BBC *Gardener's World,* when I spoke of how being out in nature is not only calming but gives me ideas for my art. People seem to like my story and why I started making collages from discarded scratchcards. I'm glad my art can also make others feel happy.

When I was younger, my autism used to cause all kinds of learning and communication problems. However, now I am able to stand up in front of groups and talk about my art and interests in the environment. I speak about being a 'Force for Nature' Ambassador for The Tree Council and, because of this, I was invited to 10 Downing Street and to COP26 Glasgow as a 'One Step Greener' Ambassador. My art has given me a voice.

I would like to thank everyone who has helped me write this book, including Russell, the editor, for all his guidance and support and Andonis Georgiou for his input with the writing. I would have found it difficult to put everything into words. I hope my message comes across through my art instead!

I also want to mention Pat, a special friend I made when I was about four years old who was the manager of the amusement and outdoor activity centre of Paradise Park, Newhaven. When I was told that he sadly died at the beginning of 2024, I thought back to the times I used to look forward to seeing him every Sunday morning for some years. Because of my limited speech when I was very young, my name for him was 'Man', later becoming 'Pat Man'. He didn't mind and we became good friends. He was a grand-father-figure to me as my own grandad died when I was only three years old.

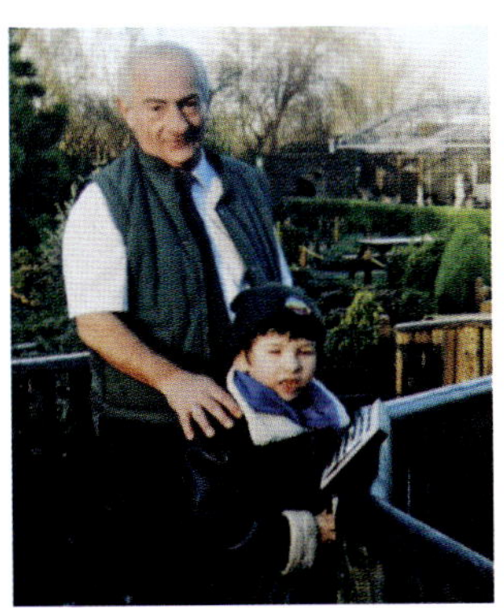

▲ *Pat Man and Robin – the dynamic duo.*

◀ ***The Garden Bridge*** *made from Italian scratch-cards, sold to Jim Knowles in the USA.*

Pat and I didn't need many words to communicate. He was only too pleased to let me collect litter with him at the amusement park when I arrived there early to help him. We used litter-pickers to clear all areas of the gardens and a special friendship developed between us. He knew I was enthusiastic to help and we used to look at the nature in the gardens together. He said we were like the dynamic duo – 'Pat Man and Robin'! Pat and I kept in touch over the years through Paradise Park. He was told in 2023 that I wanted to include his name in my book. I think he would have been happy to know I will always remember him and that he deserves being here in my introduction. The encouragement he gave me will not be forgotten.

Sticking pictures into books has always been a favourite way of mine to learn and remember. Art then became my best friend when I was at secondary school and college and it has stayed that way ever since.

James Owen Thomas

INTERVIEW WITH THE ARTIST

How did you first become interested in nature?

Nature has been something I've found very therapeutic for as far back as I can remember. As an autistic child, I had difficulty expressing my thoughts and emotions verbally, but I learned visually by watching the birds and looking at the trees in our local park, where I enjoyed feeding the ducks in the pond. And in a world that didn't make any sense to me, it was very comforting to be so close to nature and its beauty. I would get very annoyed if I saw litter strewn on the ground and feel the need to clear it up and put it in the bin. That was the beginning of a life-long habit and the discarded items I find now are recycled in my art.

I also enjoyed visits to the seaside, but my mother less so as she had to stop me throwing stones at people. And having once jumped in the lake in a park, I was clearly a high-risk liability on the beach as well!

How did your love of art come about?

When I was a small child, my mother used to take me to The Towner Art Gallery in Old Town, Eastbourne as she realised it calmed me down. By looking at art on the wall, no matter what the subject, I would become physically more relaxed and it also stopped me from yelling and screaming. When I started special school aged 4½ in Hastings, pictures were an important part of my communication and learning and even the timetable used illustrations. A PECS (Picture Exchange Communication System) was used on Velcro strips and, as I moved through the day, a picture was torn off to show what was to be done next. This visual representation of the day ahead provided predictability and helped reduce anxiety. The symbols improved communication without relying on speech and I also used pictures and symbols to ask for things.

So yes, it was visits to the gallery and the use of the PECS system at school that stimulated my interest in art and it developed from there.

How has being on the autism spectrum influenced your work as an artist?

My need for order, neatness and precision is a trait of my autism, which comes from how I want control over my environment. My fascination with colour, illustrations, pictures and nature from a very early age developed my ability to express myself creatively as an artist.

I am told that autistic people often see the world differently. I struggled being in class at secondary school and college from the age of 15 to 20 when living in Yorkshire. I found it difficult to communicate and socialise with other young people. Having autism was clearly directing my learning and interest towards art.

How did you become involved with scratchcards?

I first started to enjoy collecting bus tickets, then train tickets and eventually scratchcards. When I was 14, I remember seeing a scratchcard floating in a puddle and was fascinated by the bright colours. I took it home, dried it out and kept it in

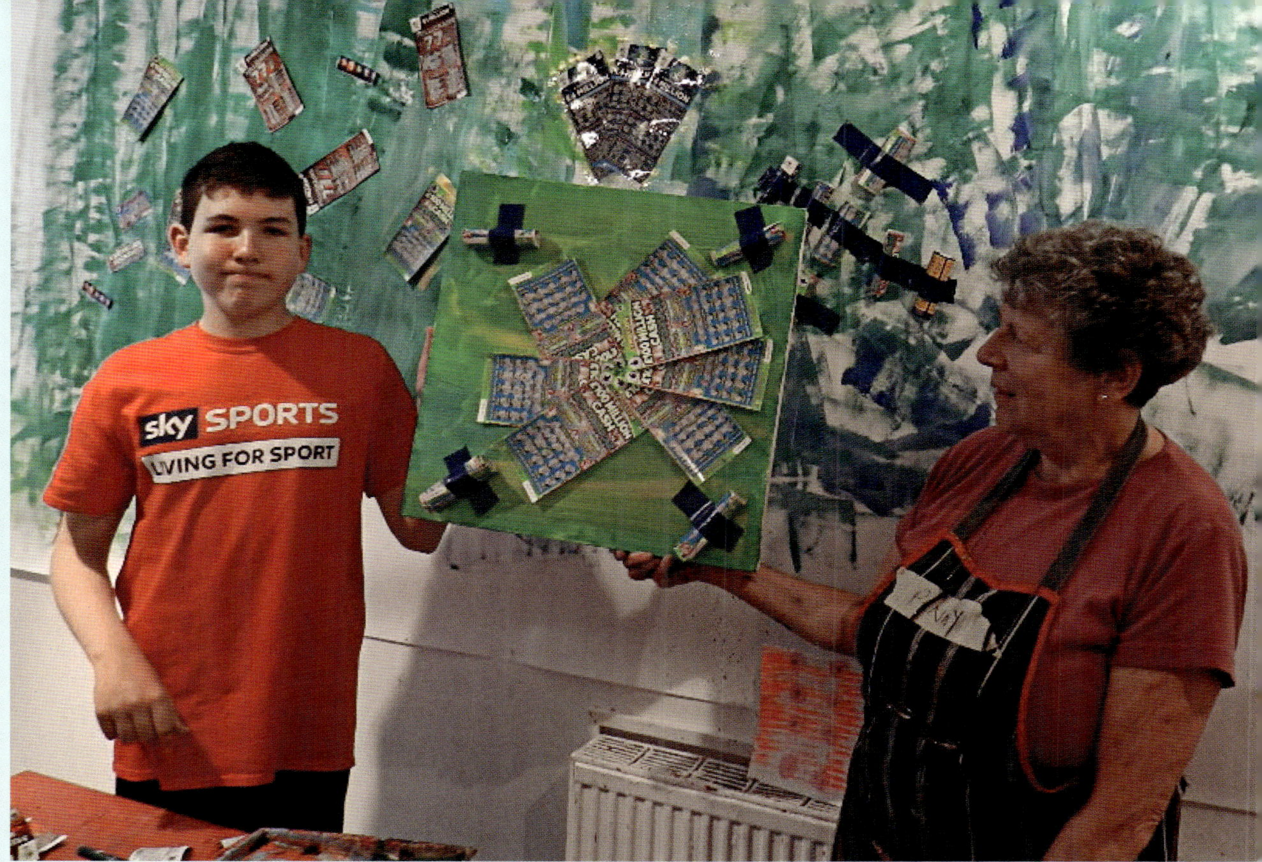

▲ *James with Penny Hobson and an early collection of his scratchcards.*

a box. This started a new interest and I collected more whenever I saw them. I began to wonder why some people threw them on the ground rather than putting them in a bin. Of course, I never liked to see them lying there so would pick them up and save them for my collages. Using scratchcards for art wasn't something that I think had ever been done before, a fact the National Lottery confirmed when I was 16 and visited their offices.

I now receive lottery scratchcards from all over the world but haven't yet found a winning ticket to make me a millionaire!

What is it about collage in particular that appealed to you?

As a very young child, if I found something particularly colourful and interesting, I would tear it out of a magazine or leaflet and stick it in a scrapbook. Anything would go in: tickets, pictures, price tags, bits of packaging etc.

Using pieces of scratchcards to create art became an extension of this and I realise now that I am creating a style that is very much my own.

How does your autism help you with your work?

Creating a collage needs lots of patience. First of all, the pieces must be sorted by colour and size and if I wish to add texture, then I add fabric. My materials are all carefully sorted in containers and boxes. I have my own ways of organising my materials and I tell people that I 'like to create order out of disorder'.

And how does your work help you with your autism?

The concentration required for my artwork helps me shut out the problems around me. The processes involved are somehow comforting to me and the repetitive nature of it is reassuring. My art also helps in my conversation with others as it's a topic I find easy to talk about.

Does your autism hinder your artistic work in any ways, and how do you overcome that?

Although I understand the value of my art in coping with stress, I realise that it can also create some problems. Having to keep checking and rechecking things slows me down. I find it very hard to know when a collage is complete, often worrying over a minor detail. It's then that I may need reassurance that it is finished.

Who are the artists you admire most and why?

I very much admire David Hockney's work and, since the age of 11, I have enjoyed visits to the World Heritage Site of Saltaire to see his art on display at Salts Mill (see page 130). He has achieved so much during his lifetime and has been able to adapt himself to using technology. I love his use of bright colours, especially in his nature and tree artwork.

What are your proudest moments?

Aged 18, I was asked to create artwork for our town's entry in the Britain in Bloom competition in 2019 and I was pleased to receive an award for doing this from Baroness Floella Benjamin at the Royal Horticultural Society headquarters in

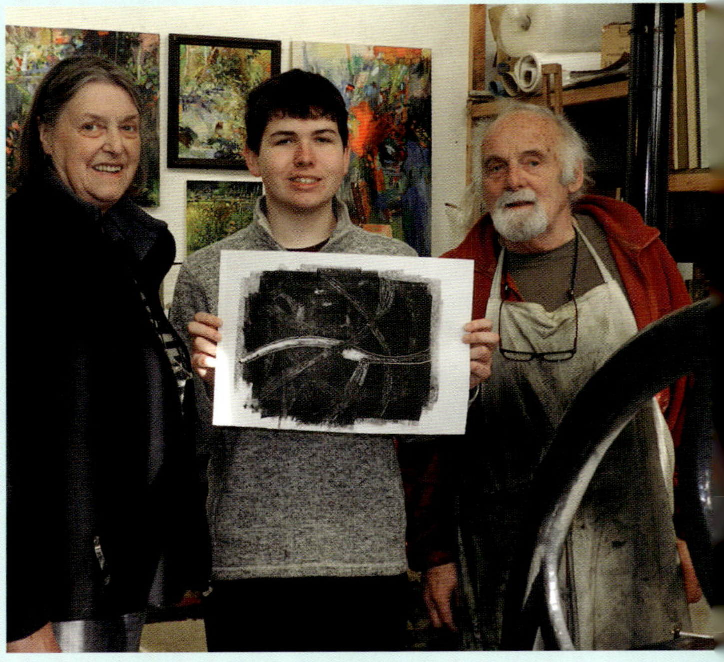

▲ *Printmaking with David and Heather Cook.*

London. The artwork I created for the event is still visible on planters in our town of Pateley Bridge in North Yorkshire.

In 2020, at the age of 19, I became involved with The Tree Council, which appointed me as one of their Force for Nature ambassadors; young people who speak up for trees and the natural world in an effort to help protect our planet threatened by climate change and man-made disasters. A year later, I was nominated by The Tree Council to become a COP26 One Step Greener Ambassador. With this position I was invited not only to meet the Prime Minister at 10 Downing Street, but also to visit the COP26 Climate Change Conference in Glasgow.

Through my contact with The Tree Council I received an invitation to be interviewed by JJ Chalmers on *Gardeners' World*. I was so pleased later to meet Monty Don when he spoke at the

Harrogate Convention Centre in December 2022. In 2022, an opportunity came up to rent a gallery space for a year in Pateley Bridge. It gave me good experience of displaying my artwork, dealing with the public and arranging other artists' exhibitions in the gallery. It had three spacious exhibition rooms where I could show my original artwork, prints, cards, coasters and tea towels.

The fact that I'm now teaching others about my collage art makes me feel very proud. I have certainly gained confidence in speaking publicly about art, autism and the environment. I've also been able to help the Caudwell Children's Charity and Alzheimer's Society by donating original collages, raising £20,000 and £10,000 respectively to support their work. I also use my workshops for charitable fundraising events including for the National Autistic Society and Maggie's Cancer Support.

What advice would you give to neurodivergent people?

Whenever I am asked this question, I can only advise what I have found helpful from my own experience. I began volunteering for the National Trust when I was 14 and this was very important to me. I used to fill the bird feeders in the hide area at Fountains Abbey and carried out survey reports at Brimham Rocks (see page 88), a natural landscape near Harrogate famous for its ancient rock formations. I used to enjoy talking to the visitors and this helped build my confidence. These National Trust sites were also where I first had my art exhibitions.

What advice would you give anyone wanting to become an artist?

I would say that it is helpful to talk to established artists. I was fortunate enough to have a mentor, Penny Hobson, who is a beachcombing artist in East Sussex. We have known each other for many years and still keep in touch. She gave me help and support when I was at school and college.

When I was at Bradford School of Art, I also gained some valuable work experience with David and Heather Cook in North Yorkshire, who invited me to learn printmaking in their studio. My main advice is to continue the type of art that interests you and makes you happy. And keep talking to other artists.

How do you think art can help the environmental cause?

As my art is based on collage with recycled materials, it makes people think more about the earth's resources and the damage by excessive waste and single-use, non-recyclable, non-biodegradable items. The environmental damage being inflicted on our beautiful planet is a global issue with more and more people taking to the streets to demonstrate and demand action to stop it from continuing.

I am concerned too but, rather than protest on the streets surrounded by crowds, I prefer to express my feelings and concerns through my art.

How do you see your future?

I hope to travel overseas in the coming years so that new experiences and places will help influence my art. I also want to continue expressing my concern for the environment and speaking up for people with disabilities.

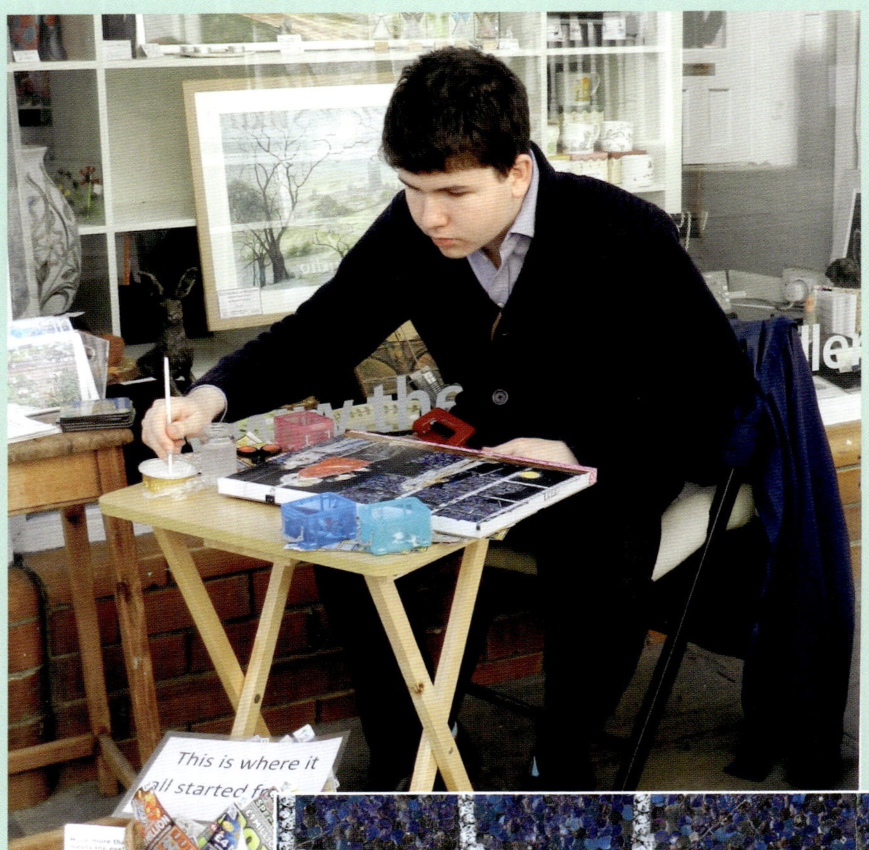

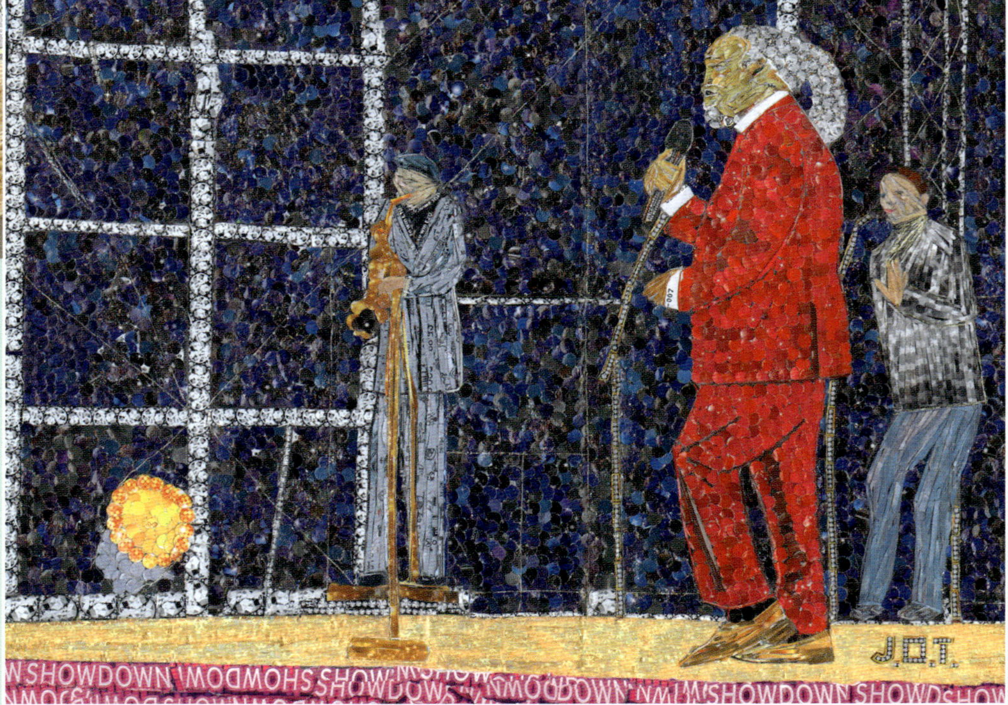

▲ James works on a collage of Billy Ocean, who he had seen in concert at Pontefract Races.

CHAPTER 1

Autism and Art

JAMES' EARLY LIFE
By his mother, Jane Thomas

James was born on Easter Monday 2001 at Eastbourne District General Hospital, several weeks premature. Although I didn't feel prepared, I was relieved to have given birth to such a healthy-looking baby boy. But my abiding memory was hearing his persistent, high-pitched screams echoing along the corridors of the hospital at night. James wouldn't keep awake during the day, a time when I found it almost impossible to rest with the noise on the ward. When the nurses tried to settle him in the nursery at night to give me some rest, he'd stay awake and cry hysterically until he was back with me again.

We stayed four nights in hospital as James developed jaundice and was the first baby to try out their new special heated cot in the hospital.

However much I tried, James' crying proved an impossible pattern to break. He would scream and clench his fists in anger or frustration, fiercely resisting my attempts to straighten his fingers. Health visitors advised me to leave him to cry himself to sleep, but that didn't work. It became too upsetting for both of us. James clearly needed help and I was at the end of my tether.

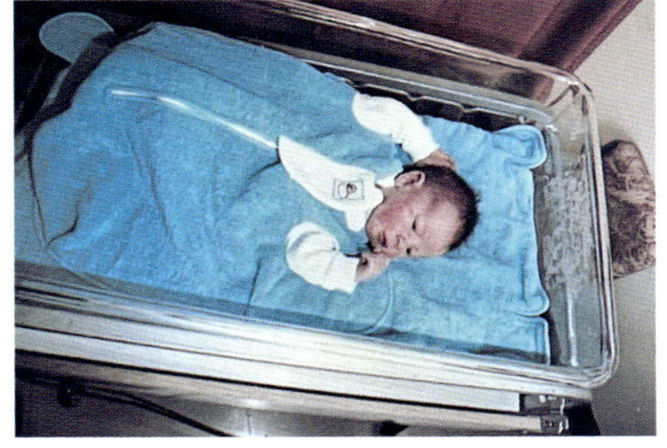

▼ *James in his heated cot.*

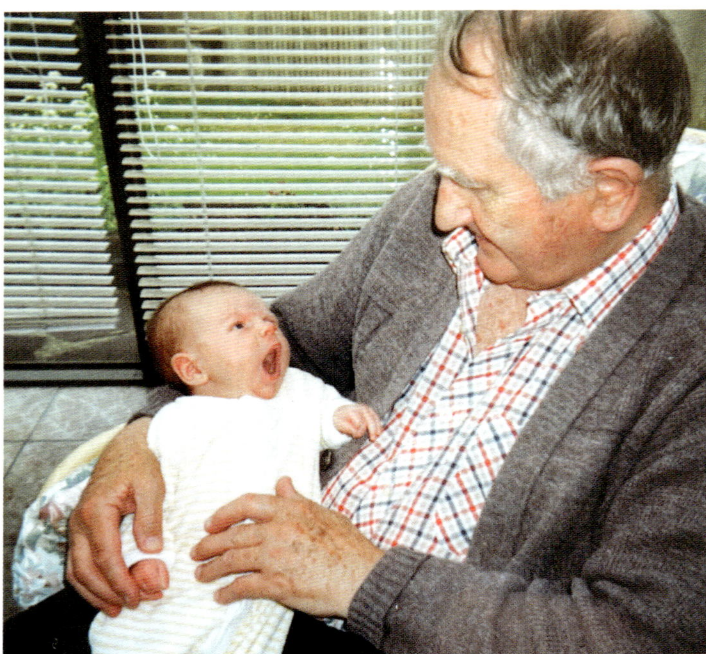

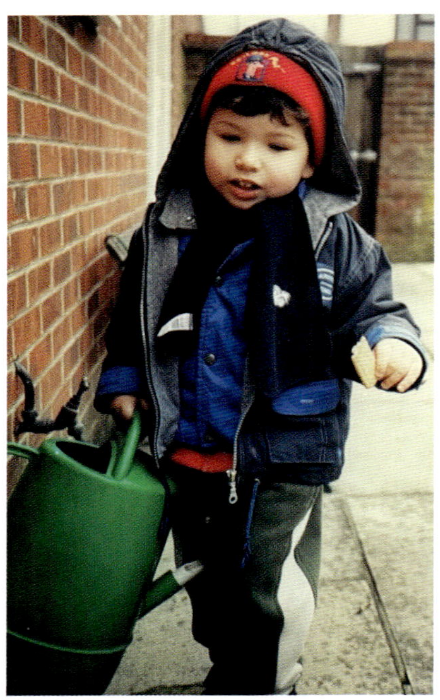

I'd no idea then that James' need to be swaddled and held tightly was due to a dairy and gluten intolerance, which gave him terrible stomach pains. It wasn't until some years later that his inability to digest certain foods was professionally diagnosed and his diet reassessed.

James was unusual in that he preferred to lie flat in his pram rather than sit up like other babies but he was fascinated by the colours and patterns on the fabric inside the pram. As a single mother juggling my job of running a translation agency as well as the needs of a hyperactive, unpredictable, demanding little boy, I welcomed the peace and quiet when he fell asleep in his pram. I would rush home from our walk to do my work, because if he woke up he would be constantly demanding my attention and screaming if the telephone rang.

Whenever James became restless, I'd take him to the park where he'd enjoy the sights and sounds of nature and also feeding the ducks. He found solace there away from everything that made him tense: electric lighting, computers, strange noises, traffic and too many people rushing around. Spending time in our garden, watering plants and flowers also helped James.

Instead of crawling, he would bounce up and down on the floor on his bottom, getting frustrated that he could not move very far. However, he did manage to reach a significant milestone and took his first steps around the correct time, just after his first birthday. It wasn't long afterwards that

▲◄ James with his grandfather, Peter.

▲ Filling a watering can in the garden.

he clambered onto the settee, using it as a trampoline. Oblivious to anyone telling him to stop, James would bounce with his arm stretched up straight into the air, keeping it in his sight and laughing hysterically. Then after this repetitive game, his mood became sullen, kicking and screaming on the settee or floor.

As a mother, I felt increasingly frustrated as I wanted my son to be happy, but in between the tears and tantrums, there were moments when he returned my love in his own special way and gave me hope. Sometimes he would pull me by my hand to stretch out on the carpet with him to enter his secret world and explore every angle of the mantlepiece and also under the table. If only for a short time, everything became peaceful away from the muddle and confusion of everyday life, where he felt nobody understood his needs. I didn't always understand him, but I tried my best.

Although James continued to display psychological, emotional and behavioural problems, he was physically strong, so doctors were not unduly concerned and simply dismissed it as the 'terrible twos'. But even when he was three, he was still running around in circles late at night, banging his face with his hands, bumping into furniture and throwing things around, endangering himself and others. He once threw a shoe in a fit of rage at a therapist's head. She was clearly hurt, but managed to calm him down by holding him tight.

On our first hospital appointment to discuss James' anti-social behaviour and the difficulty taking him anywhere, he ran around the doctor's room, tried to ransack his briefcase, turned taps on and off, pulled drawers open and repeatedly tried to escape until they locked the door. The doctor sat passively throughout as if nothing was happening and prescribed iron tablets for him!

I asked to see a different doctor and, six months later, it was finally acknowledged that there was a serious problem. After an EEG test for epilepsy, which thankfully proved negative, James later received a diagnosis of autism. I was in shock for several weeks and felt desperate as my father was seriously ill with cancer at the time and he died the following year. James' diagnosis seemed like the beginning of another end.

I knew little about autism, but being told that there was nothing I could do but join a support group made me even more determined to research this lifelong developmental disability. And if it was going to affect how he communicated and interacted with the world, I needed to find out what I could do to help him.

Whenever we were out in public, James' behaviour attracted disapproving glances implying I was a terrible parent with no control over my child.

But I was determined he should have the same experiences as so-called 'normal' children and not be kept at home, shielded from the outside world. I avoided shopping centres, where James would scream the place down, but he enjoyed visiting parks and The Towner Art Gallery in Eastbourne. He completely calmed down the moment we entered the building and gazed at the pictures no matter what their subject, absorbing the colours, shapes and textures of the art on the wall in wonderment. It provided a safe space for us both and it was a relief to be able to escape the panic and pandemonium of life outside.

Life revolved around routines – James disliked new places, different situations, too many people around him, and high levels of activity and noise would make him extremely anxious.

As James had received a formal diagnosis of autism, the local council allowed him Early Years support followed by a place at a special school. If he had been made to attend mainstream school, they understood James would have been unable to sit still for even a few minutes. He lacked concentration and would flit from one activity to another. He clearly needed specialised help in a quiet learning environment.

I wasn't really expecting him to change, although I never gave up hope that maybe one day James would show some sort of affection towards me, especially when he went off to school. He always seemed happy when he

▼◀ *A peaceful woodland walk.*

▼ *Enjoying a ride on a miniature railway with his mother.*

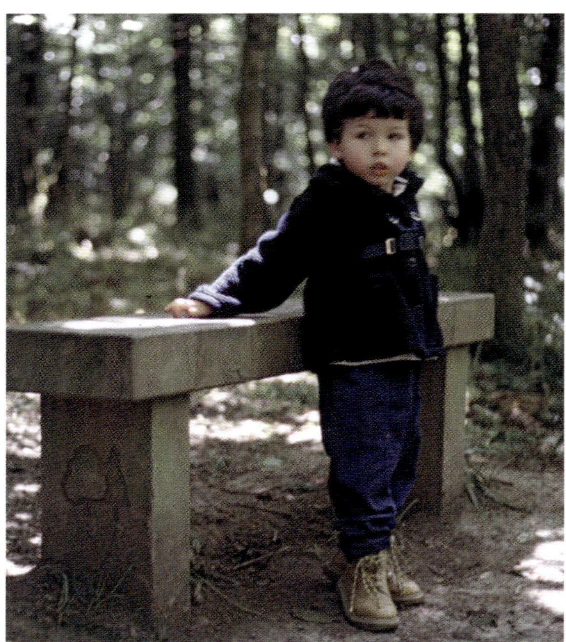

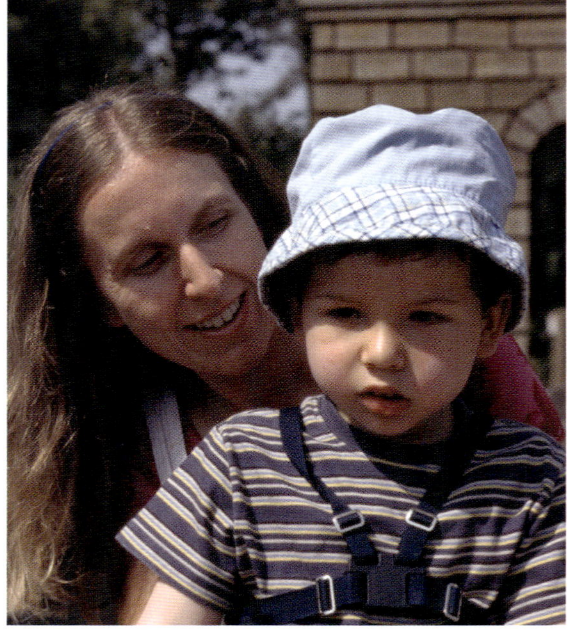

came back home, though, and we continued with his special interests whilst still living in East Sussex. He always felt at peace during our woodland walks.

James was not keen to play in playgrounds like other children of his age but always wanted to walk around the sides and edges of parks to do our best to clear litter. I always took carrier bags with us as we separated items for recycling from the litter. This stage lasted for a number of years and James' interest in recycling never disappeared.

At around five to seven years old, James continued to feel upset by bright lights, sounds and numbers of people in supermarkets, but he wanted to organise trolleys, lining them up to tidy them. It showed a sense of order in his mind. After this came his fixation on gathering coupons in shops, which he would take home to save. As well as coupons, James liked collecting bus tickets – our own and other people's that were left behind on buses (see page 140).

By the time James was six, I had already started to look around for alternative schooling. I knew James was beginning to make progress and had proved he could carry out certain tasks perfectly well, so there was no need to repeat them as was happening so often at school. He seemed bored and frustrated, needing more encouragement to learn. With his Statement of Special Needs Education (now Education Health Care Plan), it was clear that he would benefit from a calmer learning environment and therapy support.

I decided to take James to another special school for an assessment as I'd heard many positive things about its method of teaching and therapy and he joined just before his seventh birthday. After a few months, therapists said that while James was moving forward with his attention and listening skills, they were concerned that his high levels of anxiety were inhibiting his ability to concentrate. It was confirmed in an independent report that James also had sensory processing dysfunction, where the brain has problems processing sensory information. It is now called Sensory Processing Disorder (SPD).

Despite this, I remained positive as I felt more encouraged about James' future, realising how much progress he was making in his education and with his health.

For many years, with a view to improving his SPD, James attended art courses at Project Art Works in Hastings, a collaborative organisation that addresses the complex support needs of neurodivergent people. Each workspace there, whether in a corner of the art room or an outbuilding in the garden, became a sensory place of colour and texture for James. He felt happy there and became more focused on his art.

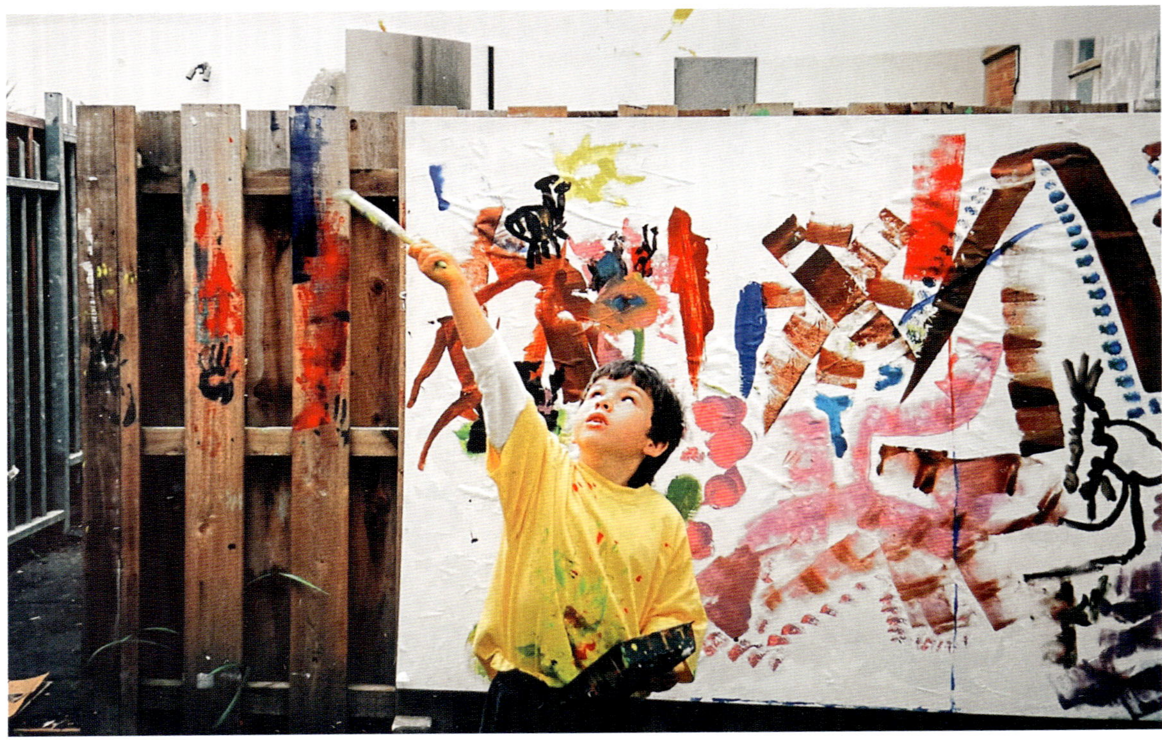

When he was in his final year of junior school in Otley, James would tell his teaching assistant all about his passion for buses. It was evident he still needed to be in his own world of structure and predictability, which involved regularly going out on buses at weekends. He was keen to discover new places and enjoy new experiences, visiting museums and art galleries where he would take part in art and craft activities. He also picked up leaflets to carefully cut out and stick into his scrapbooks. Crucially, these were times when he could relax and really enjoy himself.

At the age of 14, James' interest in collecting bus and train tickets when travelling back to the south-east moved on to discarded scratchcards. Whenever we went for a day trip, James was determined to find abandoned scratchcards or we would go into shops to ask whether they had any used scratchcards to give James. Once the local shops knew that he needed them for his art, they soon provided them for him in abundance. James sorted them by colour to keep in boxes and containers. My kitchen became his workshop, the drawers and cupboards his storage space and his colourful artwork and recycled materials would be spread across the kitchen table.

Mainstream secondary school wasn't an easy time for James and he often felt isolated from other pupils and was happier putting his emotions

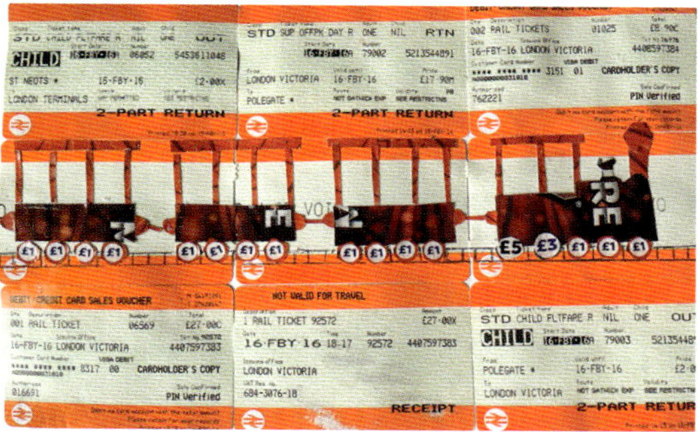

▲ *An example of James' artwork on used train tickets that he completed at secondary school.*

▶ *James earned an A* Grade for his GCSE photography for his red phone box project.*

▼ *James' collage on a found cigarette packet which he put into his secondary school sketch-book.*

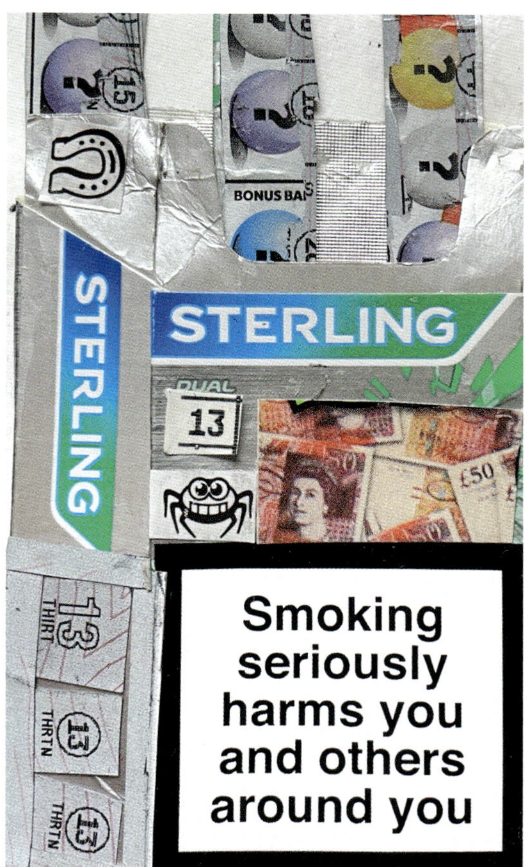

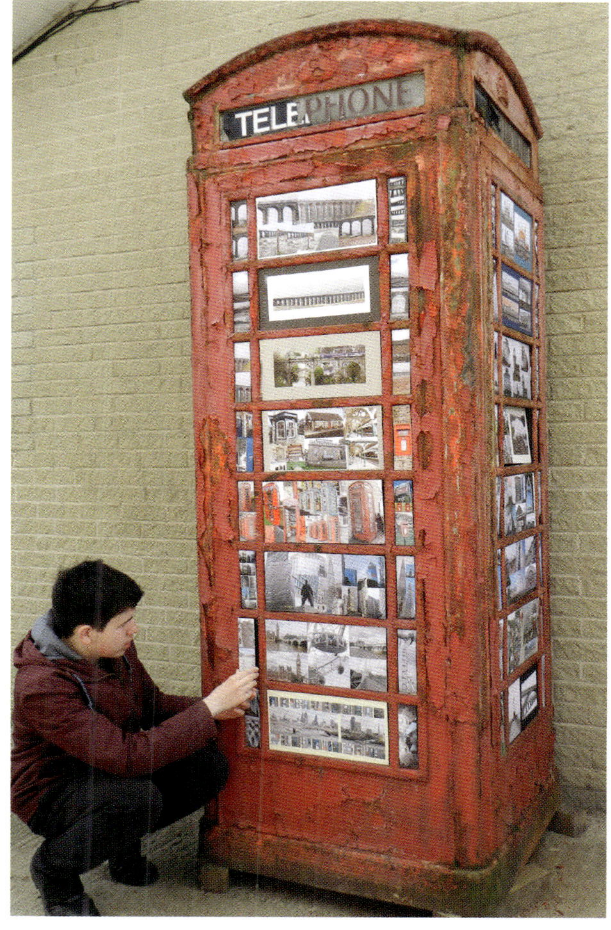

into his collages. He felt he needed to be strong to be different and the way he kept himself strong was through his artwork. At the time of making a choice for his GCSE art, he confided in his teacher, Judy Wallace, that he had a special interest in making collages from recycled scratchcards. She asked to see his work and then enthusiastically suggested he had a display in the school hall. It was with this teacher's support that James gradually gained confidence and she encouraged him to further develop his interests in photography and art. I was pleased and relieved, as James did not enjoy secondary school, apart from time spent in the art room and at the after-school gardening club.

James did very well, earning an A* grade for his GCSE exam piece as one of the options was to create art using recycled materials. He also enjoyed taking a GCSE in photography and his final project included a display of his photographs from different parts of the country on the inside of an old red phone box in a neighbour's garden.

After secondary school, James had a book of photographs printed, featuring the decorated red phone box. It was called 'How Special Memories Evolve' and he dedicated it to his grandmother, who has dementia. He was studying locally at a college in Ripon for a Trinity College Silver Arts Award and he did some practical training in horticulture. The tutors were very impressed when James also had a solo exhibition at Ripon Cathedral and students in his group were taken to see it.

James would soon begin his two-year extended diploma course in art and design at Bradford School of Art, but alongside this, he was determined to progress with his Trinity College Gold Arts Award. I was concerned the extra workload might have caused him stress, but when we researched and found out about the Theatre Royal in York running the course, we contacted the Youth Theatre Director. She informed James what he would need to do to gain the qualification and how it would end with an exciting display of his artwork. There seemed to be no stopping him and he took it all in his stride. The way he was beginning to see his autism less as a disability and more as a different kind of ability was reassuring.

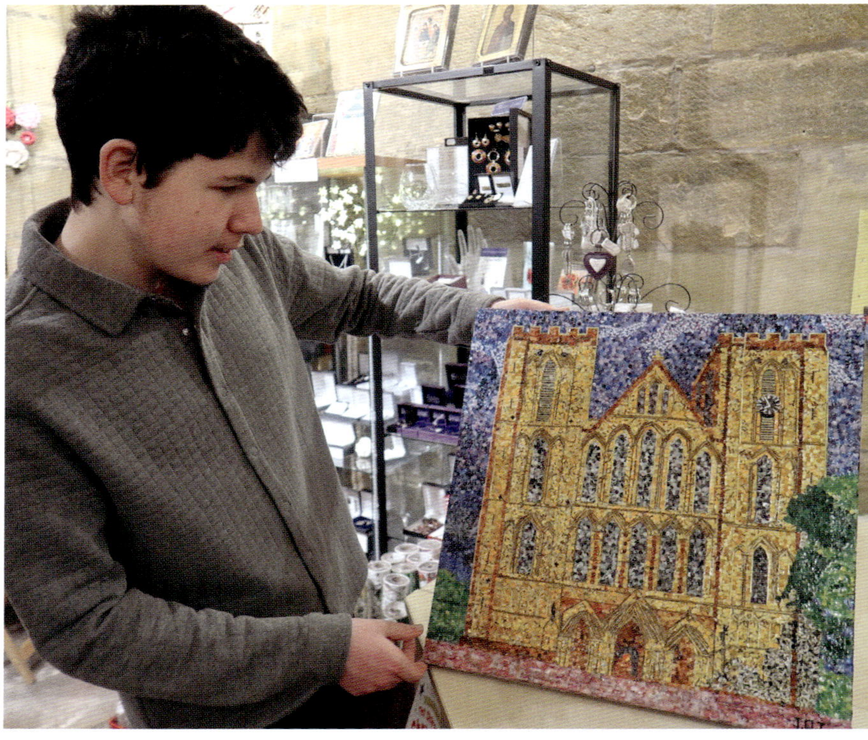

▲ *James at Ripon Cathedral with his artwork.*

COLLEGE SKETCHBOOKS

At 17 years old, James was proud to commence studies at Bradford School of Art; it had an impressive reputation and had educated many celebrated artists, including David Hockney, who had studied there from 1953. James was delighted as he had liked Hockney's art since moving to Yorkshire at the age of 11.

James had many things on his mind at the time but, in terms of his mental health, the main priority was to be away from the students who had caused him so many problems at secondary school. Other colleges offered good opportunities, but Bradford School of Art had much more appeal and stood out from the rest.

In 2019, during his 18 months at Bradford, he won a national award for his art. He also achieved his Gold Arts Award through the York Theatre Royal and had his first major commission for Pontefract Races (see pages 94–8). He received a Level 3 diploma in Art and Design from Bradford School of Art in 2019 and an extended diploma in 2020.

It could be said that James learned how to adapt his own style of artwork when finding ways to combine drawing, printmaking and photography with his own preference for collage. His mixed media art is on almost every page of his sketchbooks and shows his use of the many different materials that interested him at the time. These could be old packaging from bird-food products, donated items such as Japanese newspapers, and keepsakes from places he had visited. To a certain extent, he had already developed his own technique and style before attending college.

His method of learning visually continued as a college student and James was always keen to visit new places, museums and galleries during holidays and weekends. He wasn't comfortable being asked to share his sketchbooks with other students before projects were completed. It was a struggle for him to let them see and handle the artwork in his sketchbooks that he had spent so many hours completing. He often said that it seemed like passing over an exam paper he had finished for others to copy. He didn't mind sharing his bullet point notes and images of his completed work following a project. He spoke well in front of the class, delivering a PowerPoint presentation. He felt that his coursework was personal – all the research was based on places he had been to and artists he had met and worked with.

James felt different from the other students in his group and found their noise stressful, distracting him from getting on with his work and often preventing him from hearing instructions. His lunch breaks were solitary times spent taking walks around the city and watching the feral pigeons. For this reason, the first lockdown in March 2020 was not as problematic in terms of his work. He finally felt able to get on with his art and could have peaceful walks in the countryside for inspiration!

James had to complete various projects during each year, at the end of which there was a final major project. In the second year, this project had to be completed at home due to the first lockdown. Here is a selection of pages from his sketchbooks:

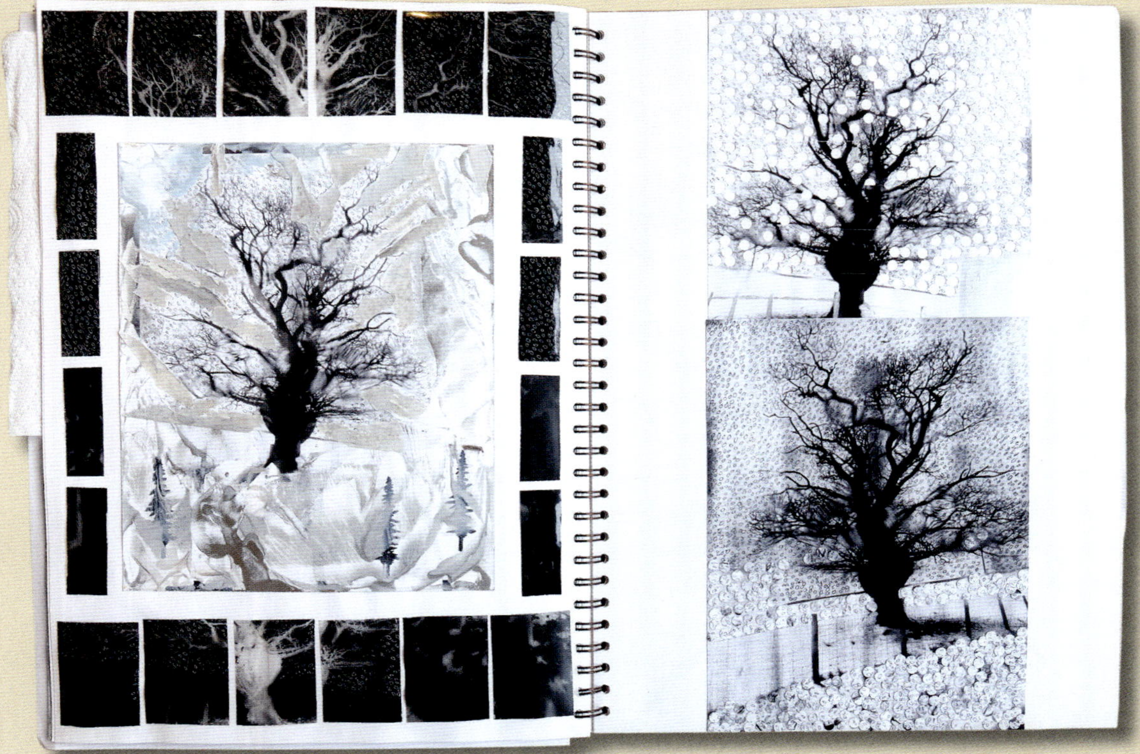

▲ James made several experimental artworks using a photograph of a single tree as a starting point. He was particularly interested in a tree that he would regularly see on one of his walks near home. He referred to it as the 'Van Gogh tree' (see also pages 120–1), imagining how it would have looked if painted in a Van Gogh style.

▲▶ In his happiest moments at Bradford School of Art, James enjoyed darkroom sessions, where he would manipulate images by using a 'solarising' technique, whereby there is a tone reversal: light areas appear dark and dark areas appear light.

▶ James scratched and drew patterns on acetate plastic before the photo development stage to make special effects. Using fluid metallic brush markers, he was also able to add shimmering colours and detail to his darkroom photographs.

(Photographs © Paul Howell)

"O'er the hills and far away..." (17th century theatre). Using fluid metalic brush markers I have been able to add shimmering colours and detail to my darkroom photographs.

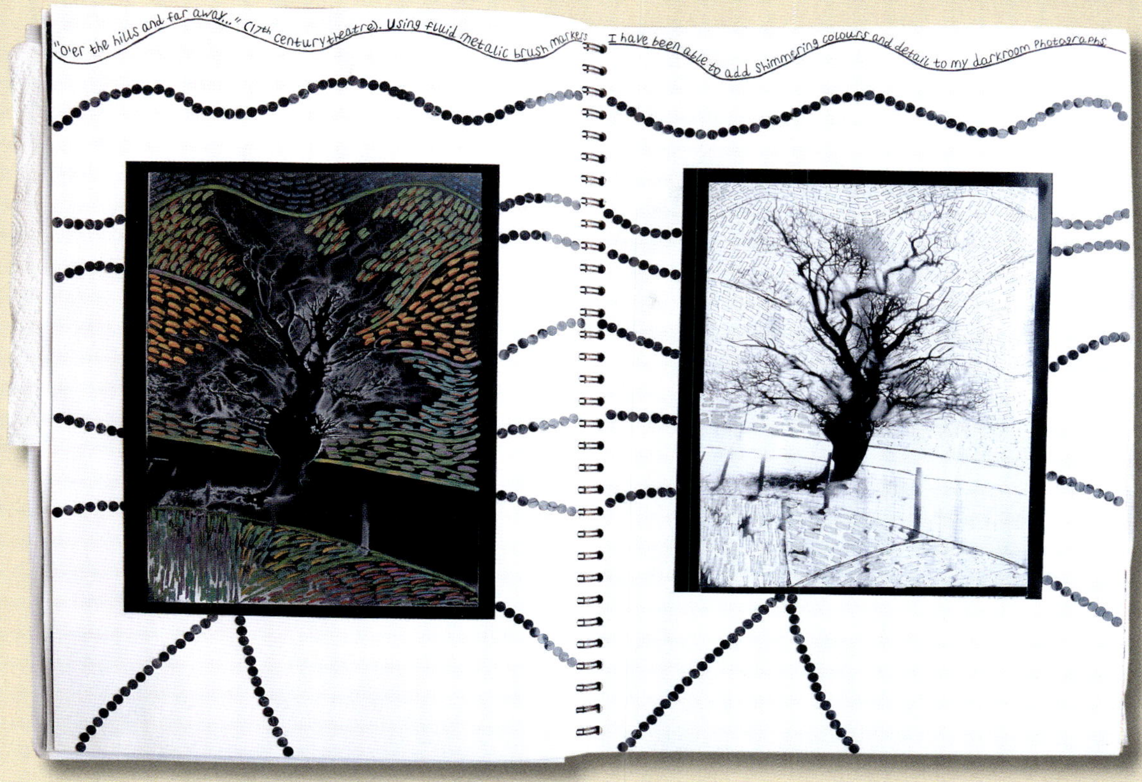

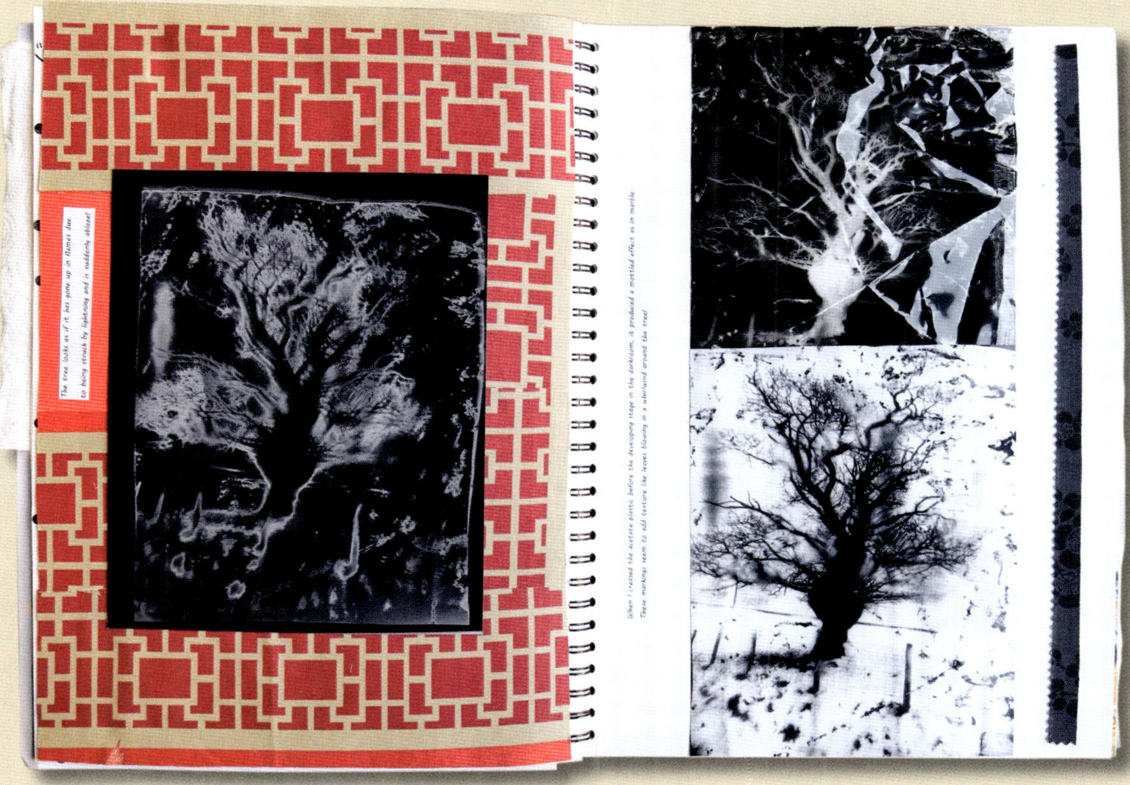

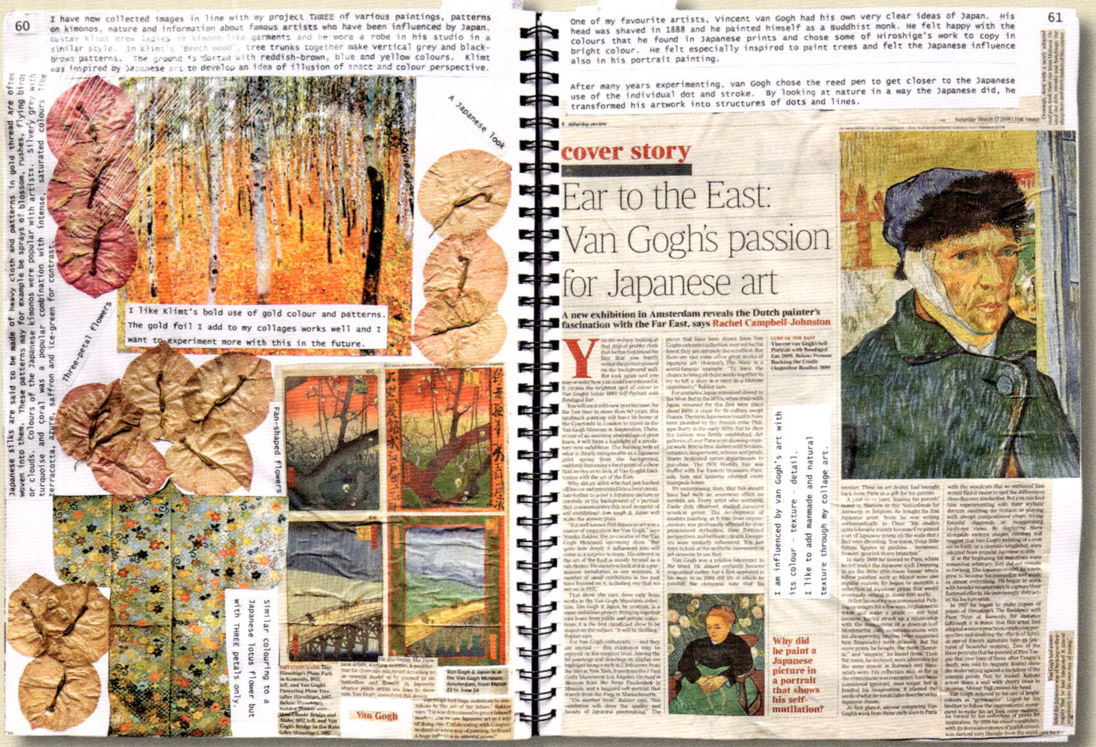

▲ This extract from James' sketchbook reflects James' fascination with two of his favourite artists, Gustav Klimt and Vincent van Gogh. He would collect newspaper articles about them, images of their work, their relationship with nature and how both were influenced by Japanese art and culture.

Klimt greatly admired the beautiful, coloured patterns on Japanese kimonos and Van Gogh loved the bold compositions and colours used in Japanese woodblock prints. It is clear from James' artwork how much he loves colour. In his sketchbook, he wrote how he liked Klimt's use of gold and explained how the gold foil he adds to his collages works and how he wanted to experiment more with this in the future.

Influenced by Van Gogh's art with its colour, texture and detail, James wrote about how he added man-made and natural texture to produce his collages, using not only the vibrant colours from scratchcards but also dried leaves, petals and bark from nature. (*Photograph © Paul Howell*)

▶ This is part of exploring the use of different materials – James described in his sketchbook his interest in the history of the cloth trade at Salts Mill (see page 130). The small sample of separated threads, stuck down into blocks of colour may come across as a simple swatch. However, threaded material has inspired James from when he was a small child, fascinated by the texture of things around him. His autism may have accentuated this trait, and it has evolved into a love of using threads of all kinds in his collages. Whether to create sunlit highlights on the bough of a tree or a forest floor, James has learnt to incorporate discarded pieces of textiles to create artistic effects. (*Photograph © Paul Howell*)

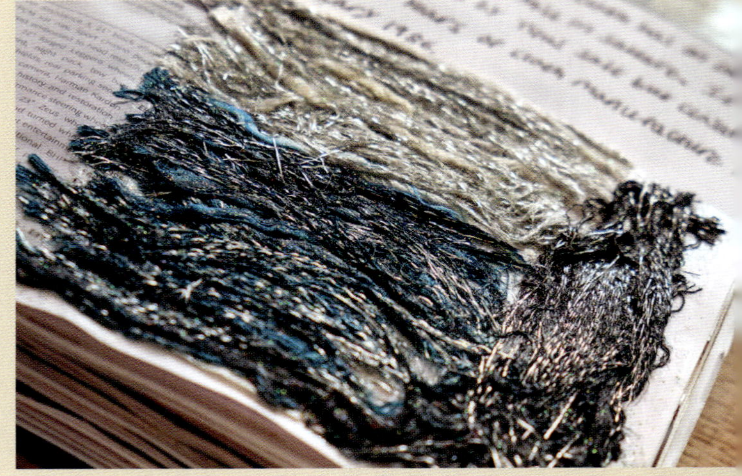

▶ Here, James used three different-sized photographs of himself to create a Surrealist self-portrait, perhaps beginning to express his own emotions in a strange, dreamlike way. His intermingling of different techniques, such as photographic collage and coloured sections of paper, possibly reflects his feelings of unhappiness and confusion.

(Photograph © Paul Howell)

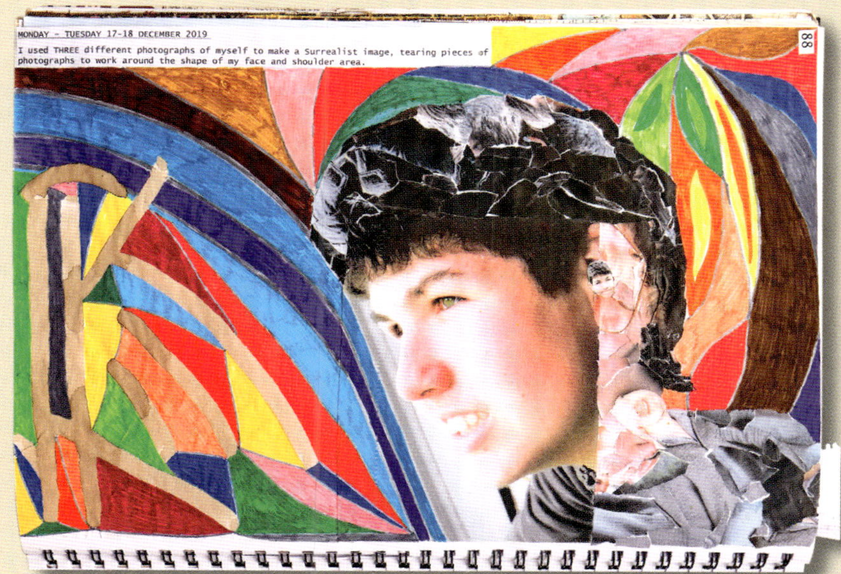

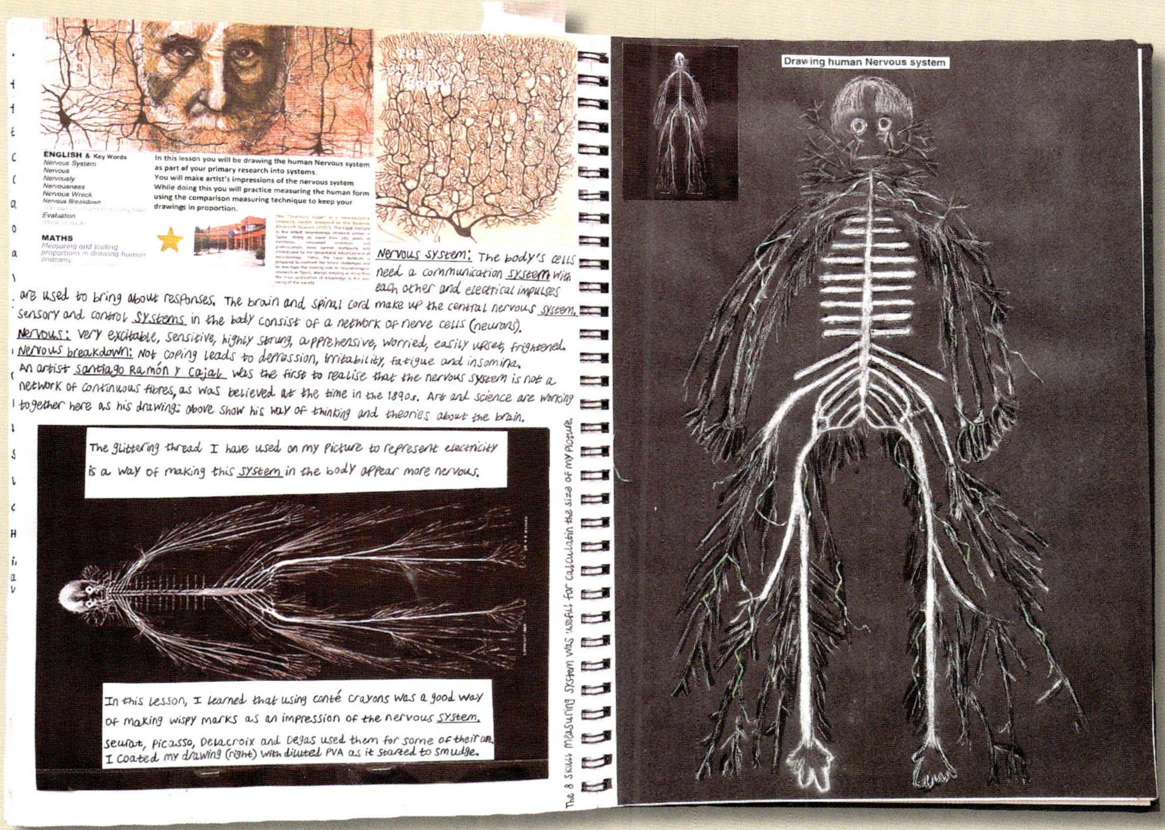

▲ In this very unusual drawing, James made wispy marks with Conte crayons and used a shimmering thread to highlight the electrical pulses that run through the human nervous system. He then coated his drawing with diluted PVA to prevent it smudging. *(Photograph © Paul Howell)*

▶ James wanted to create a copy of a painting of beech trees by Paul Nash that he had seen on display in East Sussex. James painted squares on graph paper in pastel shades to give a pixelated section of landscape with trees. By taking away the need to draw the image, he was able to concentrate and experiment with colour and tone. This mosaic style has appealed to James since he was a young child when he enjoyed making small mosaics from miniature tiles in kits, an interest he continued to develop in his collages using cut or torn materials in a variety of patterns. *(Photograph © Paul Howell)*

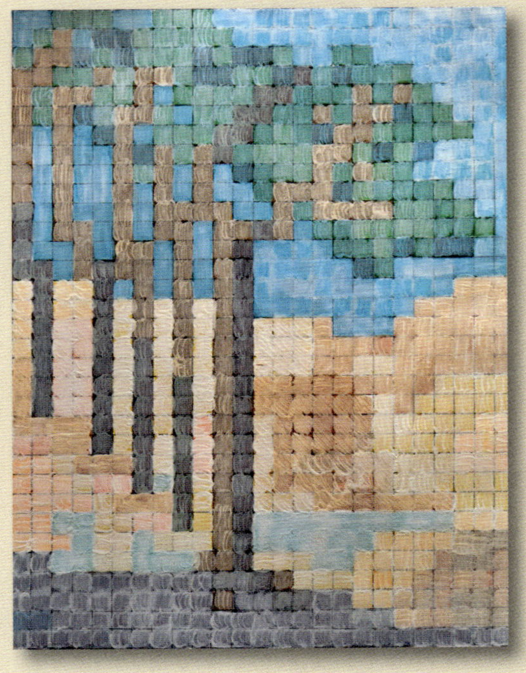

▼ James used several copies of his photographs of a schoolboy to try out different artistic techniques. Here are just two. The boy's face reminded James of a young David Hockney – not just the glasses he wore and the dark hair he had as a boy, but the roundish shape of his face. James wanted to experiment with ways in which he could 'age' this boy's appearance.

   James described in his sketchbook how he managed to avoid the acrylic paint pulling away from the shiny surface of the photographic paper using a special type of metallic paint. He then cleverly aged the face and creased the jacket by making lines with a brush and his fingernail. James used encaustic, melted natural wax – a medium he enjoyed experimenting with – to create a fiery, colourful, abstract design. *(Photograph © Paul Howell)*

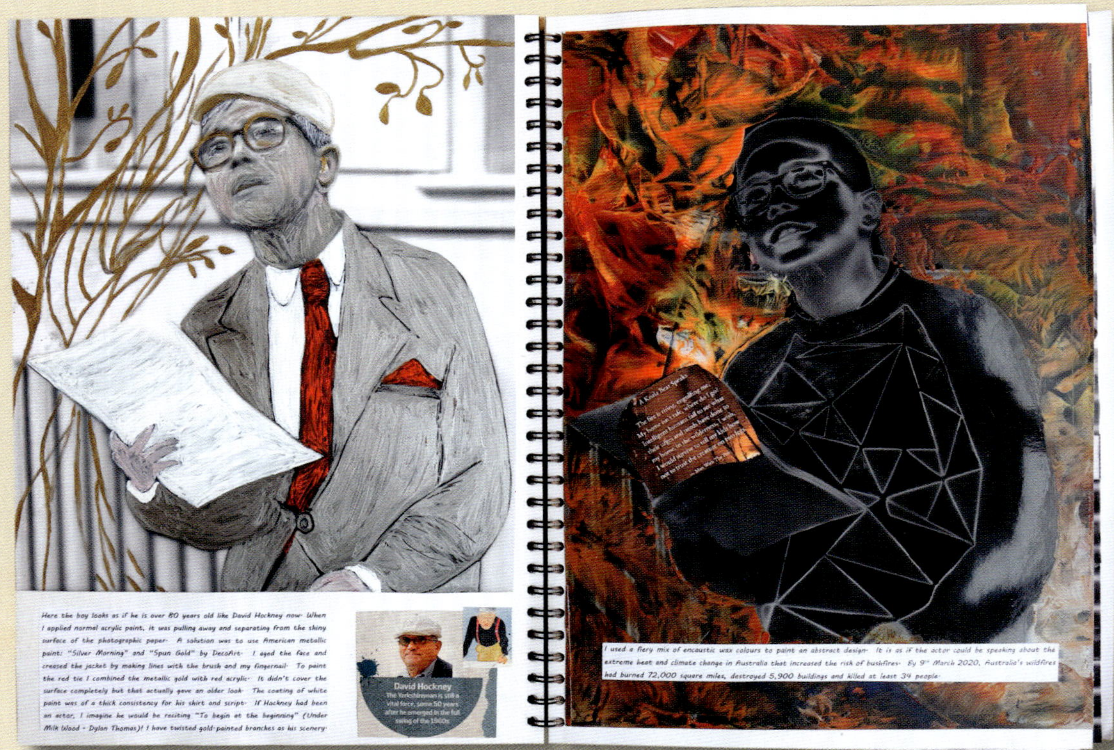

▶ From an early age, James' concerns about waste influenced his habit of collecting discarded materials. As he got older, he began to see the endless opportunities of using these waste products as the raw materials for his artwork.

After Christmas, for example, there seems nothing left to do but throw away greeting cards and envelopes. James created this artwork by collecting and mounting postage stamps to form bands in a coloured background, then cutting the greetings cards into triangular shapes.

The use of greetings cards, which have been donated to James for his artwork, has developed since this time. He now prefers to use shredded pieces of recycled cards to twist and collage into his intricate nature scenes. (*Photograph © Paul Howell*)

▼ James compared the veins in a human arm to the branches of a tree. On the left, a collaged arm shows silhouetted trees standing against a dramatic blood-red sky. On the right painted arm, the arteries and capillaries run up the length of the forearm making patterns like bark on a tree trunk, culminating in the open palm of the hand. The threads used in their spiralling pattern represent a bird's nest and demonstrate how, with most art projects, James would relate his interests back to nature and what he felt most comfortable creating. (*Photograph © Paul Howell*)

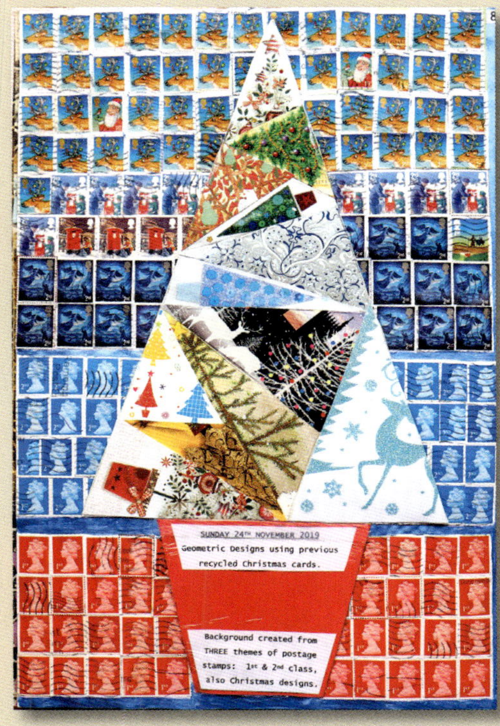

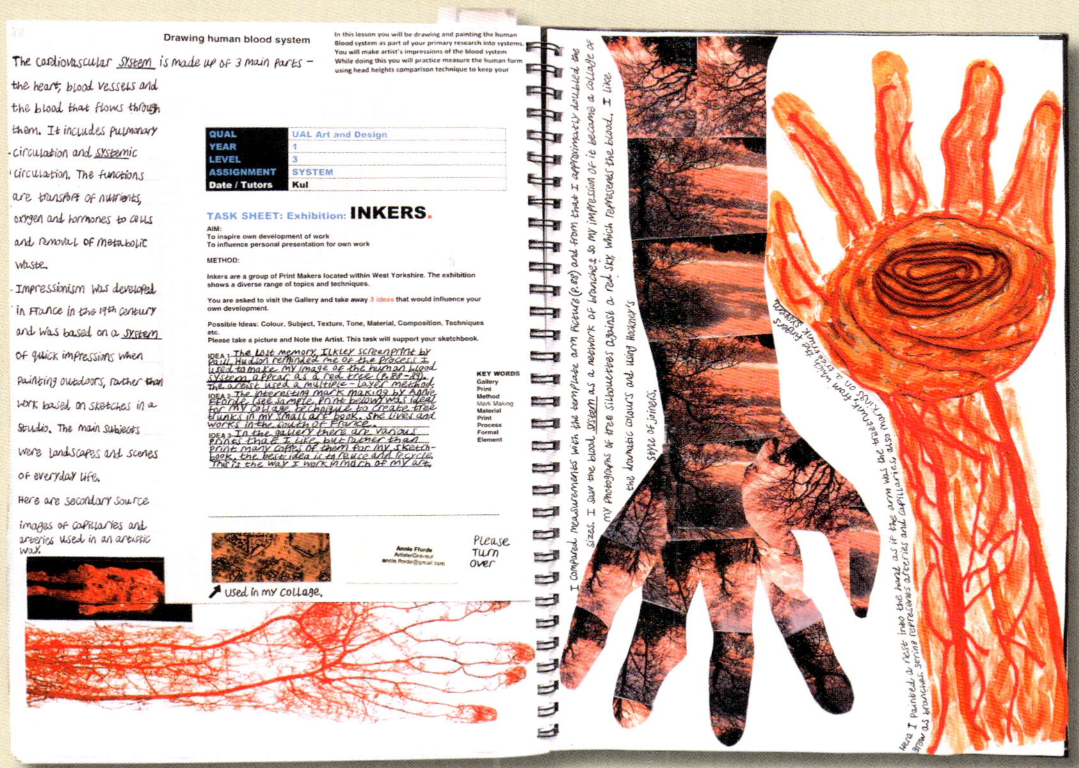

▶ As part of his course at Bradford School of Art, James enjoyed a few days' work experience with Scientific Games (SG), the Leeds-based scratchcard manufacturer. The company had heard about his collages and invited him to join their design department and sketch ideas for a new scratchcard for potential use in the Dutch market.

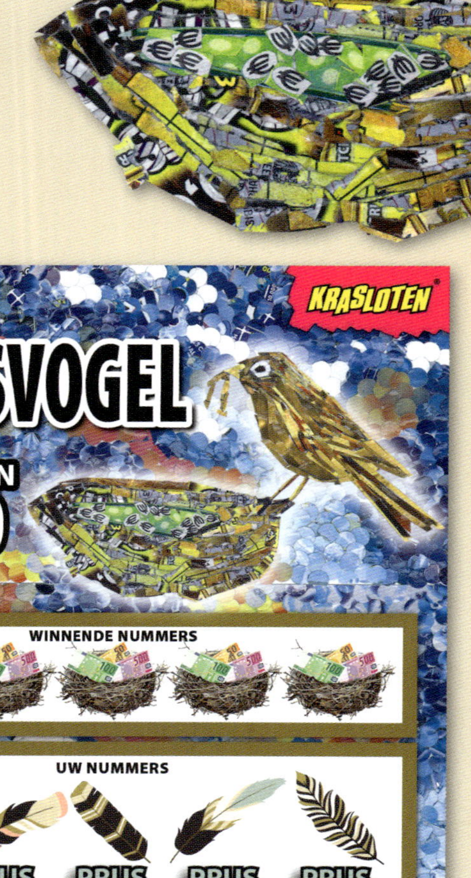

◀ Using scratchcards, James collaged a bird holding something in its beak for building its nest. This 'Lucky Bird' (Geluksvogel) idea combined the theme of recycling scratchcards with James' keen interest in birdlife and nature.

James was also shown how to use SG's computer system to transfer his artwork onto the scratchcard template and to design the background, experimenting with different symbols and fonts.

A RISING STAR

Even before James finished college, he was starting to embark on a career as a professional artist. As a student at Bradford, James was commissioned by Pontefract Races to create four pieces of artwork for their sustainability campaign (see pages 93–8).

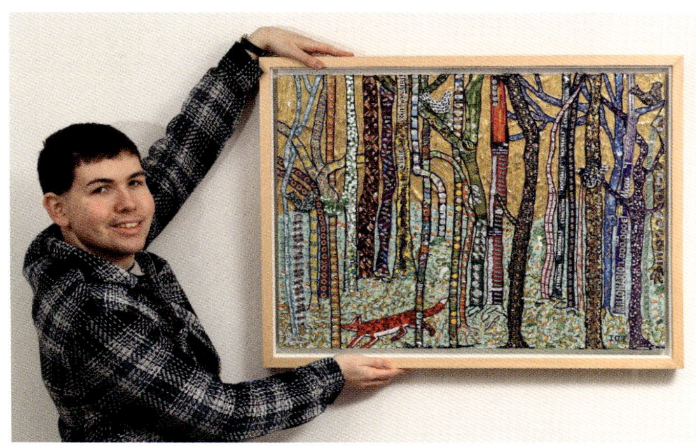

However, it was only after the barriers of lockdown were lifted and his course had come to an end that James could concentrate on beginning his art career. He continued to take commissions, created and exhibited art and used his work to promote the causes close to his heart, including trees, the environment and helping others with autism. His work is positive both for his personal development and for the environment and other people.

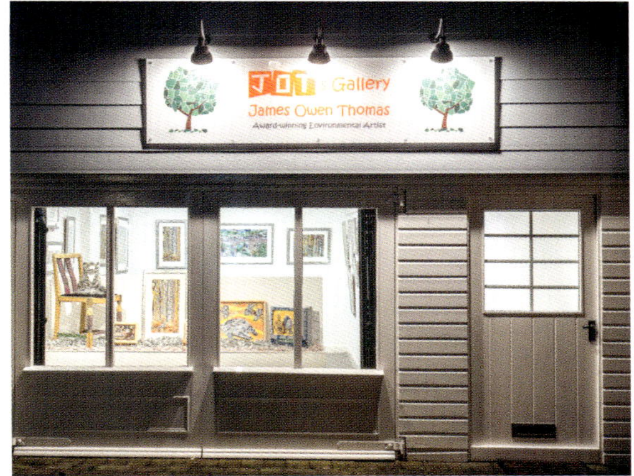

▲▲ *James at the Gallery with* **Reconnecting with Nature.** *(Photograph by Gerard Binks)*

▲*The Gallery in Pateley Bridge.* *(Photograph © Paul Howell)*

THE GALLERY

JOT's 2023 Gallery in Pateley Bridge came about almost by chance. The building had previously been rented by another artist and it had been standing empty for a year. James was still creating art on the kitchen table at home and doing local voluntary work when he was encouraged by local businessman Keith Tordoff MBE to take the plunge and get involved with running a gallery, for experience and as there was potential to develop it into a business.

As well as providing a quiet space where James could create his artwork, the Gallery also increased his confidence in speaking to visitors as they entered the building. Learning new skills when creating attractive window displays was an added bonus and so was learning how to keep good accounts of business transactions. James also invited a number of visitors such as Professor David Hill, CBE DL from the Lord Lieutenancy's Office in York, who formally opened the Gallery in June 2023. There were also visits by representatives of The Tree Council, the manager of the

Harrogate branch of the National Autistic Society, members of the Ripon City Photographic Society, a delegate from Great British Racing London and a contact from Pyramid Educational Consultants, who paid a visit and brought with her some of the climate change Picture Exchange Symbols James had helped to design. The year at the Gallery was certainly an exciting time.

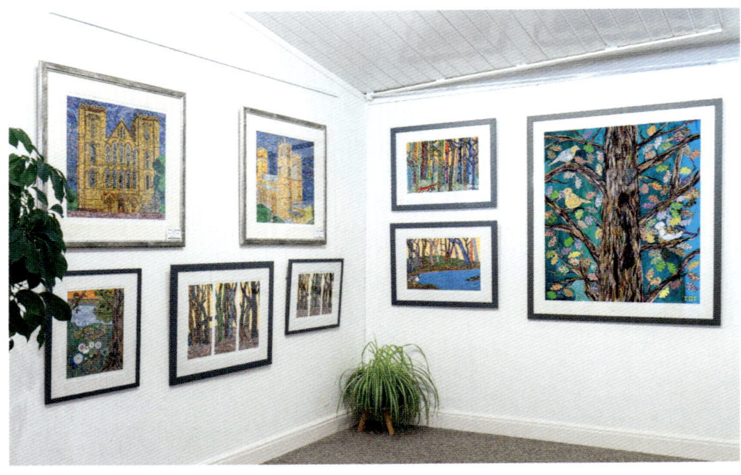

▲ *Interior of the Gallery.* (*Photograph © Paul Howell*)

COMMISSIONS

James received various commissions during the time he ran JOT's Gallery and visitors were always fascinated to watch him work. He firstly hears from customers, then discusses in detail the size of the commission, timescale, the actual image and the recycled materials to be used for creating the collage. As well as receiving private commissions to create a scene of the National Trust site of Fountains Abbey (see pages 137–9), he also received corporate commissions including one from Great British Racing, London, to celebrate the King's coronation (see pages 99–103).

Always keen to meet deadlines, James has been known to work overnight when needed as he can become completely absorbed in his work. One of his most challenging commissions was collaging a portrait of Van Gogh. The recycled canvas he used to match the customer's requirements was huge and it was to be made completely from used National Lottery scratchcards. A few extra pieces of different recycled papers were also added for interest such as some words in Dutch, which were inserts from an old book. He spent many hours preparing for the commission and dividing his materials into what he called his palette of Van Gogh colours. Working tirelessly until it was complete, he finally had the impressive collage ready in time for the official opening of JOT's Gallery in June 2023.

James continues to create woodland scenes that interest him. As artist in residence at Fishpond Wood in Bewerley, near Pateley Bridge, he was

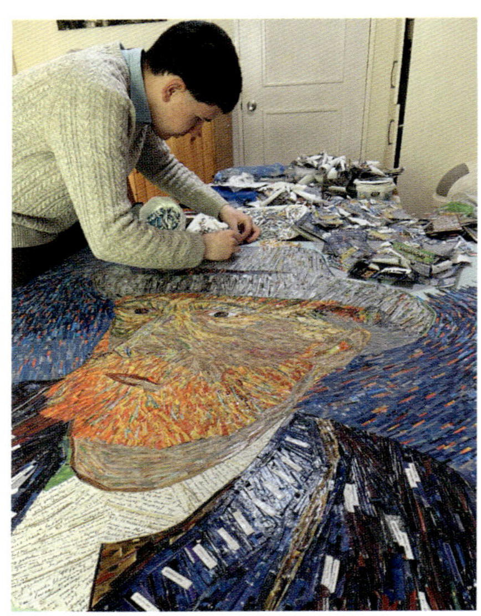

▲ *The portrait of Vincent van Gogh, one of James' largest and most challenging commissions.*

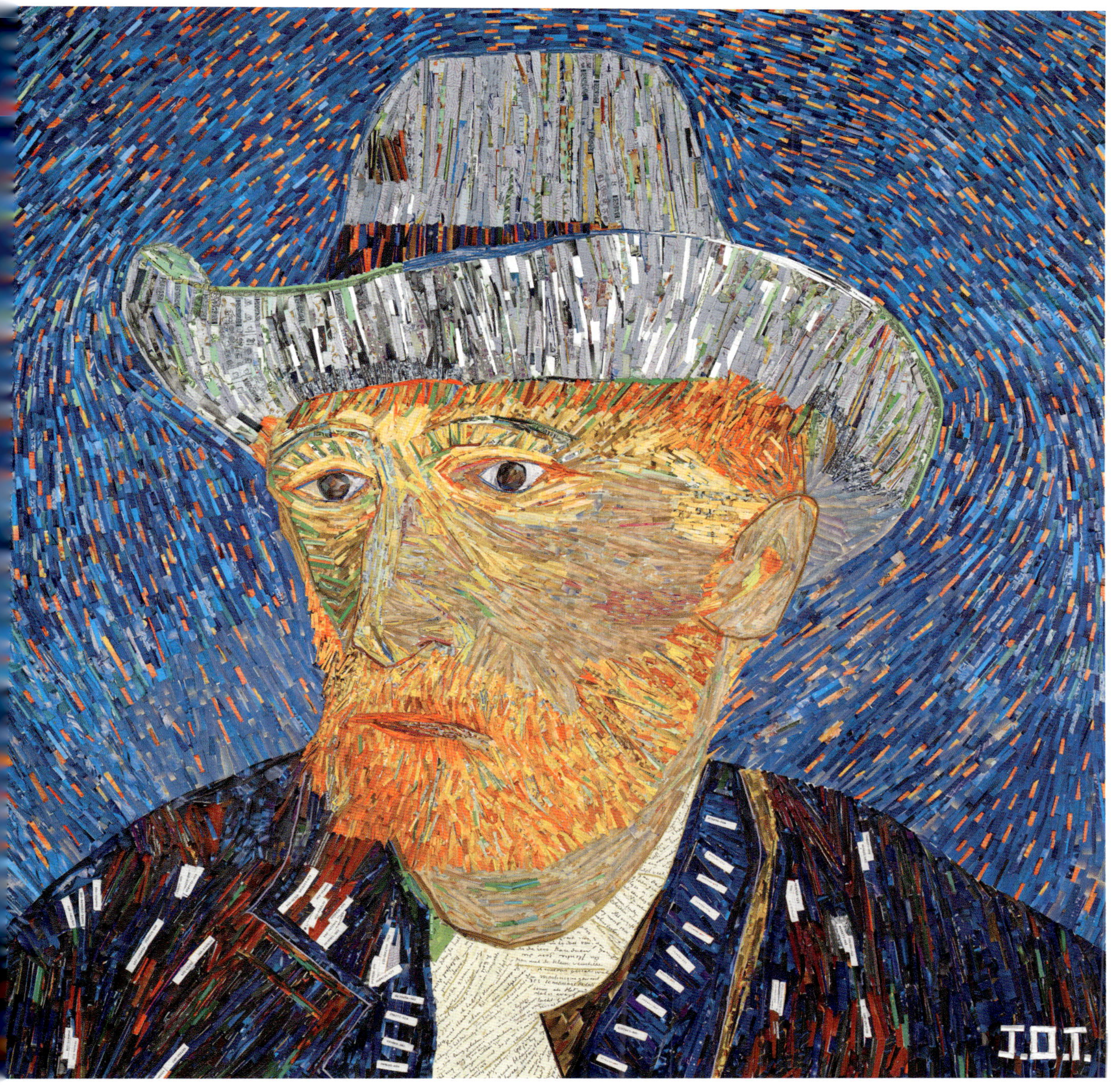

▲ *The completed portrait of Vincent van Gogh.*

pleased to be commissioned to create a collage of a tree photographed there in the woodland. He used cut pieces of fabric for the bark of the tree trunk and branches, then broke the fabric down further to create a fluffy effect for moss.

PUBLIC ROLE

One of James' main positions of responsibility is being a Force for Nature Ambassador for The Tree Council. He has been able to develop confidence to share his views and experiences on a national level. His profile was raised by his involvement in COP26 as a One Step Greener Ambassador and his invitation to 10 Downing Street. A print of James' *At Twilight* was given to Prime Minister Boris Johnson on behalf of The Tree Council with the message: 'At Twilight, but not too late in the day we hope to save the planet.'

James also made an appearance on BBC *Gardeners' World*. He was interviewed by JJ Chalmers in August 2022 and spoke about the therapeutic benefits of being out in nature and how it influences his art. James was later delighted to meet Monty Don at the Harrogate Convention Centre in November 2022.

Often going into mainstream and special needs schools and college settings, James is able to give others a voice through his art masterclasses and workshops to become a 'Force for Nature'. Like James, The Tree Council's ambassadors help inspire others to form a deeper connection with the natural world and take action to tackle the nature and climate emergencies.

James' other main interests concern special educational needs, as he was involved in the system when he started his education at special school and later transferred to mainstream education, supported through an Education Health Care Plan. James received support and advice over the years through an organisation called SENDIASS (the Special Educational Needs and Disability Information Advice and Support Service). He likes, wherever possible, to attend SENDIASS Inspire 2-gether online meetings and be part of a group of young people, who are keen to improve services for children and young people with special educational needs and disabilities. Similarly, James has attended online meetings with the Children's and Young People's Steering Group for IASSN (the Information, Advice and Support Services Network Council for Disabled Children).

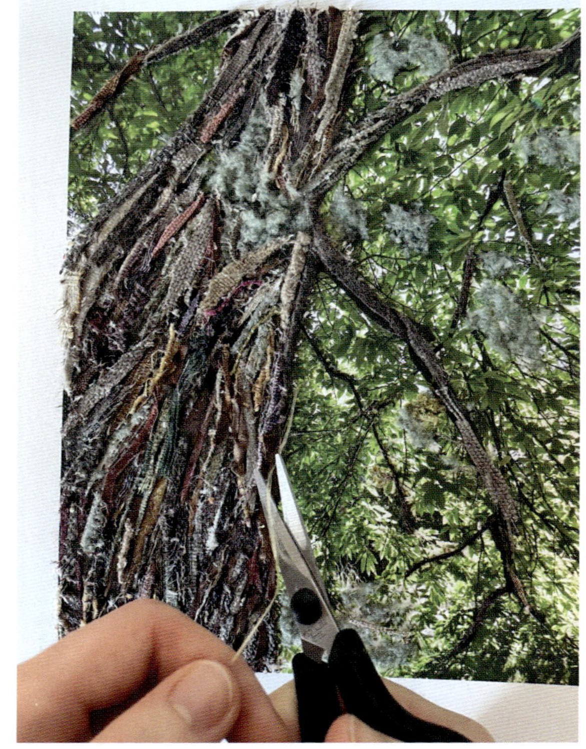

▼ *Cutting down fabric to make moss for the Bewerley commission.*

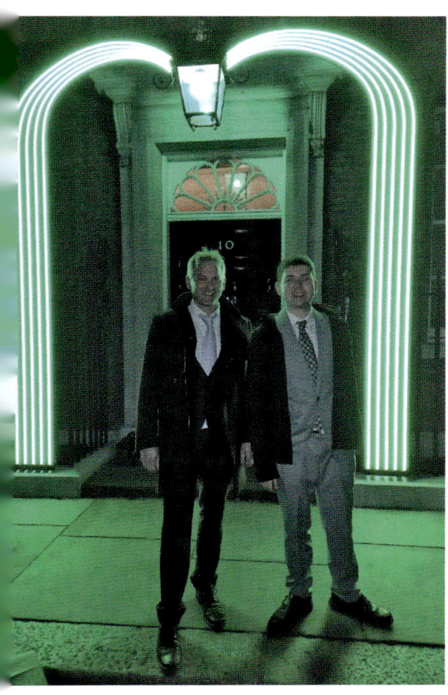

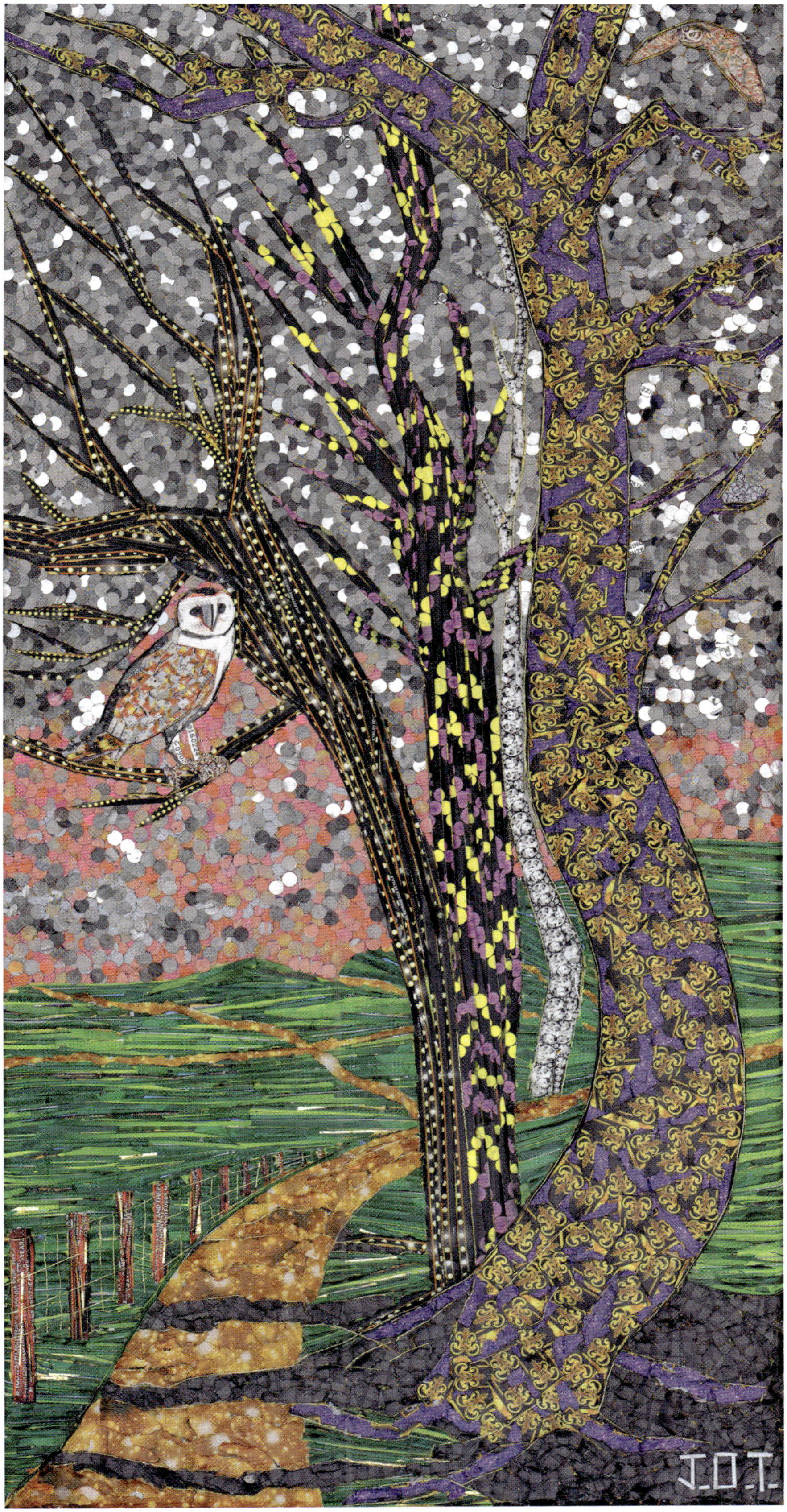

▲ *James on his visit to 10 Downing Street, with Richard Pollard of The Tree Council.*

▶ ***At Twilight***, *the piece James donated to No. 10.*

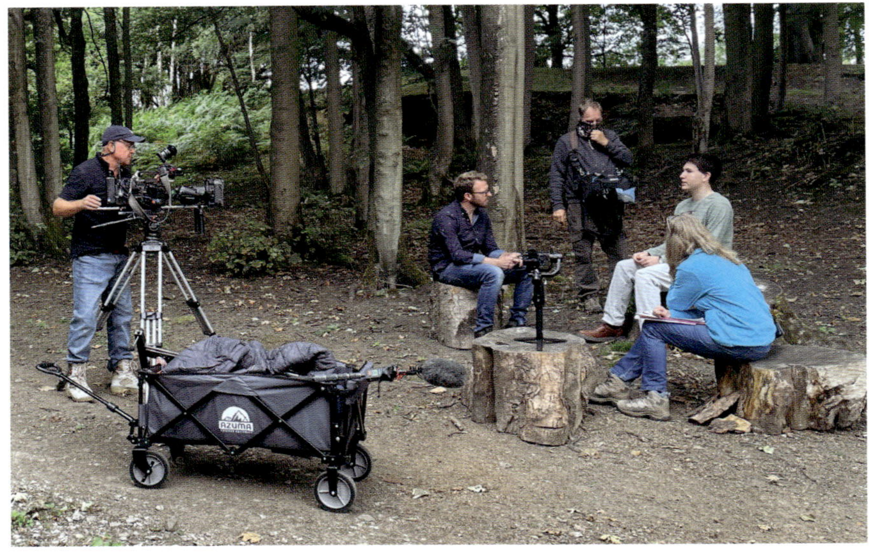

◀ *James being interviewed by JJ Chalmers on **Gardener's World**.*

▼ *James speaks to students at college in his Tree Council Ambassador role.*

CAUSES

James is deeply involved with many causes and charities.

The causes James has worked hard to support have included £20,000 of fundraising for the Caudwell Children's Charity that supports disabled children. It meant a lot to him to give something back to the charity that had helped him with therapy as a small child, as well as a cherished outing to the Sealife Centre in Brighton. For the charity's twentieth anniversary, James wrote and asked if he could help by donating the artwork he created during lockdown for his final major project at Bradford School of Art. He explained

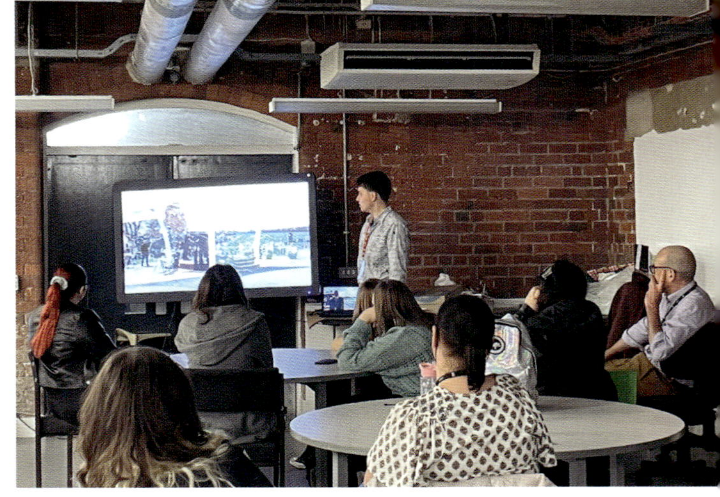

that the 11 different canvases were all individual parts of a cherry tree in blossom. This idea of a tree branching out represented hope and a positive future for disabled children. James added to the collection and produced a larger tree comprising 20 canvases to represent each of the years that the Caudwell Children's Charity had been in existence. The canvases were created using old brochures, tickets, leaflets, T-shirts and a mix of other recycled materials sent by the charity. They sold for £1,000 each to generous members of the audience at their fundraising Butterfly Ball in London.

James said at the time: 'I think this is the best thing really about my art that by doing events and fundraising for charities, it also helps my own condition and self-esteem as I can get quite low at times, and it got worse since the time of the first lockdown.'

In 2023, James raised £10,000 for another charity close to his heart, the Alzheimer's Society, as his grandmother, Joan, has dementia. The piece that he named *Seaside Memories* focused on memory through postcards. He used layers and layers of recycled materials including donated scratchcards and some of his grandmother's old postcards to create the artwork. Older memories last much better than short-term memory for people with dementia and James knew that his grandmother used to love to reminisce, talk about the family, the old days and holidays. The seven postcards used in the piece also represented the journey through the seven stages of dementia from normal cognitive function to severe dementia, where pictures and words become blurred so cannot be understood.

James has also raised money through exhibitions, workshops and donations for the Alzheimer's Society's 'Forget Me Not Appeal', for the National Autistic Society's 'Spectrum Colour Challenge' and for other charities including Maggie's Cancer Support, Harrogate Homeless Project and Shelter.

TEACHING

James' workshops are increasingly popular and he has been teaching his form of environmental art since the age of 21, when he became far more open to sharing his techniques. He has enjoyed the growing interest in his art and positive feedback from his workshops.

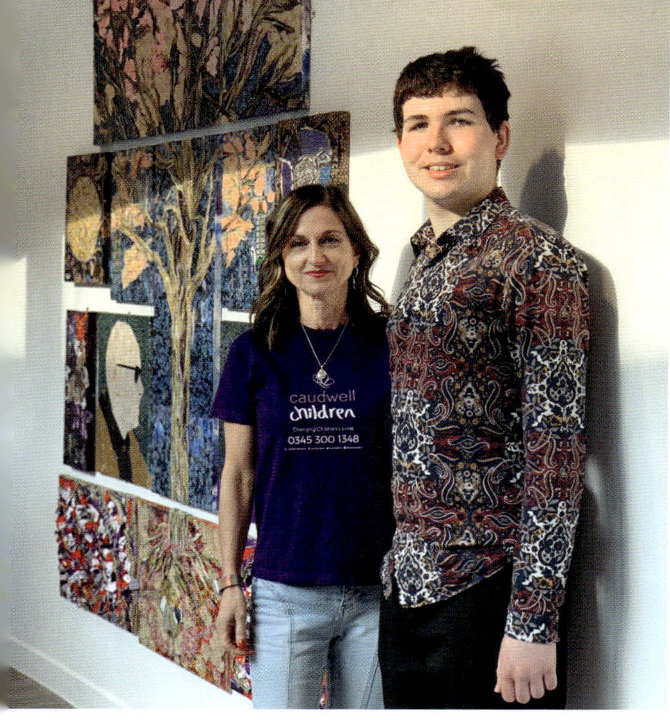

▲ *James in front of his 20-canvas artwork at the Caudwell Centre.*

▼ ***Seaside Memories**, representing the seven stages of dementia.*

Although at art college, James had been rather wary of other students copying his ideas from his sketchbooks, he decided to join the Springboard training course in 2019 at The Tetley gallery in Leeds (since renamed as Yorkshire Contemporary) so he could learn how to effectively deliver workshops. He had noticed at some of his earliest exhibitions at the National Coal Mining Museum and Bradford Industrial Museum, for example, that there was interest in him holding children's activities during weekends and school holidays. At that time, he was only 17 and felt shy speaking to a group of children who had gathered around him to join in!

The training James received at The Tetley gave him the knowledge he needed to develop structured workshops, suitable to different ages and abilities. He listened to speakers from organisations as part of the course, who talked about the benefits of art to promote mental wellbeing. James knew this from first-hand experience as he felt much calmer and less stressed when creating his collages. It was very interesting for him to hear these speakers and others who offered advice on disability awareness and equality training. When working alongside practising artists at The Tetley and assisting with their workshops, James gained invaluable experience and grew in confidence.

By the age of 21, he felt much more prepared to offer workshops himself and one he remembers well was at the Conference for the National Women's Register in 2022 in Newcastle. He wanted to make his workshop an inspiring, creative learning experience for the 50+ ladies involved. They came away very impressed, pleased to create something from materials that would otherwise have gone to waste, and thinking harder about what they consumed and threw away.

James has gone on to increase the numbers of workshops he leads at schools and colleges to provide bespoke creative projects that are designed around individual needs. His workshops take place not only in special needs settings but in mainstream education, at art clubs, WI groups, care homes and outdoor nature settings. He has even been asked to return to his former college, Bradford School of Art, to teach students on the same extended diploma course that he had studied.

As the Artist in Residence for Whitewoods Wellbeing at Fishpond Wood near Pateley Bridge, James has also enjoyed leading many workshops in the study barn in the woods, which was the setting for the BBC *Gardeners' World* filming in 2022. The study barn is such a calm setting for workshops and becomes like a sensory room in nature. James has also been assisting with the planting of new trees (oak, birch, rowan, cherry and hornbeam) to

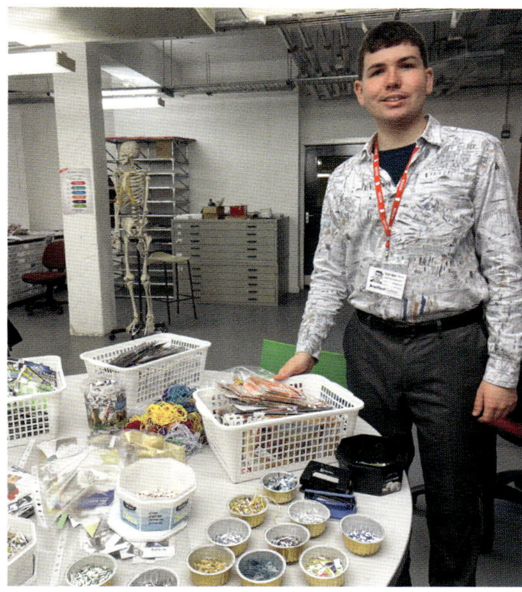

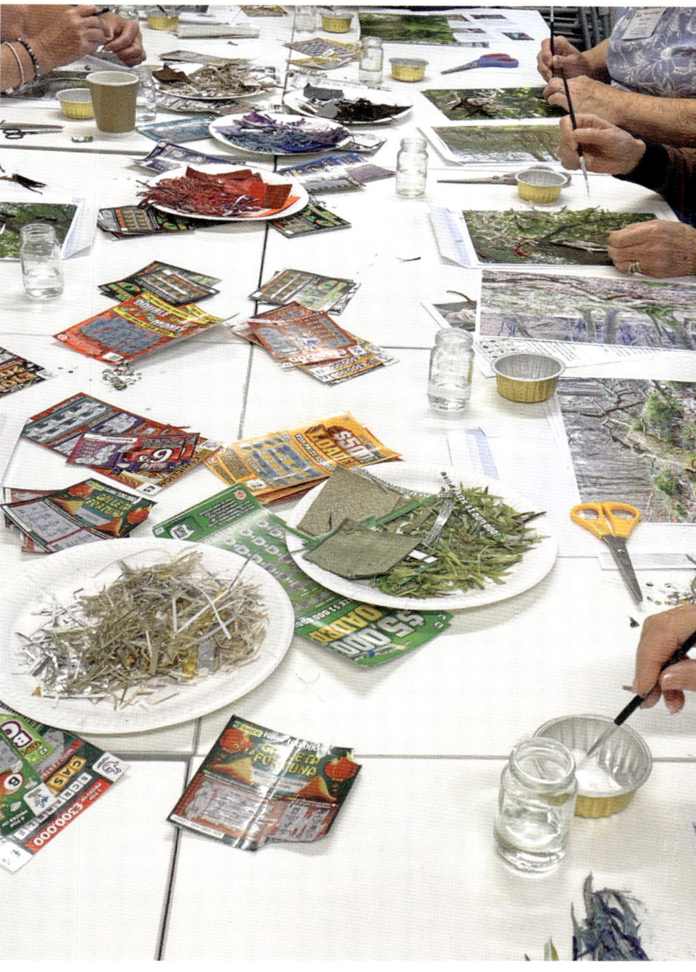

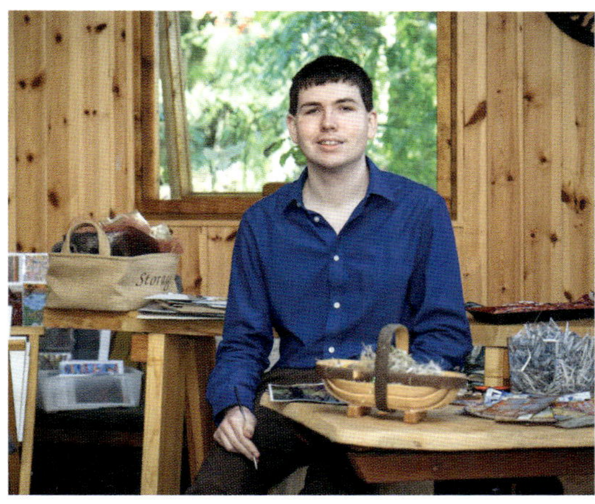

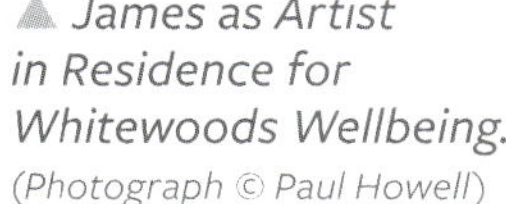

▲ *James as Artist in Residence for Whitewoods Wellbeing.*
(*Photograph © Paul Howell*)

replace the rhododendron and storm-damaged and invasive trees that are being taken out. The woods are steadily becoming more bio-diverse and sustainable, in terms of trees and wildlife, as progress is made with a regeneration plan. Being involved in this has been a positive experience for James' wellbeing.

More recently, there have been requests to run online Zoom and Teams workshops not only for children in his role as a Tree Council Ambassador, but also for adults with corporate commissions. These have been very successful and have helped to increase his experience as a teacher.

PECS CARDS AND SENSORY ROOMS

James can remember the times he spent in sensory rooms at special school and at the Chelsea and Westminster Hospital on their children's ward. Sensory rooms allowed him to feel calmer and reduce stress, anger and hyperactivity. He found them to be very therapeutic when he needed to be away from the noise, bright lights and people around him whether in classrooms or busy hospital waiting areas.

At the end of James' first year at Bradford School of Art, he created a sensory room experience by cornering off part of the college gallery to make an art installation of a small area that was calming. He used a bamboo screen that he decorated to create a peaceful and relaxing setting.

Although James did not have any photographs of the sensory rooms he used as a child, he has since established contact with Zen Sensory, a sensory and wellness centre in Harrogate. The centre displays some of his artwork in its reception area and hopes to involve James with future events and workshops.

In 2024, Pontefract Races (see pages 94–8) became the first racecourse in the country to host Autism in Racing race days. They provide an immersive space as a sensory room that overlooks their parade ring. James also provides family workshops at Pontefract Races.

At workshops for children or adults with special needs, James often takes PECS (Picture Exchange Communication System) symbols with him, which he benefited from in his own education. He could never have dreamt that as a young adult he would go on to help design some of these picture symbols himself. He worked on a joint project with Pyramid Educational Consultants UK Ltd in Brighton and The Tree Council to help design new symbols to represent the climate crisis. These symbols can be used by pupils with special needs to help with their understanding of environmental problems, spread the message about climate change and what everyone can do to prevent further damage to our planet.

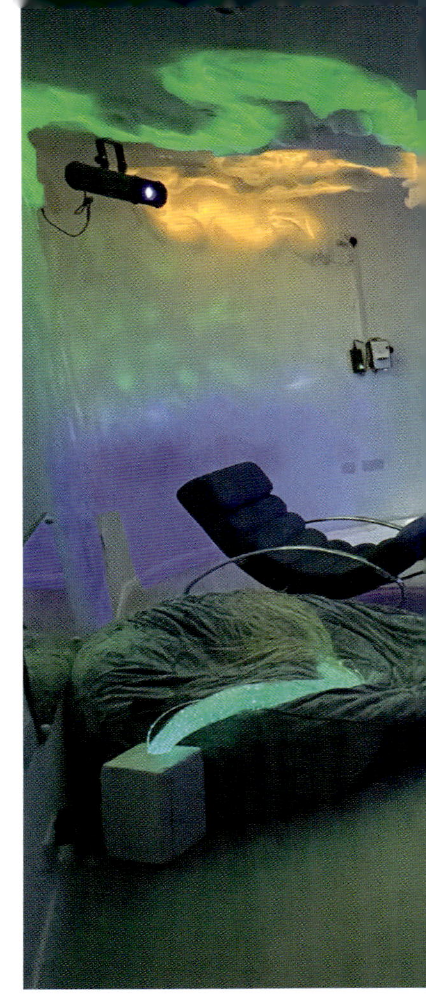

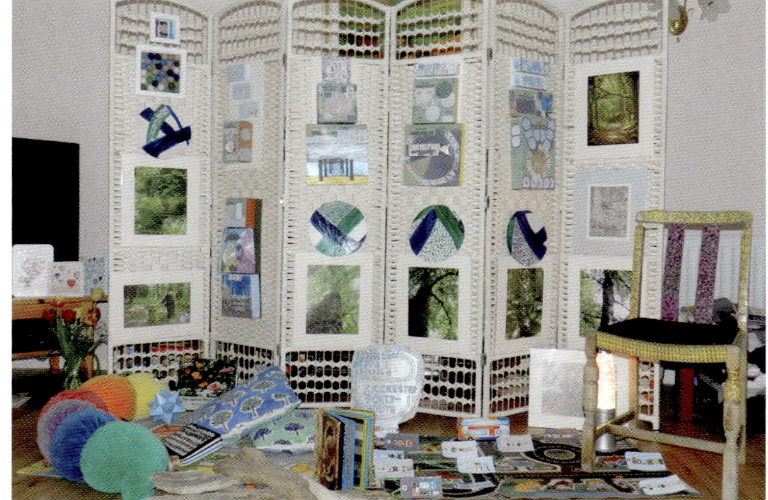

▲ *James' sensory room at Bradford School of Art.*

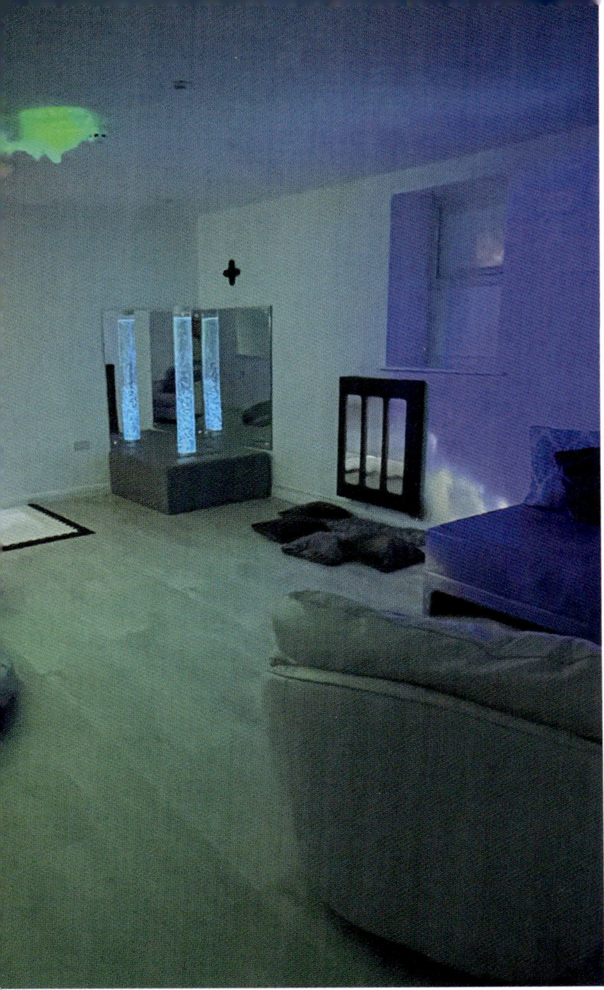

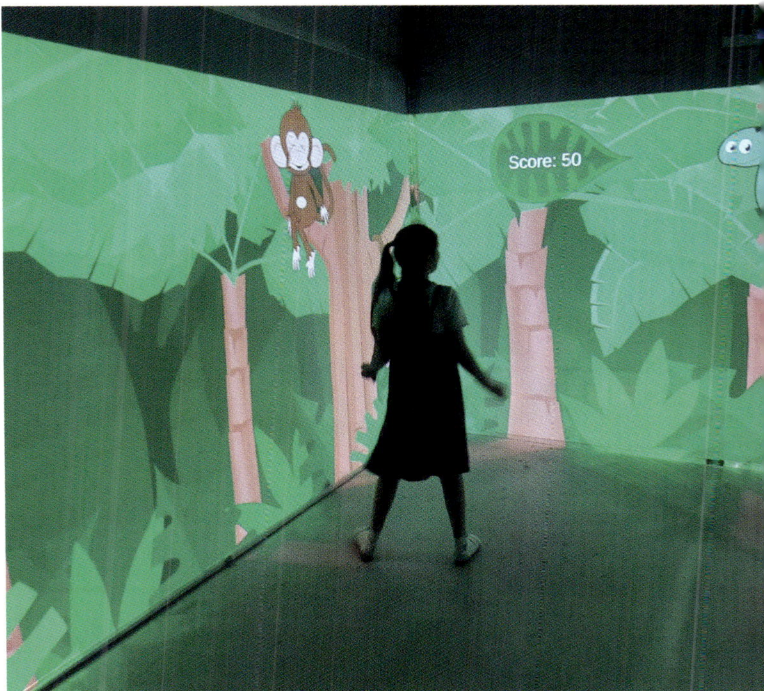

◄ *A modern sensory room at Zen Sensory, Harrogate.*

▼ *The Autism in Racing sensory room.* (Photograph © Bobby Beevers)

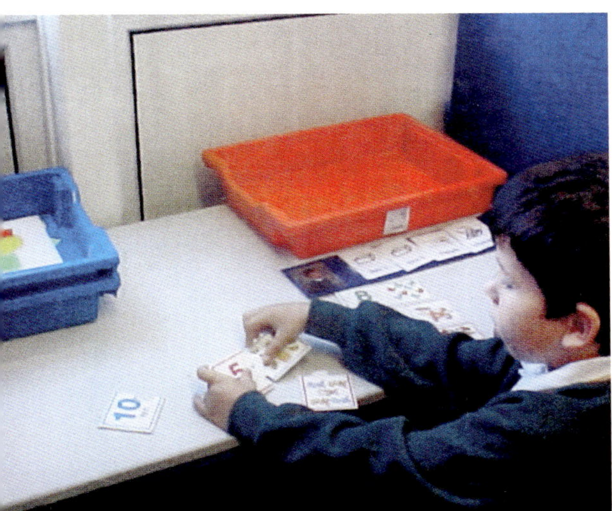

▲ *James using PECS cards as a child.*

▶ *PECS cards that James helped to create.* (Photograph © Louise Hotchkiss)

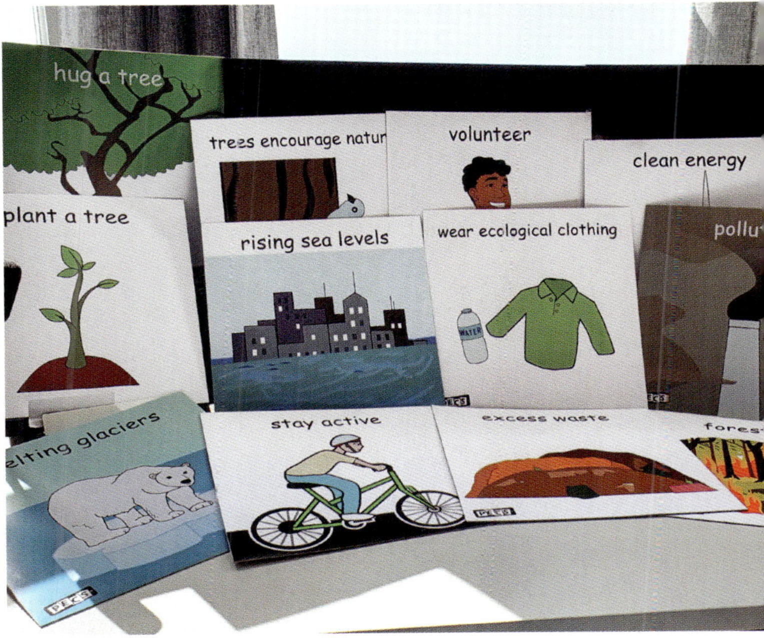

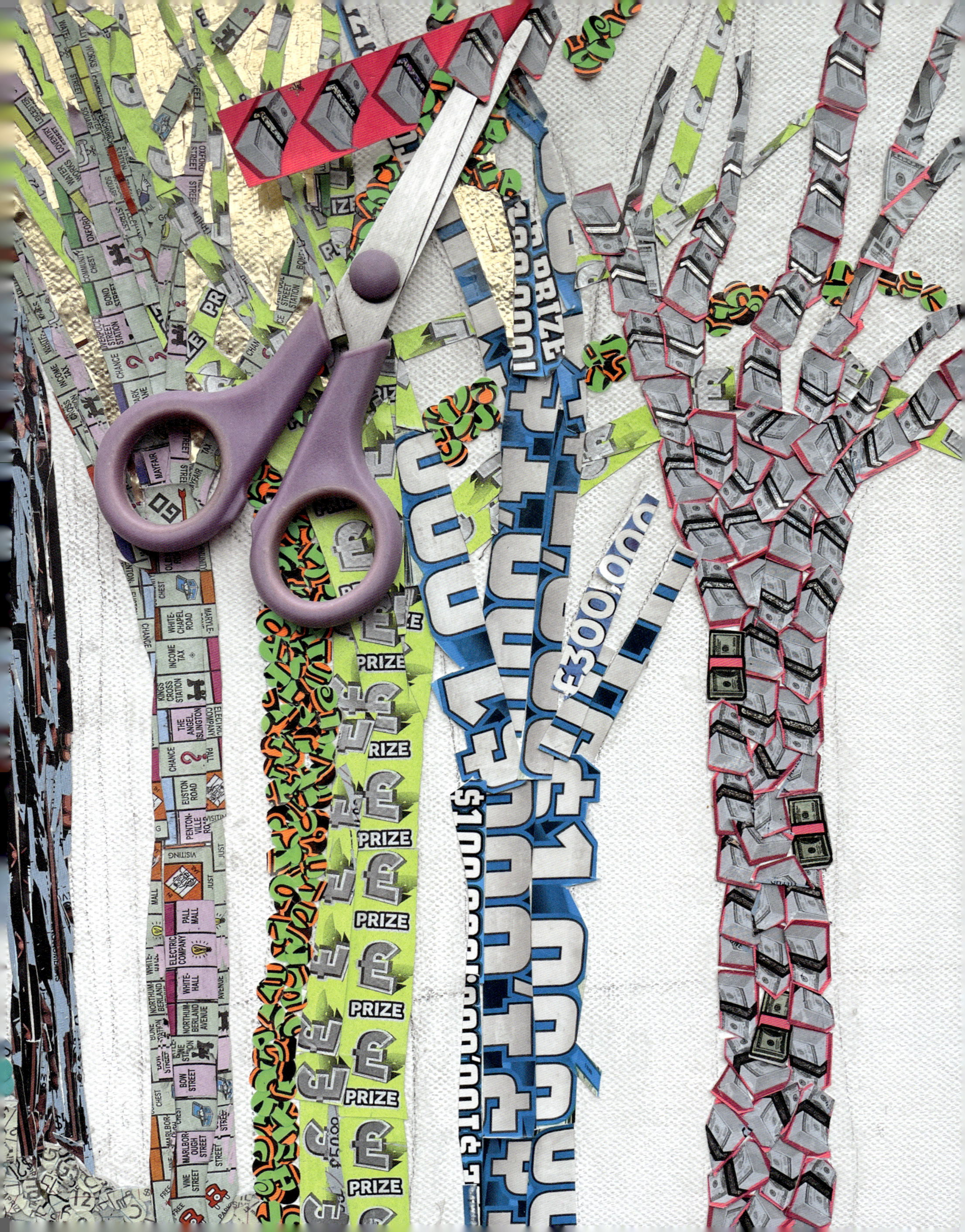

CHAPTER 2

The Collaging Process

James collages many layers of torn, cut or hole-punched pieces of paper and other recycled materials into his artwork. Reimagining single-use items, his style of art is relatively inexpensive and his methods are straightforward. However, the results are beautiful, sensitive in nature and powerfully engaging.

One of his favourite materials is used National Lottery scratchcards. As well as sourcing them for himself, James is given bags of scratchcards from a variety of places, for example from local shops. Once collected, he grades them according to colour and stores them in containers in the cupboard. Smaller boxes are then used to store the pieces he cuts, tears, shreds and hole-punches. The smaller boxes store what is left over after a project. These left-over materials are very useful for his workshops when groups like to use a mix of materials. When starting a new collage, James decides on the method he wants to use and spends many hours preparing the materials once he has a plan.

James tells people that he likes to create order out of disorder. The process of sorting materials is calming to him and helps his autism. He can become very absorbed in the whole process of preparing his art materials. Once, James was sent many sacks of materials from a client who was very enthusiastic to supply him with a huge variety of recycled materials (see page 99). It took days to sort everything out before he was able to start the commission!

◀ *The **Woodland Magic** collage (see page 1) takes shape.*

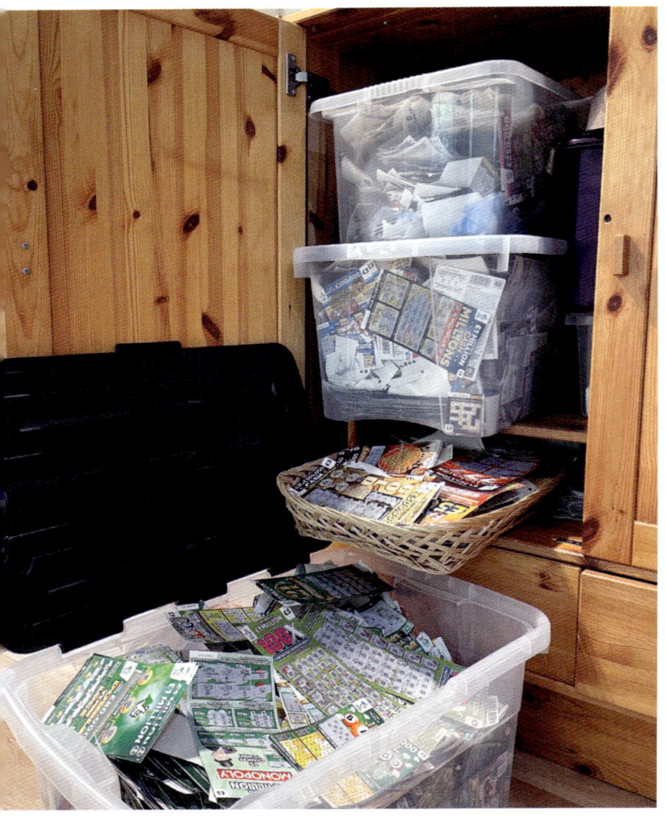

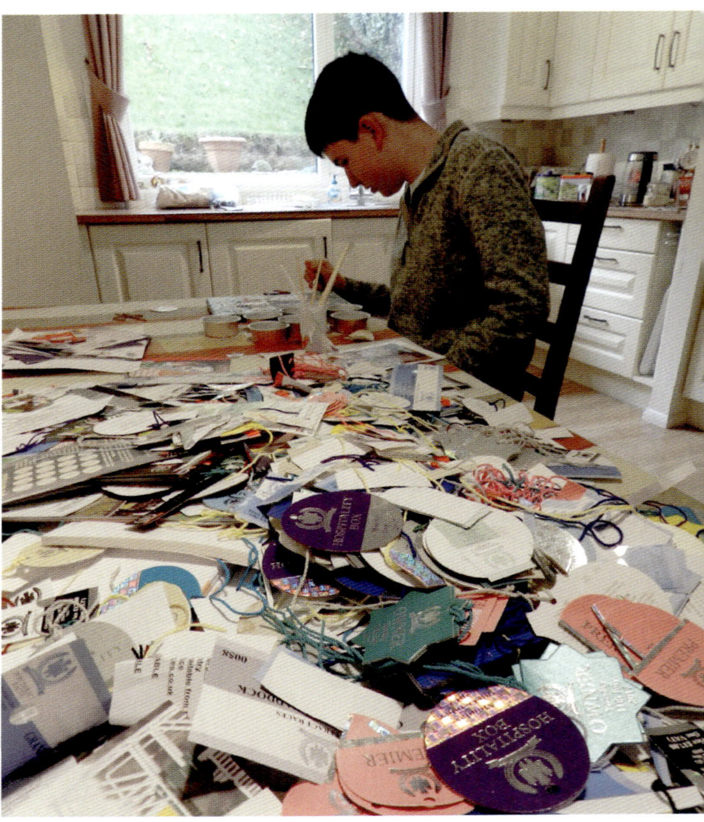

After gathering the raw materials, the initial step is to tear, cut or hole-punch the paper and sort by colour or by symbols found on scratchcards. For example, blue '£' or '$' signs may be used in a variety of ways, such as adding interest and creating clouds.

An office hole punch, a small paintbrush, a pencil, a rubber and a ruler are often all that are needed for the preliminary stages. James has a large store of canvases, bought in advance from charity shops and car boot sales. It is much easier for him to work on white canvases that have never been used before but are still sold as second-hand. However, if the unwanted canvases he has purchased are already printed with pictures, the outlines have to be sketched with a marker pen rather than a pencil. If this still proves difficult – for example on a dark surface – James has sometimes sketched onto white paper and stuck this on top of the printed canvas to make it easier to collage over. Another solution could be to paint the surface of a dark canvas with white paint before the collage, to make sketching easier, but James avoids this method as he doesn't like to use paint. It all depends on how dark the surface area is and if pen markings are visible enough for the outlines.

▲◀ *A cupboard full of donated scratchcard materials.*

▲ *James with an array of materials on his kitchen table.*

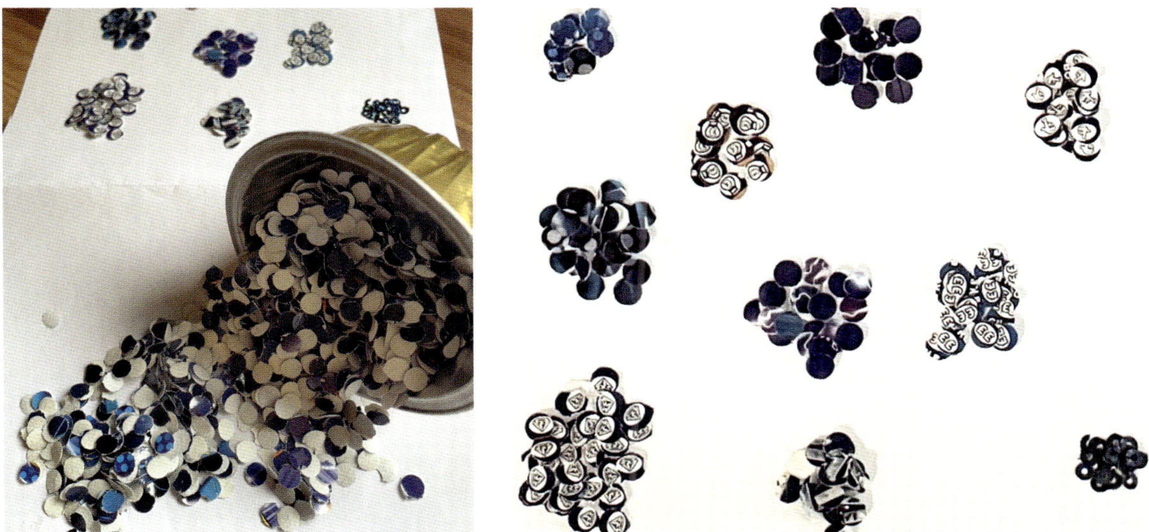

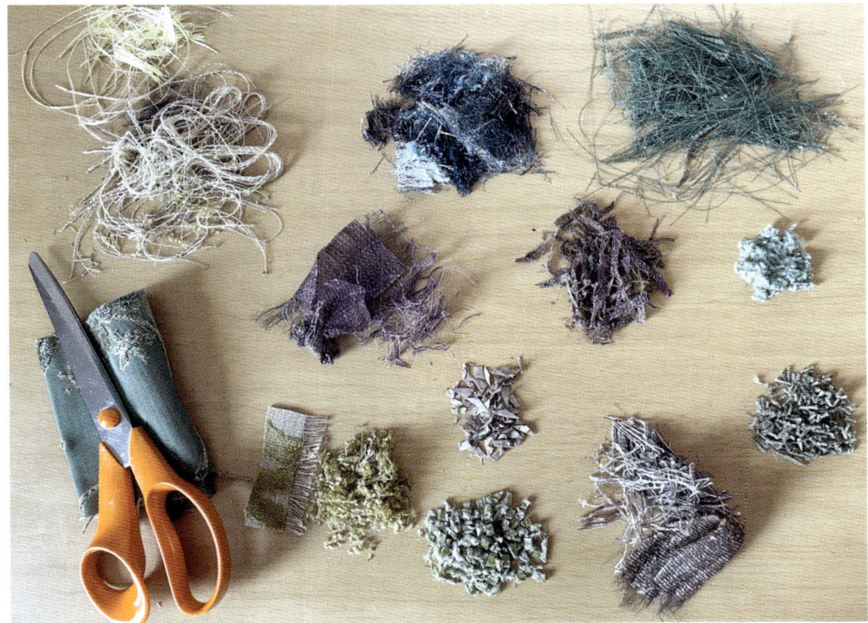

Once sketched, ideas come from the materials available to him such as scratchcards, threads, strings and torn strips of recycled papers from old magazines. Sometimes James knows he will need to work with certain tickets, brochures and fabrics supplied by a client. In addition, only certain colours may be needed. Great British Racing told James he should work with the royal colours of red, gold and purple for the artwork celebrating the King's coronation (see pages 99–103), but he could also add black and white

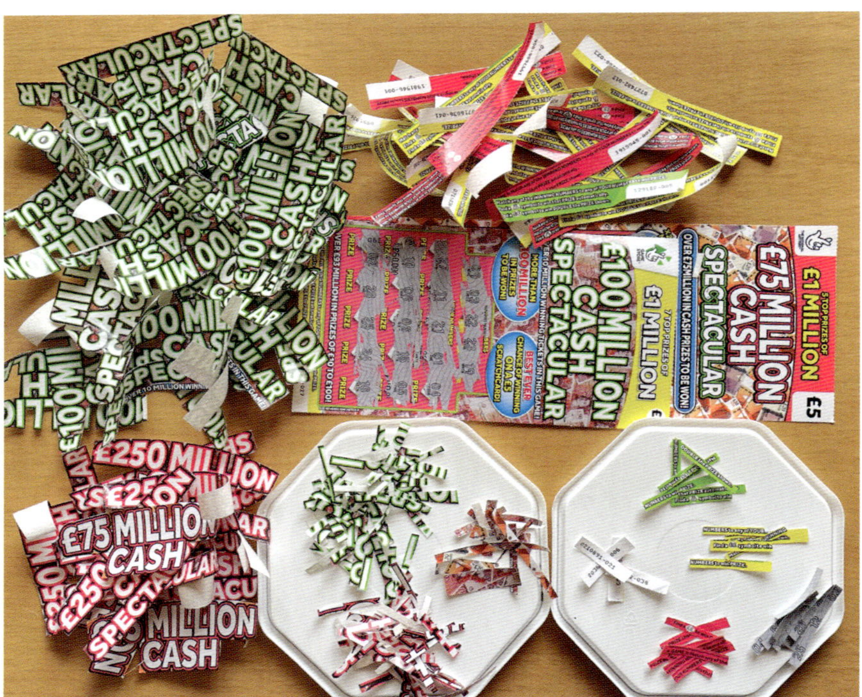

◀ *The repetitive use of words from scratchcards forms striking patterns and adds meaning to some of the artworks.*

▼◀ *Some basic tools – eraser, pencil, scissors, hole punch, glue brush and ruler.*

▼ *Water-based sealants and varnish provide a glossy and sometimes glittery finish, as well as fixing the many pieces of the collage firmly in place.*

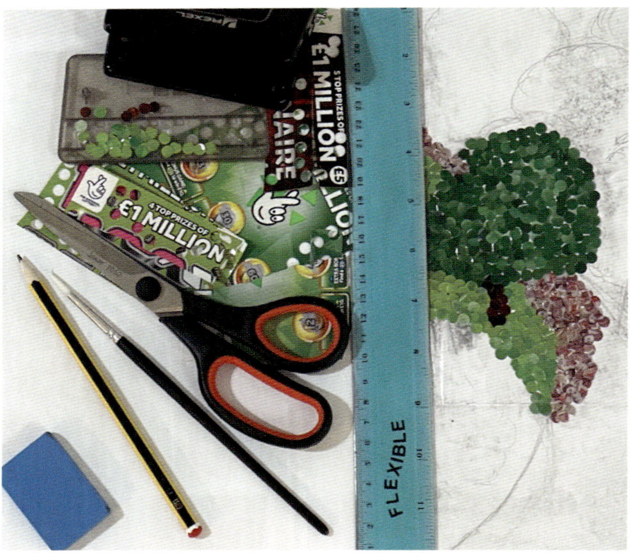

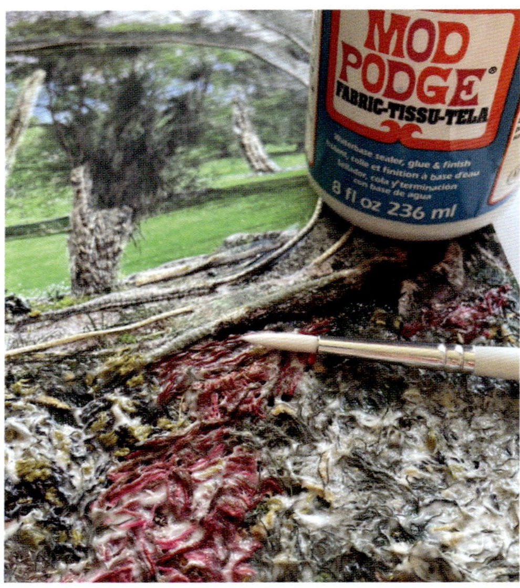

into the collage. James often starts a collage without fully knowing how it will develop and, in the case of this coronation piece, he was concerned how he would create the horse's mane and tail until he found an old black plastic carrier bag at home, which he cut into thin strips. Problem solved!

STAINING PAPER

For some artworks, a paper shredder can be used to create more texture and give a raised, three-dimensional appearance. When using card, it is made easier to shred by peeling off its backing (**a**, **b**).

A natural stain can be given to the pieces of shredded paper by adding them to water in a bowl with used teabags to soak for several hours or overnight. Different tones can be achieved by experimenting with other teas, such as Earl Grey or camomile. After soaking, the water is drained off (**c**) and the paper pieces allowed to dry out, leaving strands that look like dried-out pasta.

Excess water can be dabbed away using kitchen paper. Then, when either damp or completely dried, they can be used to give a crinkly texture for the bark of trees etc. (for example in the 'Erik the Red' series of tree collages on pages 68–9).

Alternatively, the damp strands of paper can be flattened between sheets of kitchen paper with a rolling pin (**d**). This method is useful for creating smoother textures e.g. paths and roads (see *By Moonlight* on page 118–19).

IS IT FINISHED?

James uses several different techniques in each collage and it often takes him a long time to build layers of texture until he is satisfied with the end result. He invests a great deal of time layering and experimenting until the composition aligns with his vision. There are occasions when he finds it difficult to know when a piece of artwork is finished and sometimes he has to return to make adjustments to improve it.

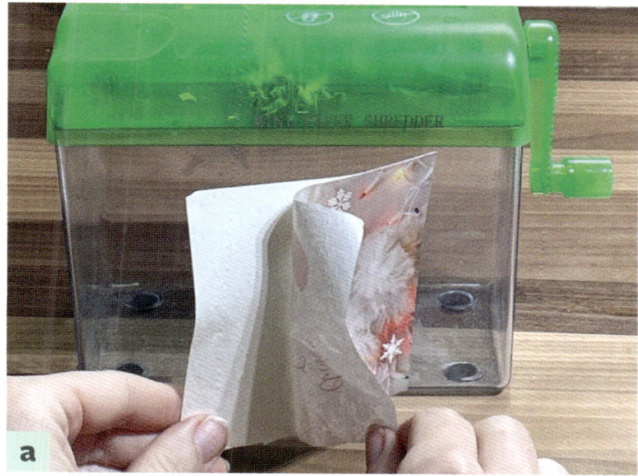

Peeling the backing off card before shredding.

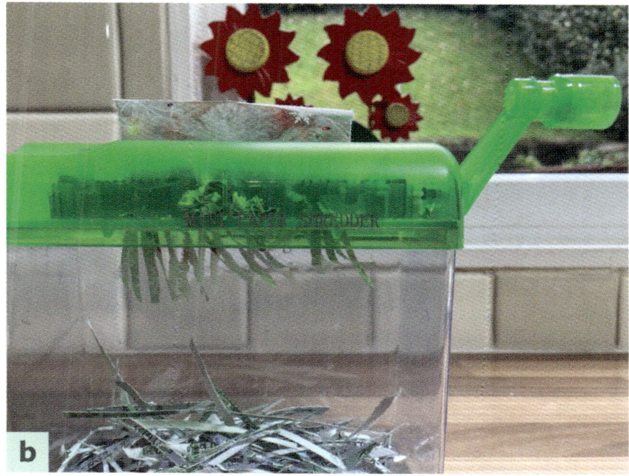

Shredding the card.

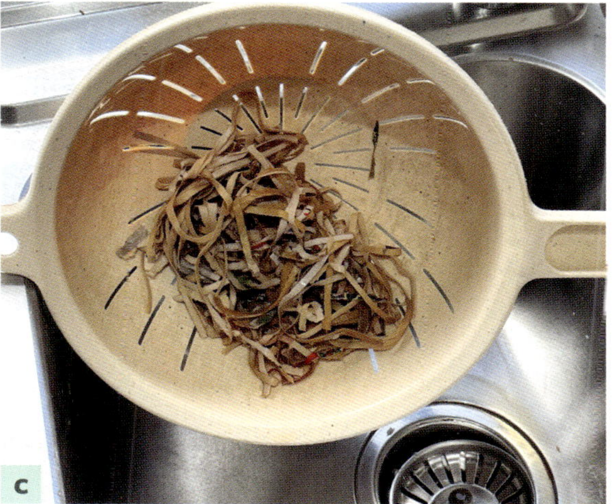

Tea-soaked strands of paper after draining.

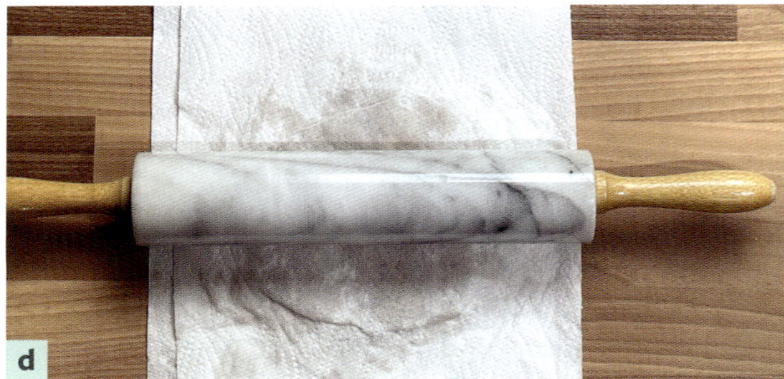

Using a rolling pin to dry damp card strands.

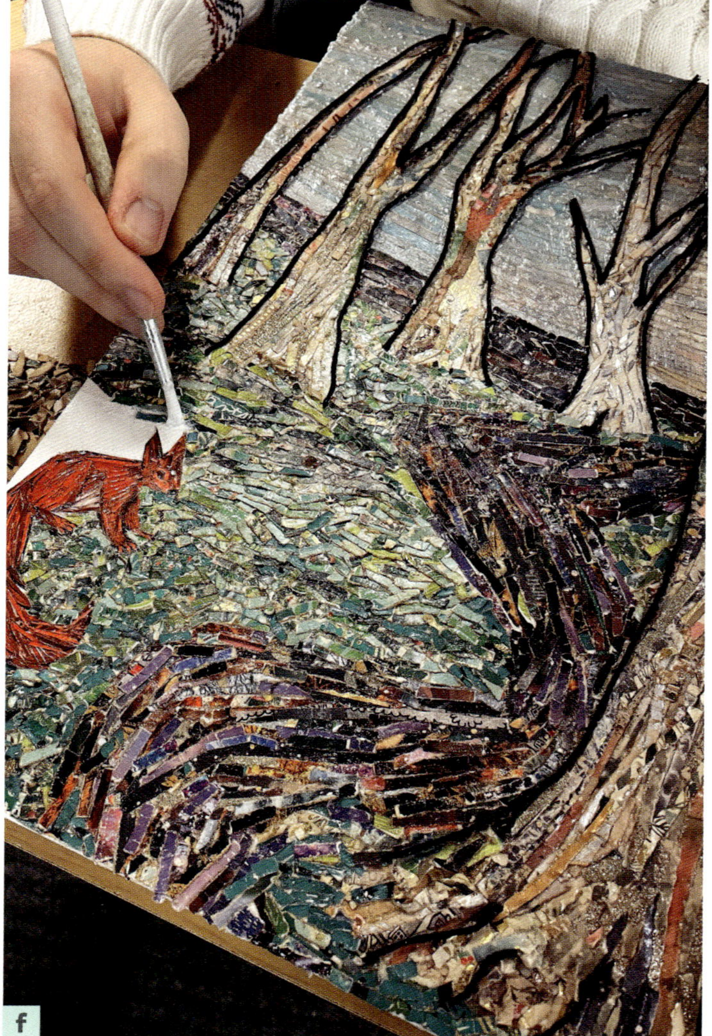

The remainder of the collage nears completion.

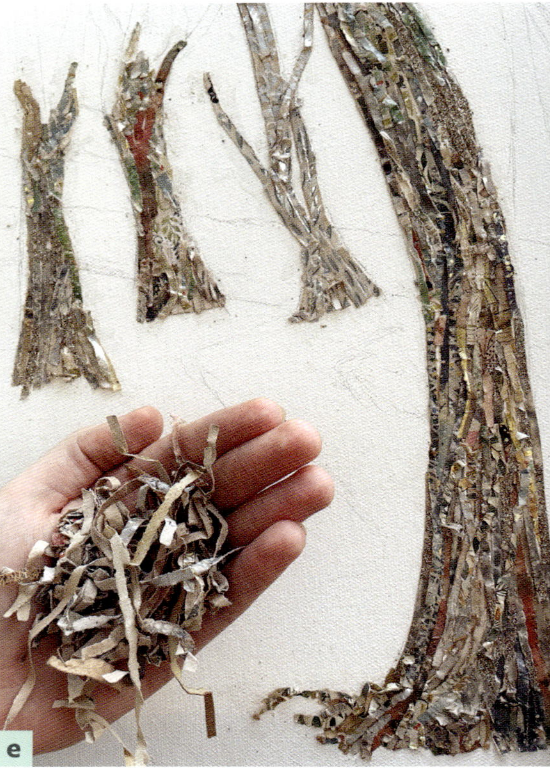

Applying tea-stained shredded paper to the tree trunks in a collage.

The process is ideal for staining old Christmas cards and providing them with a more natural brown colour rather than a bright white background (**e**, **f**). Shredded scratchcards do not necessarily stain as well because of their shiny finish, but they can still be used to create texture in collages (see the pathway in *Woodland Magic* on page 1).

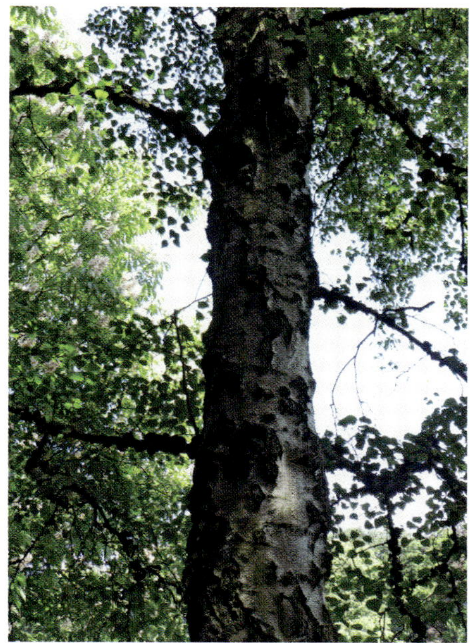

▲ *Original photograph of a tree.*

PHOTO-COLLAGE TECHNIQUE

This technique transforms a photograph fully or partly into a collage. The first step is to decide which area of the photograph to collage and apply just a small amount of glue with a brush – then various materials can be applied depending on the desired effect. Thin strips of different fabrics placed next to each other make a good effect for bark. Different shades of brown, beige and green go well together, but adding in more unusual colours like purple also can be effective. Fabric can be cut into smaller pieces as required. Cutting it finely creates a fluffy effect to use in areas of moss etc. Gold and silver threads pick up the light when highlighting areas. Brown and green threads are good for lining edges. Small pieces of torn, cut or hole-punched paper from recycled scratchcards, packaging and magazines add texture when layered into the collage.

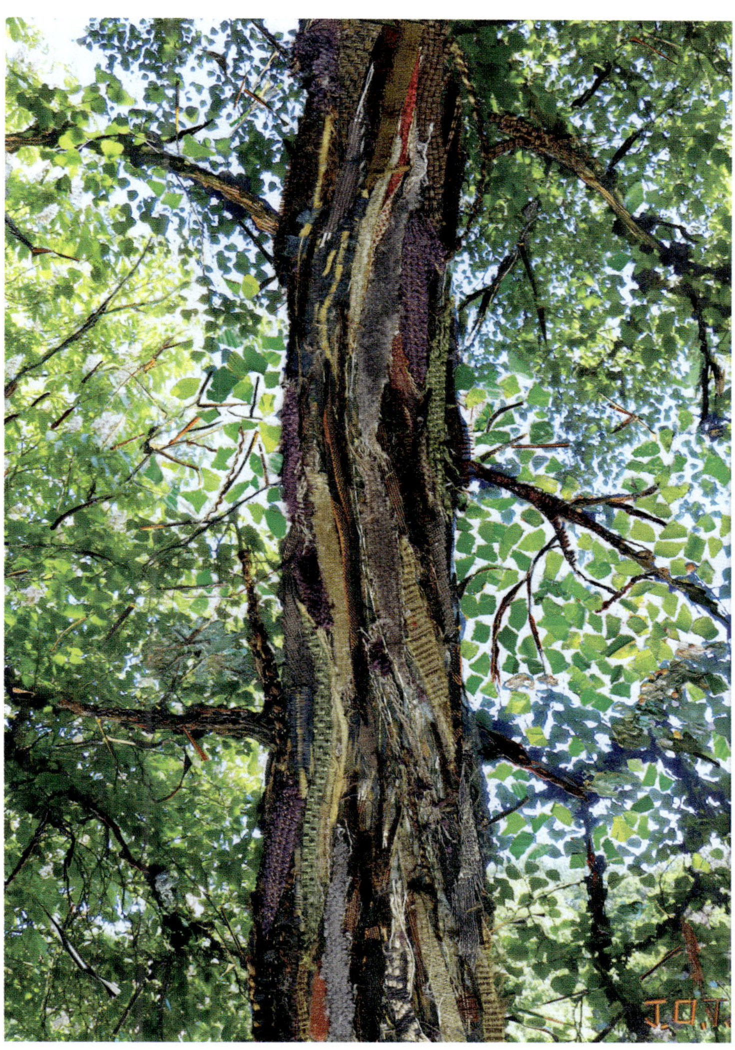

▲ *The same photograph almost fully collaged with fabric for the bark and torn paper for the leaves.*

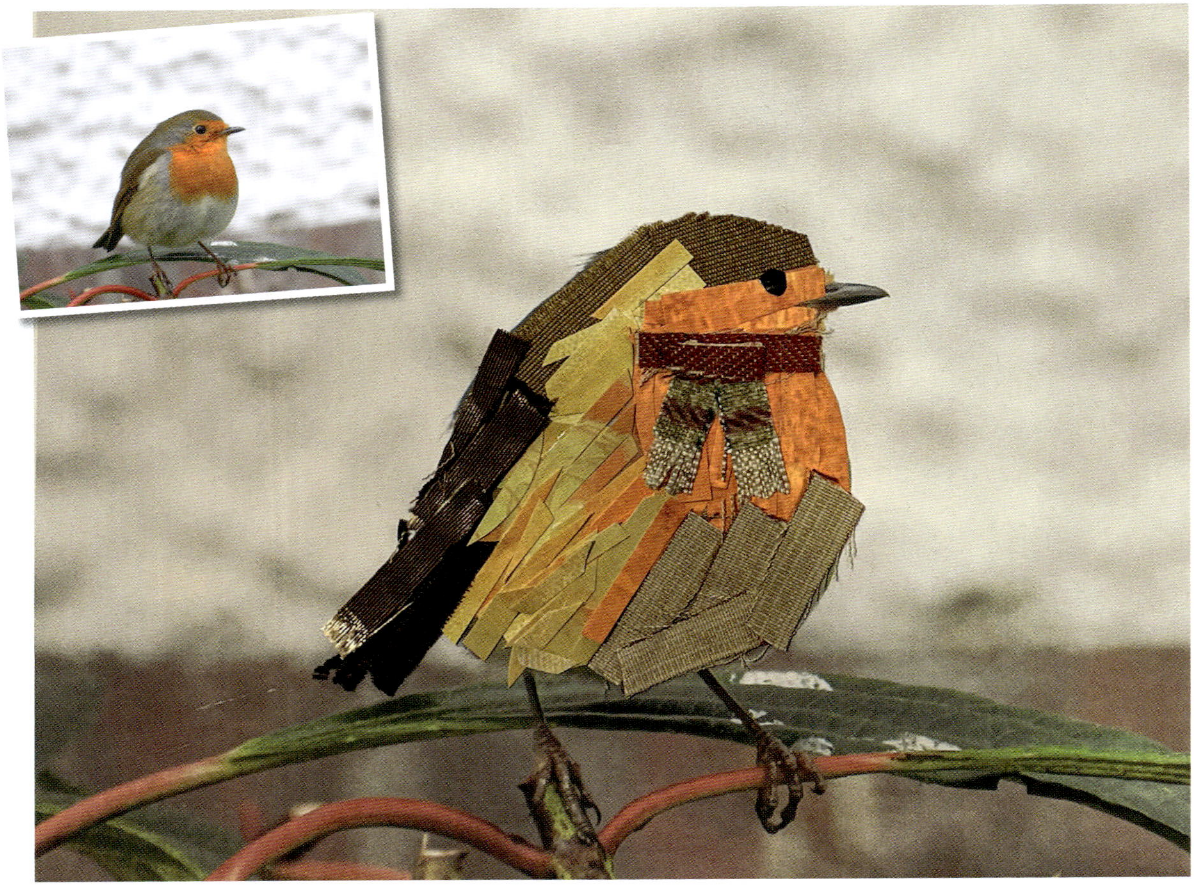

▲▲ Original photograph of a robin, taken by James.

▲ The photo-collaging in this case (undertaken by someone at one of James' workshops) was kept to just the robin itself, in gold and brown fabric and with cut strips of orange scratchcard.

▶ This photo collage of Brighton Pier shows James' concern for the environment. Plastic is forever washed up on shore, so he used plastic sequins from recycled clothing for the beach. It brings a sombre environmental message to the artwork.

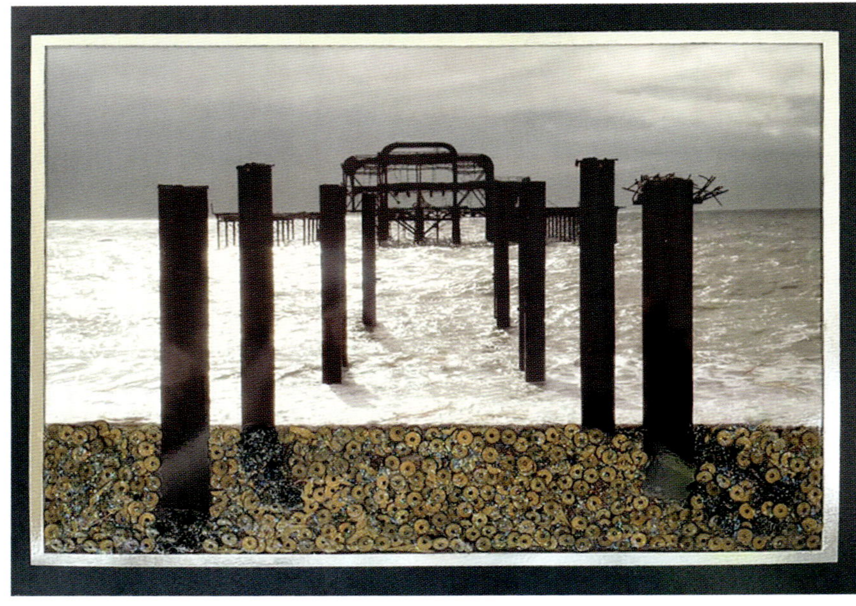

ENCAUSTIC TECHNIQUE

Occasionally, James uses an encaustic wax technique. He was introduced to this method of painting with beeswax by Brian Nelson, the founder of Encaustic Art Plus and Encaustic Art UK, who is well aware of the therapeutic nature of the craft.

Working with encaustic wax enables James to create unusual and abstract shapes for dreamlike landscapes, whether used as a solid background or torn up for other effects.

When James' interest in encaustic art developed, he purchased a starter set that included an

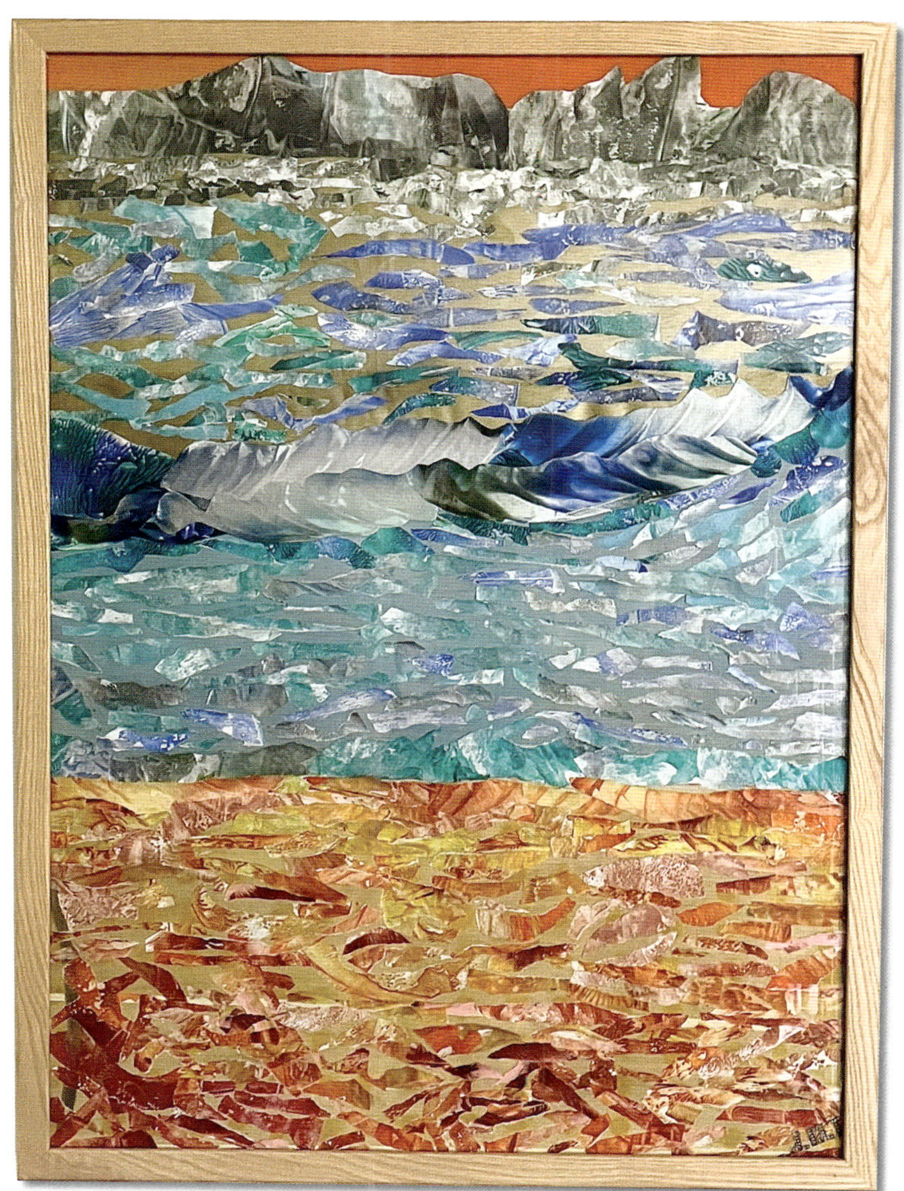

▶ James tore strips of encaustic paper for his piece called **A Changing World**. This piece shows the effects of climate change, with ice melting into the ocean and sea levels rising.

encaustic art painting iron, a selection of wax block colours, painting cards, a metal scribing tool and a short guide book. Care should, of course, be taken when using the painting iron and any appropriate safety advice followed. Once James had used the painting cards, he started to work with some of his own recycled card material with a glossy surface.

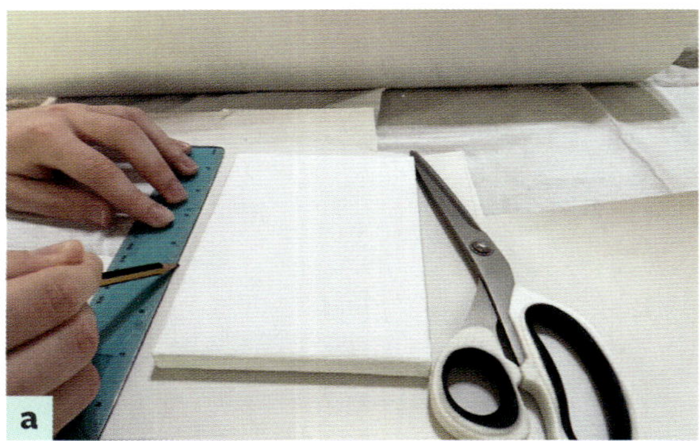

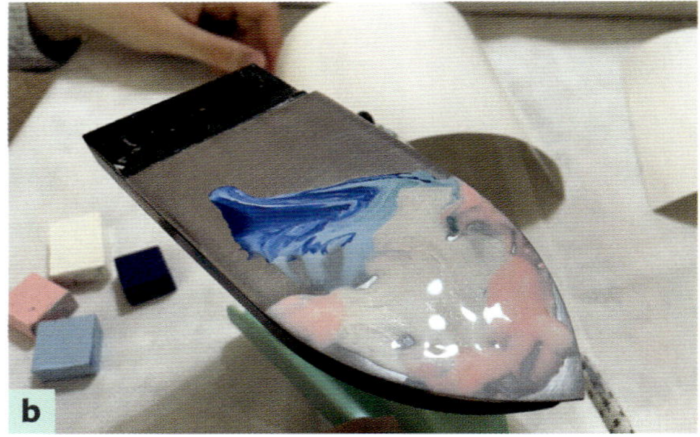

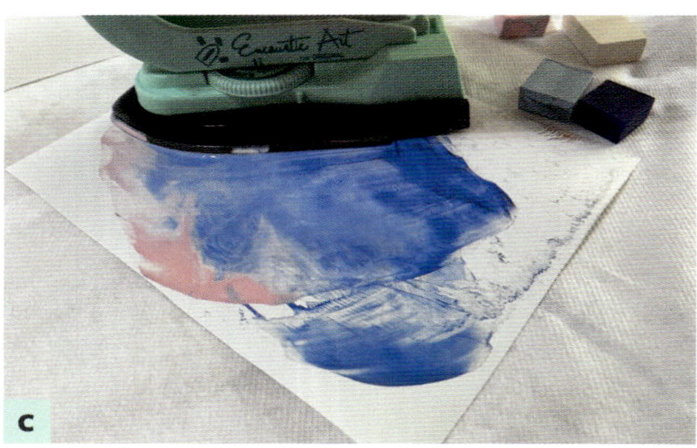

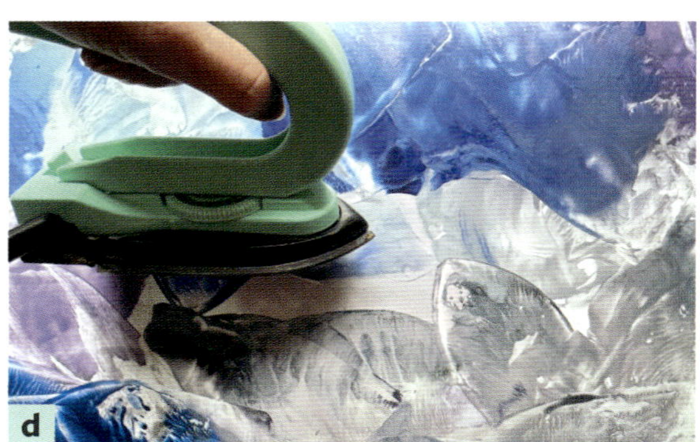

a *Measuring recycled card that will be used for ironing encaustic wax, which will then be covered over a canvas.*

b *Blocks of encaustic wax can be combined onto the surface of the specialist iron to melt and achieve various results.*

c *The wax is applied and smoothed onto the card using the iron.*

d *For a slightly different effect, the wax-covered iron can be dabbed up and down onto the card.*

e *Wax can be layered, scraped and dabbed to produce different textures. Papers covered in encaustic pigment can be torn into strips to form jagged patterned backgrounds.*

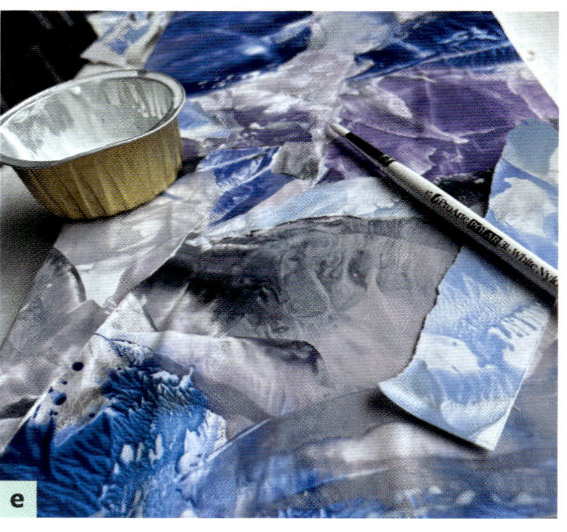

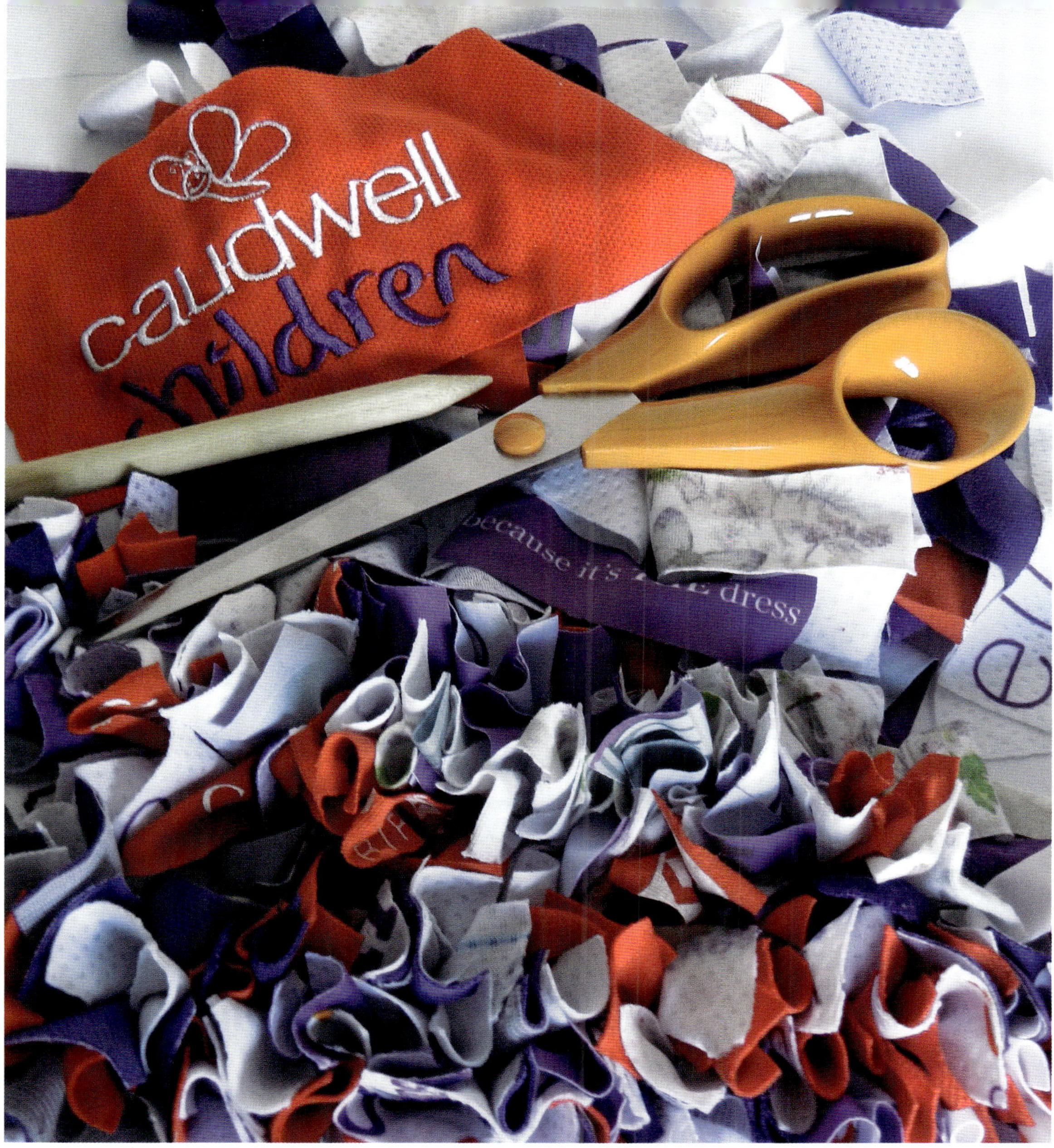

RAG ART

Scraps and fibres play a part in many of James' pieces, for example in *By Moonlight* (see page 118–19), where the complete background was created from an old black T-shirt which was cut into many small pieces and given a glittery coating of varnish to fix it for a starry night-time appearance.

In some of the fundraising collages for the Caudwell Children's Charity, he also cut the Caudwell logo and name from t-shirts and added them to his collages.

▲ *Cut-out Caudwell logo among other scraps.*

COLLAGING NATURAL MATERIALS

Natural materials can be incredibly useful in collage. Tea leaves scattered onto pathways, for example, can make an effective muddy appearance, or dried leaves and dried petals can be added to synthetic materials. An example of this can be found in *Within the Woodland.*

▶ ***Within the Woodland*** *uses real leaves on the ground.* ▼

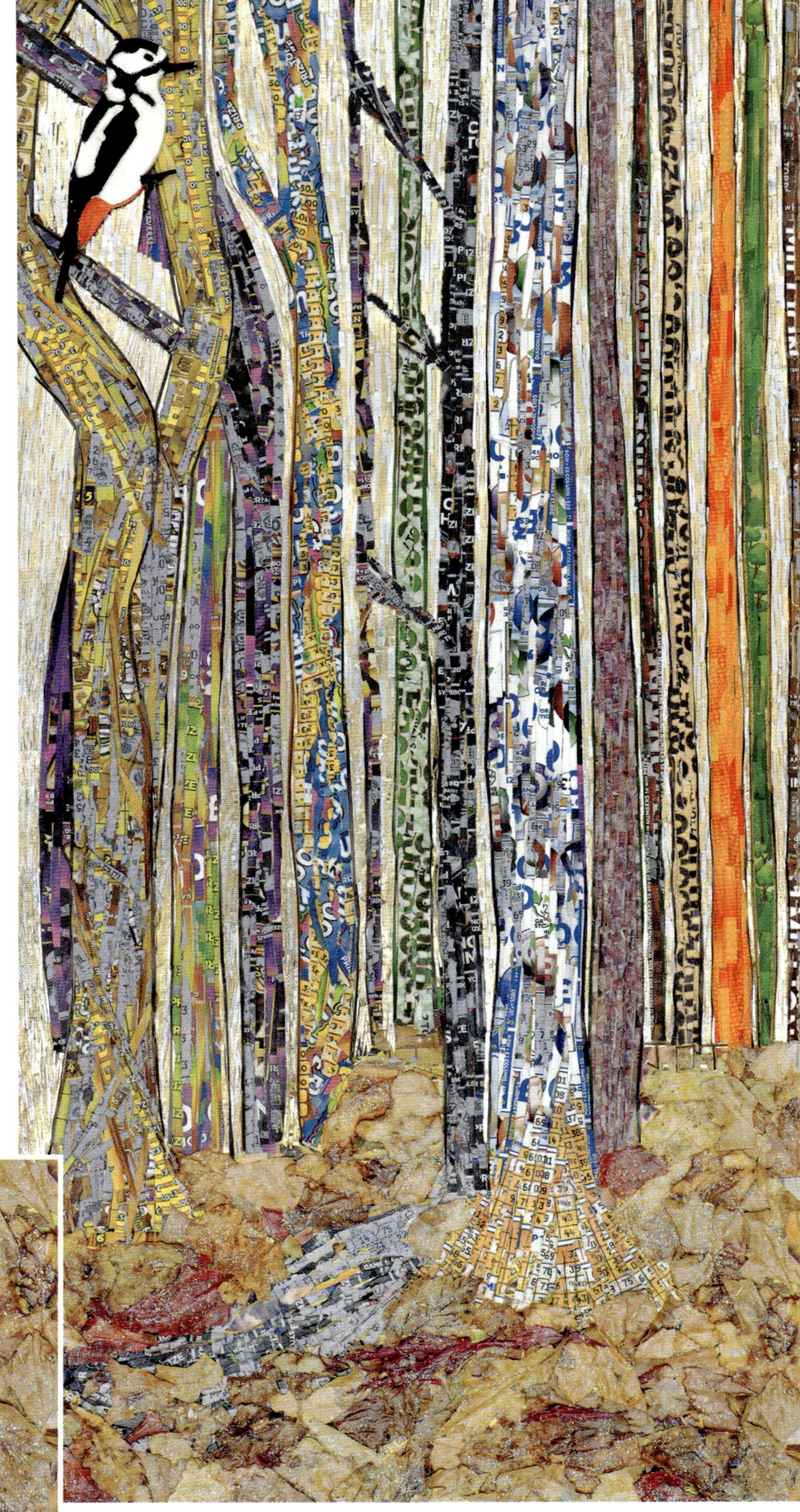

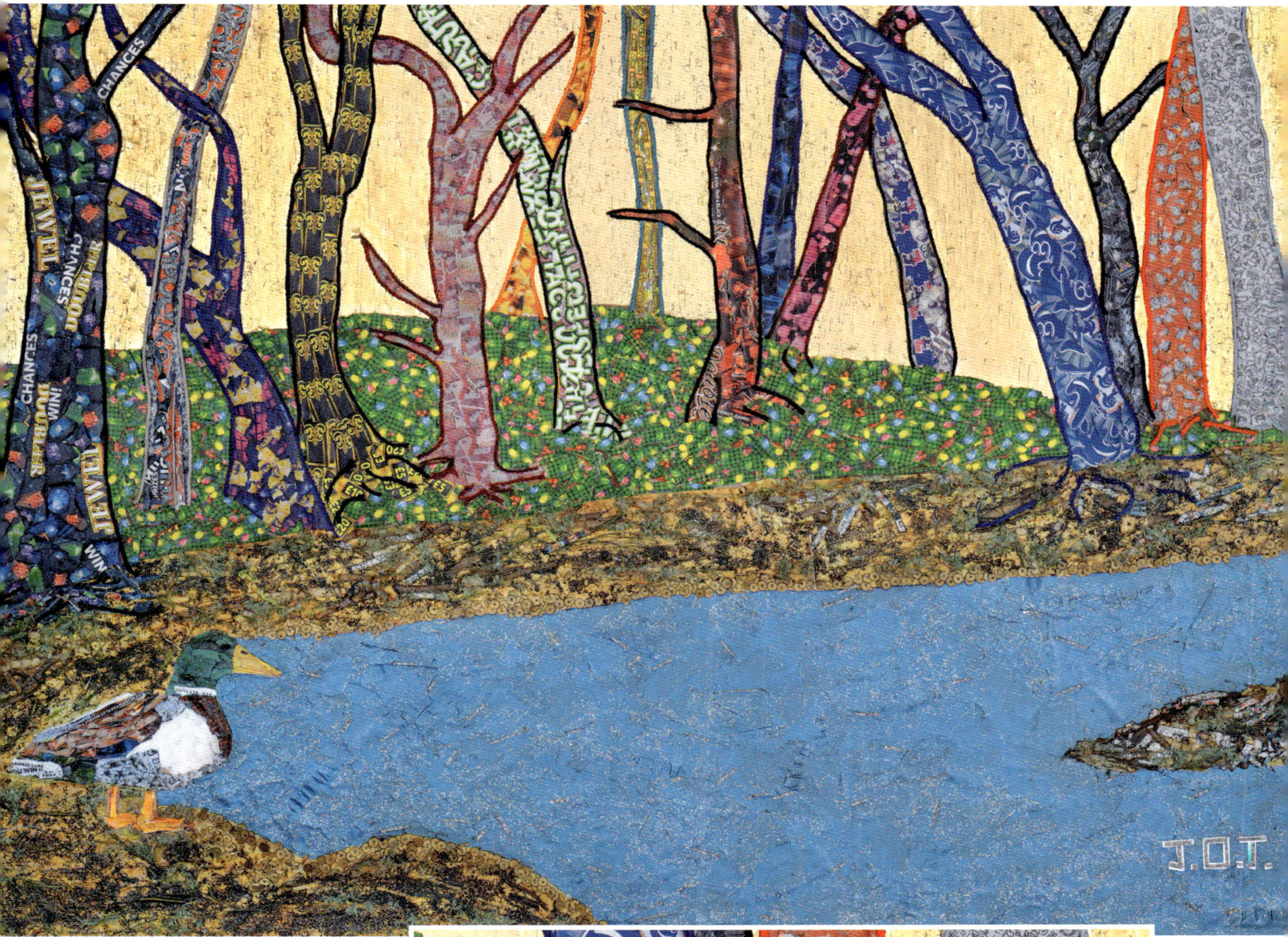

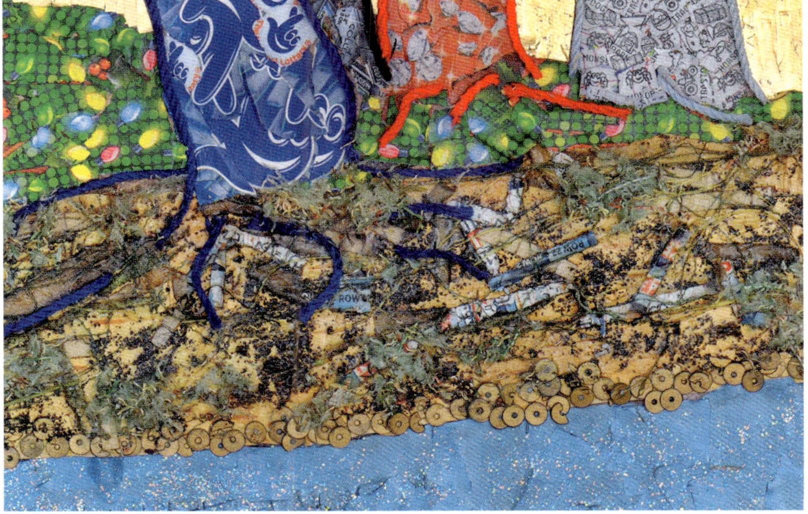

▲ In *Fishpond Wood*, silver birch bark was used as a base on the path, along with tea leaves and sequins. ▶

CHAPTER 3

The Artworks

GARDEN CREATURES

It is amazing what can be seen from a window overlooking a simple household garden. As a child, James would often stare out of his window to see what birds or small creatures would visit. He would often say to his mother that it felt like they were his pets, except that they could come and go as they pleased. His mother asked him if he would like a cat or dog of his own, but James found the sound of a dog's bark distressing and a cat's natural inclination to hunt birds and mice too upsetting to watch.

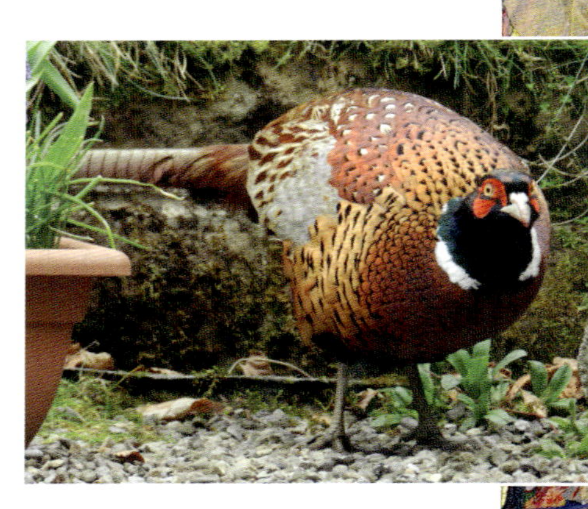

▲ *A pheasant in James' garden, and the collage it inspired.*

James was happy to look at wildlife entering his garden. As he fed the birds every day, they became almost tame. Blackbirds, sparrows, pheasants, robins, wood pigeons and doves visited most often. He gave them names as he recognised the same ones coming back again and again for their food. They often perched on the kitchen windowsill, staring through the glass, waiting for snacks. And when James was in the garden, they would follow him around hoping he'd give them more food.

James found it very calming. He especially liked watching blackbirds fill their beaks with currants and take them off to their nests to feed their young chicks. Wildlife such as rabbits, hedgehogs and mice join the birds in exploring his garden. He now keeps his camera to hand, taking photographs of them to refer to as he incorporates all these birds and animals into his art.

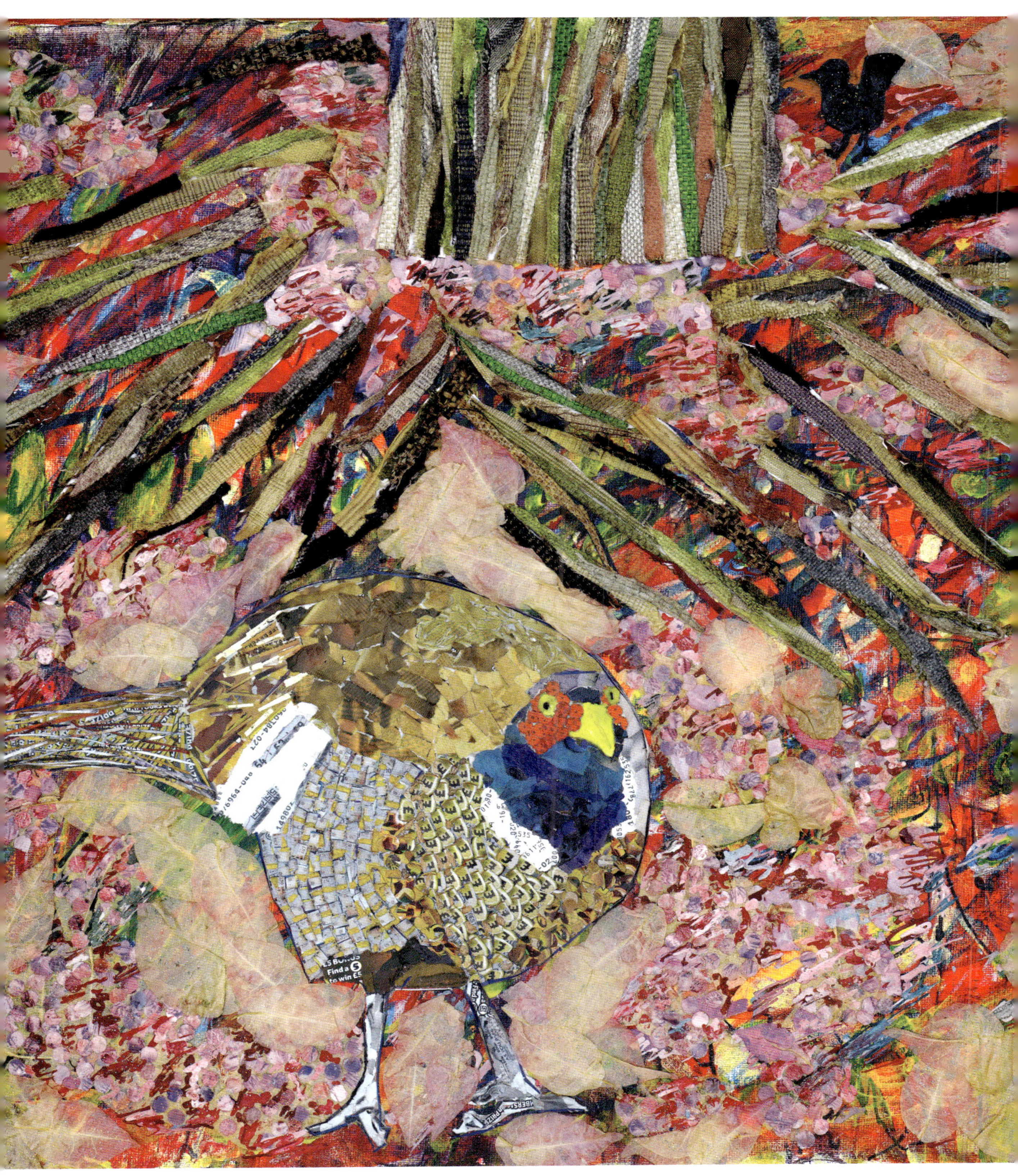

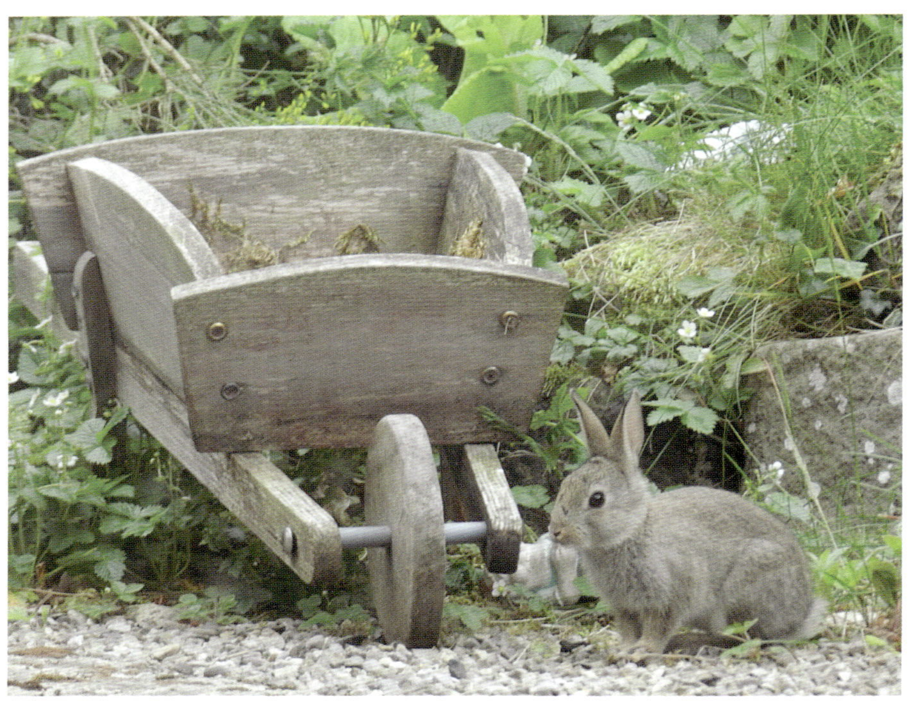

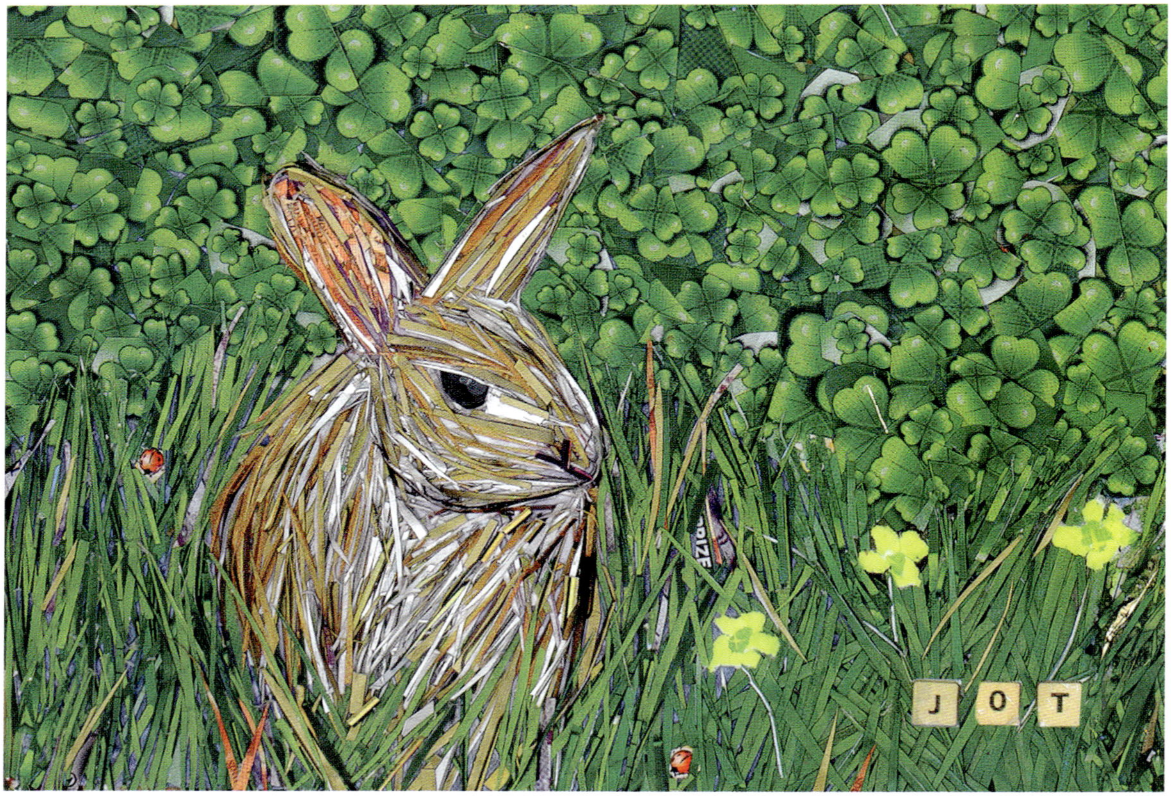

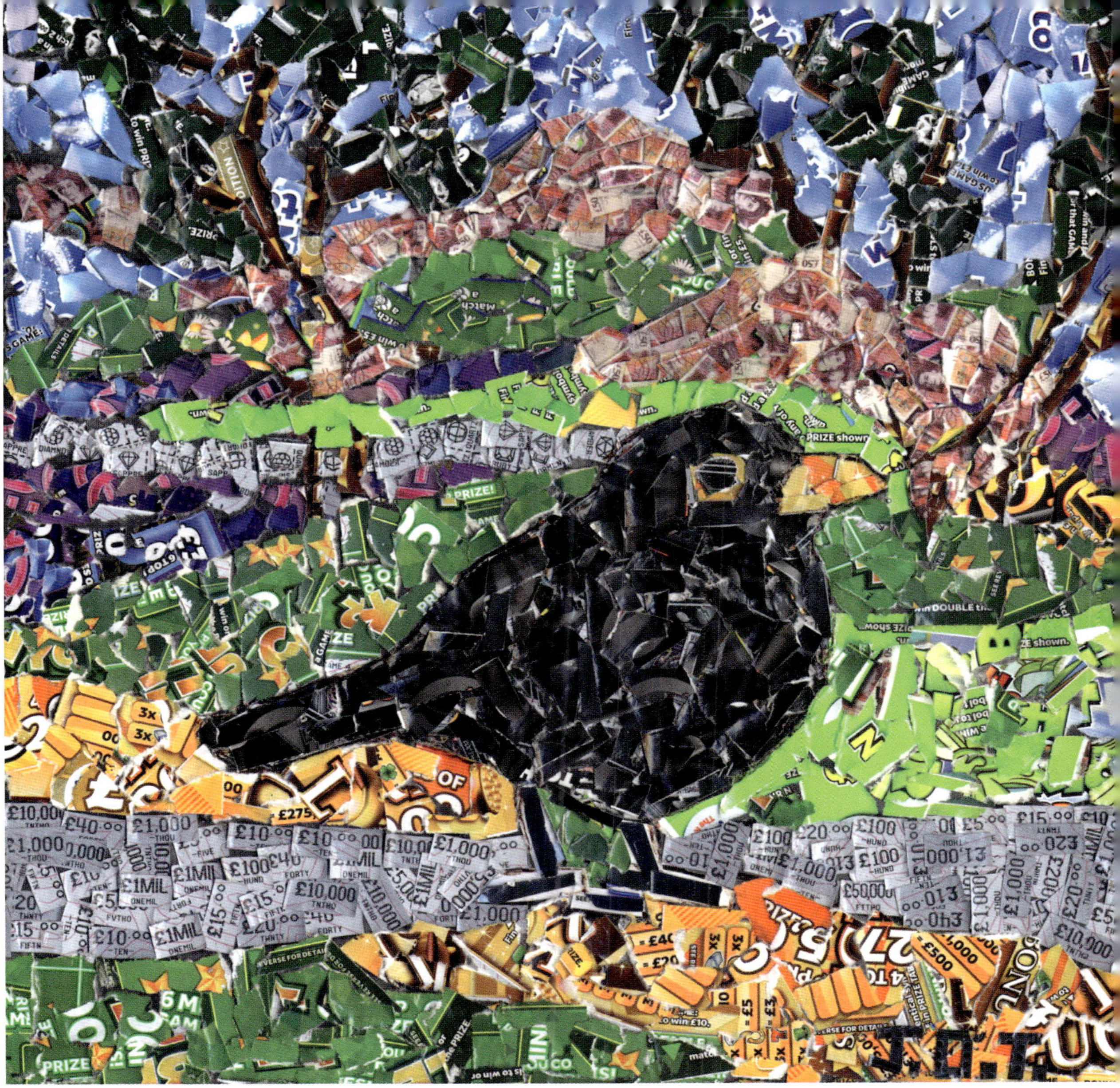

Some other photographs James has taken
and the artworks they have inspired.

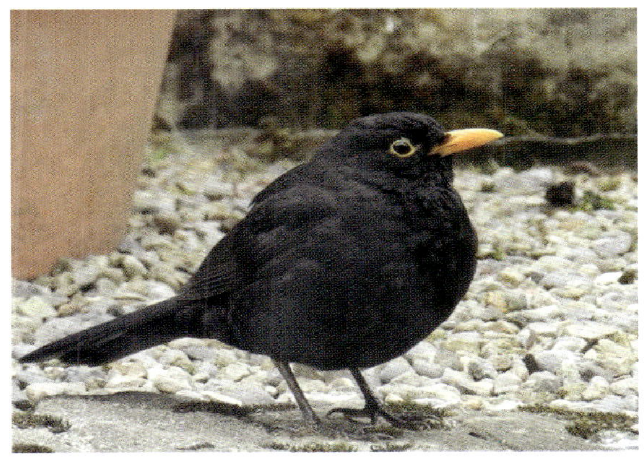

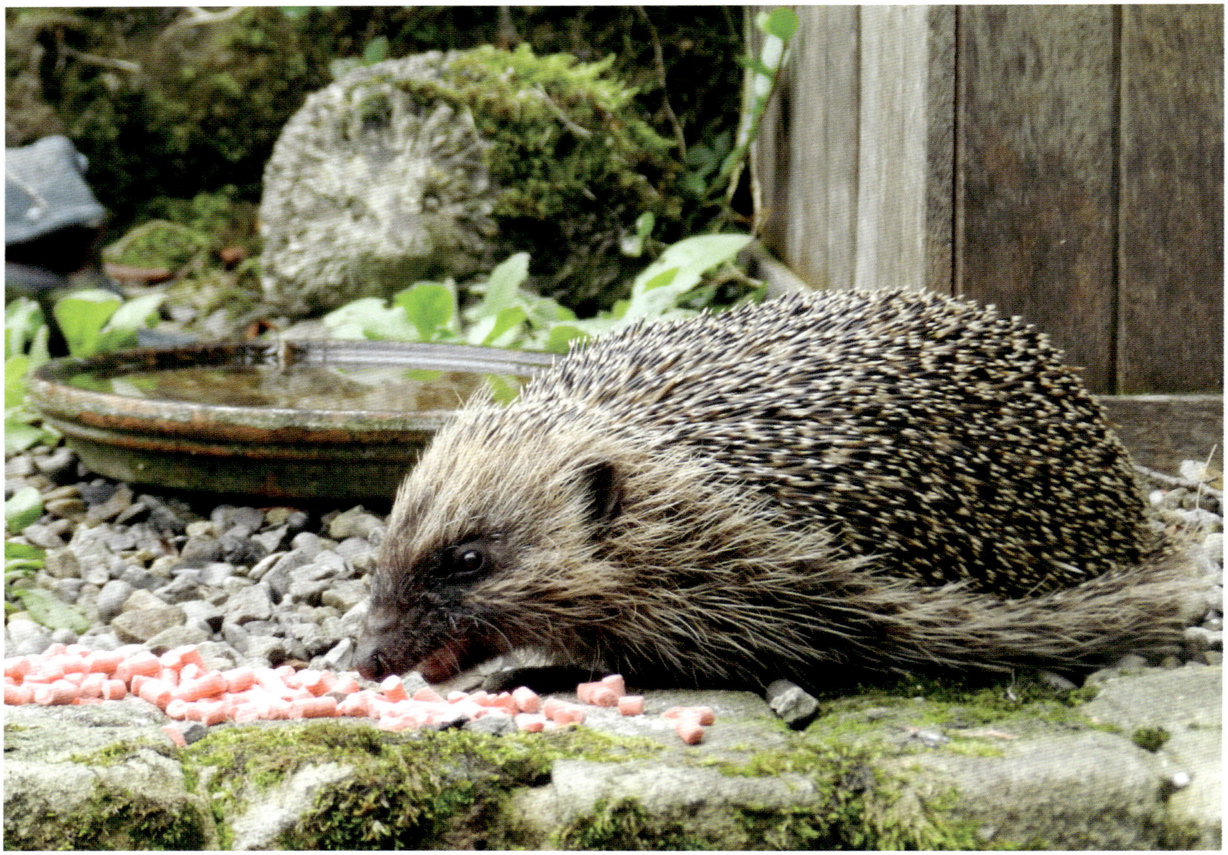

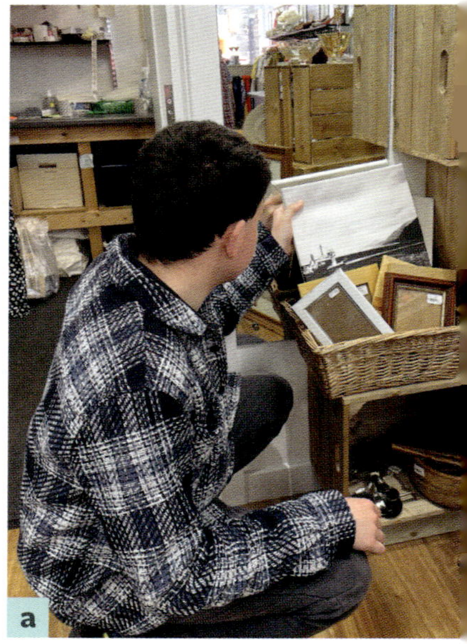

HEDGEHOGS

For the artworks that follow, James was inspired by a hedgehog.

The first thing he does is find a support on which to make the collage, usually going to the local charity shop to find second-hand canvases (**a**). They may be hidden in a basket among photo frames and books, etc, or stacked against a wall. In this case he chose a set of three canvases, on which he would use different techniques, but all on the theme of hedgehogs.

When something catches his eye, he'll take a closer look. If he's lucky, he'll find just what he's looking for. In this case he found a small, stretched canvas with a dull, black-and-white photo that could easily be covered by his collage art. He also found a couple of small, white canvases. It doesn't matter if there are slight dents and marks on the second-hand canvases as the collaging process will hide these types of imperfection.

James was also inspired by a walk along a path that winds through some local woodland with a river running through it. He chose a point of view and roughly sketched out the position of the trees (**b**).

Finding a canvas.

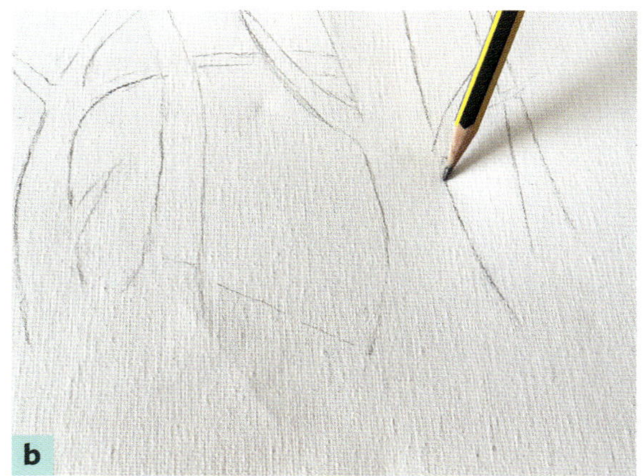

Sketching the trees.

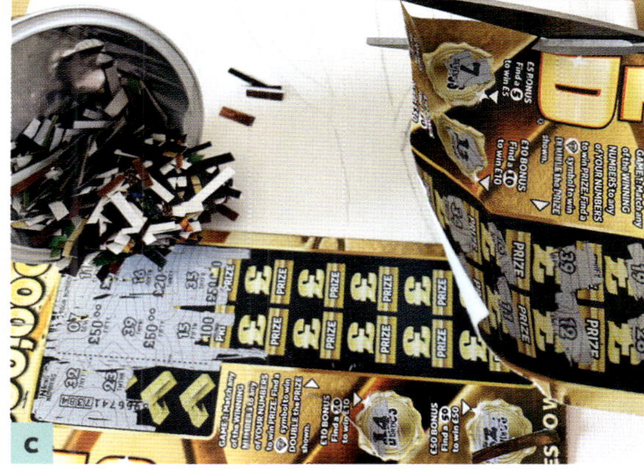

Trimming the cards.

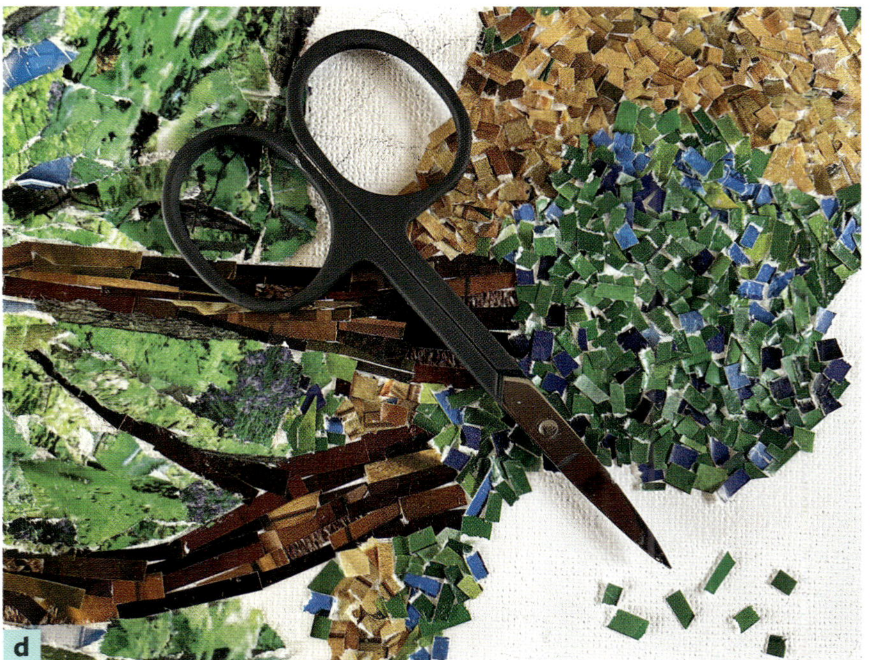

Colour variation on the tree trunks and cutting squares for the grass and bluebells.

BARK

James has always been fascinated by the feel of bark, whether it has a coarse and rugged texture or it is fine and smooth – he once saved some strips of silver birch that are as smooth as paper!

The varied and intricate textures of tree bark can be represented through collage in many ways. In other artworks, such as *Árbol de la Vida* (*Tree of Life*), James cut and twisted up different types of fabric to simulate the rough texture of a tree trunk.

Looking through his collection of discarded scratchcards, James searched for colours that would match his ideas. Here, some scratchcards with brown and gold edges (**c**) are trimmed to make up the trunks and branches of the trees.

He mixed up the different shades of brown and gold to give vitality to the tree trunks and make them seem three-dimensional (**d**).

For the grass, strips were cut from green scratchcards, then cut down further to make tiny squares that overlap to create the effect of separate clumps of grass. With several layers, the appearance of thick grass can be convincingly represented. This is time-consuming but gives a richer result – far better than a surface that appears too flat.

James wanted to add the appearance of some delicate bluebells growing across the forest floor, so he dotted in a scattering of blue-coloured offcuts to represent the springtime blooms.

The woodland setting that would be the hedgehog's home was taking shape nicely (**e**).

Both the path and the grass are dotted with minute fragments of recycled scratchcards. Layering the scraps makes a good textured surface, hinting at mud, leaves, twigs and dappled light on the woodland floor. The sky is made from torn pieces of blue paper from old magazines, made into a base coat and later partly covered by torn pieces of green paper, also from magazines (**f**). The hedgehog's face was made from brown magazine paper, then its spines were made from small strips of grey scratchcards. Thin strands of gold thread and black dots of paper were used for its eye and the nose was added to complete the hedgehog.

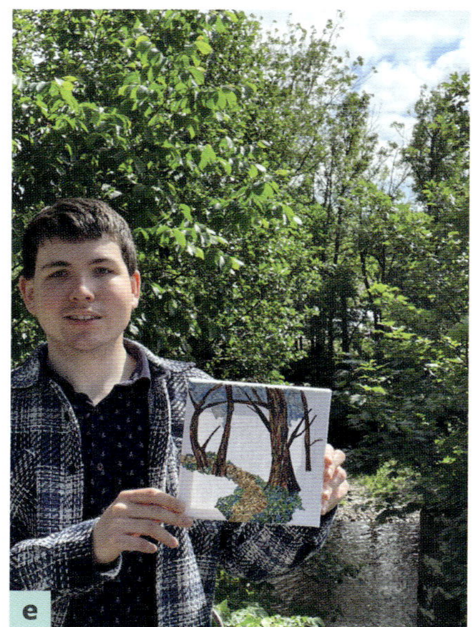

James occasionally revisited the actual scene to see what other details he might want to add and to gain some more inspiration from nature.

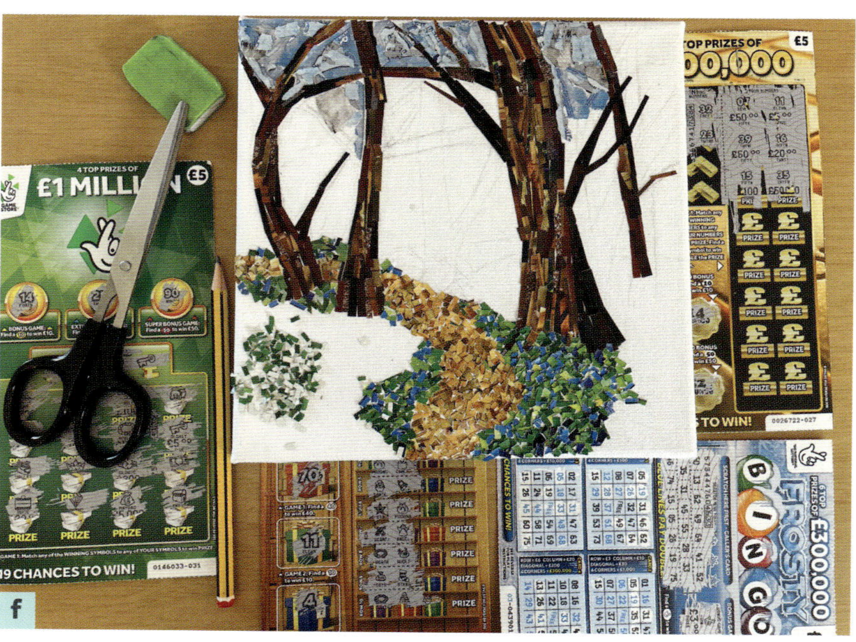

Working on the sky as the piece takes shape.

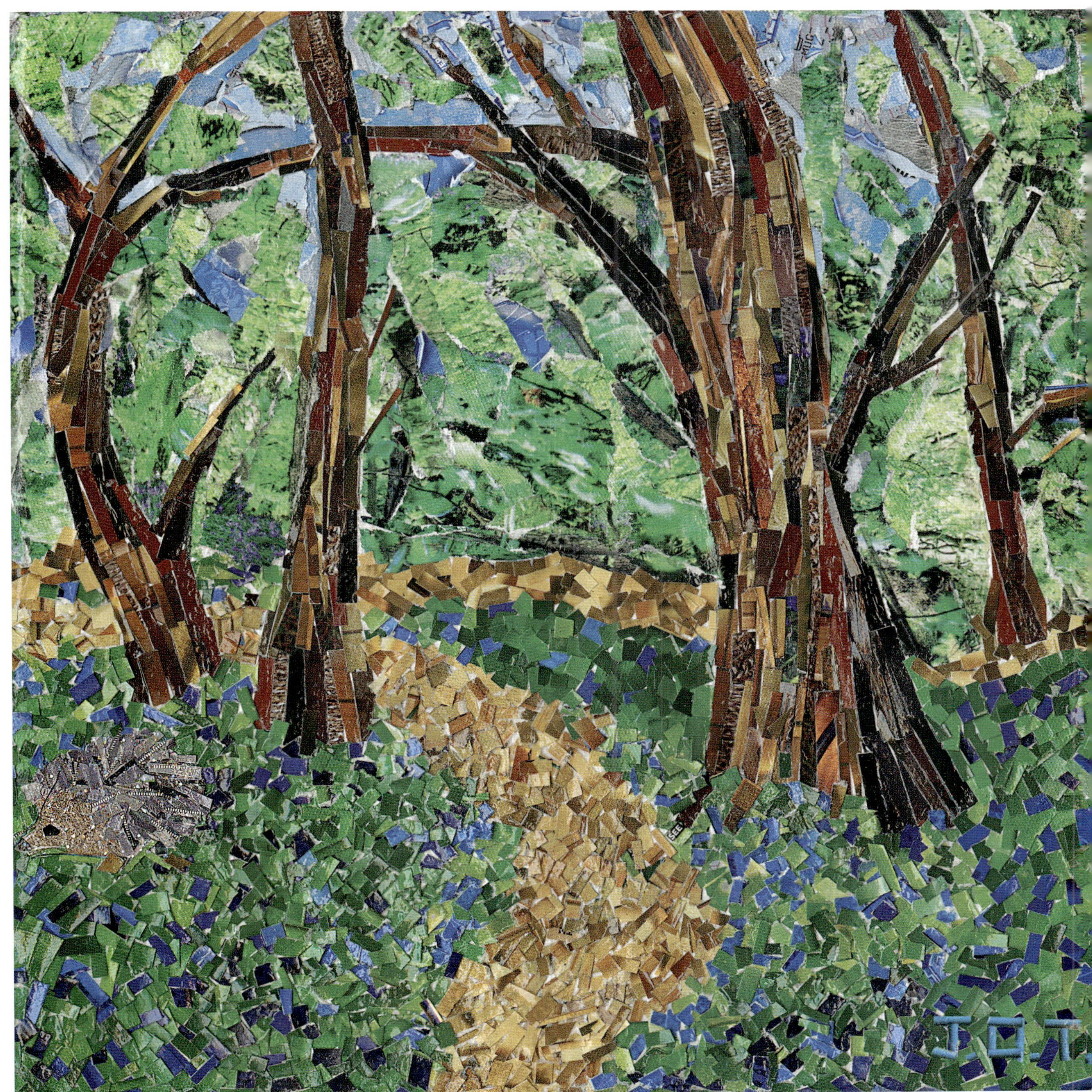

▲ *The completed piece.*

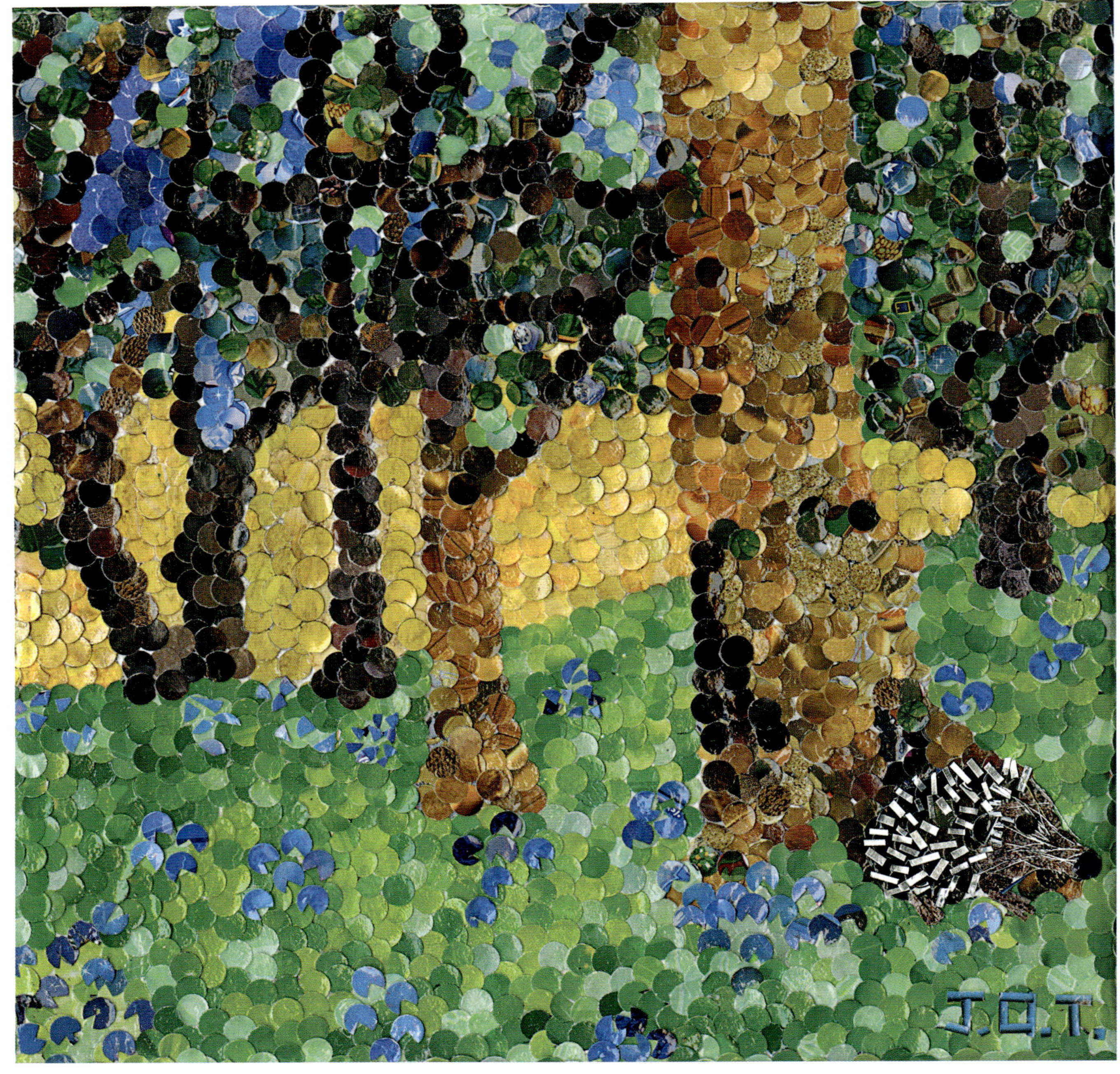

James created his second artwork from the same scratchcards as the first, but this time he hole-punched them. With a bit of patience, nail scissors can be used to cut a very small piece from each of the circles to shape it as if it were a bluebell. He added patches of these onto areas of the grass and he highlighted the hedgehog with tiny strips of silver scratchcard to help it stand out from the woodland floor, making sure it didn't blend into the overall composition too much.

▲ *James' second hedgehog piece, collaged with hole-punched scratchcards.*

James created another variation on the hedgehog theme, working over an old collage using remnants of glittery fabrics, one of which had sequins. These made an ideal textured surface for a path and grass at night-time. He made the sky from torn pieces of colourful magazine paper and the trees were created from money symbols found on various international scratchcards. These little hedgehogs were collaged with fibres of gold thread. He also used gold and silver strands of thread to outline and highlight the trees. Finally, to finish the scene, James applied a glittery varnish onto the background, giving the effect of shimmering moonlight.

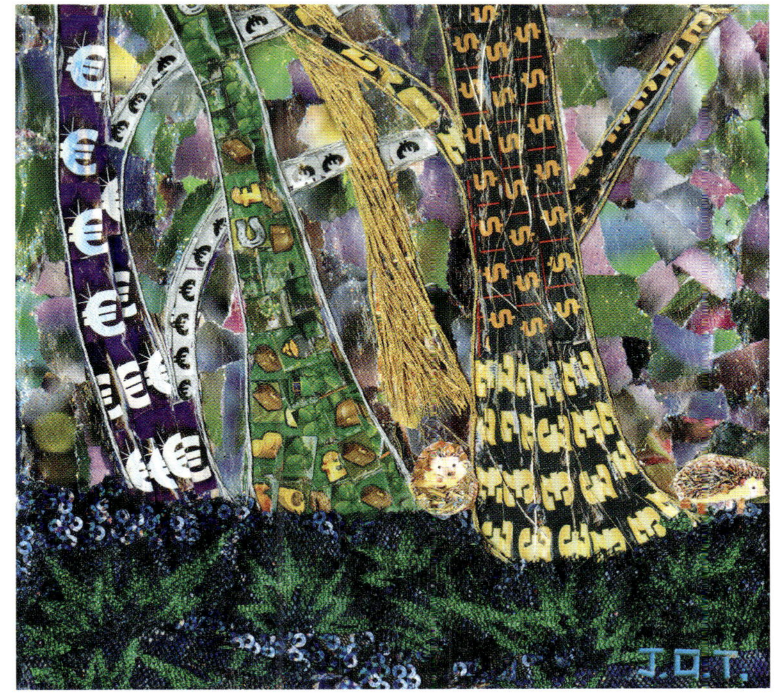

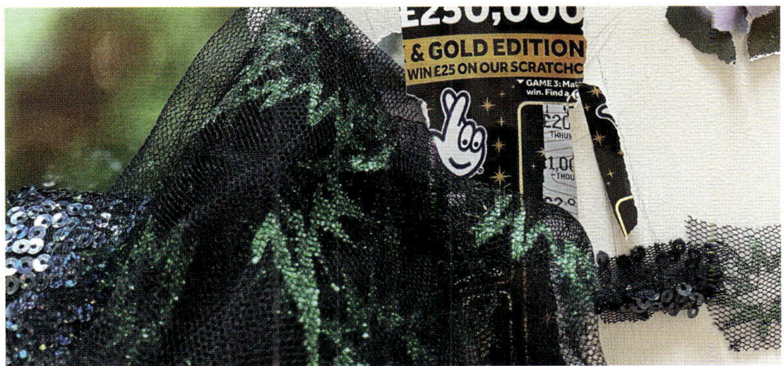

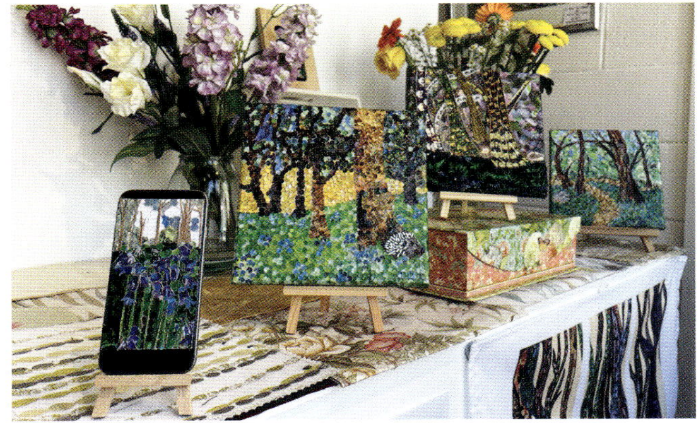

▲ *James' third hedgehog piece, made using glittery fabrics and sequins.*

◄ *All three pieces of art were displayed in the window of JOT's 2023 Gallery.*

ANIMALS OUT AND ABOUT

James' inspiration has, of course, come from many places other than his garden. His earliest childhood memories are filled with images of all types of creatures, from butterflies and field mice to Highland cattle and horses. Living in East Sussex until the age of 10, he enjoyed being taken to visit the Raystede Centre for Animal Welfare near Lewes. He used pieces of torn paper to decorate their colouring sheets.

James was particularly fond of the peaceful sanctuary area around the lakes where he bought seeds to feed a wide variety of birdlife. There were also many dogs, cats, rabbits, donkeys and goats, which he liked to watch whenever he went.

In 2010, when he was 9 years old, James entered a Raystede art competition, drawing and colouring their three-legged cat, which had always fascinated him. His picture was put into the following year's Raystede calendar.

In East Sussex he also used to visit Drusillas Zoo, although he spent much of his time looking for quiet areas, as well as opening and closing doors for people. His fixation with doors lasted a couple of years.

MOUSE

After moving to North Yorkshire, James used to enjoy visits to the Hesketh Farm Park near Bolton Abbey, where he saw sheep, lambs, calves, pigs, goats, hens, chicks and tortoises. He gained enough confidence to get up closer to animals and liked to have guinea pigs sit on his lap and was even allowed to comb them. It was probably here, aged around 11, that he was allowed to hold this tiny mouse! Some years later, James decided to create an image of it in a beautiful forest where the tree trunks would provide shelter and a place to run about and hide.

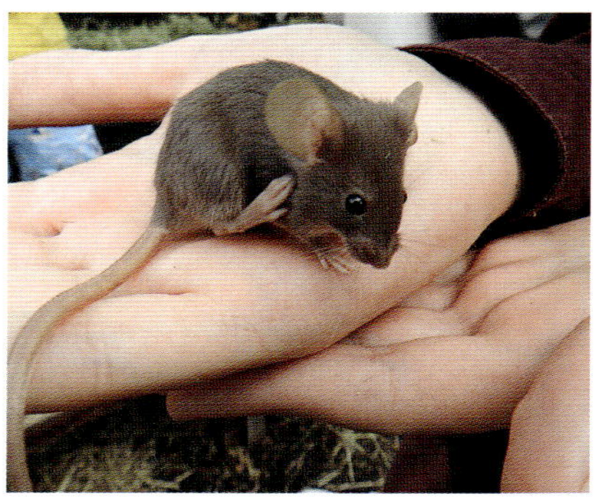

▲ *The mouse at Hesketh.*

Reusing three canvases with images of trees printed on them, James collaged over the images but changed the designs of the trees, using scraps cut from different coloured scratchcards for each tree, then defining them with bright green, blue, red and black threads. The sky is collaged from gold foil. He made a sketch of the mouse that allowed him to test where to place it, positioning it where he thought the composition worked best.

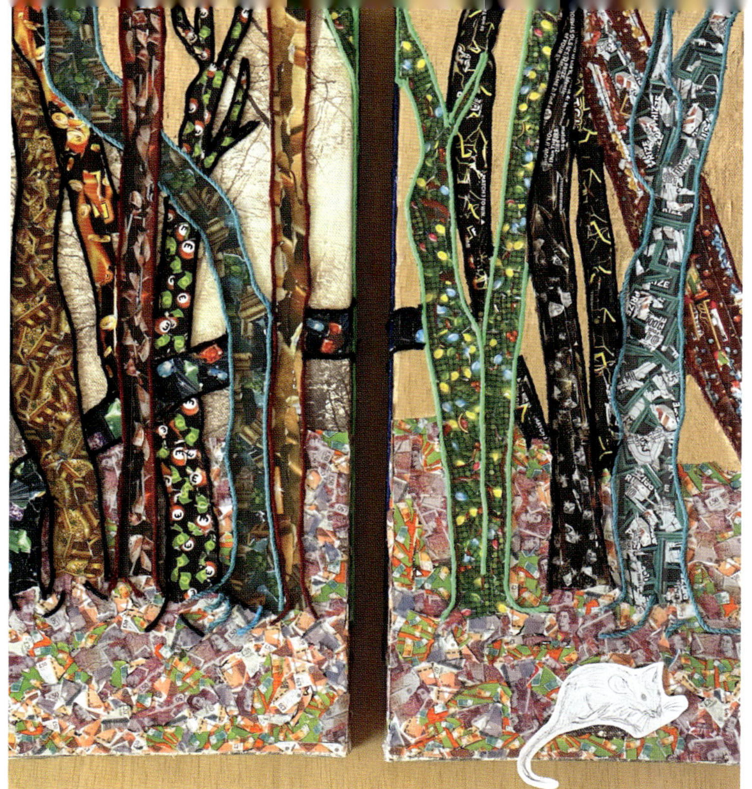

◀ **Woodland Triptych** *in progress. Some of the original canvas photograph can still be seen on the left as James collages gold foil over it, and the mouse is currently still a cut-out pencil draft.*

▼ *The completed* **Woodland Triptych***, with the now-collaged mouse placed in the central panel.*

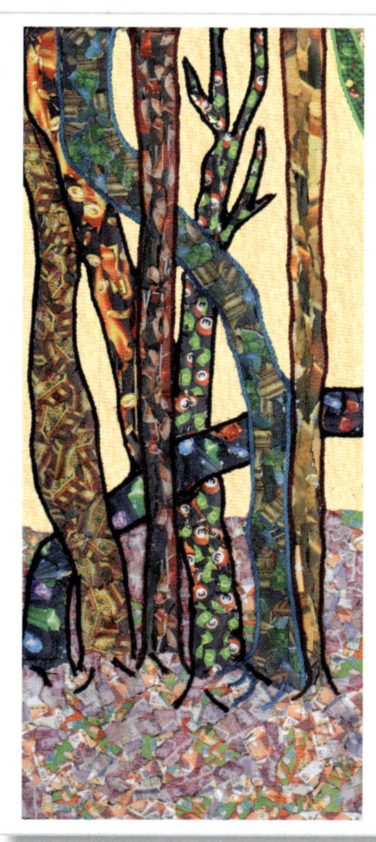

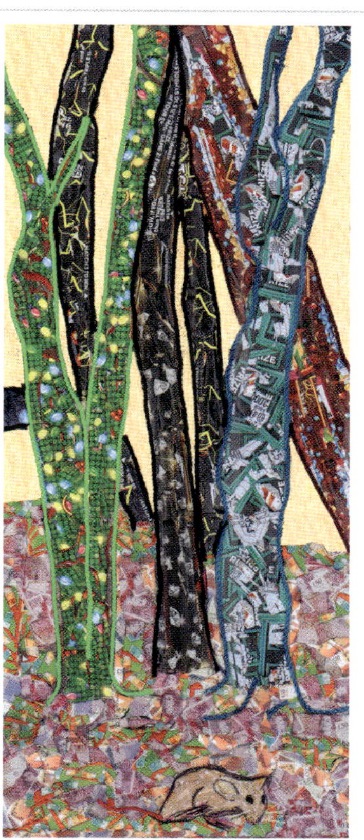

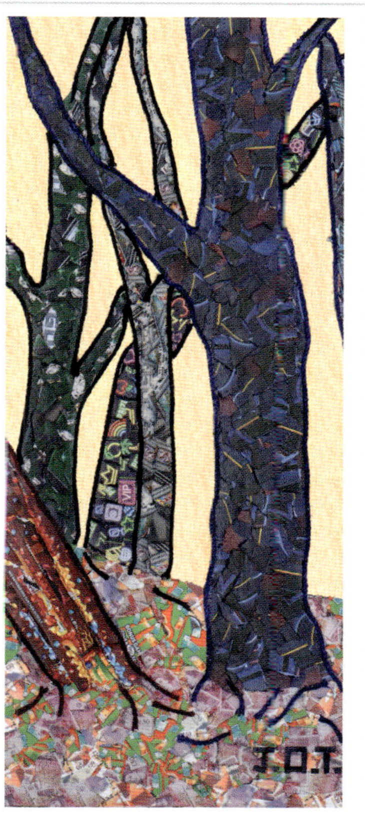

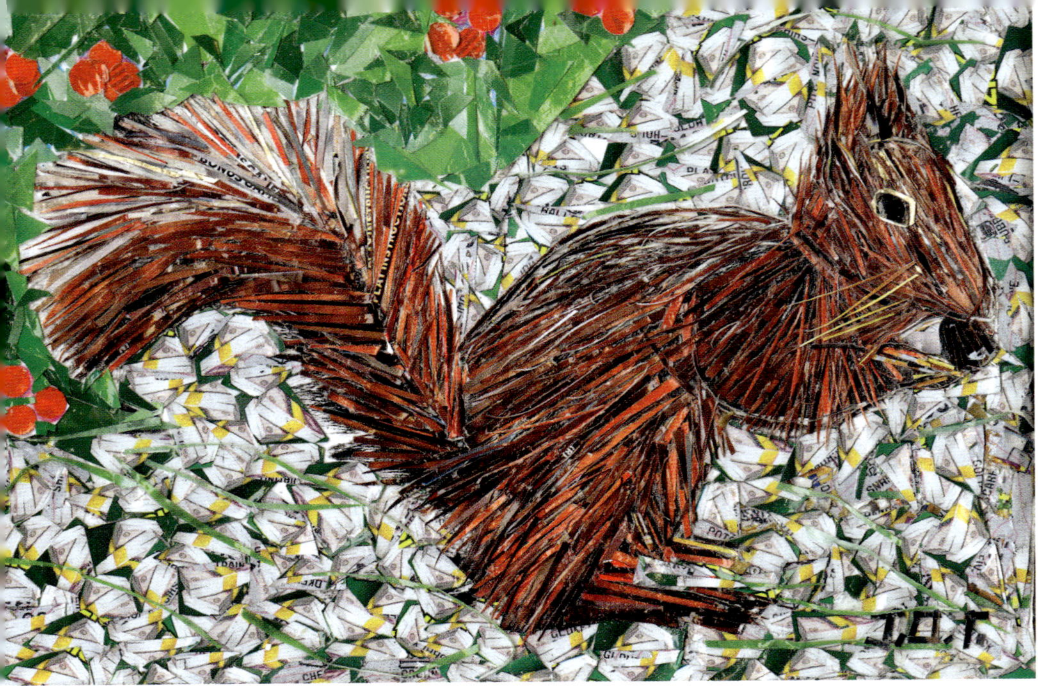

SQUIRRELS

In 2023, James was invited to visit The Yorkshire Arboretum at Castle Howard near Malton in North Yorkshire as the Arboretum was interested in exhibiting his artwork. He took with him a collage of a red squirrel that he had created some years previously for the National Park Authority.

As James had never seen a red squirrel before, an employee of the National Park Authority had sent him a photograph of one in Wensleydale on which to base his ideas. He used red berries in his scratchcard collage as he intended it to become a Christmas card. The squirrel is standing on an imaginary path of motifs of money; its fur is depicted with long red and grey strips; the grass in the background consists of various shades of green; and the berries are hole-punched patterned pieces for a decorative effect.

Spurred on by his visit to the Yorkshire Arboretum, James was inspired to create a series of collages that he called his 'Erik the Red' series. *Erik the Red* was created from scratchcards, lined with recycled string, sitting on a bench made from strips of old Christmas cards that had been soaked in tea-stained water. The dots of colour in the background are hole-punched scratchcards and the bark on the tree is fabric strips.

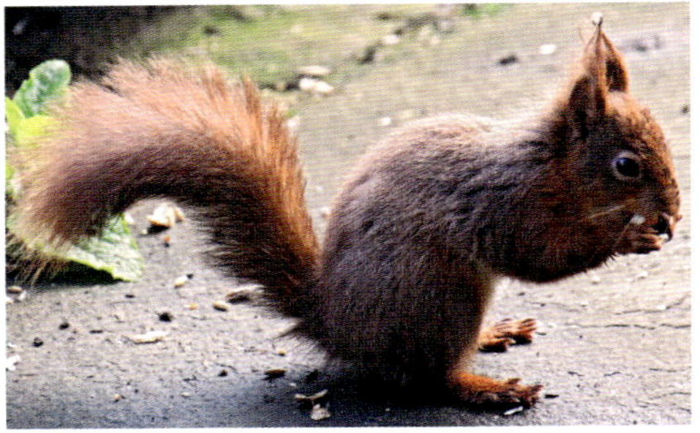

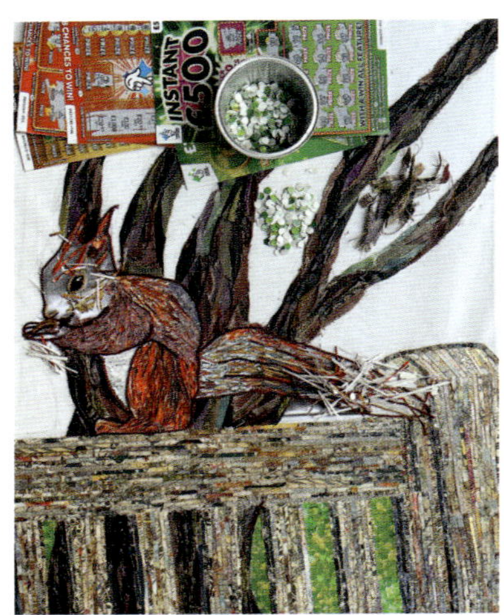

▲ Work in progress on
Erik the Red.

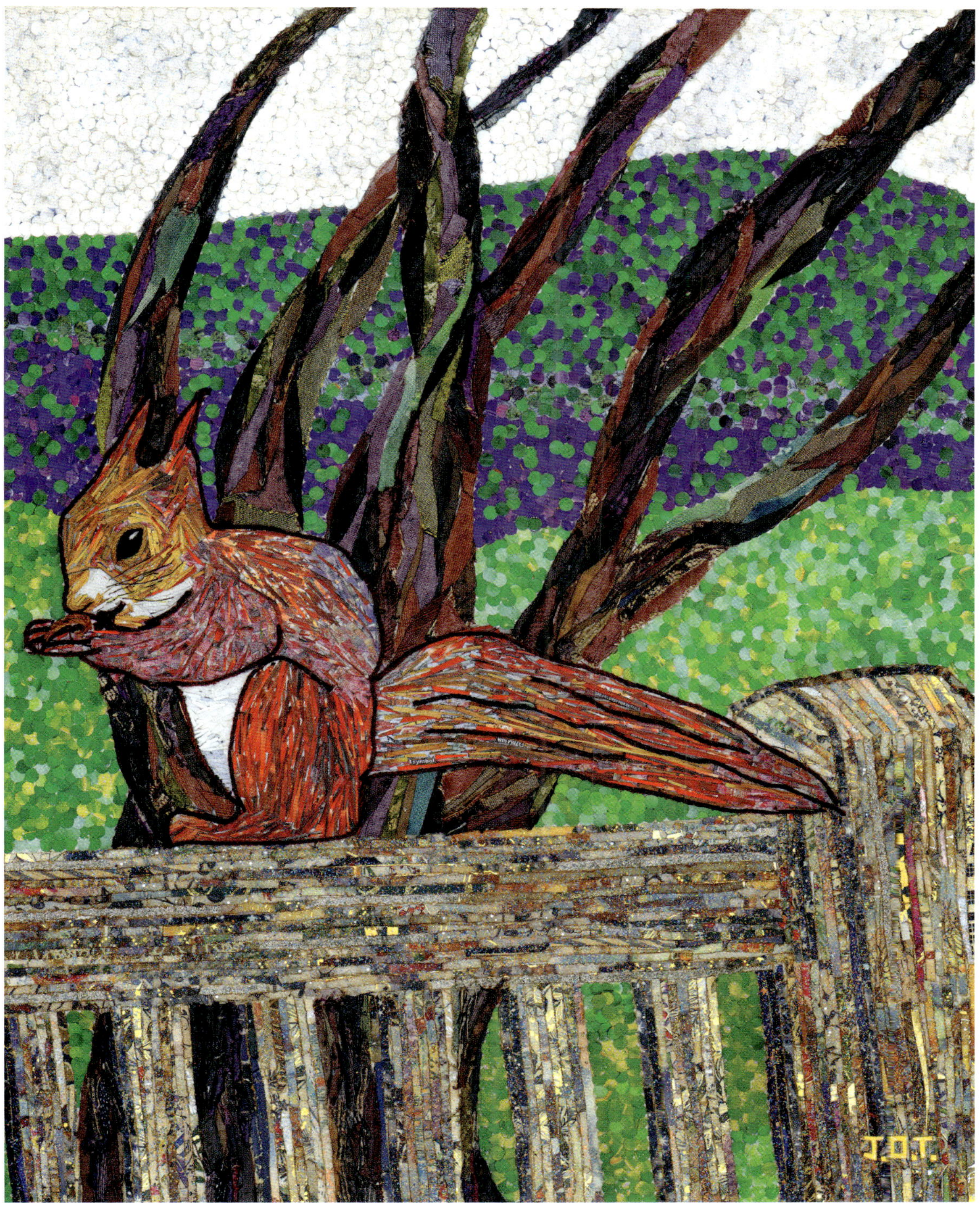

▲ *Erik the Red.*

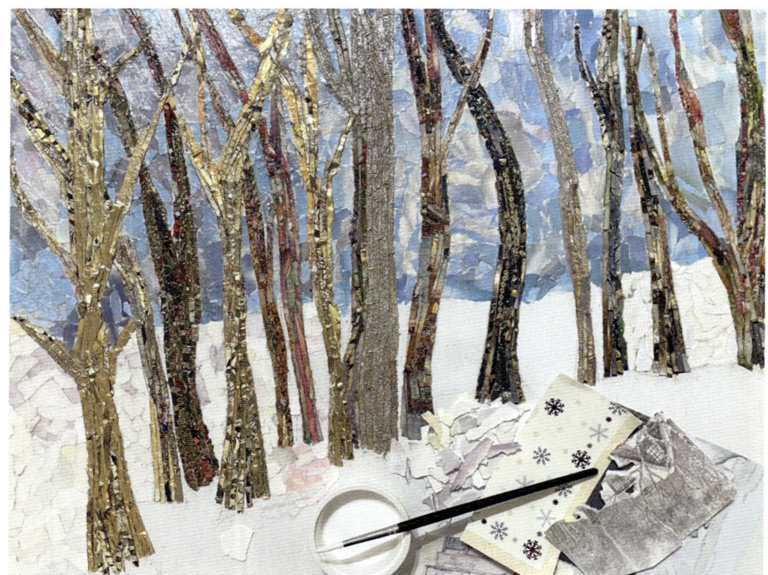

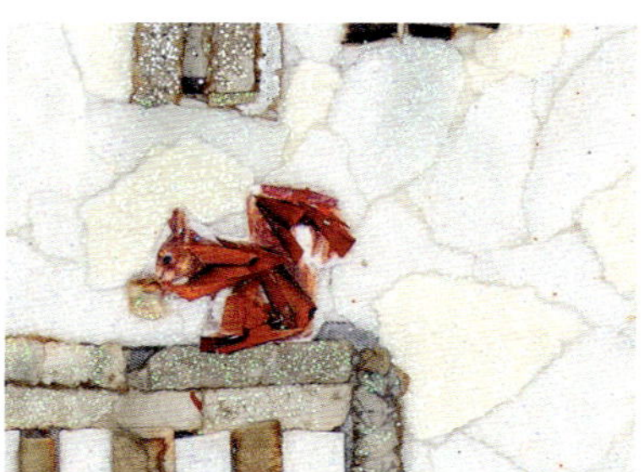

Winter is entirely made from old Christmas cards.

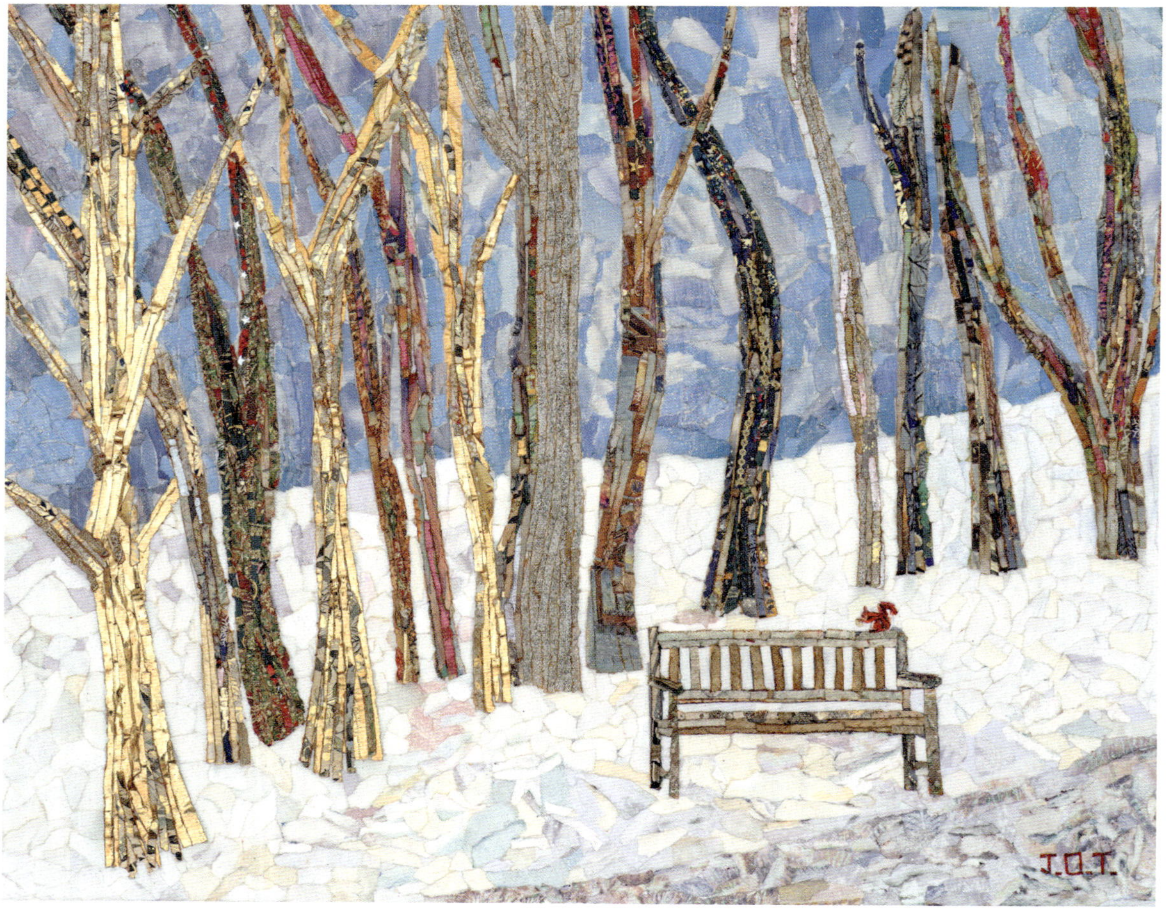

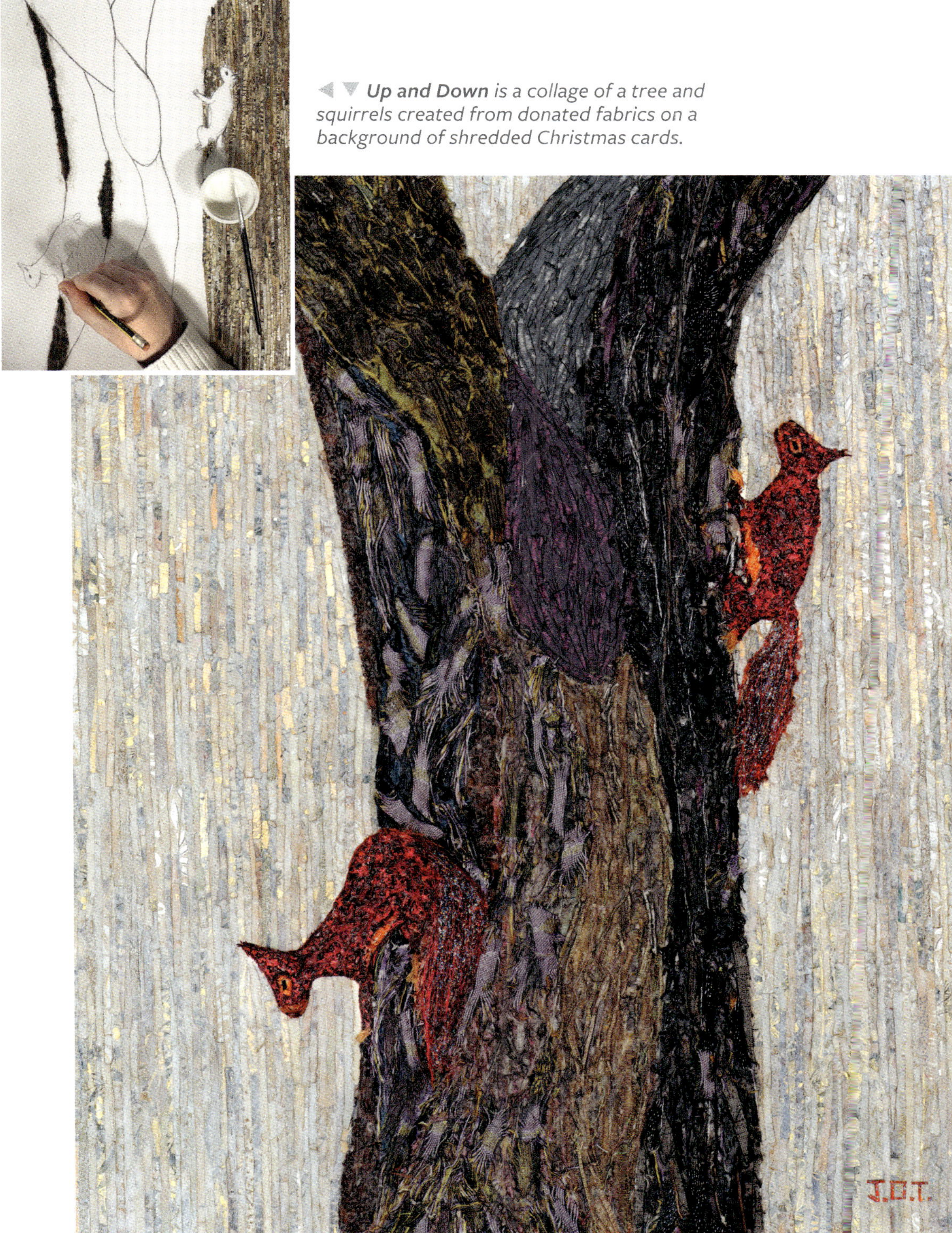

◀ ▼ **Up and Down** is a collage of a tree and squirrels created from donated fabrics on a background of shredded Christmas cards.

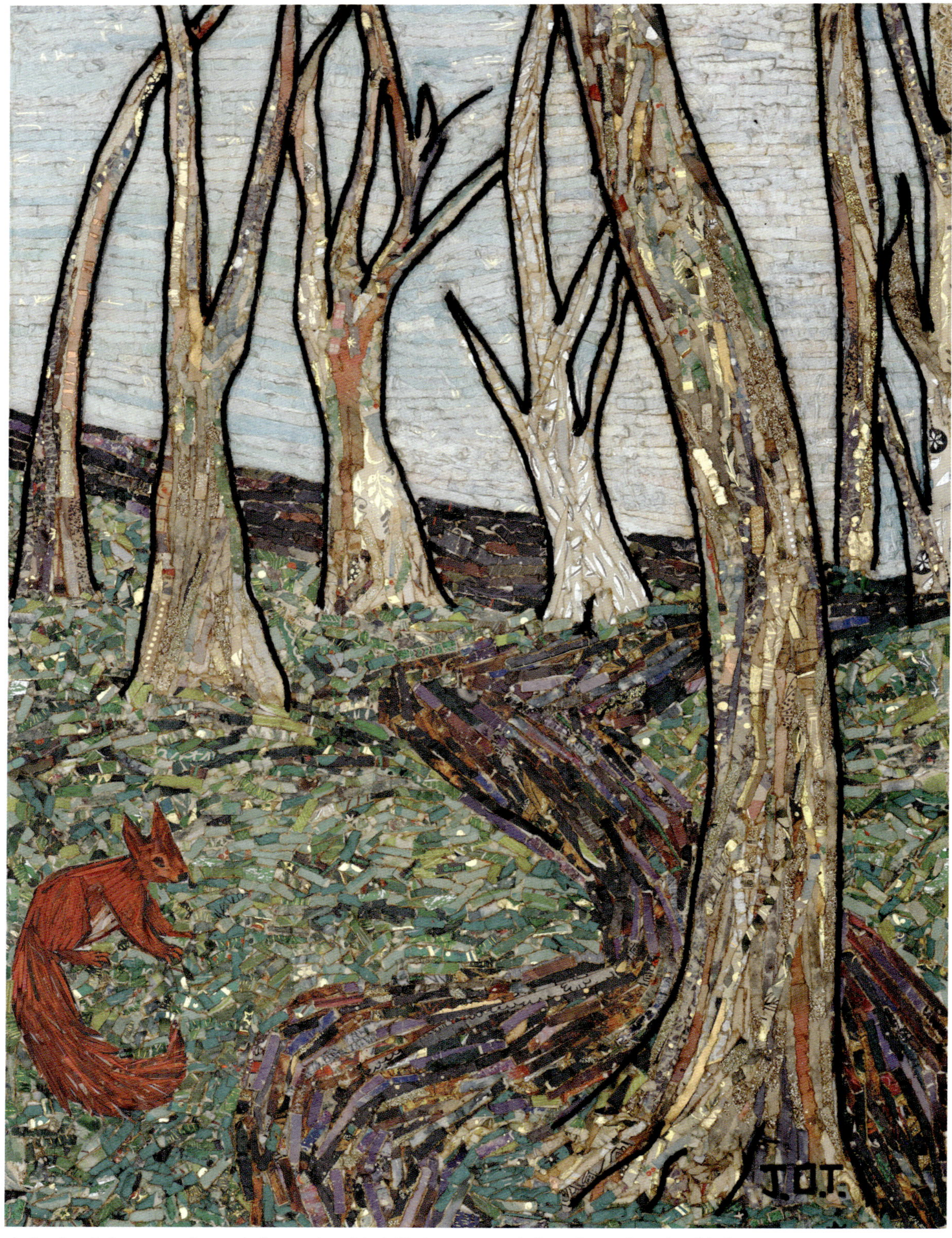

 In the Arboretum is made from shredded Christmas cards but the red squirrel is from scratchcards.

HIGHLAND CATTLE

On a trip to the beautiful market town of Settle in North Yorkhire, James took some photographs of the Highland cattle he came across by the roadside. Some of them had mismatched horns, one facing up and the other down. Inspired by these cows and thinking they looked funny with asymmetrical horns, James was inspired to create a collage using a combination of scratchcards and fabric.

After sketching out his design, he teased apart some fabric to produce the mustard-yellow strands for the Highland cattle. Using both thick and very thin strands in the two animals helped to emphasise the perspective in the artwork. The thick strands were ideal for the coat of the cow in the foreground (set over a base of scratchcard strips, for depth), while very thin cotton was used for the cow set in the middle distance.

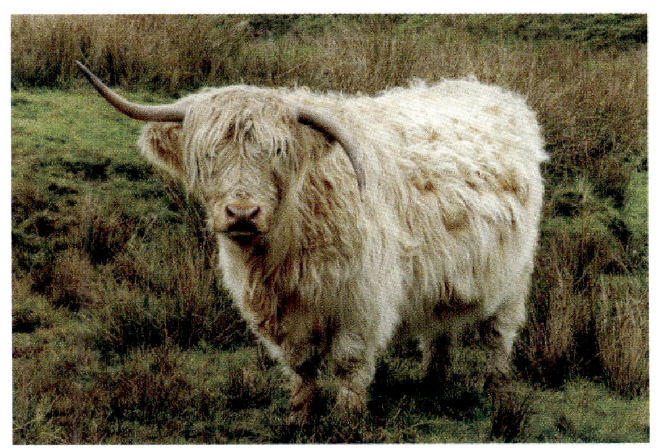

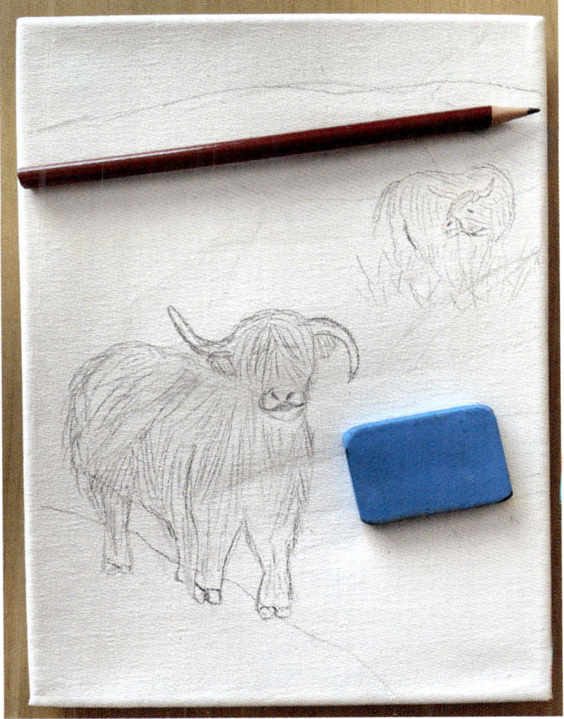

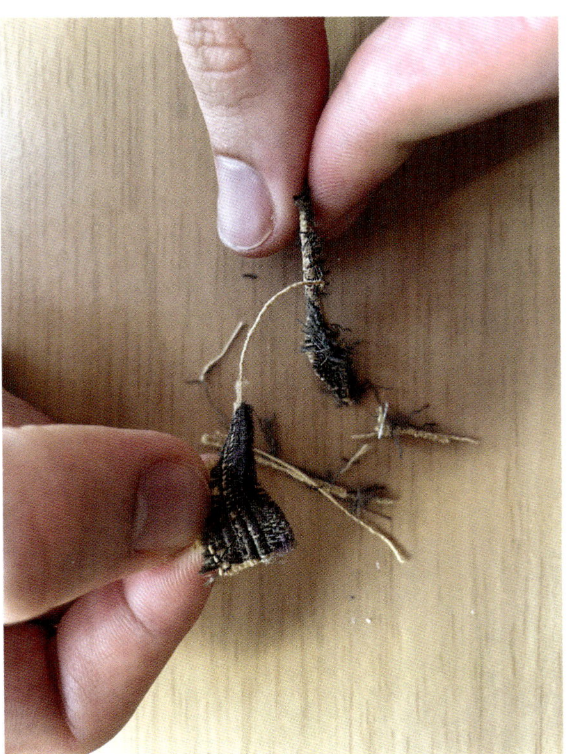

▲▲ *A Highland cow with mismatched horns.*

▲ *James' initial sketch on canvas.*

◀ *Teasing the fabric apart.*

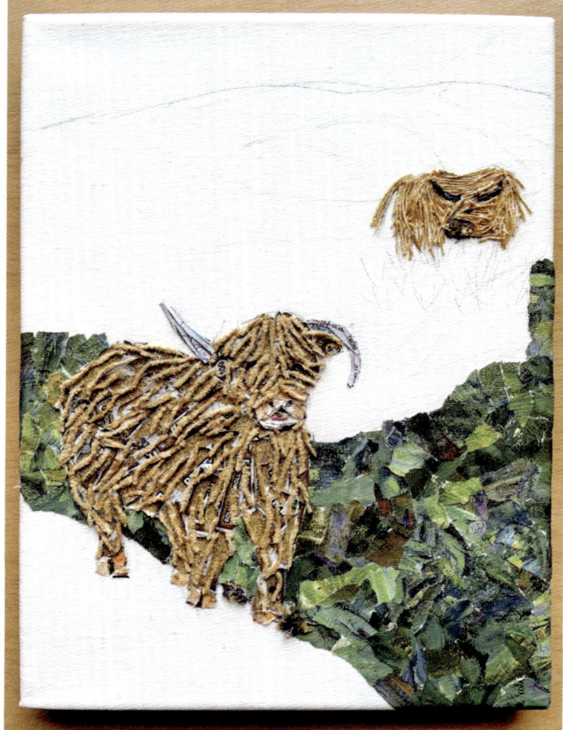

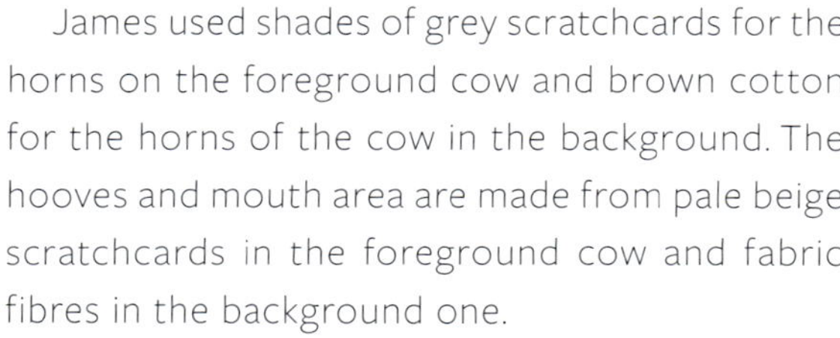

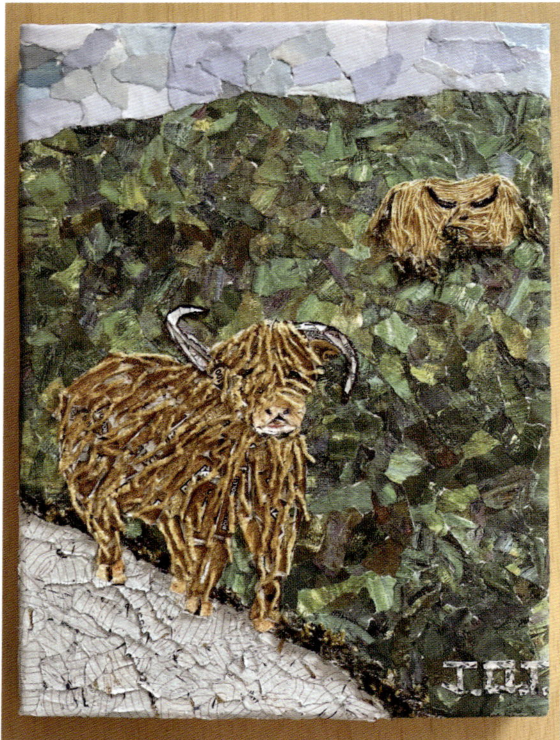

James used shades of grey scratchcards for the horns on the foreground cow and brown cotton for the horns of the cow in the background. The hooves and mouth area are made from pale beige scratchcards in the foreground cow and fabric fibres in the background one.

The grass in the image is made from torn magazine paper, as is the sky, but pieces of grey scratchcard were torn up for the path and cut in strips for the horns. The horns on the cow in the foreground were also outlined with thin cotton strands.

Finally, James made one small but important change. After learning that the mismatched horns are usually caused by some sort of accident when the cattle are young, he decided at the last minute to correct the damaged horn so that they both pointed skywards, as people would expect.

▲◄ Applying the strands of different thicknesses.

▲ The collage nears completion.

▶ After a little horn adjustment, the collage is finished!

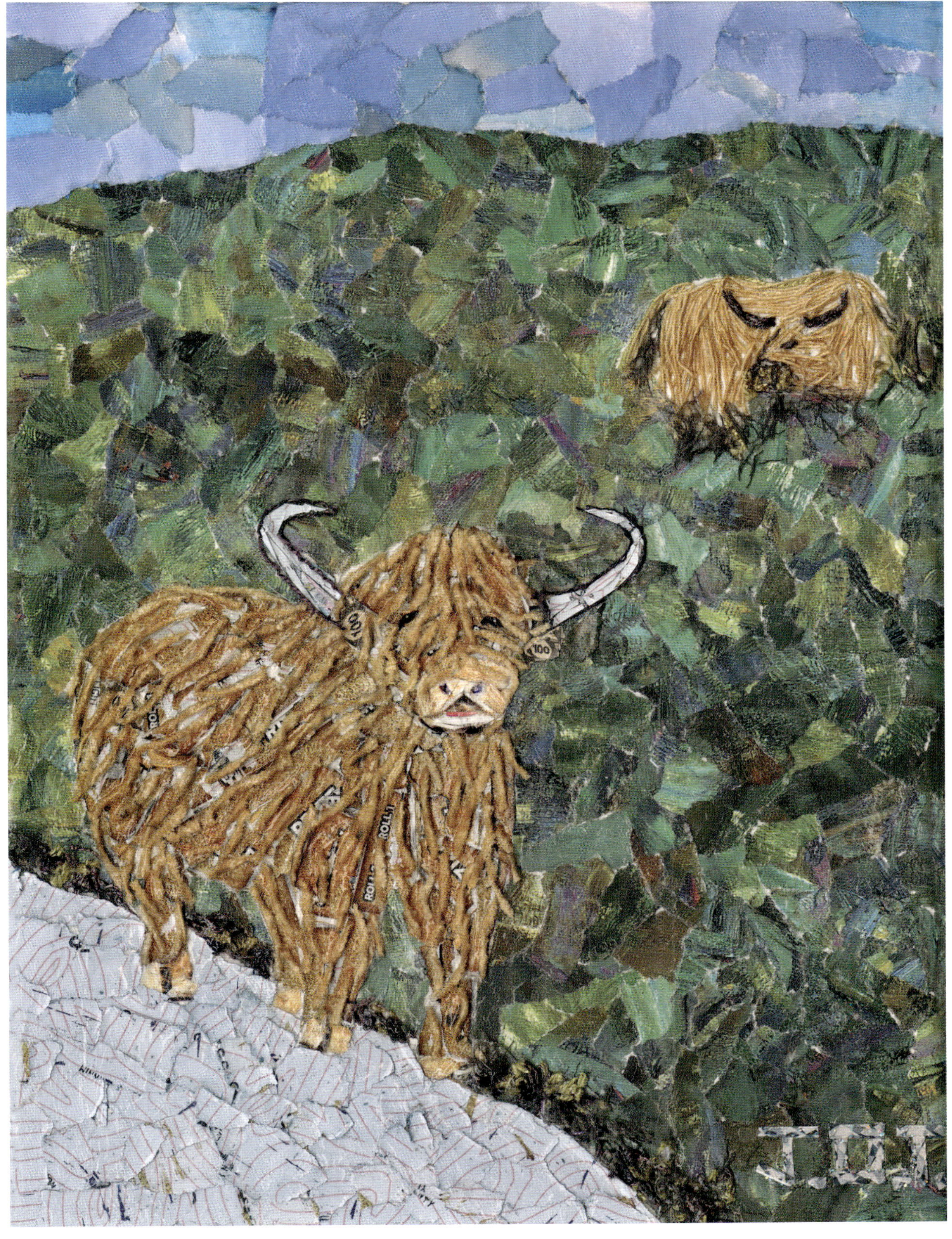

ROSIE THE PIG

James has been lucky enough to live in the beautiful area of Nidderdale in the Yorkshire Dales for many years. It is officially known as an Area of Outstanding Natural Beauty (AONB), and for good reason. On one of his many walks in this region, he came across a lovely pig named Rosie, who lived on Corn Close Care Farm. This is a very special farm that provides visitors, including disabled and neurodivergent people, with a chance to interact with the farm animals as a way to improve their mental health and general wellbeing. Seeing Rosie plod about in her pen or taking a rest certainly cheered James up, making him feel calm and less anxious.

Sadly, Rosie died some time ago from old age and arthritis and James found it a great challenge to adjust to her not being there. He really wanted to make a piece of artwork to remember her by.

The photograph James used as a base interacts so well with his materials that it really is hard to tell what is photograph and what is art. The absolute focus of the piece is Rosie and her bristly texture!

The short lengths of thread are similar to what James used for the Highland cattle, laid in different directions to match the lie of Rosie's coat. Sequins, a mixture of fibres broken down from donated fabric swatch books, and some grey felting wool have been used to pick out the foreground and thread is used on the fence in the background. Yet, some elements of the original photograph have been left as they were, ensuring that Rosie remains in a convincing and undistracting background.

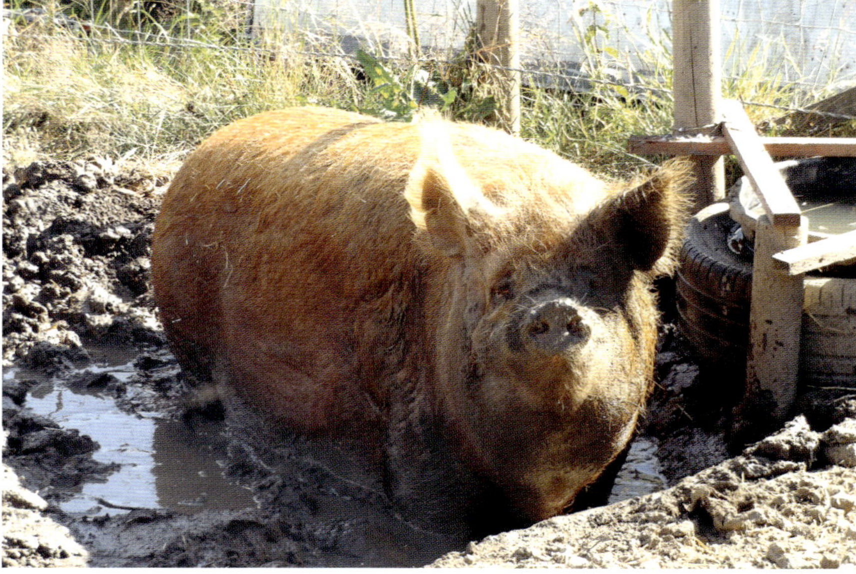

◀ *The original photograph of Rosie, over which James collaged.*

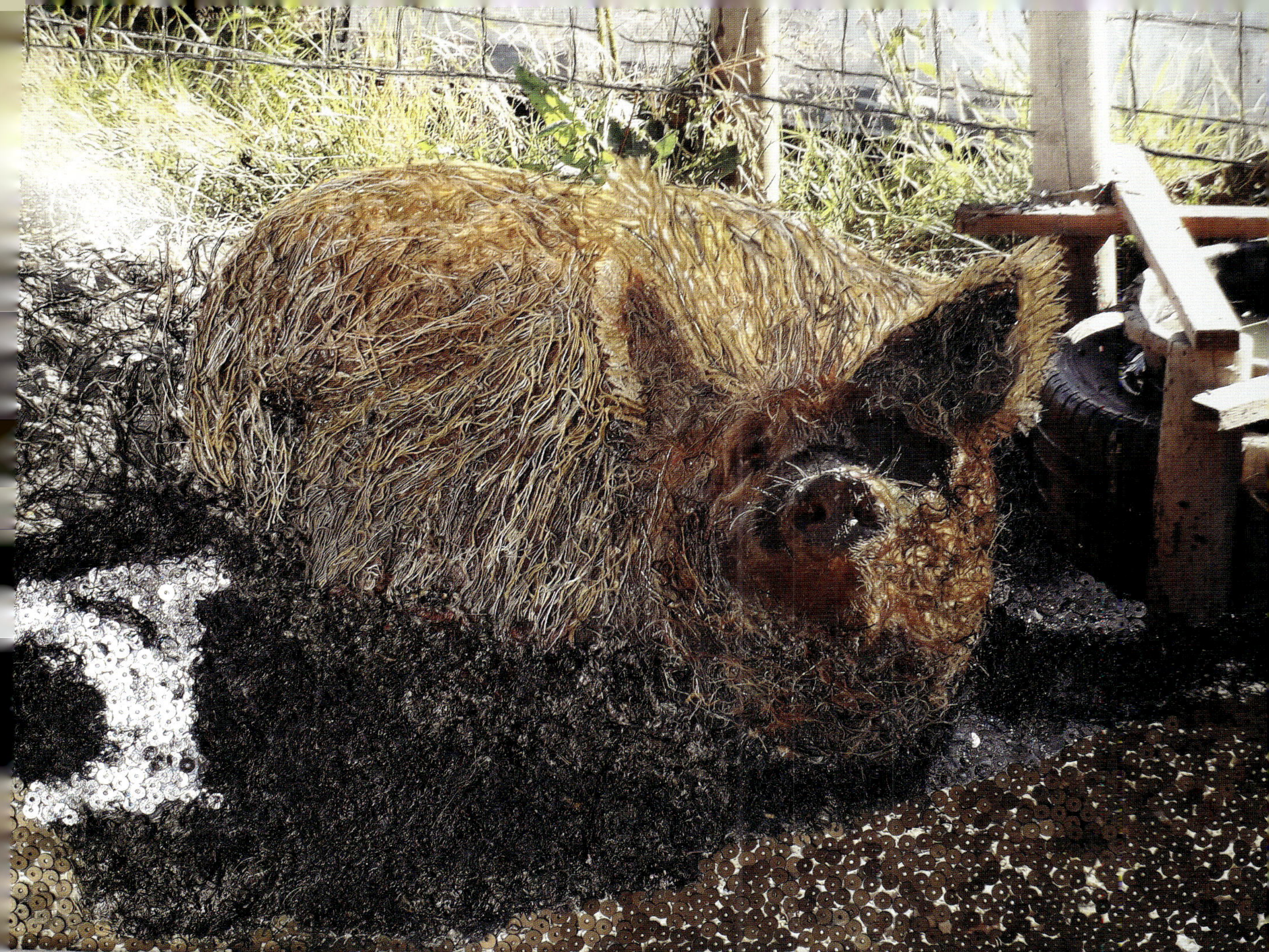

When James donated his collage of Ros e to Corn Close Care Farm, they wrote:

We are extremely grateful to James for conating this wonderful collage to us to raise funds for our Care Farm. We fell in love with the picture as it really depicts the character of Rosie so well. We decided to keep it and donate the money ourselves to purchase equipment for vulnerable people to use when working with the animals and in the vegetable area. The quality of the collage and the way he has brought the picture to life is a wonderful tribute to her and we will always cherish this beautiful piece of artwork and remember Rosie as she was such a character at our Care Farm. James' generosity has made a real difference to the people who attend our Care Farm.

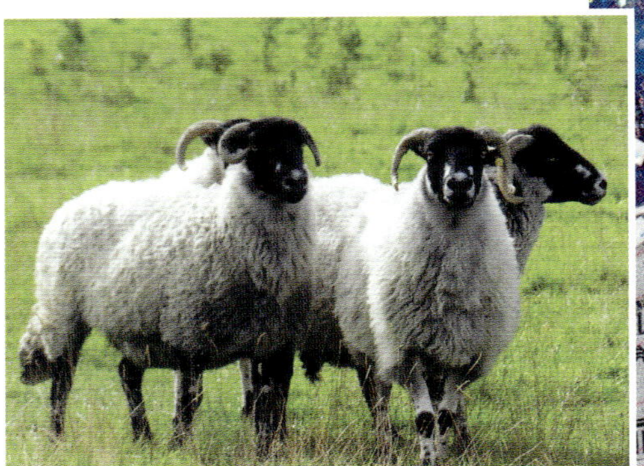

SHEEP

Swaledale sheep inspired James to create *First Snow of Winter*.

The use of thin strips of white paper hints at a thin covering of snow, and the small white squares in the sky represent falling snow, with more snow settled on the hilltops. The labelled trees and stars in the background are cleverly cut-out motifs from scratchcards, as are the triangular green gems that form the hedges behind the sheep. The purple, green and black of the foreground are cut-out pieces of scratchcards, and the hills are reused, green magazine paper cut to random shapes.

▲ *Swaledale sheep.*

▶ *First Snow of Winter.*

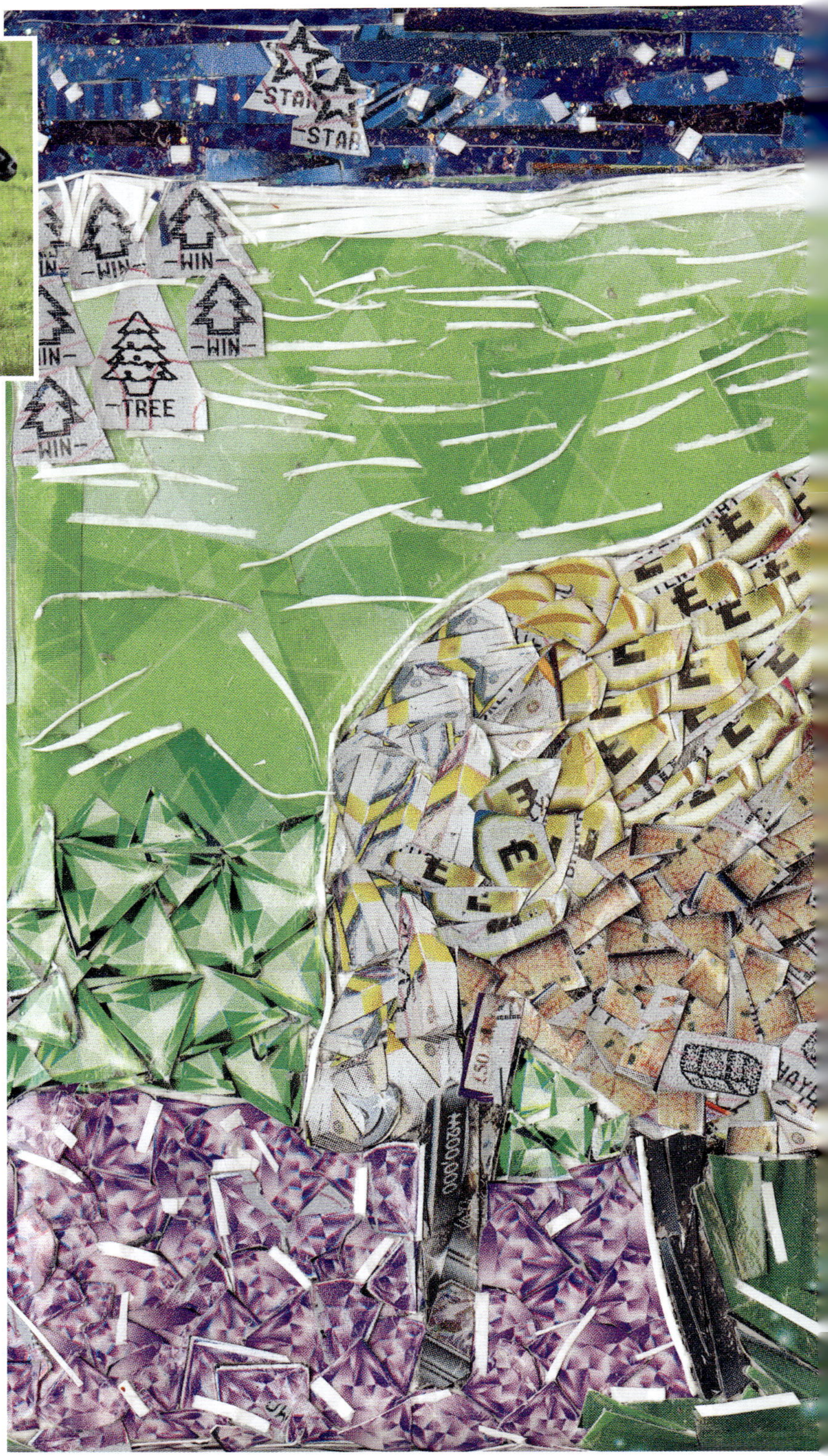

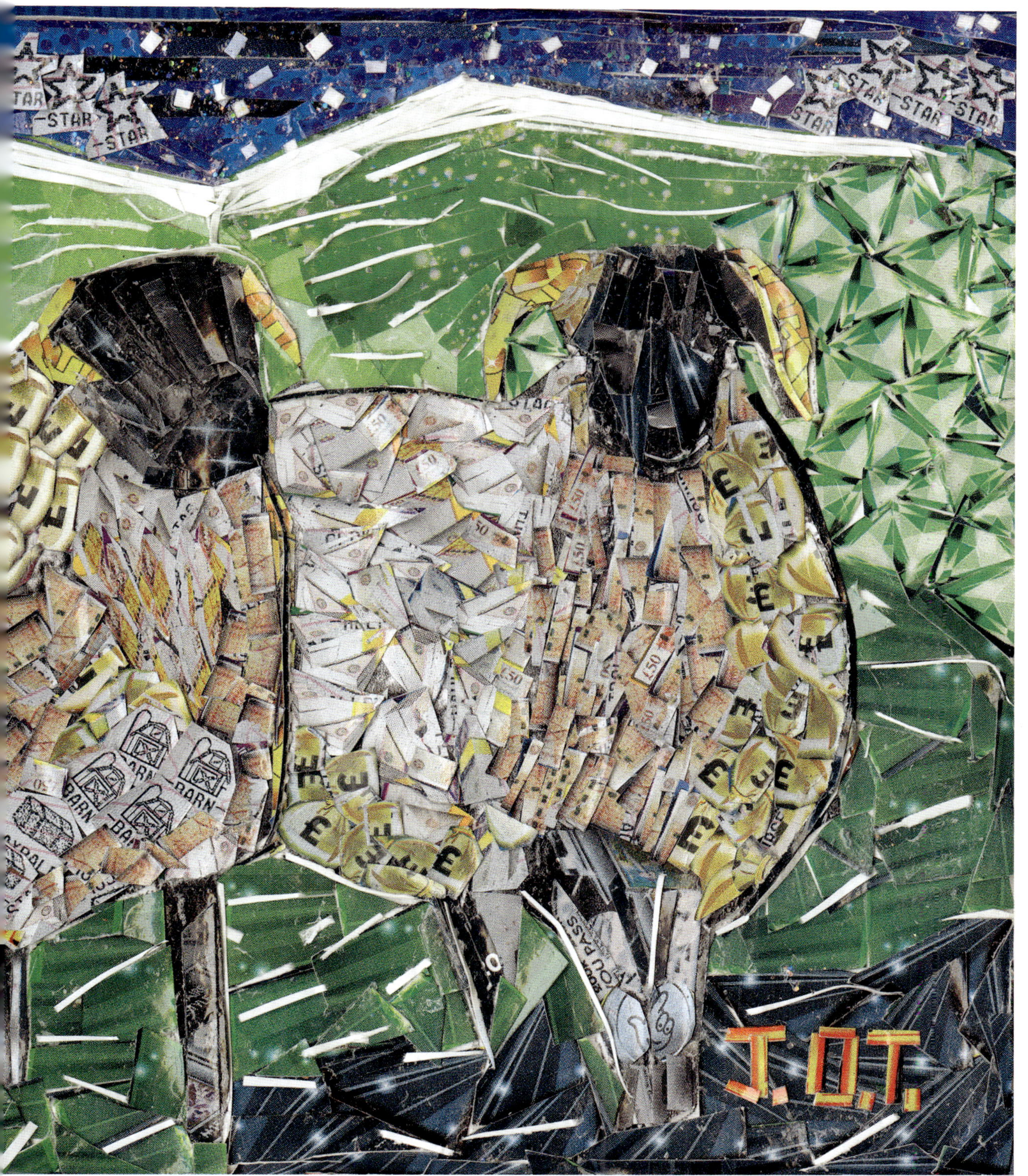

BIRDS

James' interest in birds first began when a family friend gave him his first ever I-Spy book and he was delighted to receive a certificate when he had seen and ticked off every bird in the book. As well as birds in the country-side near home, he was able to find seaside birds when visiting family in East Sussex and he clearly remembers his excitement of finding out the names of birds when on holiday in Northumberland, especially approaching the Farne Islands by boat.

PIGEON

Pigeon at Home is one of James' early collages. It has been a popular design for prints and cards, even at the National Coal Mining Museum, as there is a link between miners and pigeons. James read that the pigeon was known as the 'poor man's racehorse' and that pigeonkeeping was a popular hobby for many in the mining community. If you happen to watch the British TV soap *Emmerdale*, you might even spot a print of *Pigeon at Home* on set, above the kitchen cooker in Tug Gyhll, the home of characters Tracy and Nate – James is fortunate enough to have had three of his prints selected for use around the set.

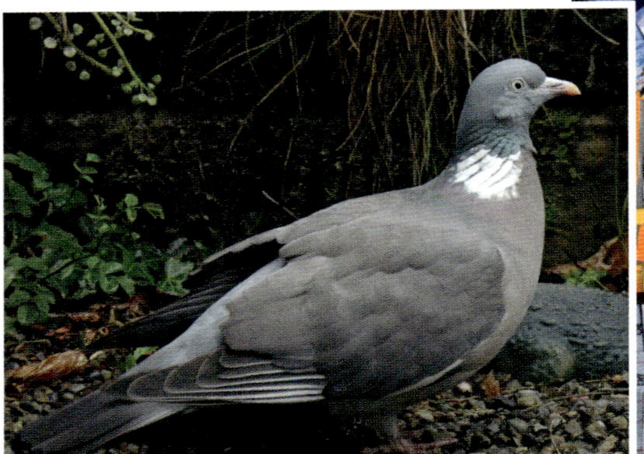

It was lucky that James still had the original *Pigeon at Home* collage available when he heard from a couple in London with an enquiry about purchasing the artwork. James learned that their young autistic son, Olly, had a special interest in pigeons. It made James feel happy to think that his artwork was giving this young child pleasure. Just like James when he was much younger, Olly seems to be developing a special interest in nature.

▲ *Reference photograph of a wood pigeon, used for* **Pigeon at Home.**

Pigeon at Home. ▶

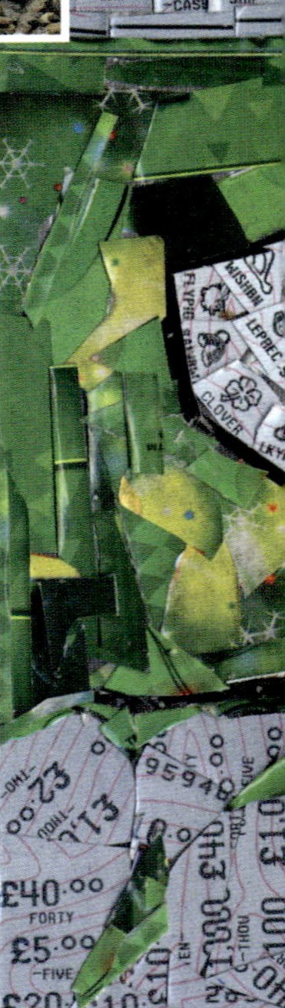

HERON

Herons, with their long legs and necks, have a dignified appearance whether they are standing or flying. They use their long legs to wade in shallow ponds or around the edges of lakes and use their beaks to strike at prey swimming below the surface of the water. They play an important part in maintaining the balance of aquatic ecosystems, but they face threats from the loss of vital wetland areas, which not only support their feeding habits, but also provide nesting areas.

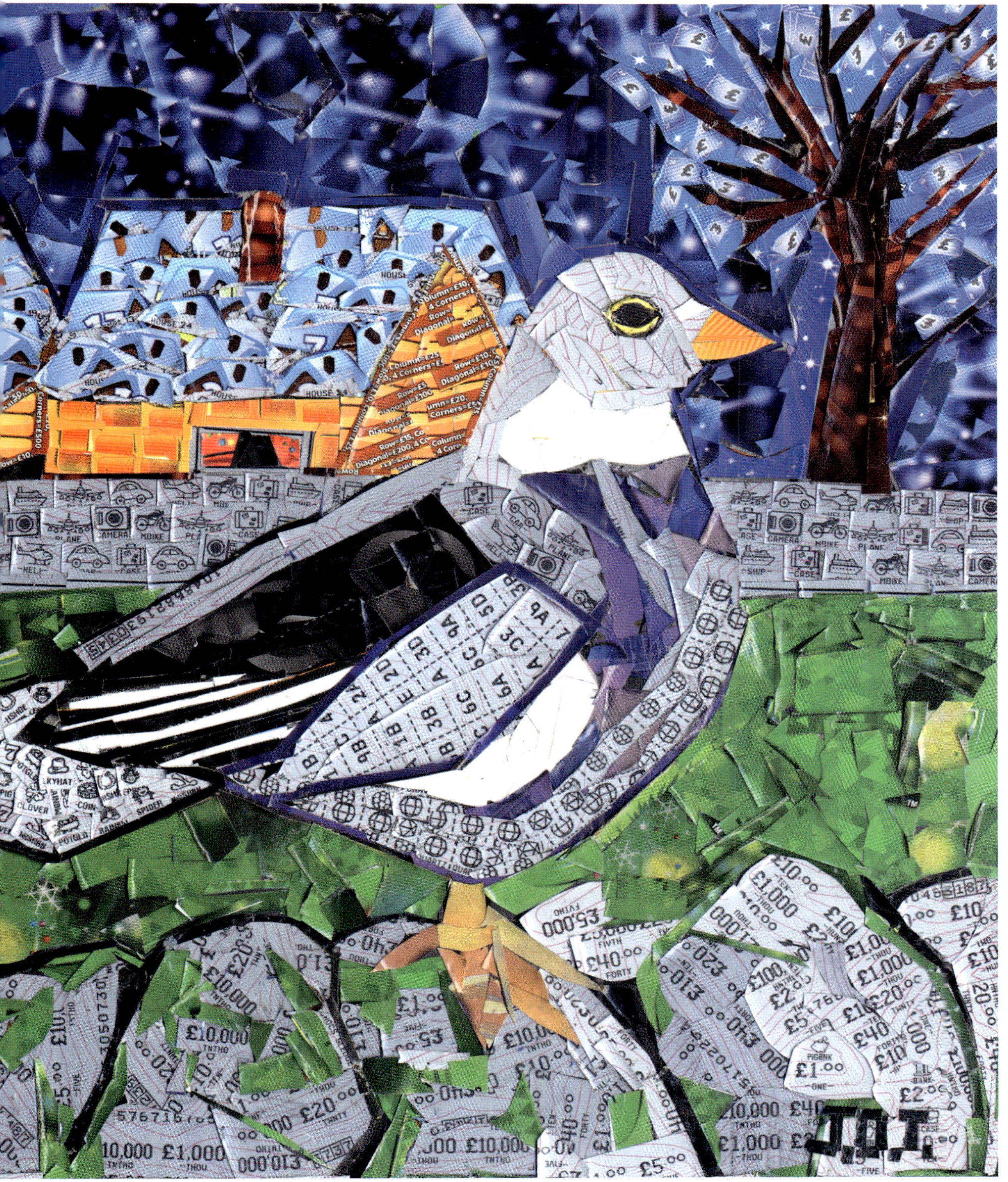

James decided to make a collage of a beautiful heron based on a photograph taken by a friend at Kew Gardens and drew a grid over a copy of the photograph so that he could easily transfer the image onto an old, pre-used canvas in the correct proportion. James learned this traditional technique from his art teacher at secondary school.

He ignored the original background image on the canvas, drawing just the heron and a few other details as a guide in putting together the collage.

James adjusted some details after his initial sketch to make the figure of the heron in the final collage clearer. The original long leaves rising up around the heron were too distracting and, by knocking them back, the bird is far more imposing and it becomes very much the focus of the foreground, rather than being a bit lost.

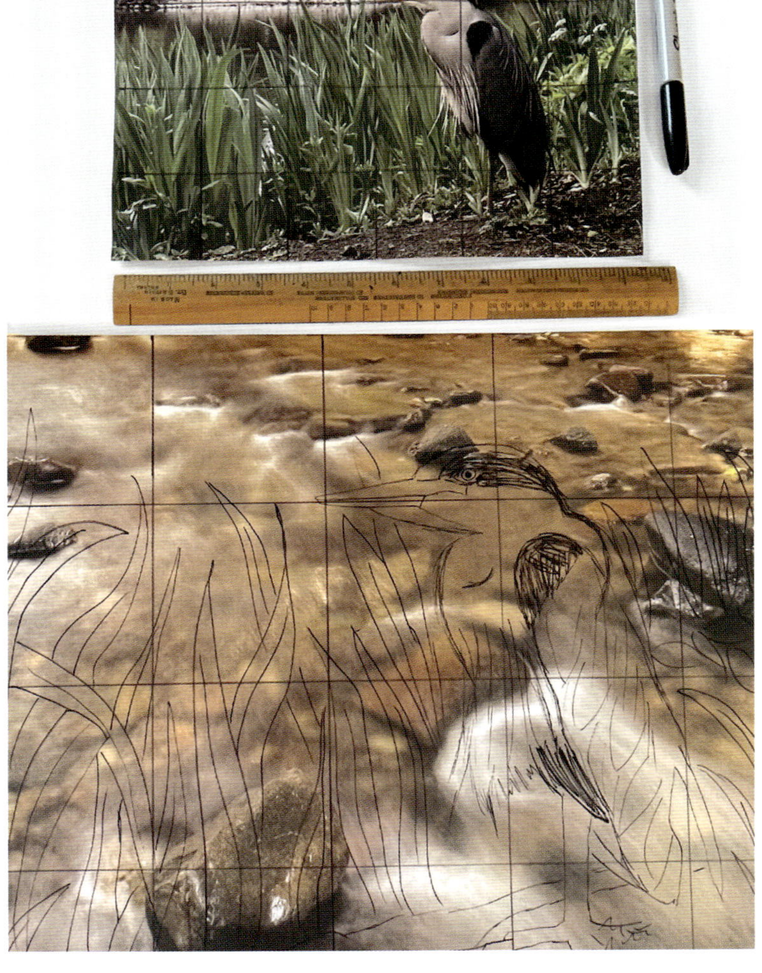

▲ *Using the grid system to transfer a heron image from a photograph onto canvas.*

▶ *The finished heron collage.*

In the full composition, the tree trunks rise flamelike in the background and a spray of purple flowers decorates the woodland floor on the far bank. The golden glow of sunlight is hinted at by the use of gold in the sky and each tree is individually picked out in particular colours using different sets of scratchcards. The grass and flowers on the far bank are depicted using long strips for lush, new growth and the brown squares of old cushion fabric on the bank in the foreground resemble freshly churned mud. Long, green scratchcard strips act as young reeds or tall blades of grass. The water consists of old blue fabric combined with plastic bag fragments. The heron's underfeathers are cut from scratchcard strips but the wings are grey and black pieces of old magazine carefully clipped into larger individual feathers.

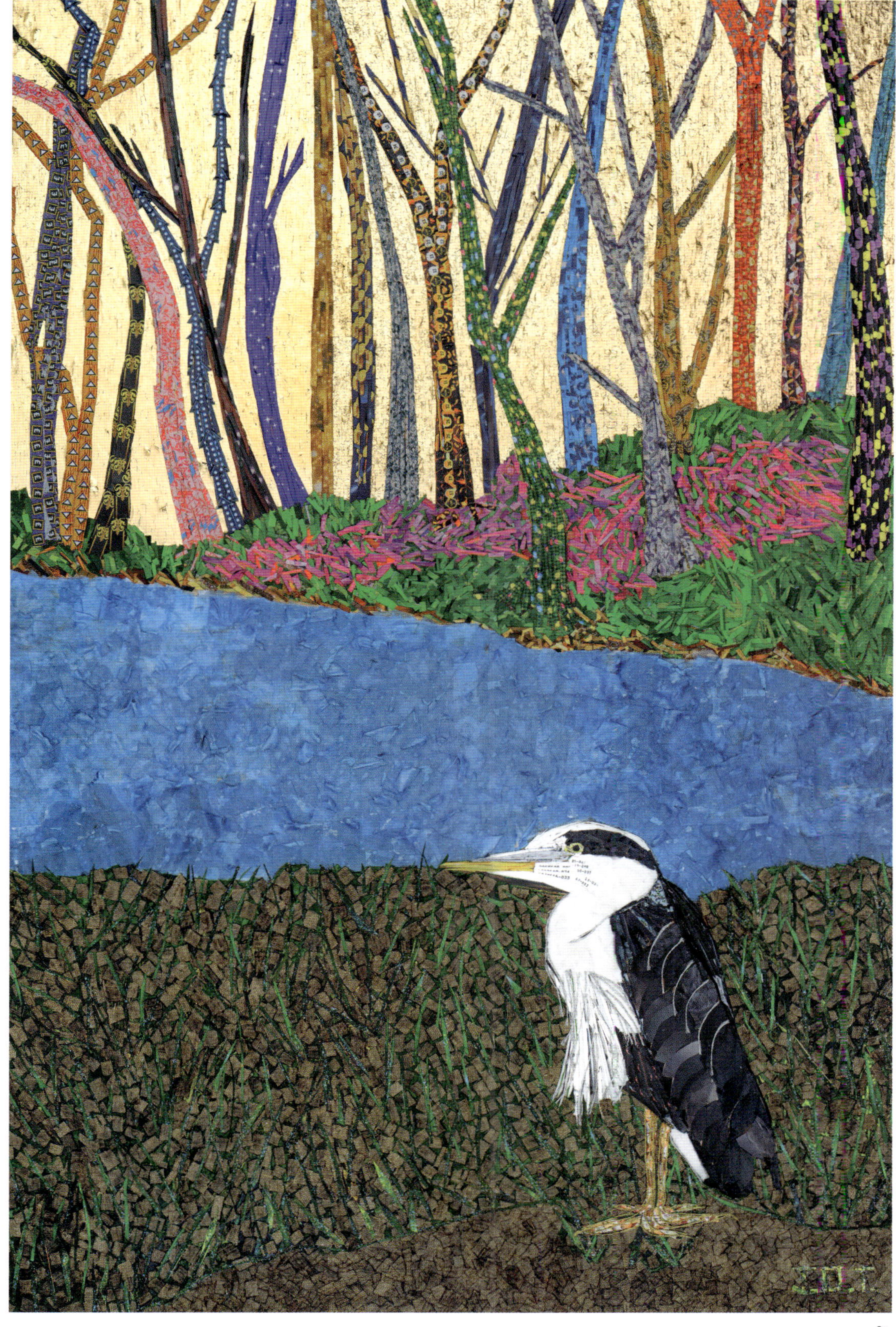

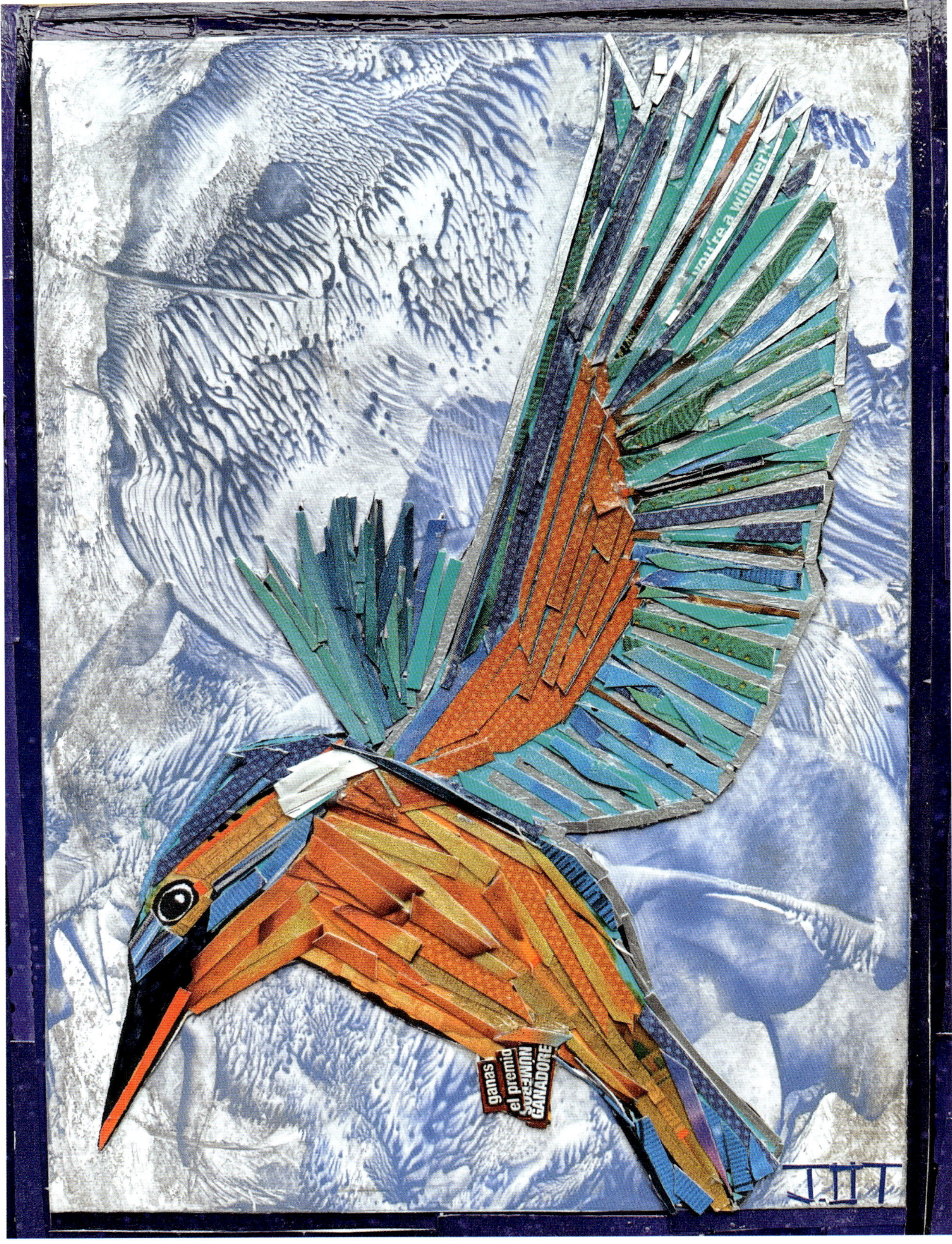

you're a winner!
ganas
el premio
NON-WON
GANADORE
J.T.T.

KINGFISHER

The bright and iridescent kingfisher is another bird that lives around water, feeding on fish found in rivers and lakes, and around shoreline areas. They are famous for their exceptional vision and diving techniques that allow them to dart down from a position above the water to grab their prey, lightning fast, from the water below.

In this artwork, James has captured the split-second stall of a kingfisher as it spots its prey below. He cut the scratchcards into long strips that have the look of feathers. Using reference photographs, James chose strips with the appropriate colours, including silver, to represent the variations of blue and green in the coloured feathers.

He used encaustic wax to give a feeling of movement in the sky behind the split-second stillness of the bird, and also for a softer, simpler background in which the kingfisher would not be lost. The light blue and white colour of the air creates a softer, more abstract background to contrast with the bird's precisely defined plumage. Its black, piercing eye – very much the focal point of the picture – focuses on a fish below and there's a sense that this is the very moment at which the bird will shoot down to catch its prey.

◀ *Kingfisher collage with encaustic wax background.*

▶ *Finished blue tit collage.*

BLUE TIT

In contrast to the dive of a kingfisher, here James has depicted an ascending blue tit in a slightly different manner, though still in an encaustic wax sky. With this bird, James was thinking of the blue tit he cared for and gave water to in the garden when it hurt itself, and the way it was able to fly away again afterwards. Its feathers are represented by hole-punched cards in the appropriate colours rather than the thin strips of the kingfisher's wings. This, along with the cool palette of yellows, greens and blues, gives the bird a gentler look, more peaceful and harmonious than the dynamic colours and striking long strips used for the kingfisher. On an artwork of this size, of course, the hole-punched circles didn't allow enough definition for the more detailed areas, so James cut them down as required – for instance, around the chest stripe, the blue cap on the bird's head and the pointed tips of the wing feathers.

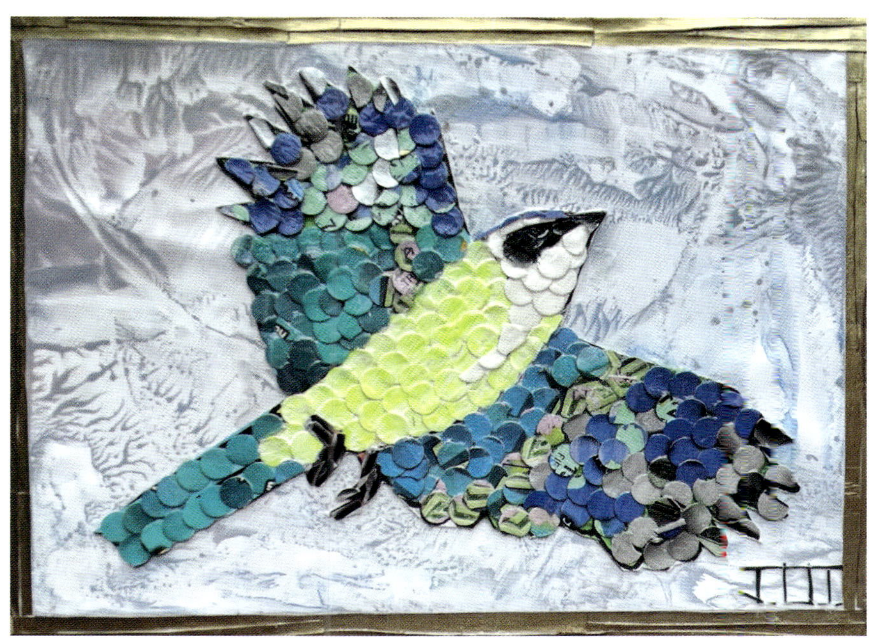

SWANS

A single swan gliding gracefully on a body of water is considered by many to be the epitome of natural grace. They maintain that powerful presence when flying in formation as a flock.

James gathered a variety of materials including hole-punched pieces of used scratchcards, threads and strings, small pieces of card on which he had used encaustic wax and old beads.

He tore up larger pieces of paper on which he had previously applied the encaustic process. These would make up the sky. He used short lengths of thread to represent the tips of each swan's feathers. Then he cut up different international scratchcards into a variety of shapes and hole-punched others to make up the different parts of the of the birds' bodies and wings. Some beads he had originally found in a charity shop were made into the glimmering bodies of the black swans.

Bank note symbols of various nations from scratchcards make up the wings of the white swans. James used symbols of British pounds for the Bewick's swan and of American dollars for the Tundra swan. The encaustic wax for the fantasy sky goes well with the swans from different parts of the world taking flight in unison. Behind the white swans are black swans found throughout

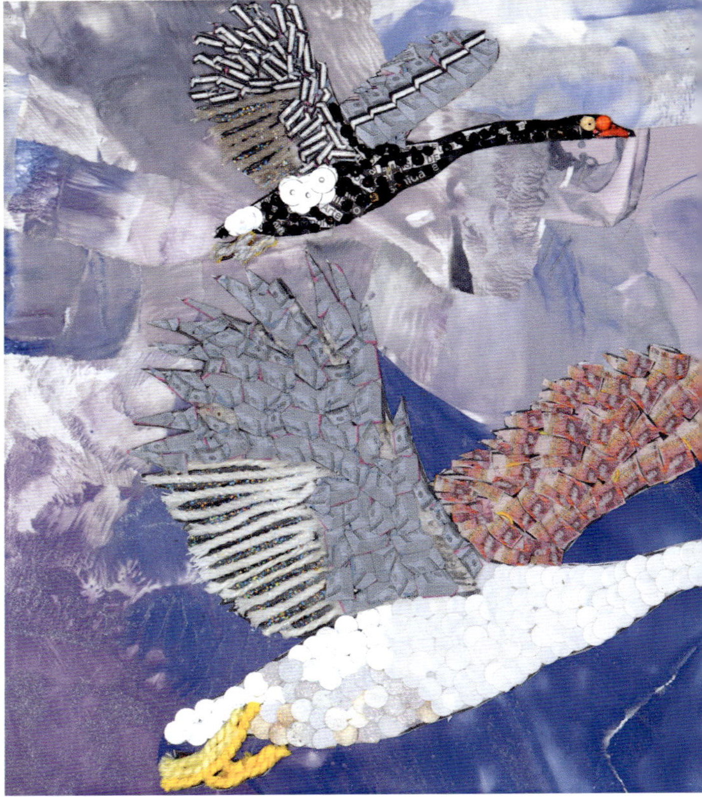

Australia and introduced to New Zealand and other parts of Europe. He worked with English and overseas scratchcards to depict the wings.

James believes that if we do nothing to tackle climate change, the cost to our planet and to nature will be huge. The encaustic sky here is fragmented and disturbed as if the swans are flying through stormy and uncertain times. It goes against the usual depiction of peaceful skies and looks more dynamic as James is making a statement that extreme weather and climate change are costing us all so much and require urgent action to be taken.

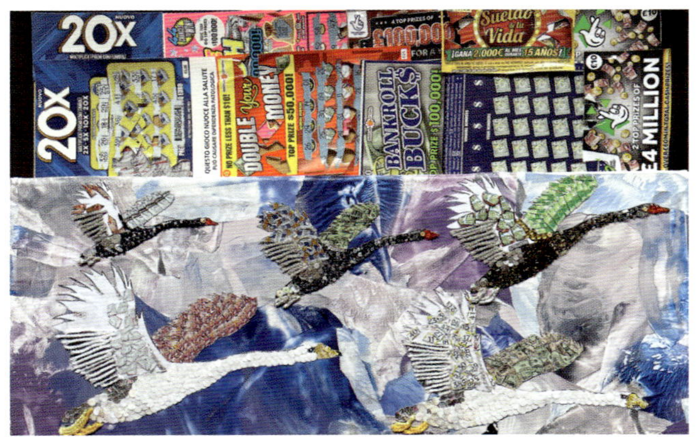

◀ *In Unison alongside some of the scratchcards used.*

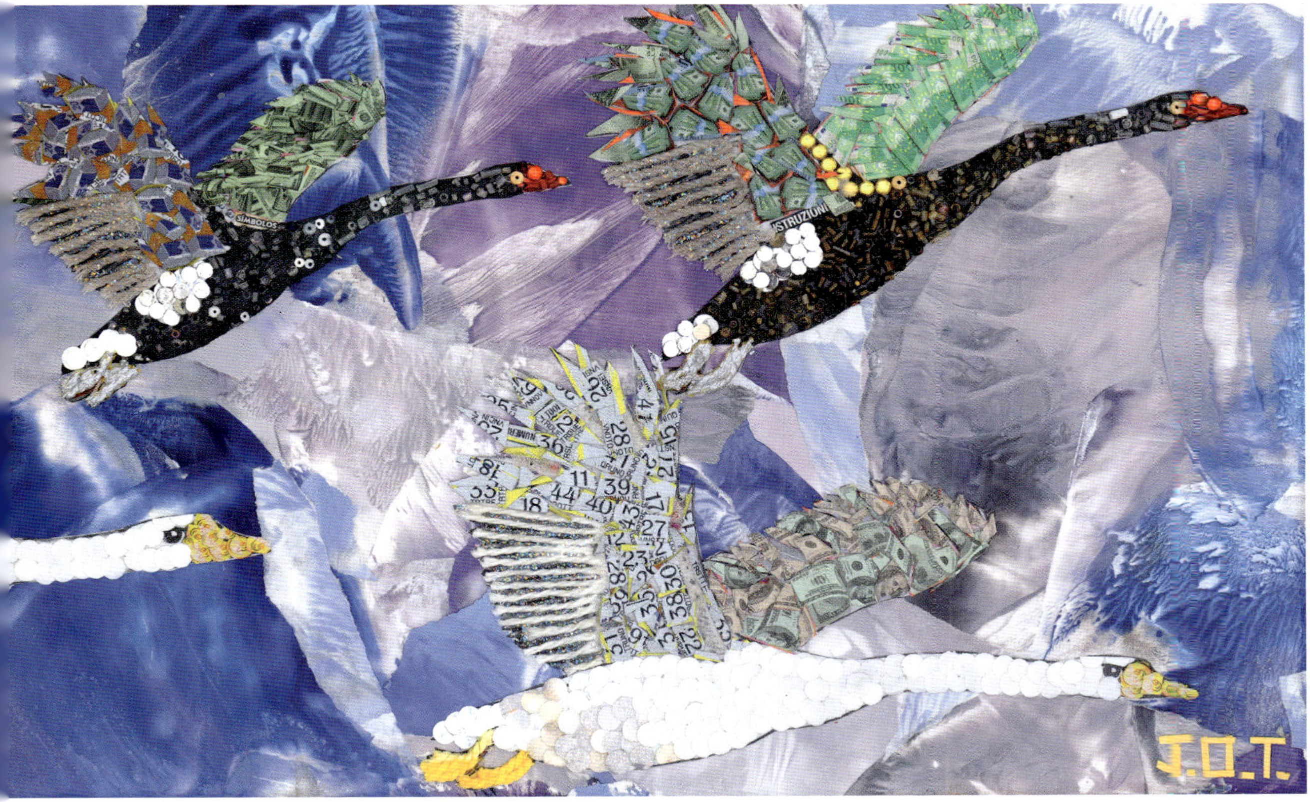

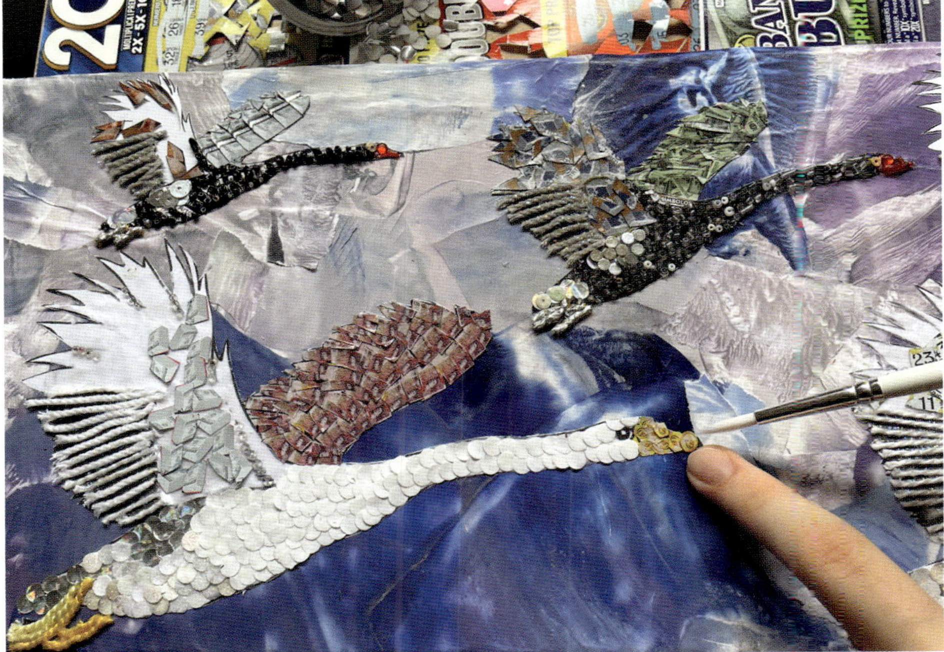

In Unison – the completed collage.

Gluing on symbols for the beak.

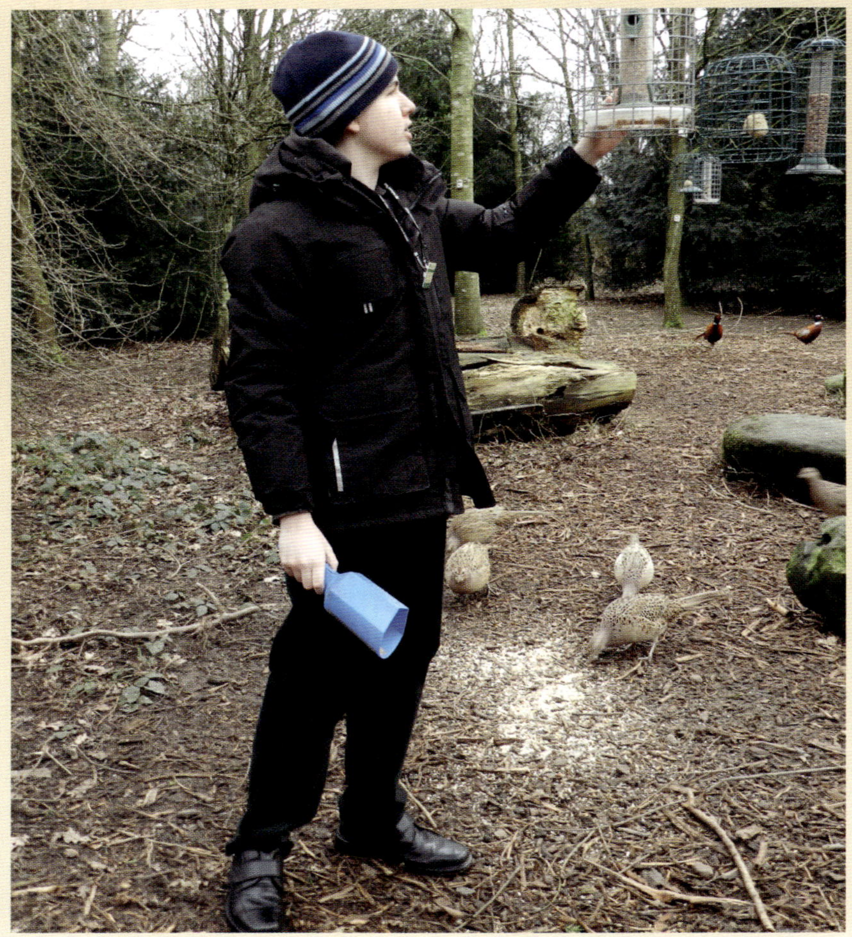

NATIONAL TRUST VOLUNTEER

James' love for and knowledge of birds led him to become a volunteer at the bird hide in Fountains Abbey between 2014 and 2019, where his responsibilities extended to the upkeep of the hide as well as feeding the birds. Cleaning out the hide became a labour of love. He would sweep away debris and fallen leaves and answer people's questions as they came to observe the birds in their sanctuary. James appreciated how his tasks linked him to the birds. The bird hide became a sanctuary for him, his own type of sensory room. Pheasants followed him around the hide waiting for nuts and seeds to fall as he filled the bird feeders, and squirrels rushed to collect as many nuts and seeds from the ground as they could find.

At Brimham Rocks, where James volunteered between 2015 and 2018, he recorded grid references of where he found certain species, and would photograph the birds. As James had his first ever exhibition at Brimham Rocks' information centre, he liked to keep them informed about his artwork so would email his photographs to them.

Bird Album

Photos he had taken at Fountains Abbey and pictures he saw in magazines and books inspired James to create this selection of collages. It demonstrates the wide variety of birds depicted in his art.

Avocet ▶

Blackbird ▼

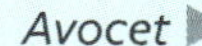

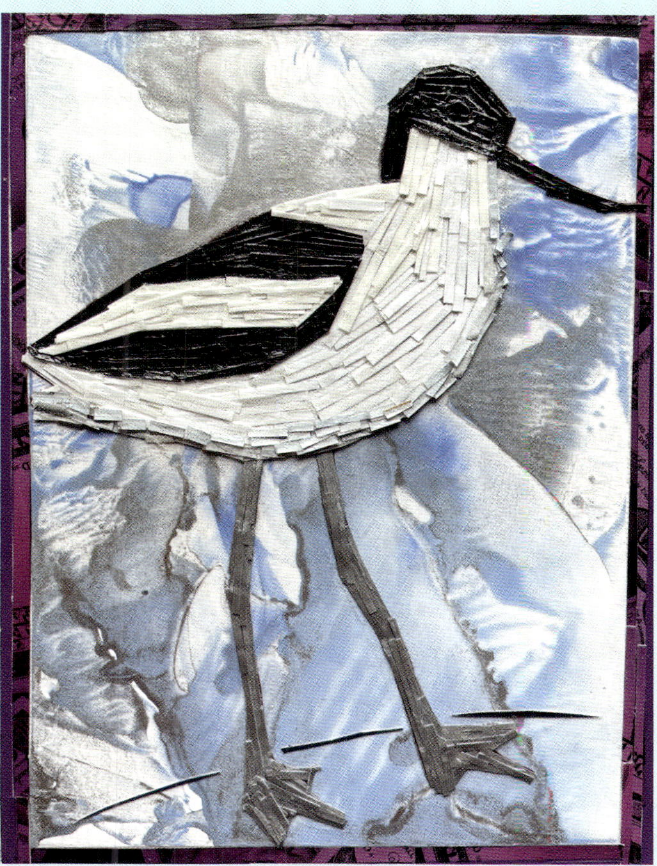

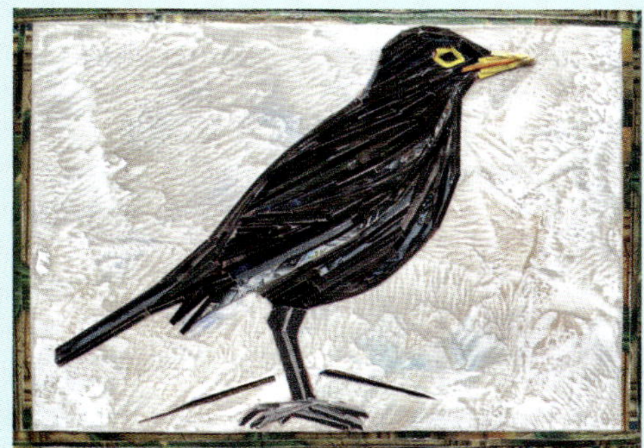

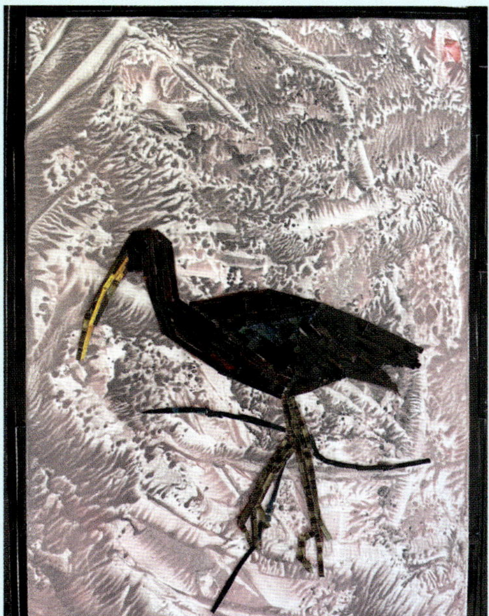

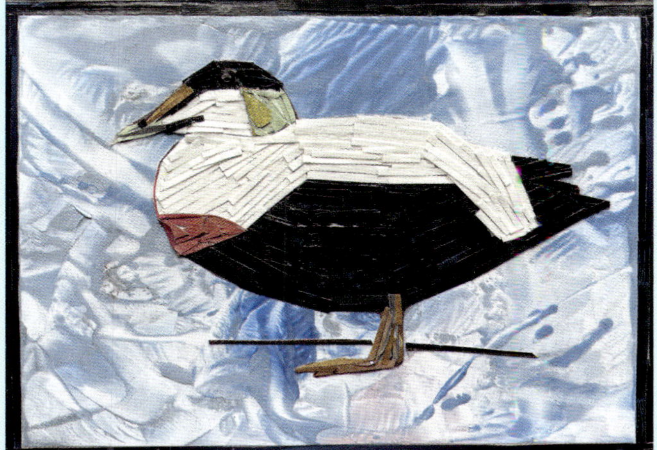

▲ *Eider Duck*

◀ *Ibis*

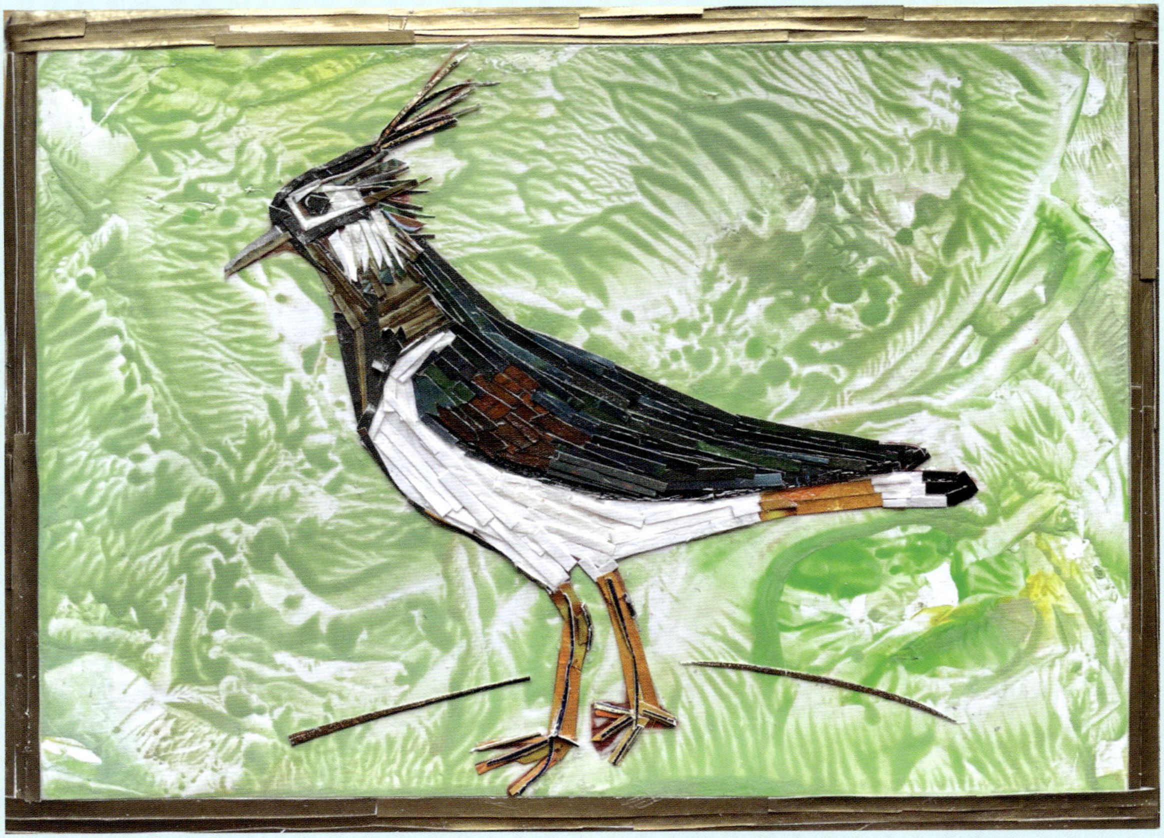

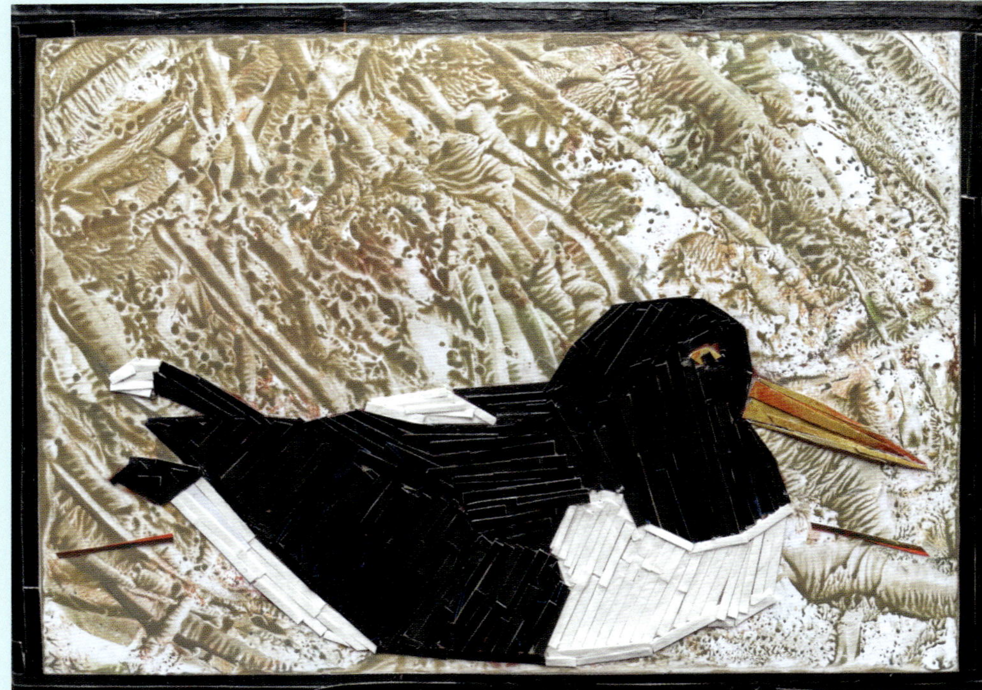

Lapwing

Oyster-catcher

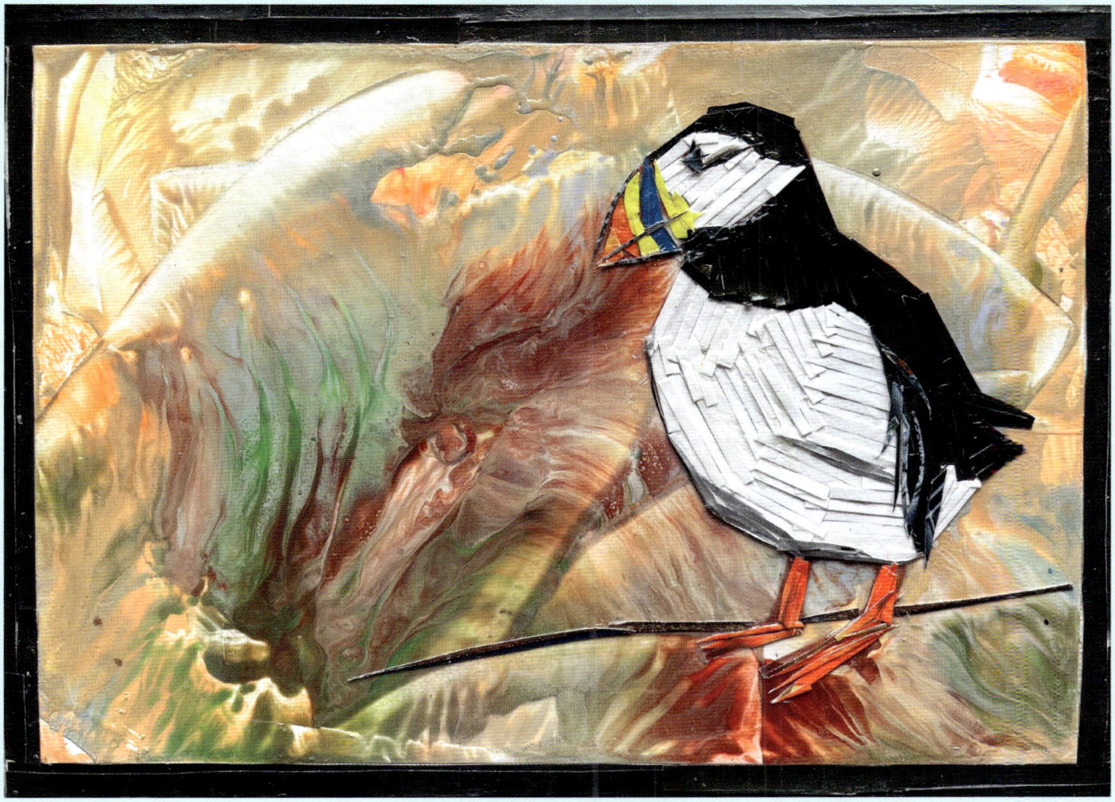

▲ Puffin   ▼ Raven   ▼ Razorbill

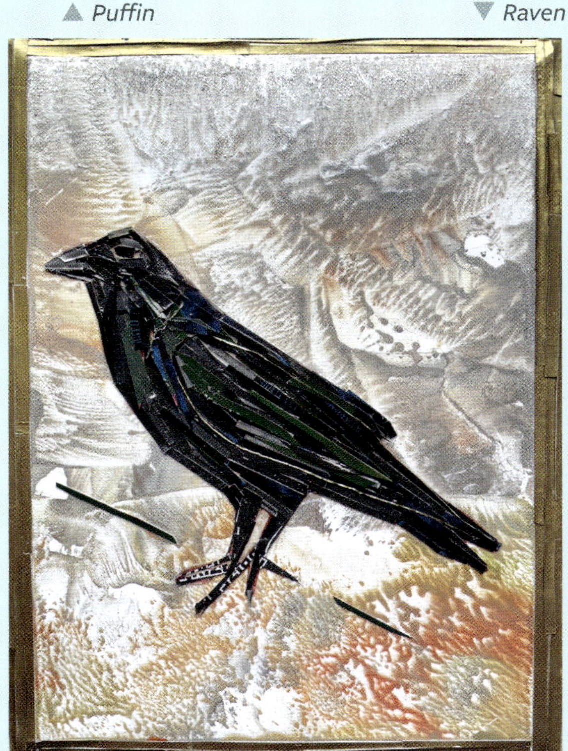

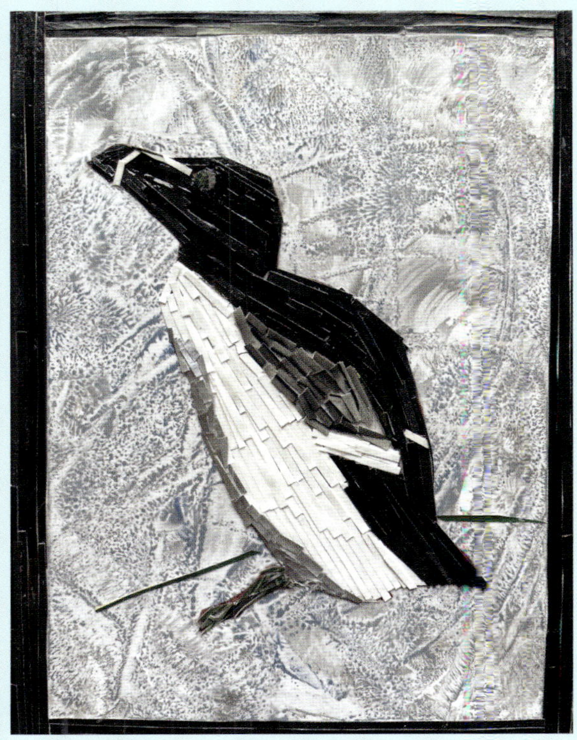

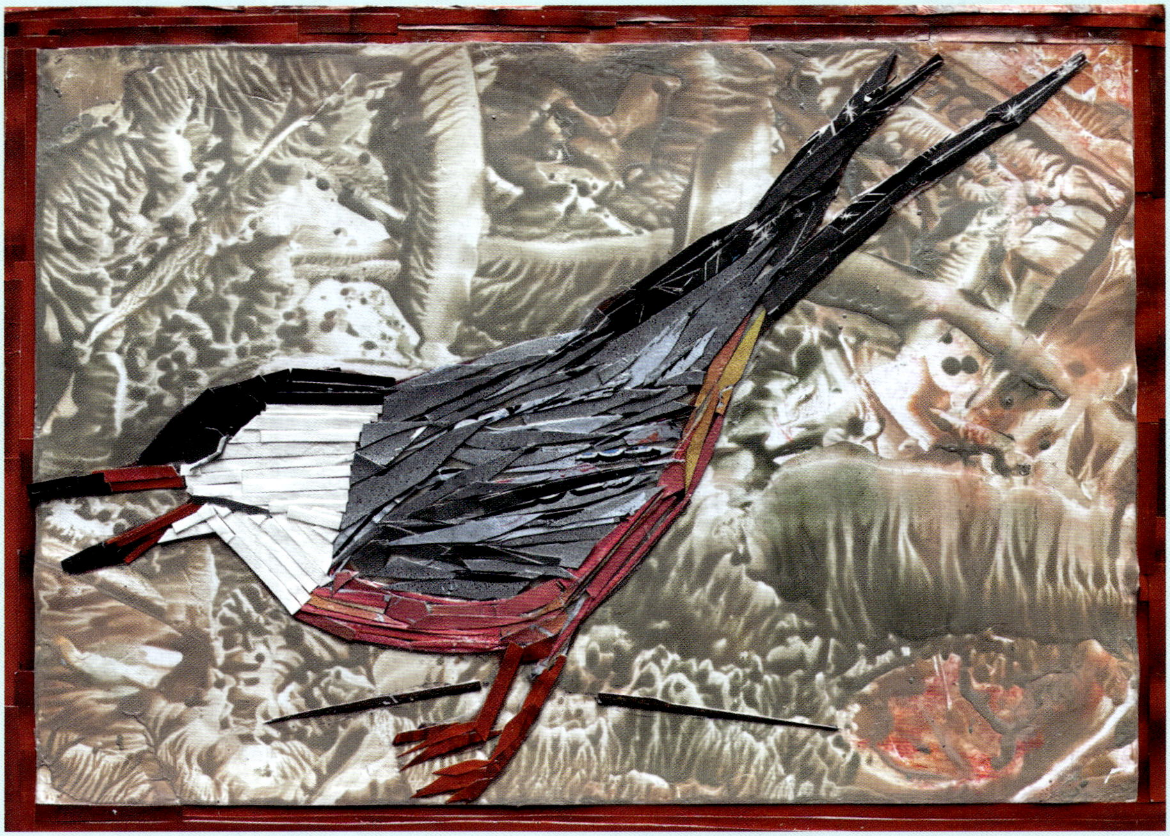

▲ *Roseate Tern*   *Great Spotted Woodpecker* ▶

▼ *Tufted Duck*

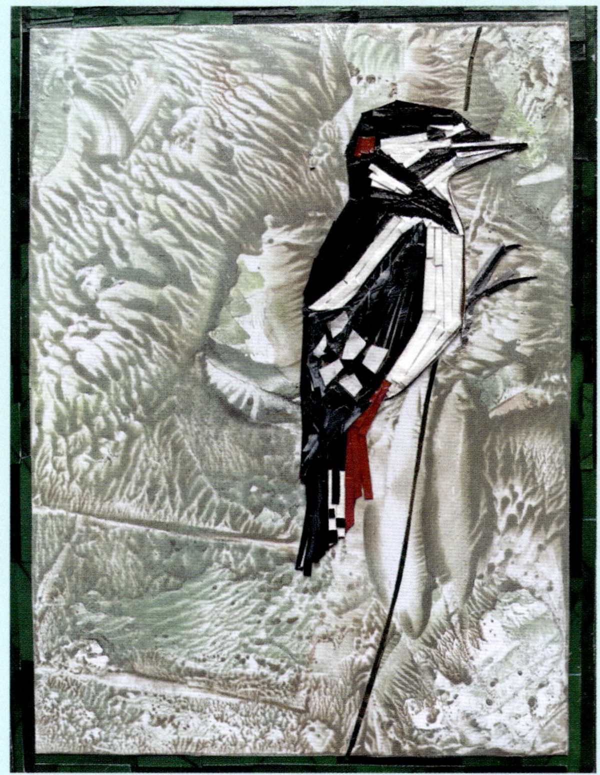

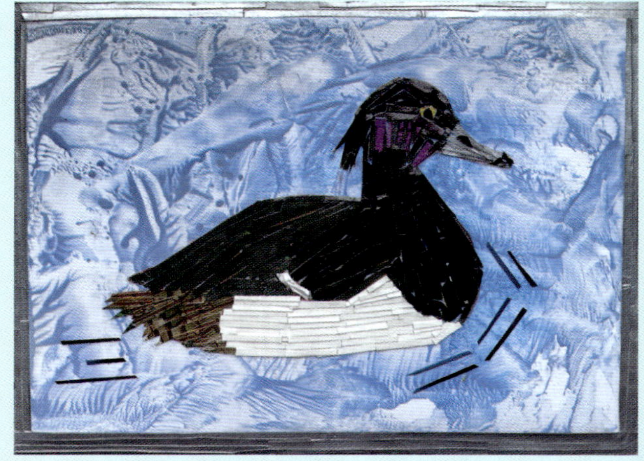

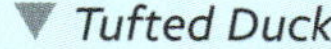

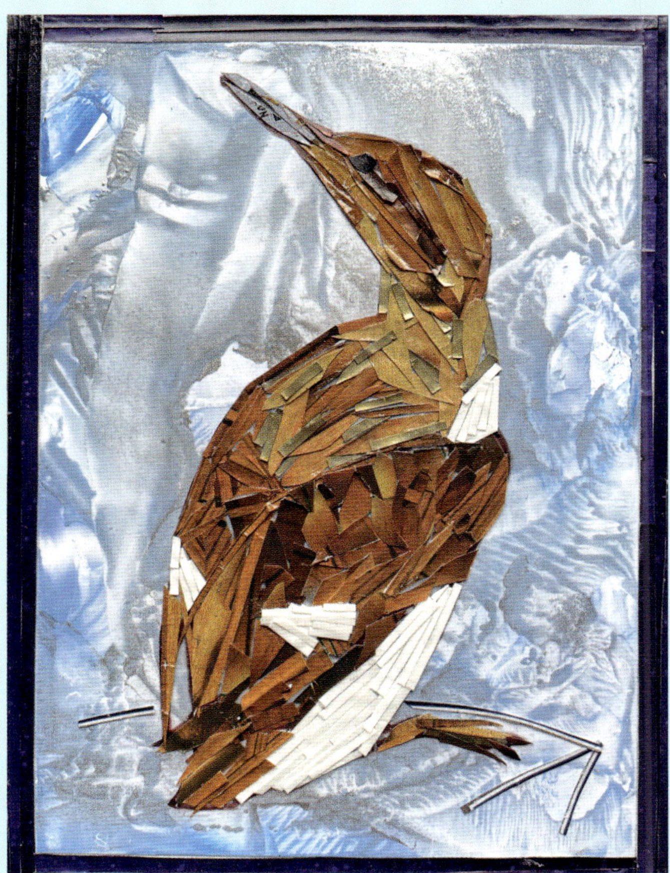

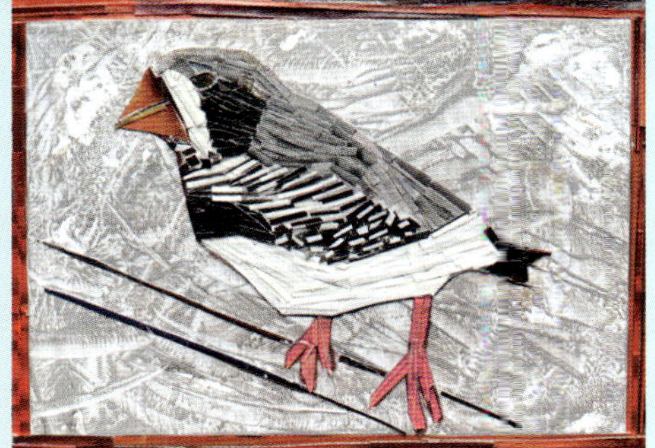

◀ *Guillemot*

▼ *Zebra Finch*

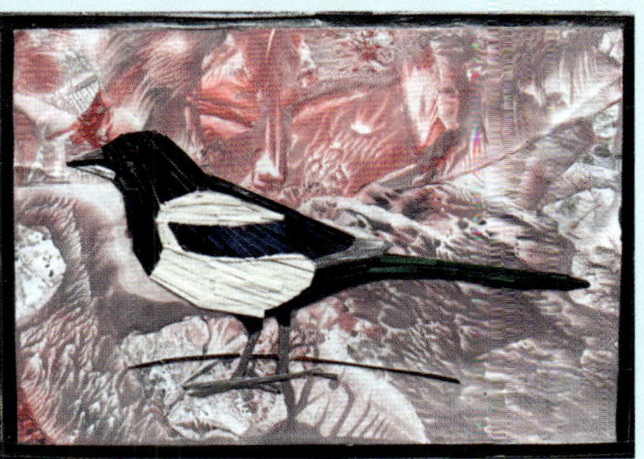

▲ *Magpie*

◀ *Kittiwake*

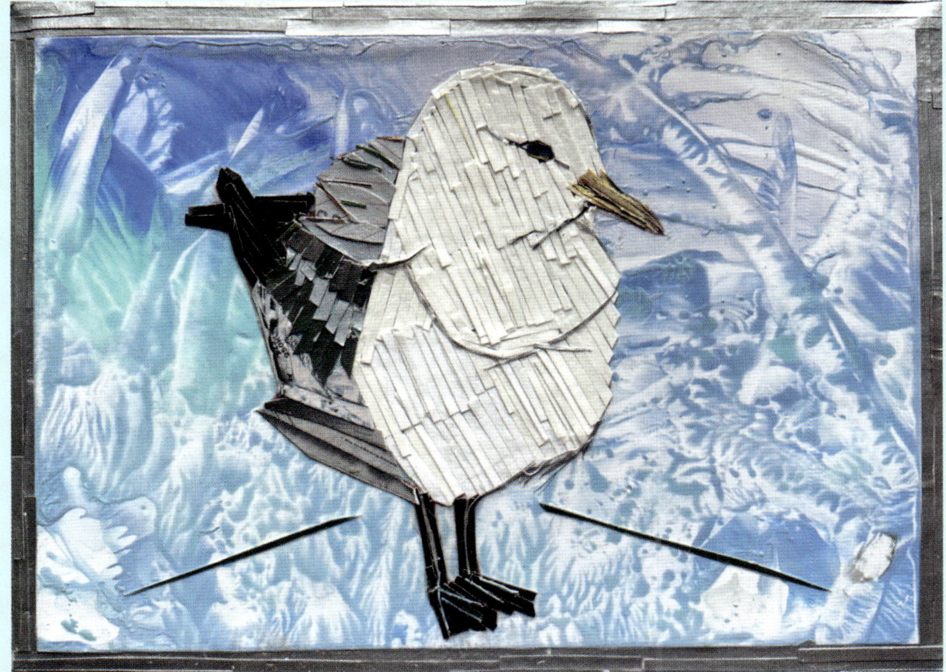

HORSES AND DONKEYS

James had always been a little intimidated by horses. Their huge size, when up close, could seem a little overwhelming. However, he always admired them from afar. Observing them over a fence or drystone wall standing in the fields, or trotting along a country lane with a skilled rider at the reins, sparked his imagination.

PONTEFRACT RACES

A pit pony artwork that James created after taking a photograph at the Beamish Museum (see pages 106–7) – and that appeared on the poster for his 2018 exhibition at the National Coal Mining Museum for England – caught the eye of Richard Hammill, Chief Operating Officer and Clerk of the Course at Pontefract Races. He contacted James to commission him to create four pieces of

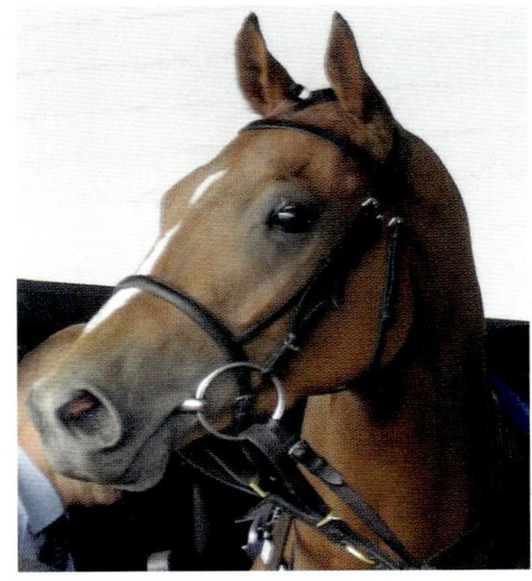

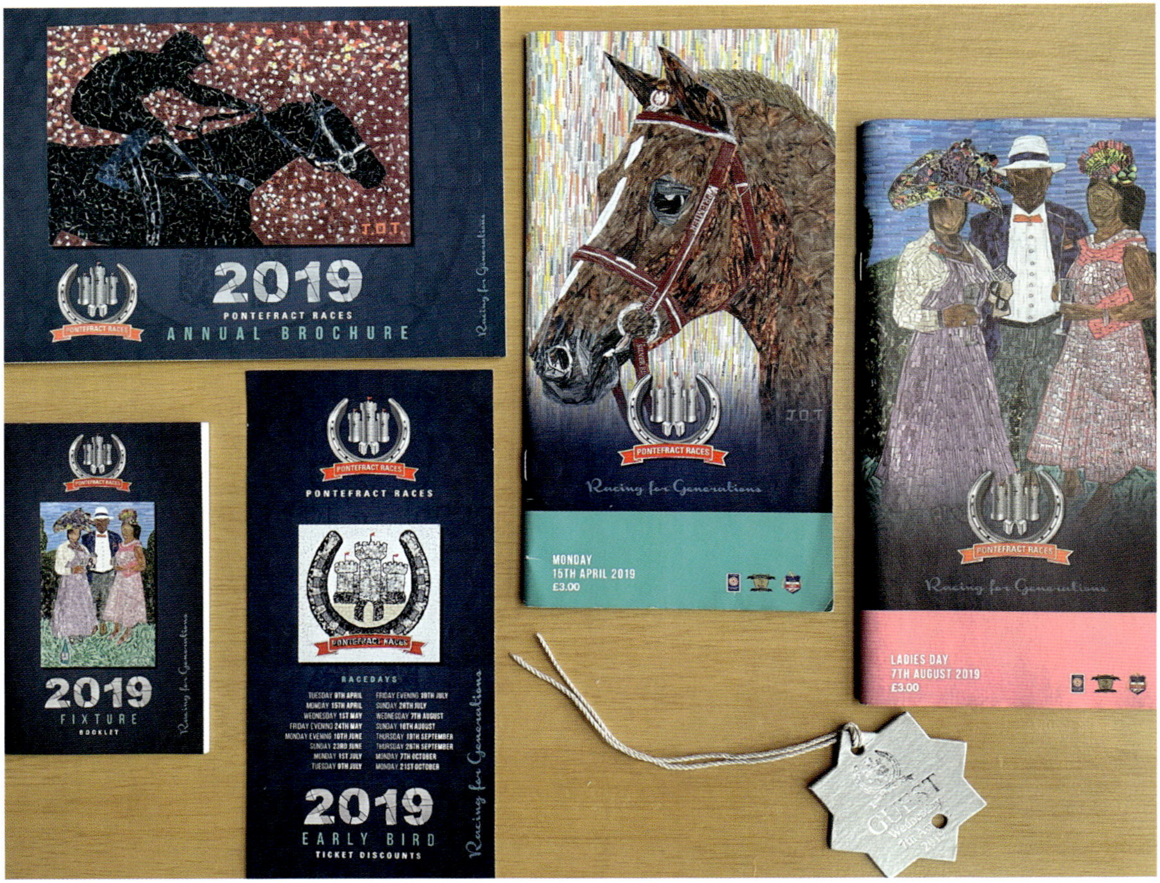

▲ *The main reference photograph of Crownthorpe.*

▶ **The Thoroughbred.**

▼ *James' artworks on the Pontefract marketing literature.*

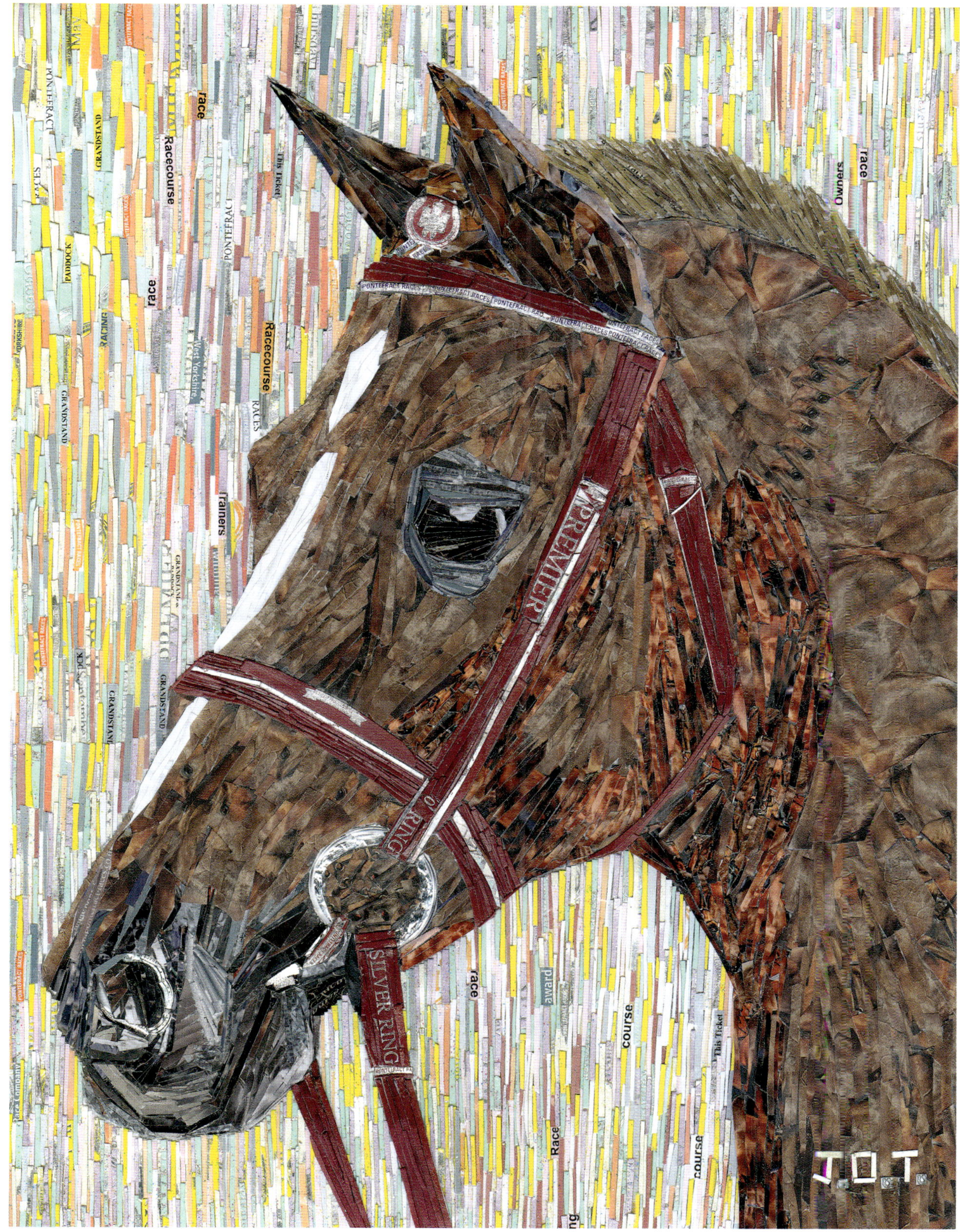

PREMIER
SILVER RING
T.O.T.

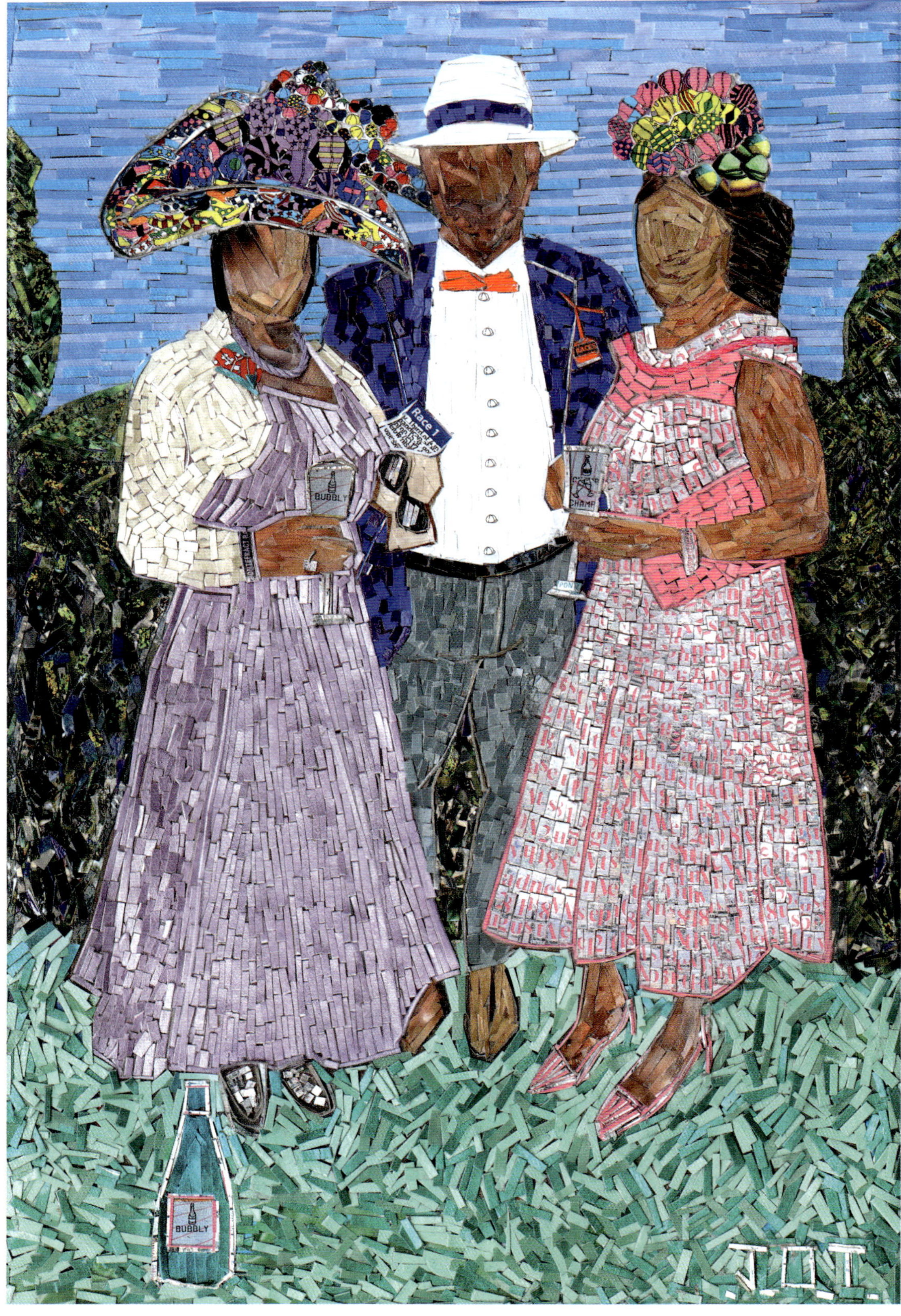

Race 1
BUBBLY
CHAMP
RACES
BUBBLY
J.O.T.

artwork using their previous race days' tickets, badges and old brochures that might otherwise have been thrown away.

James sat at his kitchen table for many hours incorporating them into four artworks: *Ladies Day*, the Pontefract logo, *The Thoroughbred*, and *Final Furlong*. These pieces are displayed in glass cabinets at the racecourse and they were reproduced on the covers of marketing literature used to promote the 2019 season.

For the first of the horse images from this commission – *The Thoroughbred* – James used various cut-up pieces from horses photographed in the old magazines that Pontefract Races had supplied. He varied as many colour tones as possible to match the colours of a horse called Crownthorpe, but also referred to other pictures to make sure he created an accurate image. The word 'PREMIER' on its bridle came from one of Pontefract Races' tickets, as does the logo between the horse's ears. The background was made from strips of tickets in pastel shades.

▼ *The pit pony poster for James' National Coal Mining Museum exhibition.*

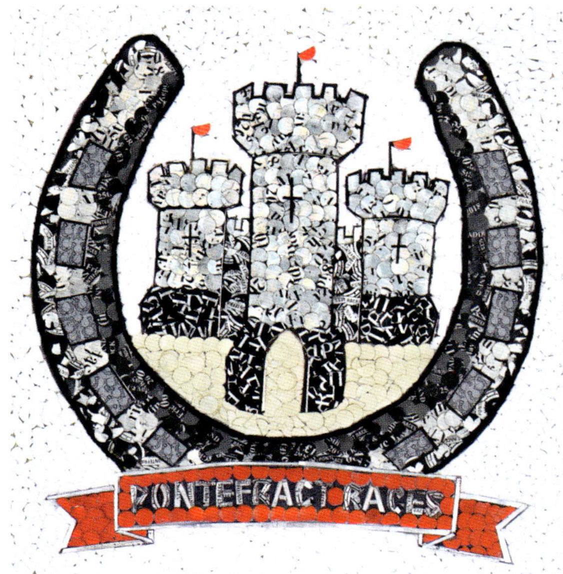

▲ *The Pontefract Races logo. Race meetings date back as far as 1648 and it is said that the early races took place in meadows near Pontefract Castle. James used hole-punched circles and semi circles that overlap in a neat, tidy way – a style that he really likes.*

◀ ***Ladies Day**, based on a photograph of the winners of the best dressed competition.*

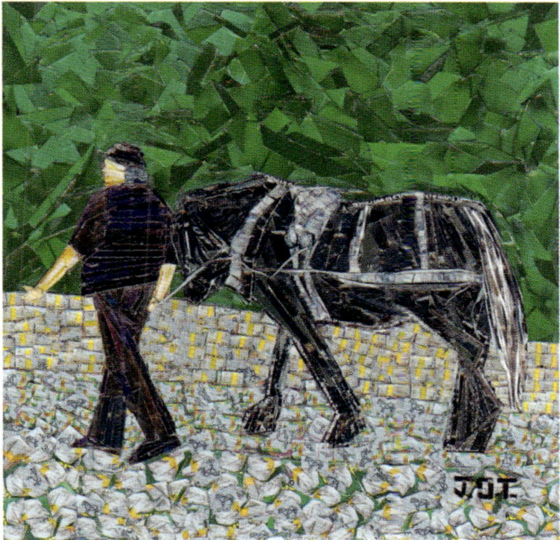

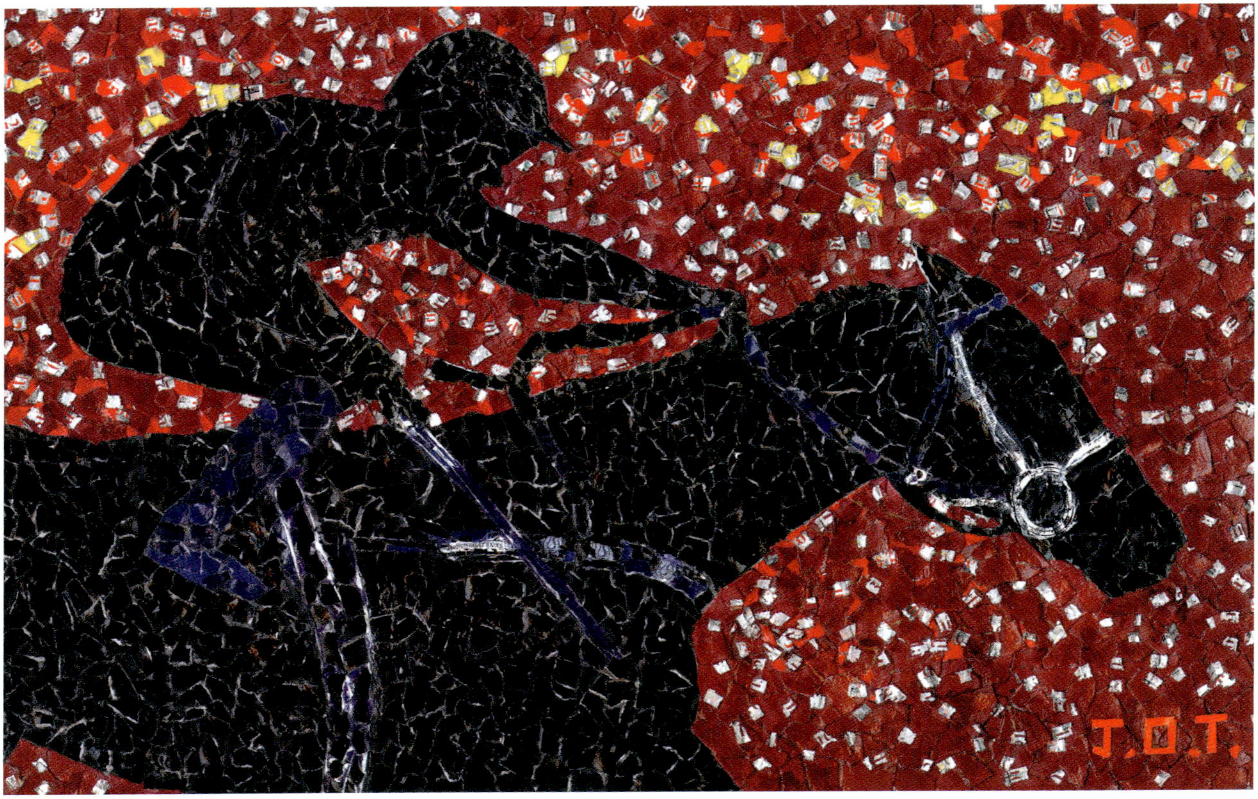

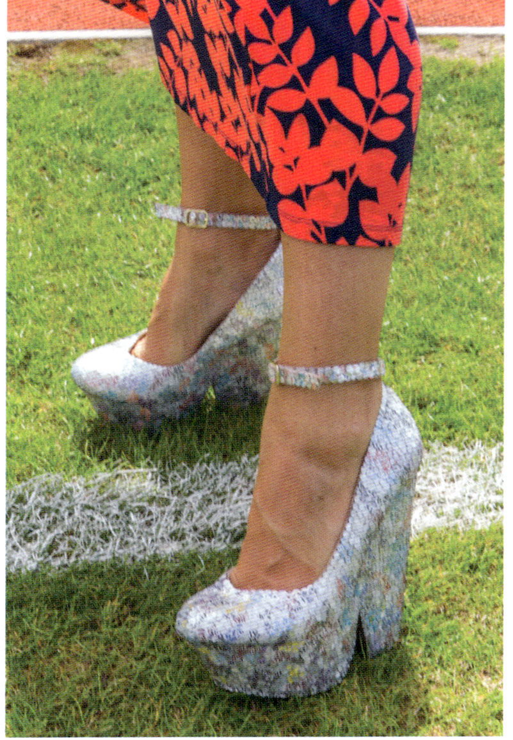

▲ *Final Furlong.*

◀ *As a little extra, James used left-over pieces from his Pontefract Races logo to collage a pair of shoes for Ladies' Day, modelled at the event by one of the judges!*

For the second horse artwork, *Final Furlong*, James needed to hurry to meet the racecourse's deadline but still spent hours working on it until he was happy with the finished result. The horse and jockey were made from small pieces of black magazine paper in a mosaic style showing rough white edges of the torn paper.

He knew what colours he wanted for the sky to enhance the silhouette, but the maroon clashed with the bright orange, red and yellow colours. He added more and more layers, but still didn't feel happy until he found that small pieces of silver blended in well. These extra pieces gave a feeling of speed on the horse's final part of the race.

GREAT BRITISH RACING

James later learned that *Final Furlong* had been used in a report on sustainability in the horse racing industry. He got in touch with the British Horseracing Authority to introduce himself and it wasn't long before he was contacted by Great British Racing (GBR), the promotional and marketing body of the British Horseracing Authority, and was asked to create a collage for them as well. In this case it was to commemorate the coronation of King Charles III.

Eager to include any horse racing paraphernalia in the intended artwork, James asked if they would send him some unwanted materials relating to horses that he might be able to include in the collage. They were keen to oblige and said they could send something in the mail.

James is used to sorting through discarded materials on his dining table at home, but it would not be large enough to deal with this load. He soon found that the floor space indoors was far too small to begin selecting the items he might use for his artwork. Thankfully, the double garage allowed just enough room to sort through all the items.

James also attended a race meeting to take some reference photographs (**a**).

A large canvas would be needed for this commission. He really wanted to convey the size and power of a racehorse. After drawing up the contours of the image, he slowly selected certain pieces of the donated materials and began the long process of cutting and sorting them into colour and texture type. James was asked to focus on the colours of the Royal Silks for the collage (red, purple and gold).

Slowly, the image started to come together. The tiny cut pieces started to shimmer into the bigger picture. James used circular pieces of text on white paper for the sky, broken up by sections of torn GBR business cards for an interesting patterned effect. The crown was made up of shiny

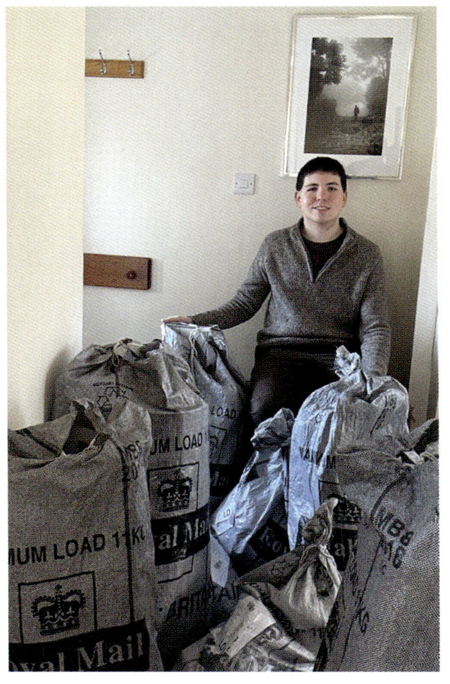
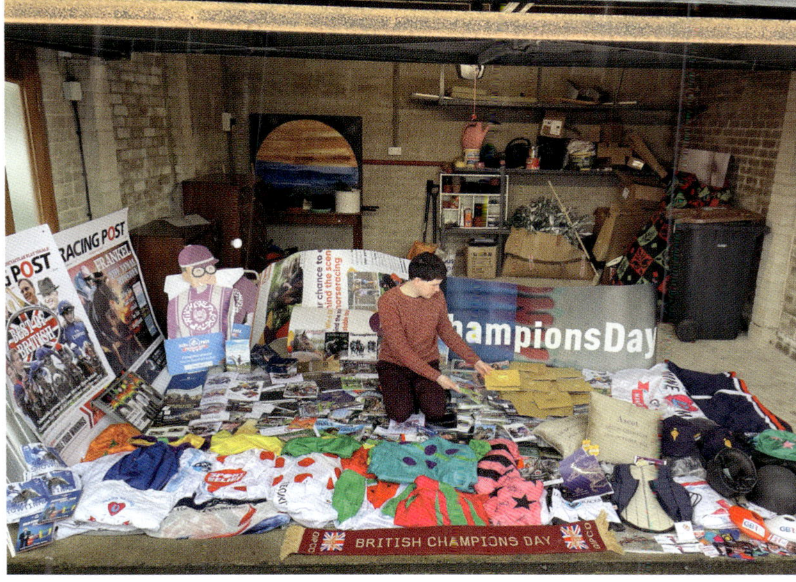

◄ ▲ *James with his consignment from Great British Racing, and sorting through it in the garage.*

pieces of scratchcards and old beads. James also collaged worn racing silks to form the Royal racing silks for the jockey. Gold squares from old Ascot cushion covers made an ideal path (**b**) and GBR gold brochures were hole-punched to form the lettering needed for the artwork. The body of the horse was created by tearing up sections of magazines depicting black colours, often photo-graphs of other black horses (**c**). The texture of the mane and tail came from cut strips of used plastic bags.

Lengths of coloured thread from previous race day tickets were cut and run round the still abstracted shapes to accentuate the contours (**d**). GBR were delighted that James cut out the names of each of the racecourses in the country to use as the horse's reins.

On the all-important day at Pontefract – 3 May 2023 – James turned up with his collage for the big unveiling, alongside Richard Hammill, who made a speech praising James' work and noting his blossoming career.

James was interviewed and photographed and he chatted to many members of the public, who asked him how he made the collage, how long it took to make and even whether he could ride a horse! He was very proud to have made this piece celebrating the crowning of Charles III, which shortly went on to be presented again, both at Thirsk Racecourse on 6 May – the day of the coronation – and in September at the St Leger Festival in Doncaster.

Some of the remaining materials that GBR had sent to James could not be used on his canvas. The items included caps, helmets, children's riding clothes, horse rugs, reading books and DVDs. James was given permission from GBR to pass them on to a local riding school, the Bewerley School of Horsemanship (now SJ Equestrian

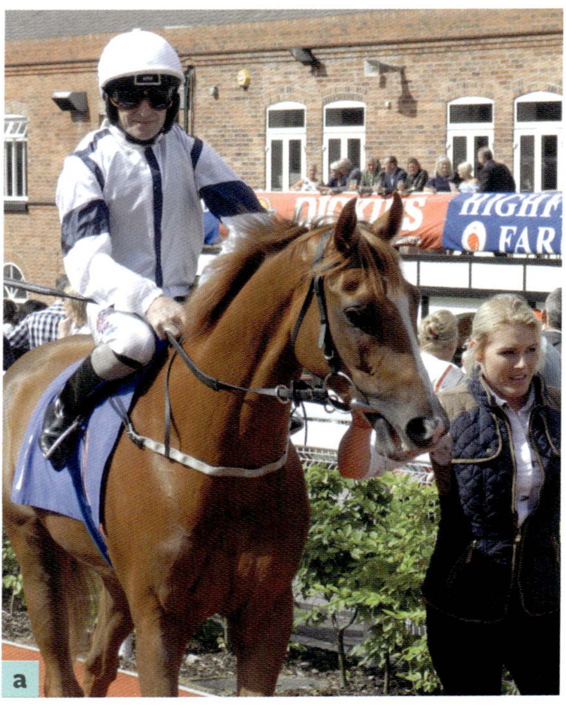

James' main reference photo for the Great British Racing piece.

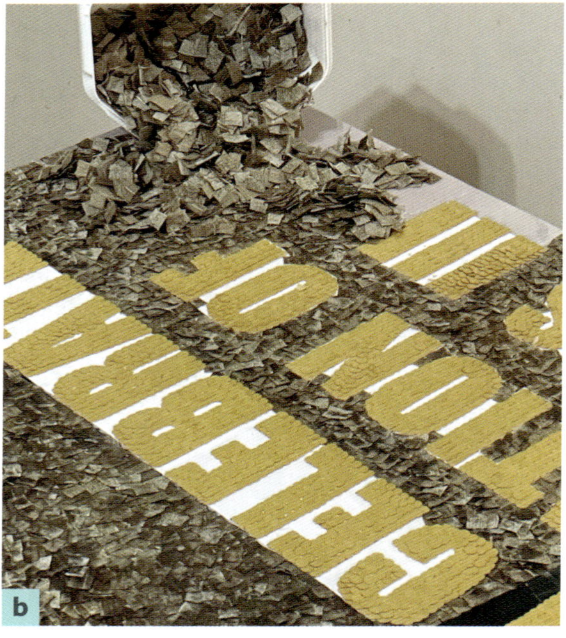

Some of the many golden squares cut from cushion covers and applied to the path in the foreground.

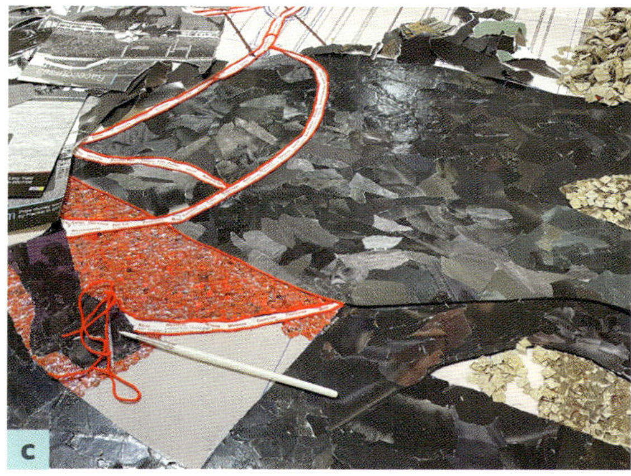

Working on the black body of the horse using torn sections of black and grey magazine images.
(© PA Media and Great British Racing)

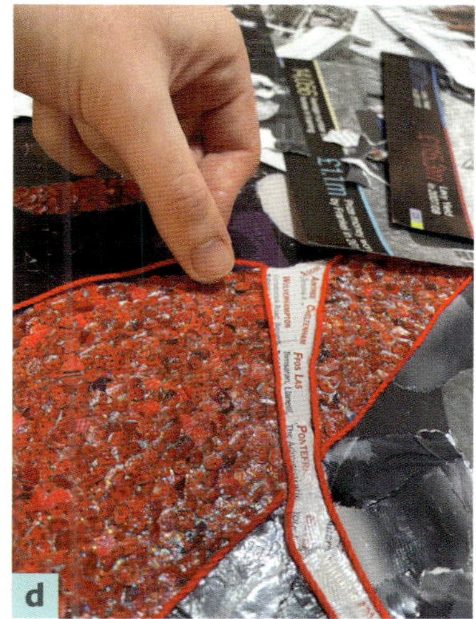

Using coloured thread to define some outlines.

▼ *James unveiling the Great British Racing piece at Pontefract.*

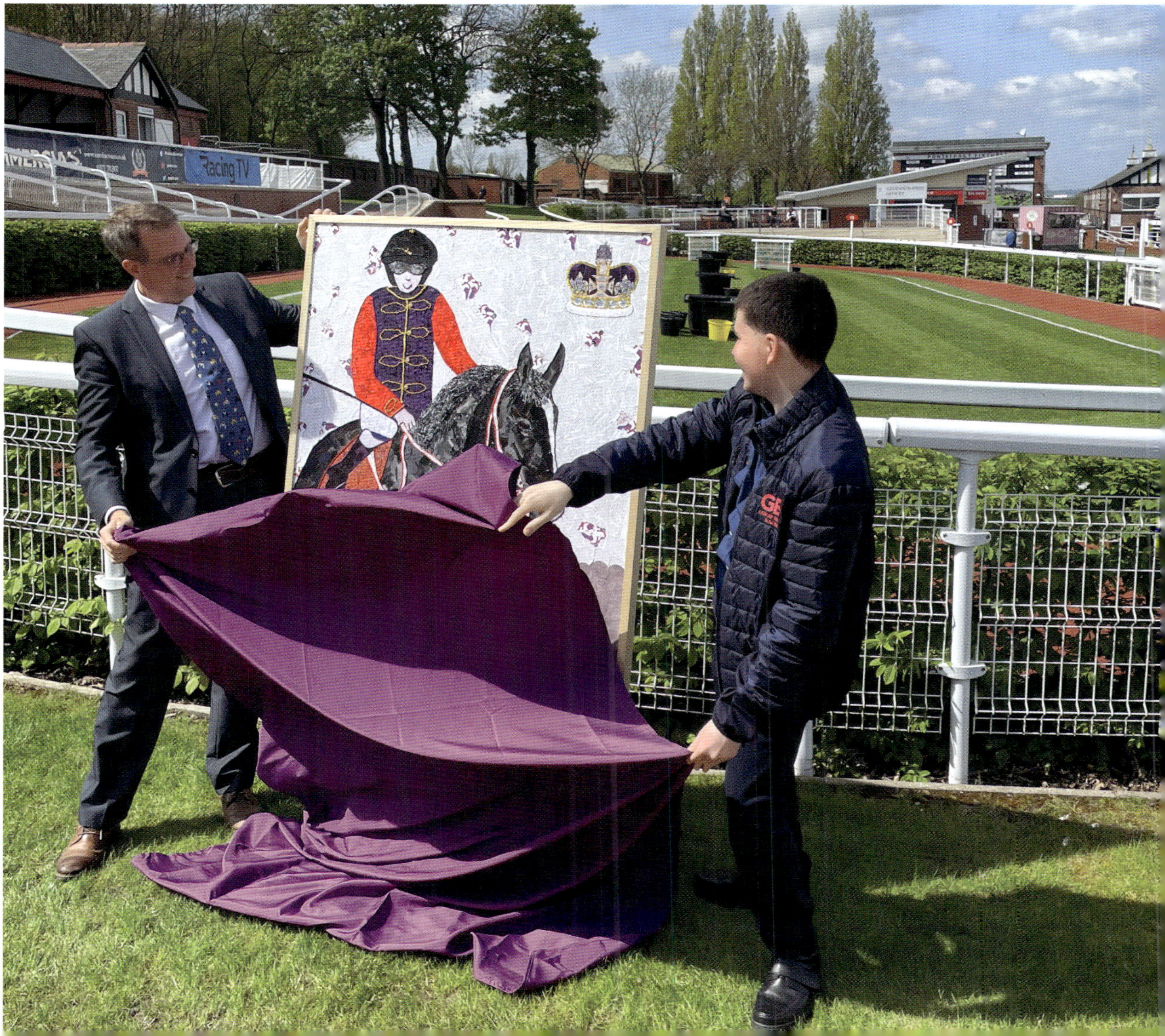

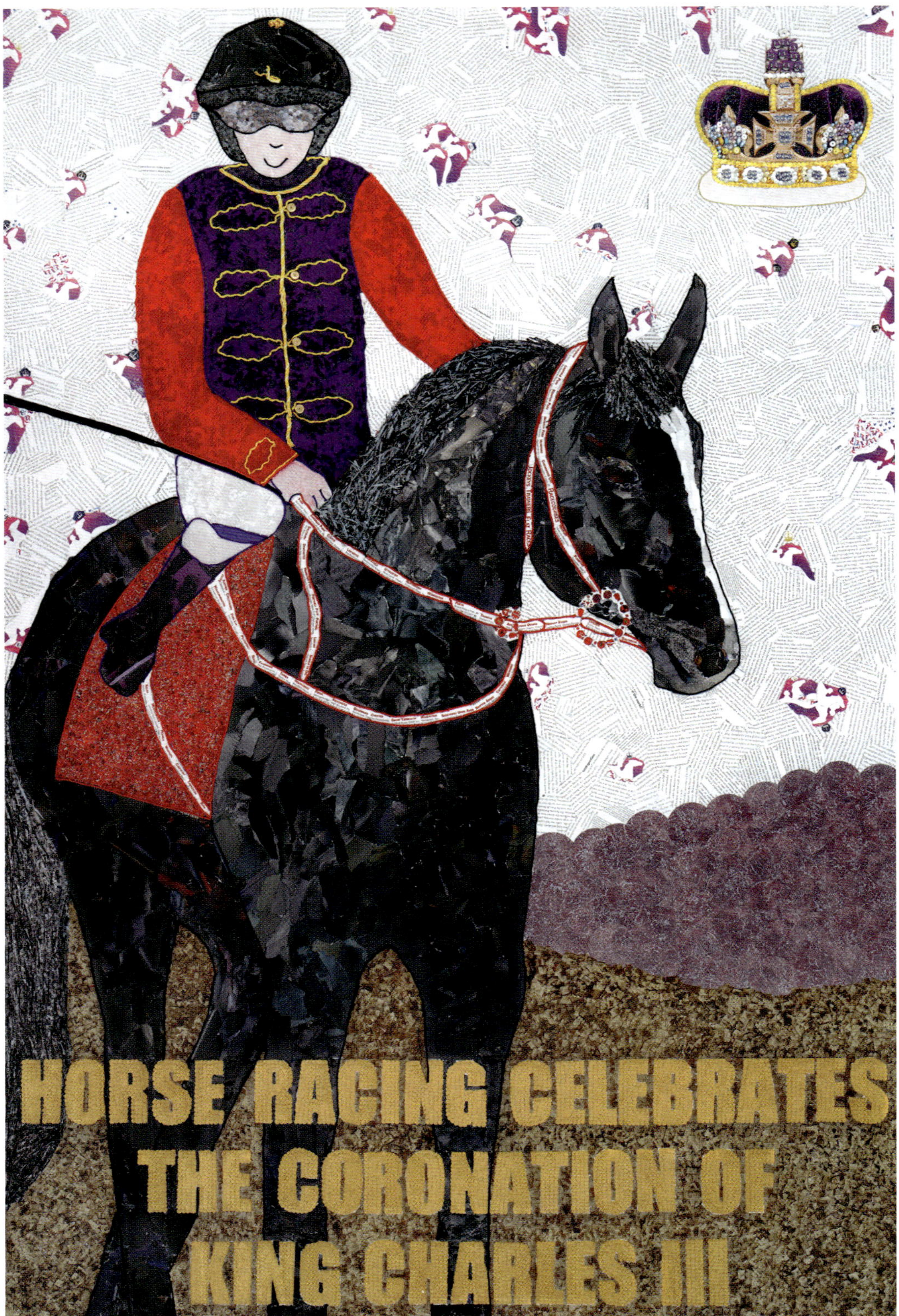

The completed commission for Great British Racing.

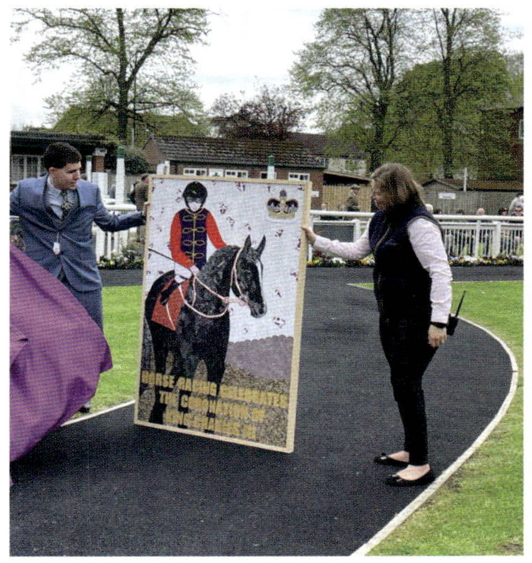

▲ *The unveiling at Thirsk Racecourse.*

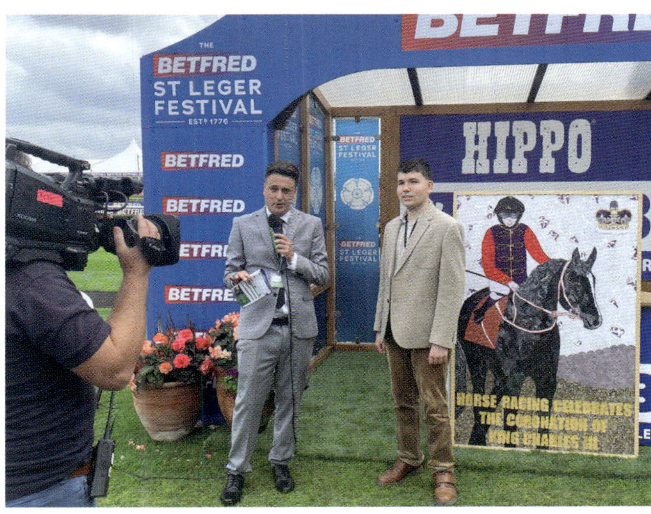

▲ *Interview with Bobby Beevers – an autistic presenter and founder of Autism in Racing – at the St Leger Festival in 2023.*

Centre, near Brimham Rocks) – so much better than having to discard them. The staff were delighted to receive these and James was invited to visit. The supervisor, June, introduced James to the horses and one called Sky quickly became a favourite.

DONKEYS

James visited The Donkey Sanctuary in Eccup near Leeds during the summer of 2023. The Donkey Sanctuary states that their animal-assisted therapy sessions are 'designed to help develop life skills, specifically self-esteem, empathy and managing emotions in vulnerable children and adults'.

James immediately felt relaxed in the company of the donkeys, who were very friendly and came close to meet him, boosting his confidence immensely. Even with their playful antics, he had a very

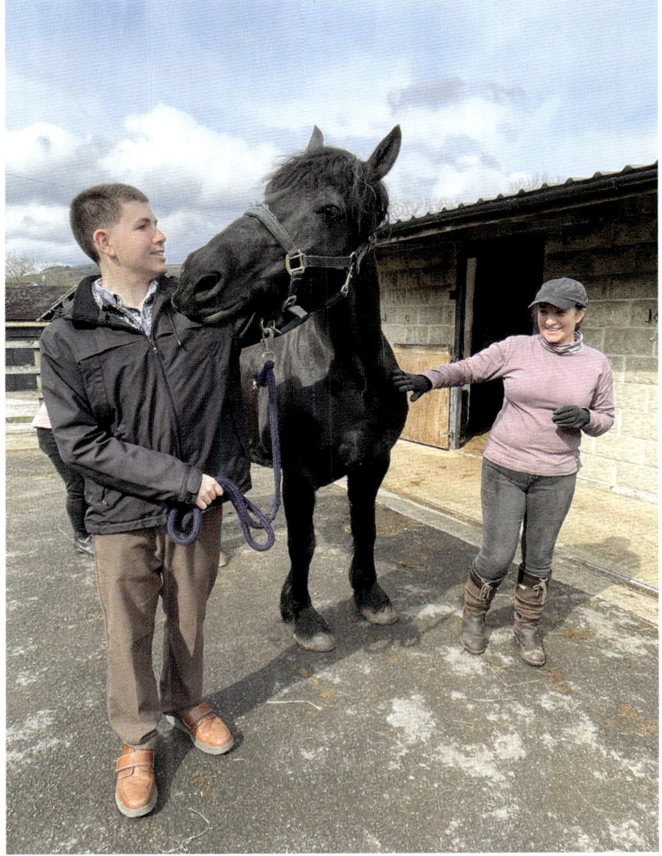

▲ *James with Sky at Bewerley School of Horsemanship.*

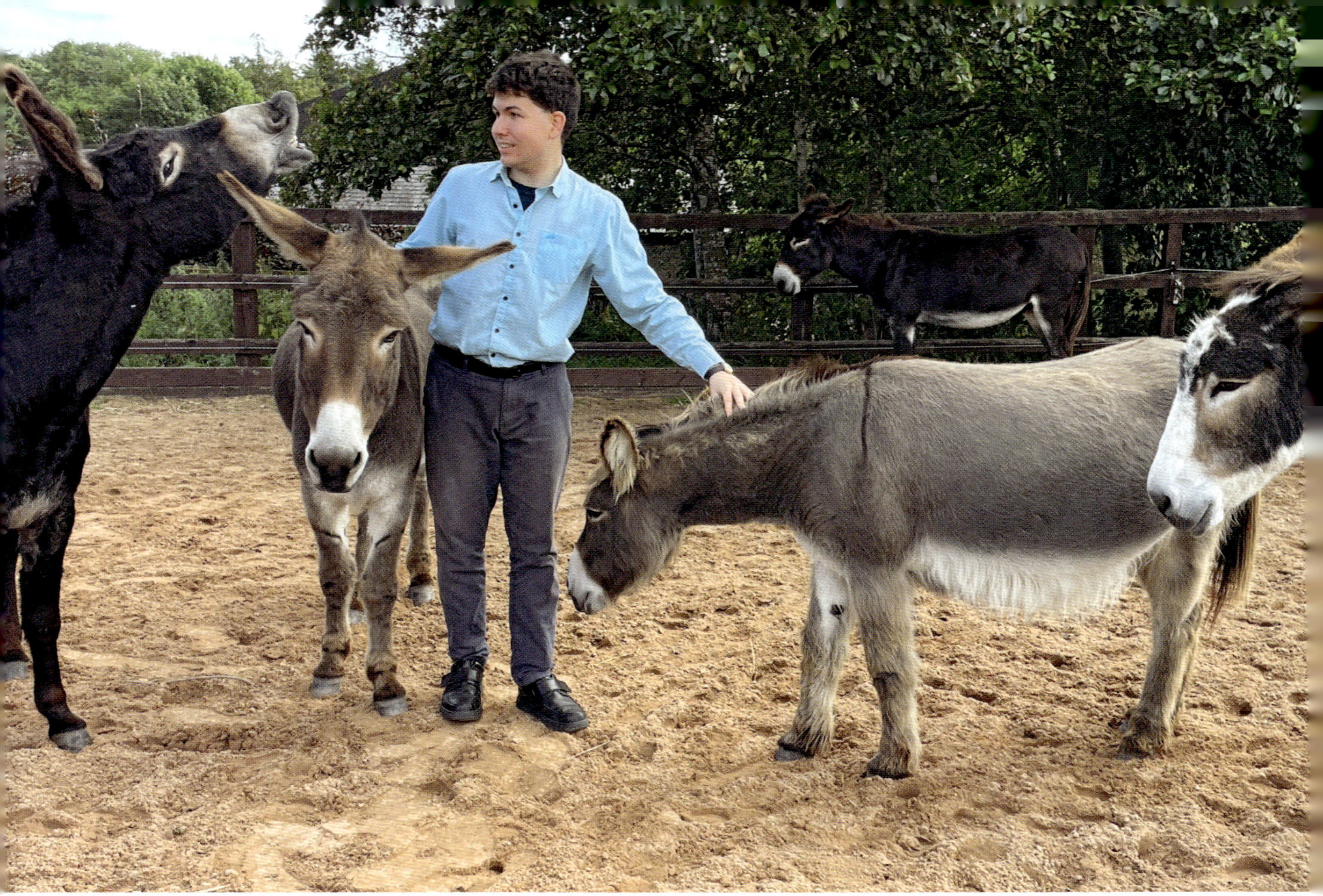

positive experience, feeling safe and happy. It was good to laugh with them as they played together. He also felt totally at ease leading one of them on a walk along a woodland area and he soon built a strong rapport with these gentle creatures.

James was pleased to support the Donkey Sanctuary by donating some of his Christmas cards to their gift shop. The donkeys were collaged with dark-grey felting wool on top of torn pieces of brown, black and grey magazine papers stuck on as a base coat. The background was collaged from the same Pontefract Raceday tickets that James used for *The Thoroughbred*.

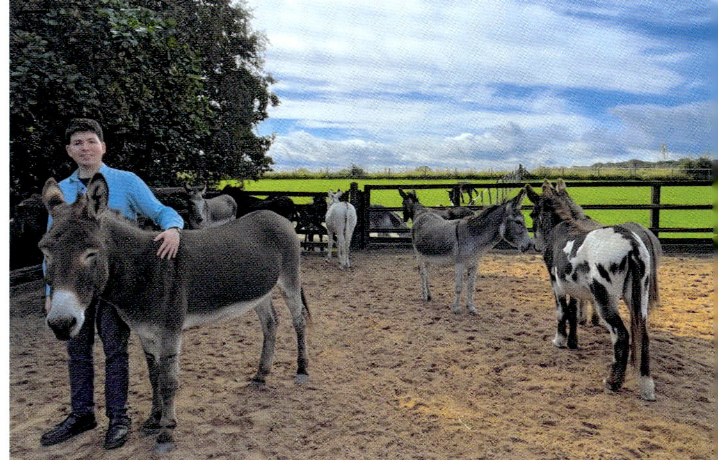

▲▲ *Making friends with the donkeys at Eccup.*

▶ *James' collage of a couple of friendly donkeys, which he also adapted into a Christmas card design.*

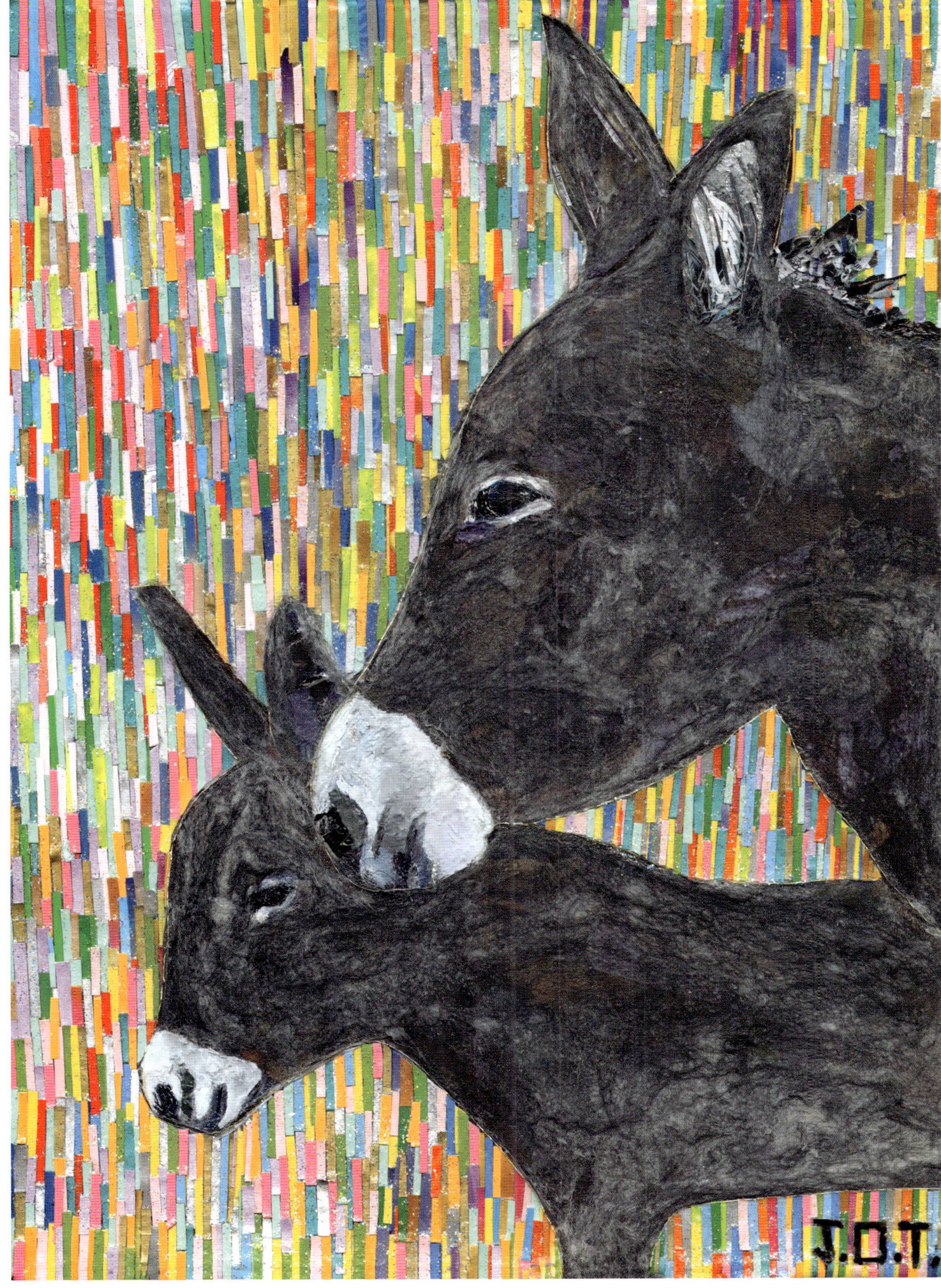

J.O.T.

COAL MINING

James has strong connections to the coal mines of the North of England. From his grandfather back to his great-great-grandfather, his family were all miners, and all named Peter Thomas as well! The earliest of these relatives about whom we have information was a miner at Askern Colliery, James' great-great-grandfather.

The second Peter Thomas was a talented musician and was able to play the piano, trumpet and violin. He went on to become a band leader and led many musical events in the surrounding districts. This was all in his spare time – his main work was down in the mines. Being over six feet tall, he had to continually crouch down or work on his knees in the constricted coal seams. Due to his long-term exposure to the coal dust, he sadly eventually died from 'black lung disease', pneumoconiosis (also known as CMDLD, or coal mine dust lung disease).

To learn more about his family's coal heritage, in 2018 James visited the National Coal Mining Museum near Wakefield. He also went on a daytrip to the Beamish Museum in Co. Durham, learning about the history of coal mining in the North East. James took a photograph there of a pit pony being led by a re-enactor, from which he created a collage. It went on to be used as a poster for his 2018 exhibition at the National Coal Mining Museum, where it would gain the attention of Pontefract Races (see also page 94).

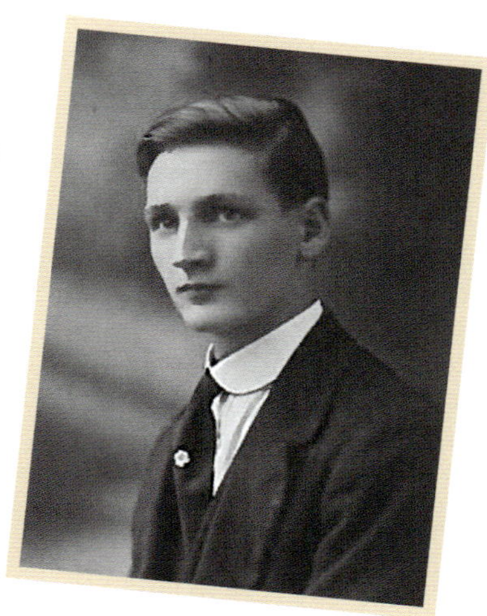

▲ *James' great-grandfather (the second Peter Thomas) at the age of 17.*

PIT PONY

In the pit pony collage, the various shades of cut pieces of green scratchcard in the background represent the hedge and James carefully cut patterned money symbols for a textured pathway. Horse and horseshoe symbols from scratchcards are used for the cobbled road. Black, brown, maroon and purple strips of scratchcard were used for the miner's clothing. Strips of banknote symbols were used for the horse's reins, bridle etc.

Walking towards the mine, miners and pit ponies of the past would have seen the tall head frame rising high above the ground where the mineshaft drops deep down into the earth. And at its top, the massive sheave wheel that connects the mine cage and skip lifts to the winch by the strong cable.

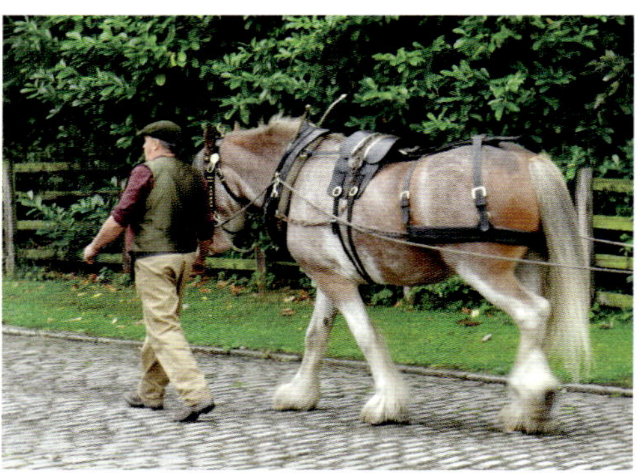

▲ *James' pit-pony reference photograph.*

▶ *The completed pit pony collage.*

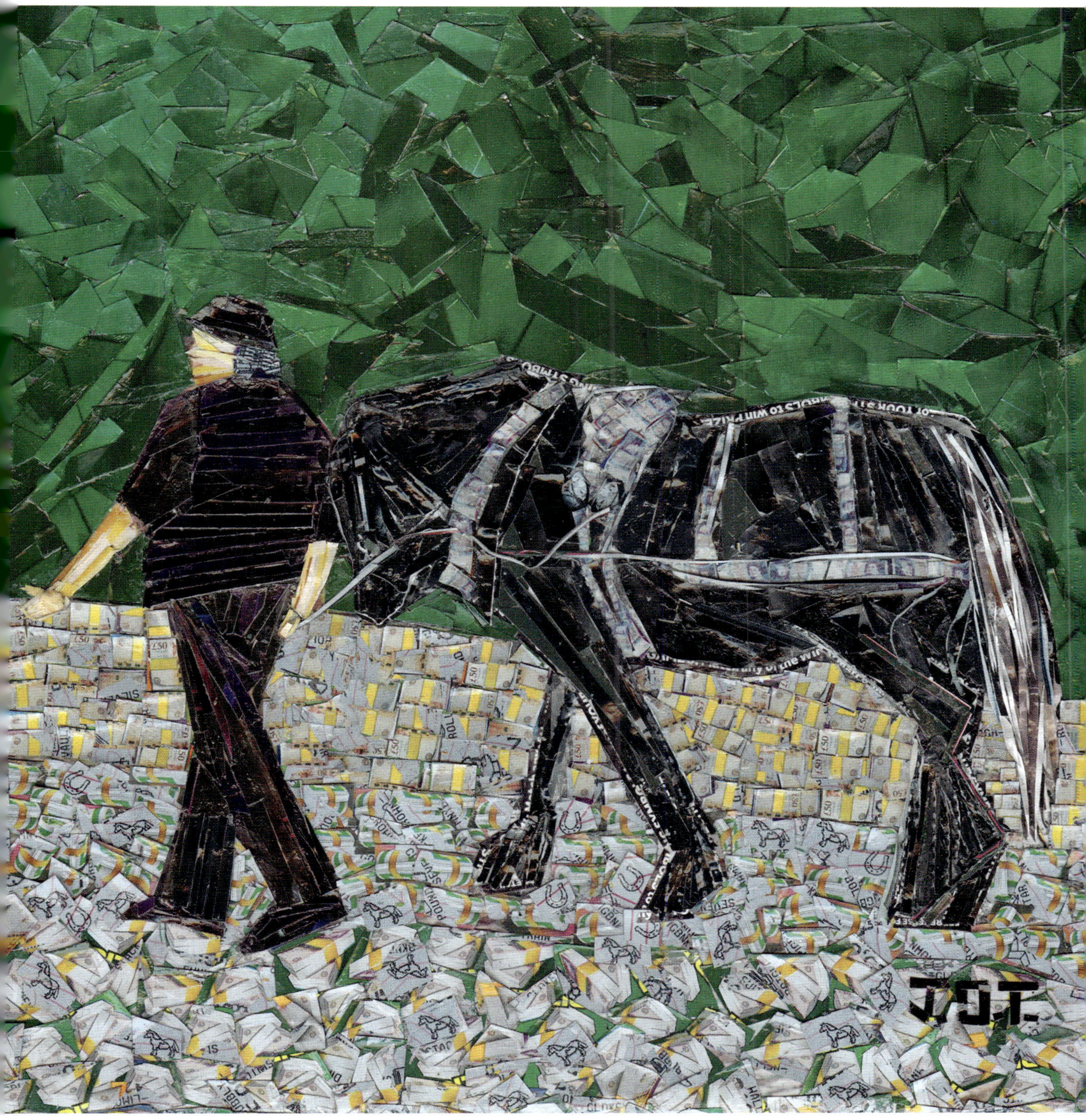

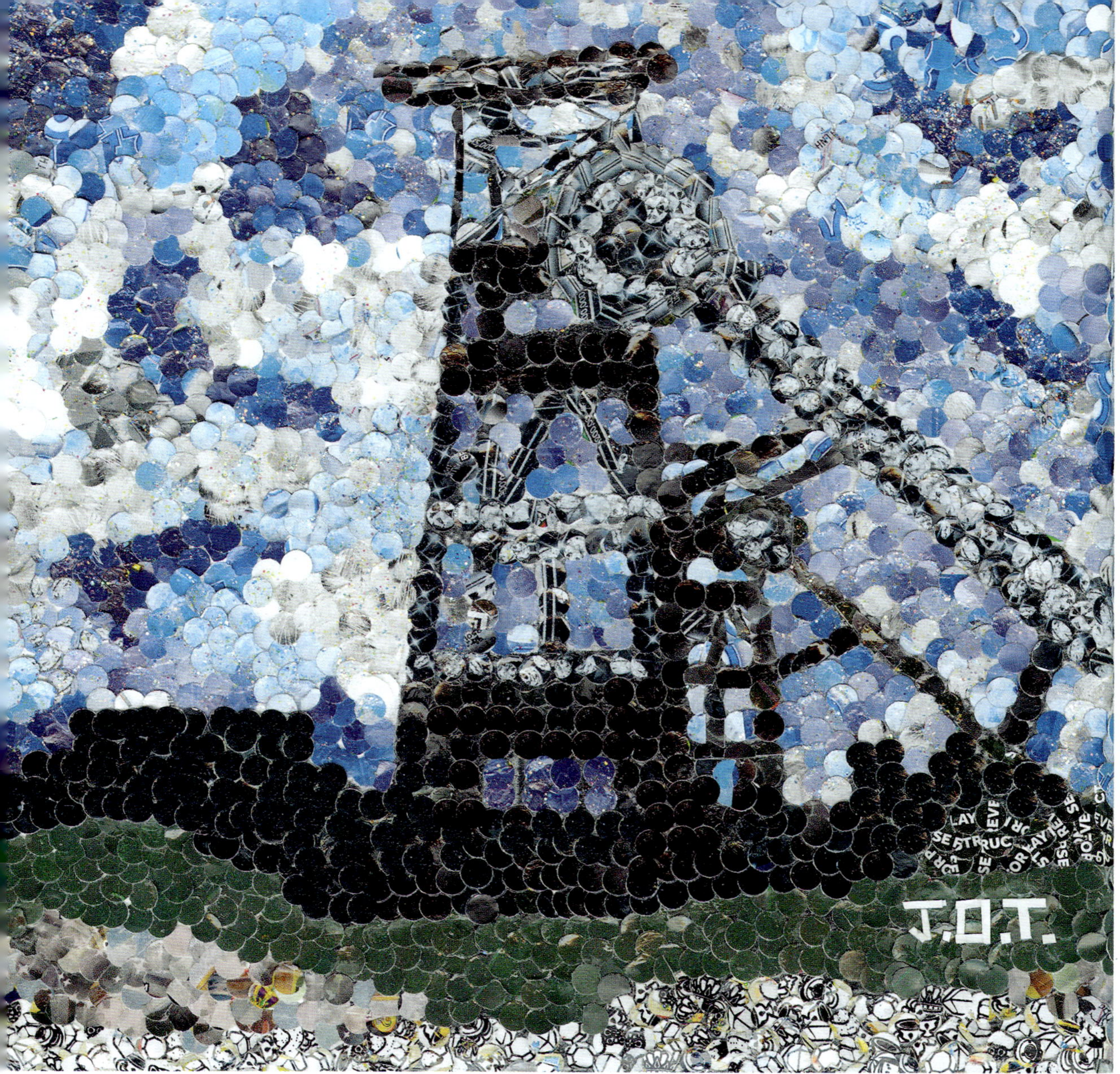

UPTON HEAD FRAME

For another piece, based on photographs of Upton Colliery – where his ancestors were once miners – James used his hole-punch method. This not only showed the pit tower and the variegated sky, but also suggested the layers of ground through which the shaft has been sunk. He used shades from a wide selection of scratchcards, adding words and symbols of diamonds to differentiate the mining wheel from the sky. The sky is a mix of blue and grey shades of patterned scratchcards with a glitter varnish then applied.

▲ A depiction of Upton Colliery's pit tower.

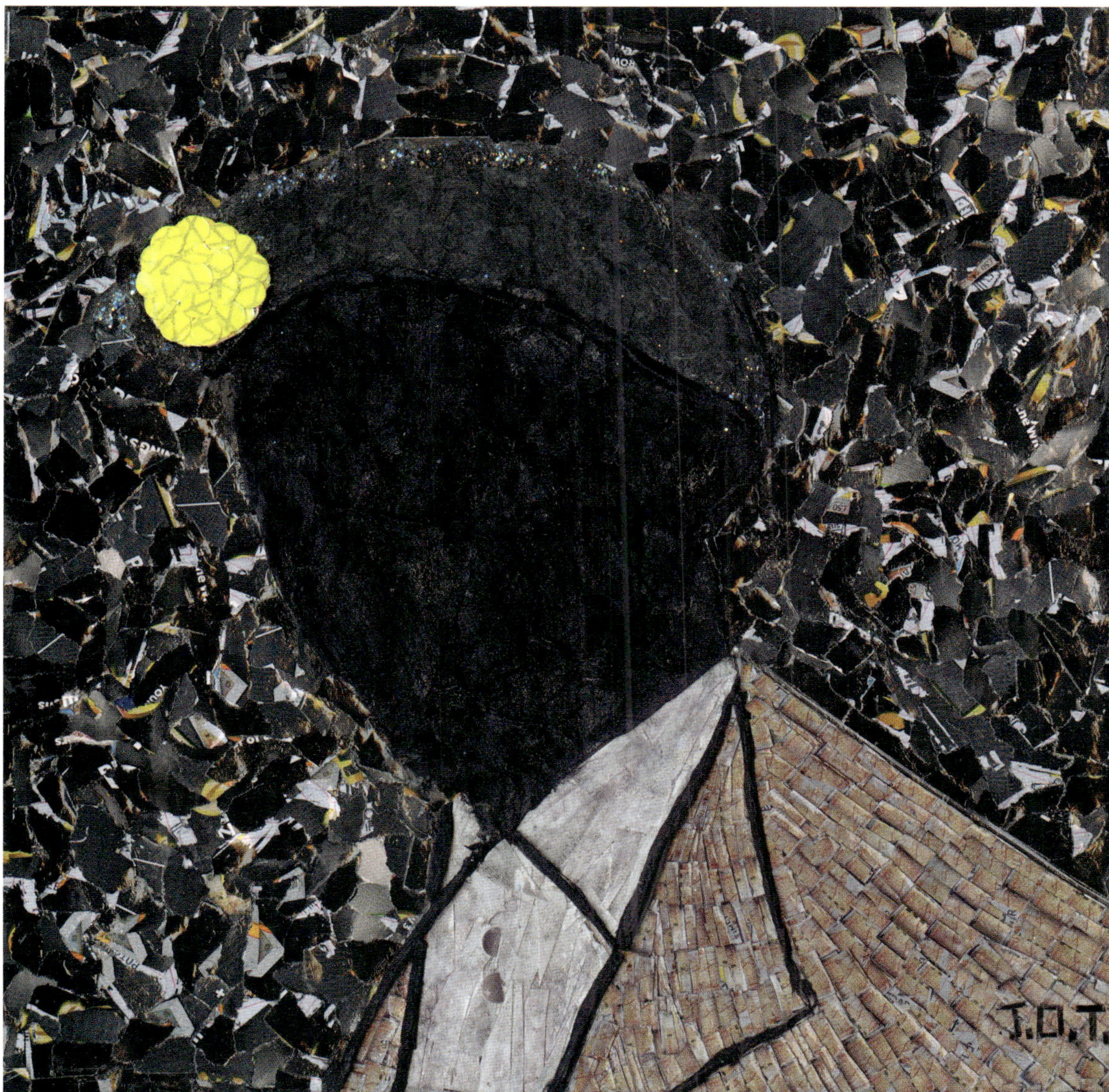

▲ *The Miner.*

THE MINER

The average miner, working in dark and harsh conditions with only a lamp or a helmet light to guide his steps, would have found the atmosphere in the mine claustrophobic and the lack of fresh air stifling. Another collage, *The Miner*, is based on James' great-grandfather, who wore his flat cap in the tunnels rather than a hard hat to protect his head. However, James added a light as if it was a hard hat, and some glitter varnish at the top of the cap gives the impression of the light reflecting. He collaged the face from layers of thick, black recycled paper that he tore to create texture. The blackness represents the years of exposure to coal dust, rather than James re-creating the face of his great-grandfather. The clothes are grubby, showing a grey, dirty-looking shirt made from off-white scratchcards. The old brown jacket was made from a repetitive pattern of cut sections of bank note symbols.

CANARY IN A COAL MINE

In the dark distance within the tunnel, a bright yellow speck would often have been seen back in the nineteenth century and even early in the twentieth century. This yellow dot was not the light of another miner's helmet or a

▼ *Canary in a Coal Mine.*

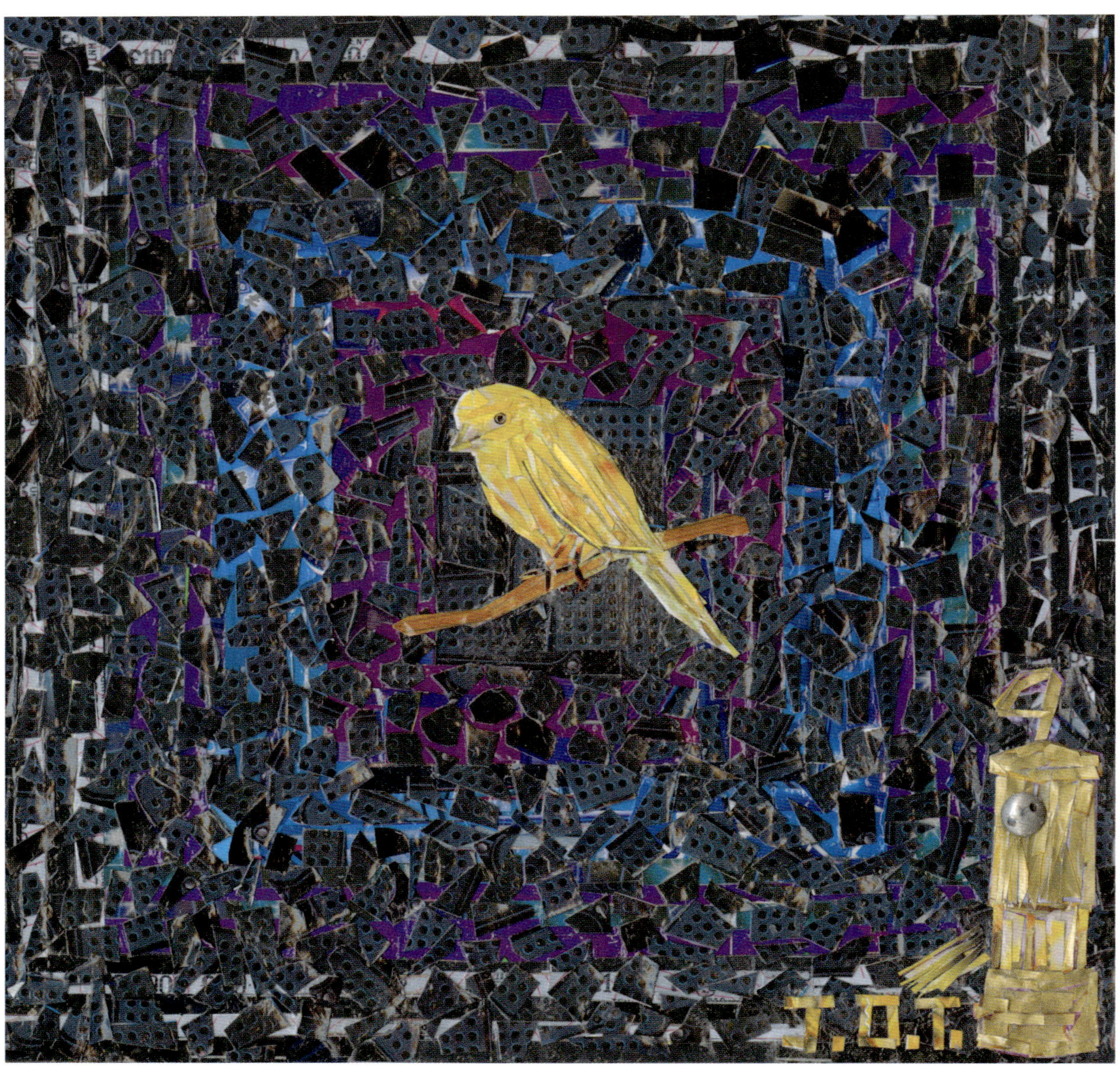

lantern on the tunnel wall, but a little canary in a cage reflecting what little light there was.

Canaries were used as an early warning system to protect the miners from deadly gases that were undetectable by human beings. While the miners worked hard hacking out the coal, they would also keep an eye on the canaries in their cages along the tunnel walls. If a bird, with its sensitivity to the toxic gases, started to gasp or flutter about in a state of distress, the miners took it as a sign that they would have to evacuate the mine immediately.

In this collage, James picks out such a canary centre-stage, small and innocent, but clearly of some importance. The concentric squares that form the background hint at a box or cage, and have the feel of a dark tunnel moving off into the distance. The background was collaged first, then the canary over the top. James created a base of concentric squares from black, purple, blue and other coloured scratchcards. The dimpled scratchcards came from a design called Pinball Multiplier based on an amusement arcade game. When James has a project like mining, for example, he selects the colours and looks for any patterns he can re-use in his artwork to make texture.

THE MINER'S HOME

James was also keen to show the other side of a miner's life – the hard work of his wife at home, diligently cleaning, and ironing perpetually grubby clothes. This piece tells the story of a miner who has probably just come home from his shift and removed his damp coat and trousers, which are being dried by the fire. His wife already has other clean clothing hanging on a line.

James looked at reference materials to get a good feel for the domestic details of a bygone period. Even then, he still had a little fun – for example, on the mantelpiece there is an image of 'Hols' and a 'Boat' symbol. Though the miners very much looked forward to their holidays, palm trees and boats would have been out of the question. A mug symbol is by the fire next to a whistling kettle, ready for the miner's tea. The fireplace is banknote symbols and there are hole-punched black dots of coal. The clothing is off-white pieces of scratchcard and the apron is a decorative pattern of diamond symbols to add colour. The miner's boots on the stool are made from '£' symbols.

The dotted lines from the borders of scratchcards form the washing line and some of the hems on the clothing.

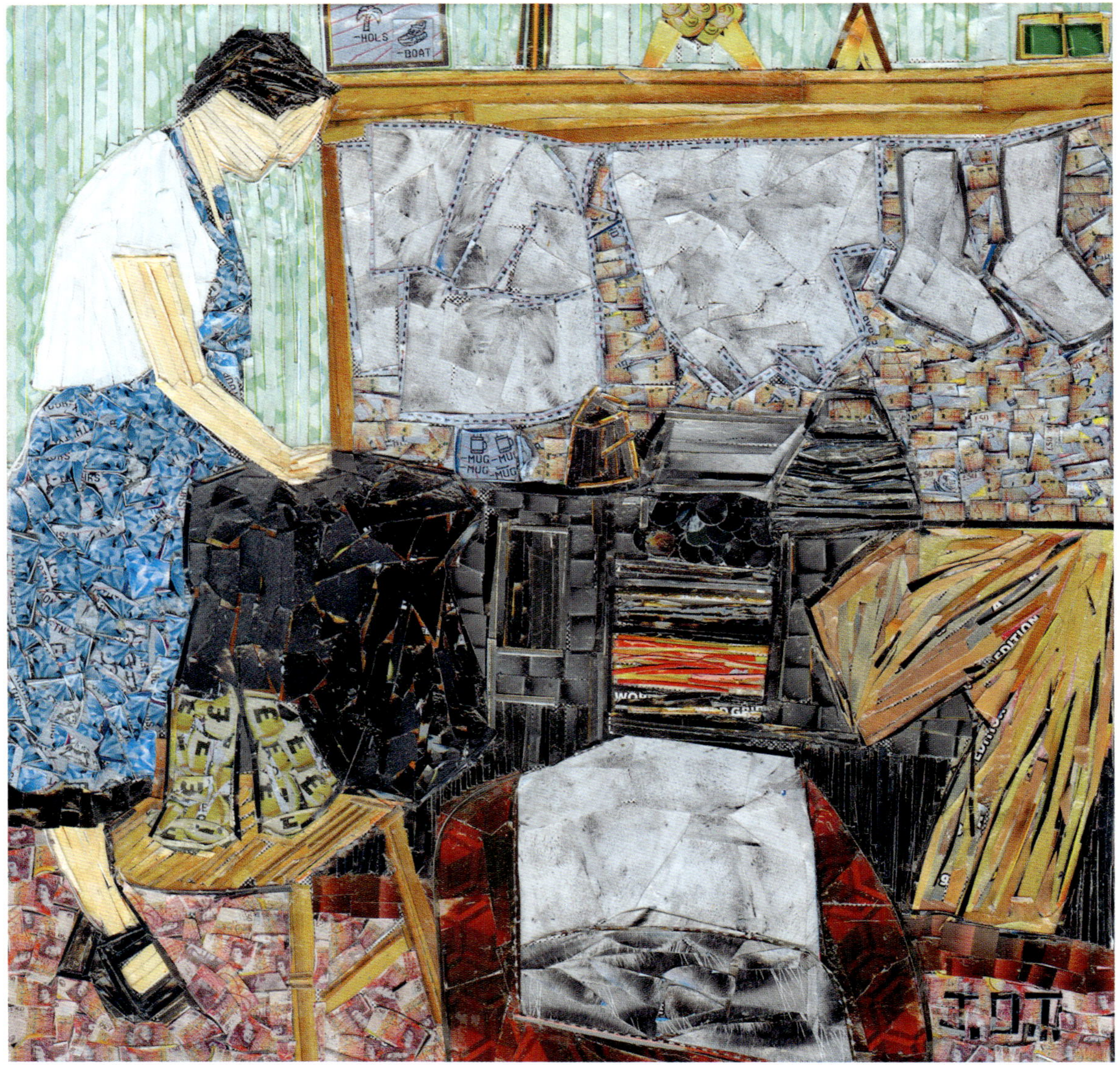

PADDY TRAIN

James' uncle – once a miner in the West Yorkshire village of Upton – would often tell of his experiences working in the mine in the mid-twentieth century, recounting stories about the close-knit community to which he belonged. He would travel in a Paddy cart along the tunnels, deeper and deeper, ready to do his dangerous job in the darkness under the earth, the way illuminated by the small light on his helmet. A poignant image, and one that inspired another of James' collages. Unusually, he has used discarded ink cartridges to depict the tunnel walls, and a flattened drinks can forms the bulk of the train. He cut out a piece from a scratchcard called 'Cash Vault' to represent a wheel.

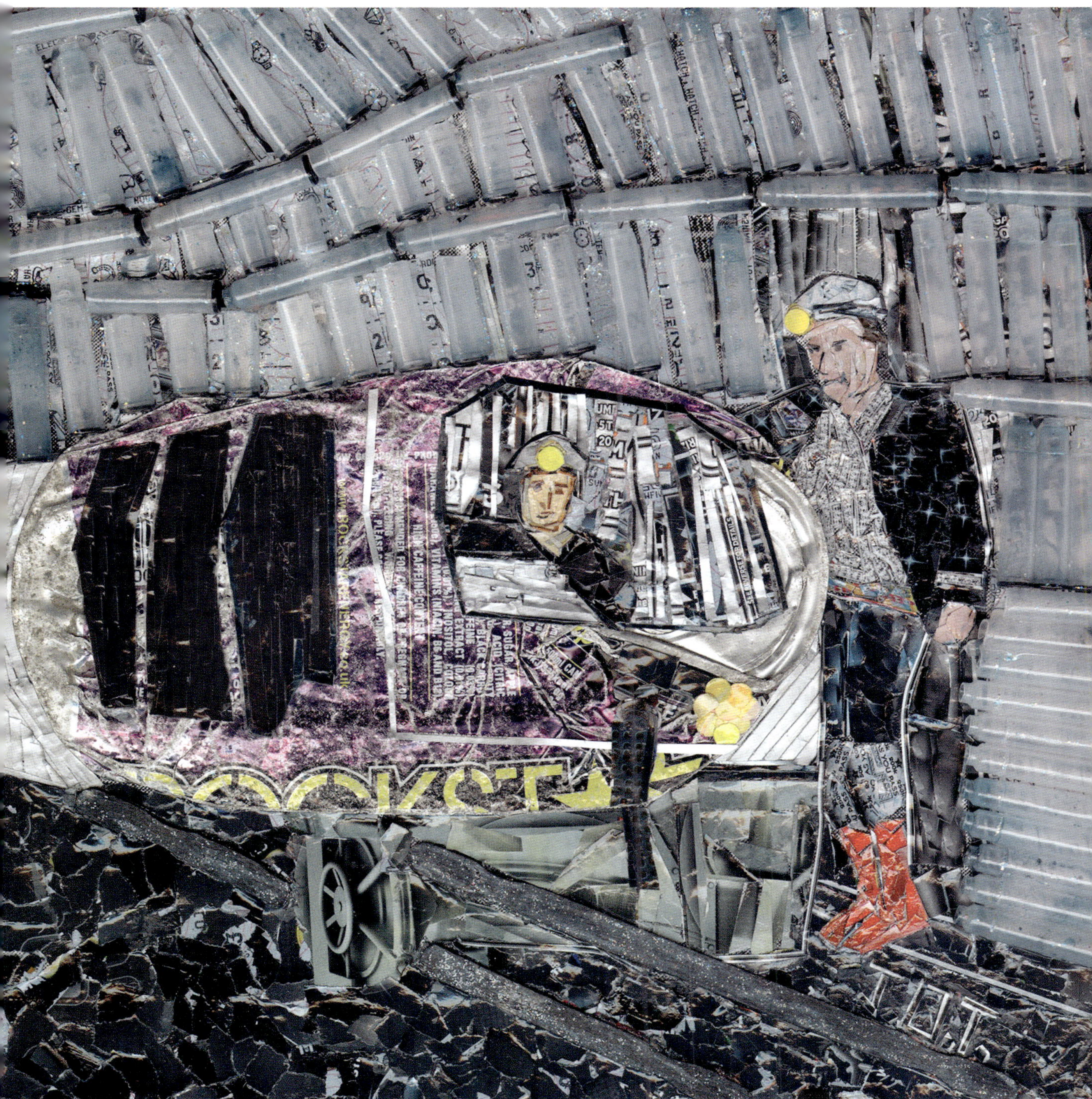

A Paddy train in a mine.

PORTRAITS AND PEOPLE

James' grandmother, Joan, who was married to the last Peter Thomas, has always been a fervent advocate of James' creative endeavours. She used to spend hours with him when he was a young child, colouring. She came to stay with her daughter and James in Yorkshire during the first lockdown but after nearly three years she moved into a care home for a higher level of support.

ISOLATION

While she was living with James, he collaged *Isolation*, a picture of her based on a photograph that had been taken when she lived in Sussex. The green, white and brown mottled design in circular hole-punched pieces creates a colourful wallpaper design. James wanted this to blur into the background as the focus is more on the bare wooden table in the foreground, which uses many hole-punched shades of brown scratchcards. It is empty apart from a saucer and spoon.

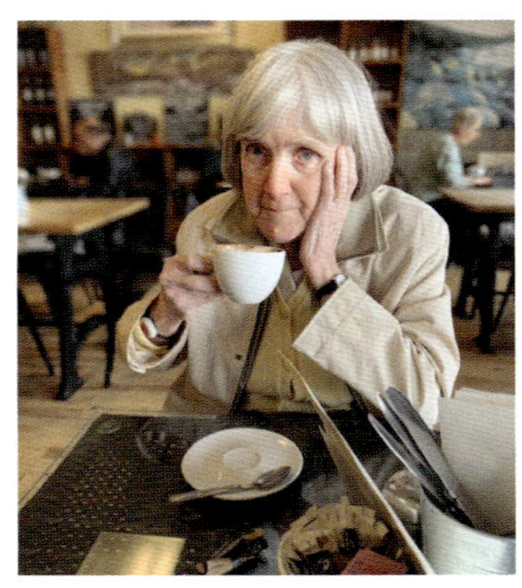

▲ *The reference photograph for* **Isolation**.

▶ **Isolation**.

Joan is holding her plain white cup of coffee (made from circular pieces of white scratchcard material). James looked especially for rainbow symbols from scratchcards for her clothing – coloured for her cardigan and grey for her outer jacket. This represented the isolation felt by many elderly people during lockdown and linked to the care given by the NHS. Joan's face is made from small, flesh-coloured strips of scratchcard and her expression shows weariness and loss of hope, as if all she had to look forward to is her warm drink. She props up her face with her hand and James made her wedding ring shine using gold paper.

He submitted *Isolation* for a competition looking for the best contemporary visual art by and for learning disabled, neurodiverse and disabled artists at the Level Centre in Rowsley, Derbyshire. They wanted to fill the Level Centre to celebrate 'The Art That Difference Makes'. Two pieces of James' artwork were chosen as part of a public exhibition at the Level Centre during summer 2022.

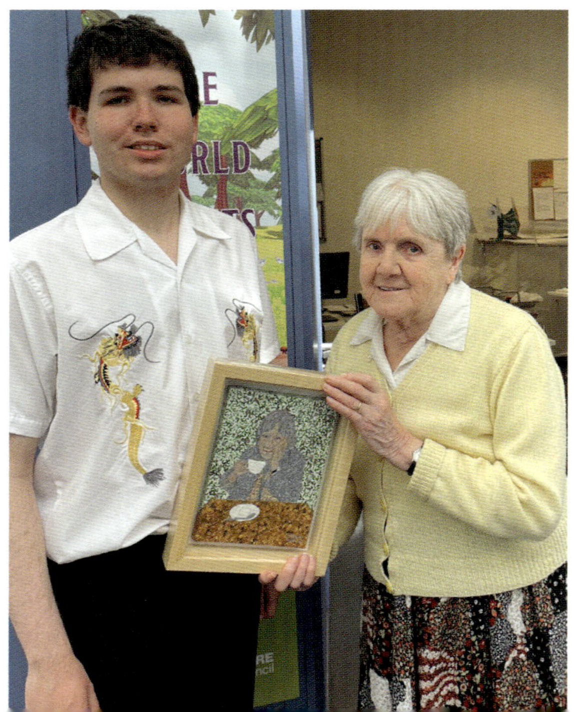

▶ *James and his grandmother with* **Isolation** *at the Level Centre.*

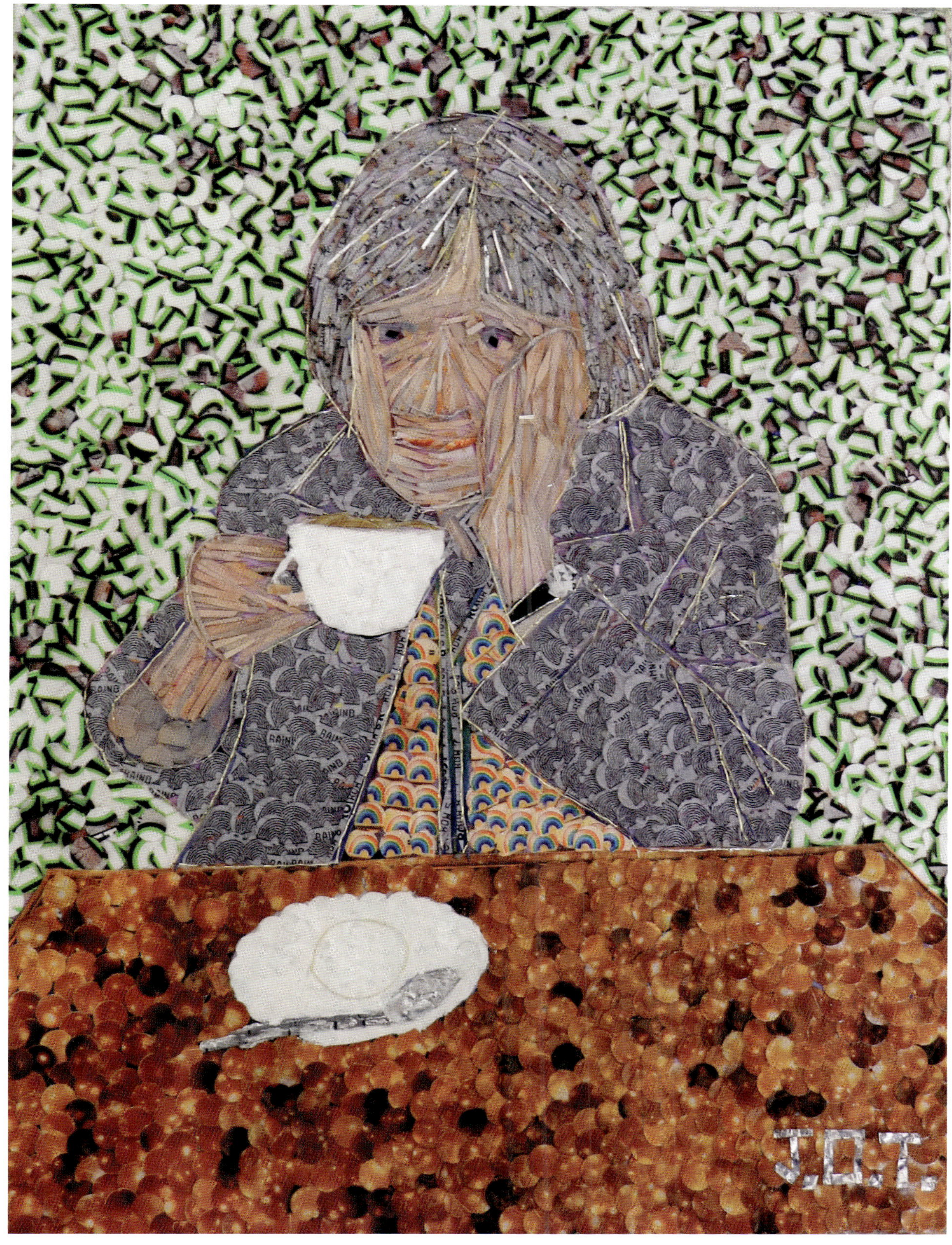

J.O.T.

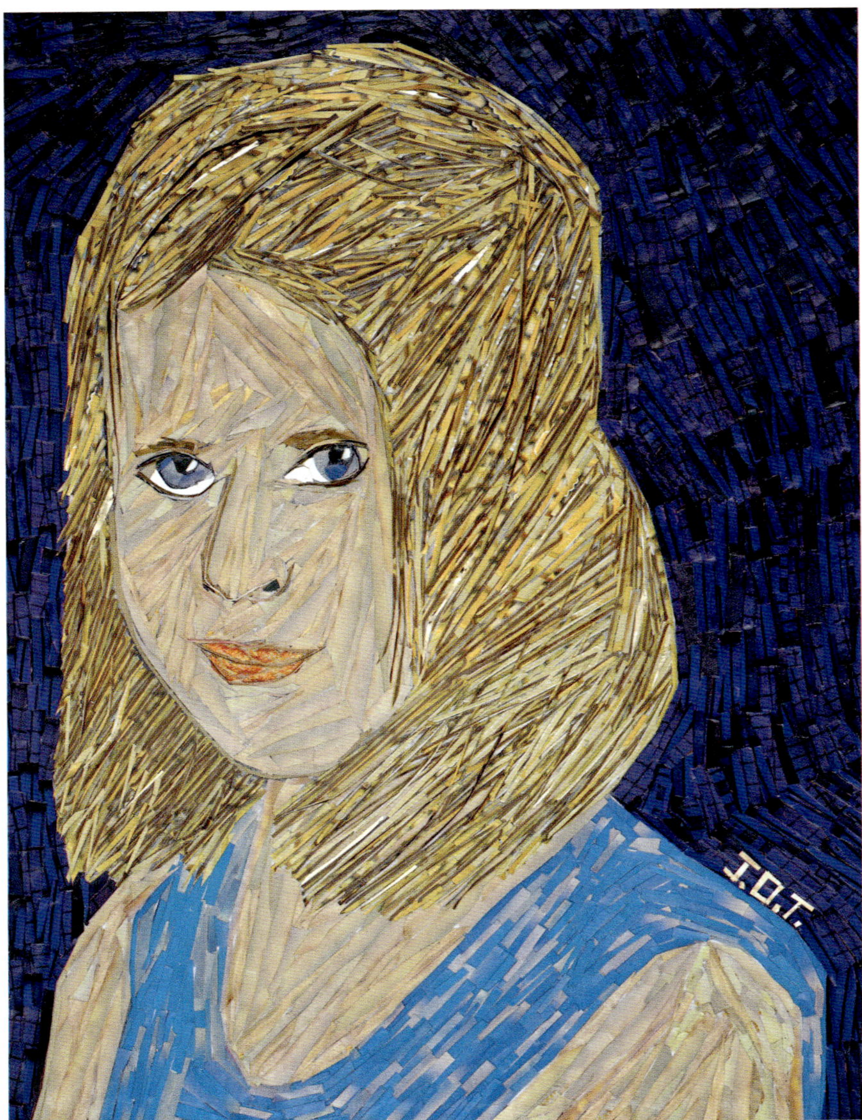

◀ *Portrait of a*
Young Woman.

PORTRAIT OF A YOUNG WOMAN

James' mother, Jane, has been a constant means of support for him and even though he finds it difficult to show his feelings due to his autism, she knows how much he has appreciated her over the years. *Portrait of a Young Woman* shows her as a girl in 1976.

Jane had been sketched in Plymouth by the well-known artist Robert Lenkiewicz. James liked to imagine how it would have looked if Lenkiewicz had painted her portrait instead. He looked for golden yellow strips of scratchcards for the fair hair colour and applied these in many layers. The hair is straight but he wanted to make it flow in different directions. It was quite difficult to find the right skin tone shades for the face and lips as he did not want to add any paint. The eyes stare out intensely.

In 2021, James held an exhibition at Horticap, an independent charity in Harrogate that provides horticultural training for adults with learning disabilities. During the exhibition, James was approached by a visitor who was so touched by his portrait of his grandmother that she asked if he could create a similar portrait for her, this time of her own late mother, Marlene.

MARLENE

Upon receiving a photograph of Marlene, along with various personal items such as pieces of black fabric, a patterned black-and-white piece of textile and some brown buttons that once belonged to her mother, James set to work.

He adopted a similar theme as with the artwork of his grandmother with hole-punched scratchcards for the table. The picture could be regarded as another scene of isolation with a lady on her own at a table, but this has a far happier feel. The colours are soft pink and James has collaged dried Bougainvillea petals in the background to give a summery feel. The lady is about to enjoy a slice of cake, which means it's a treat – perhaps a special occasion. Fingers-crossed symbols for good luck are on Marlene's

clothing in a repetitive pattern, as though wishing her all the best. Two of her buttons have been stuck onto the patterned jacket, which is made from green-and-pink hole-punched scratchcards. The jumper is a combination of fabrics that used to belong to Marlene. Thin strips of flesh-coloured scratchcards define the face and various shades for the hair.

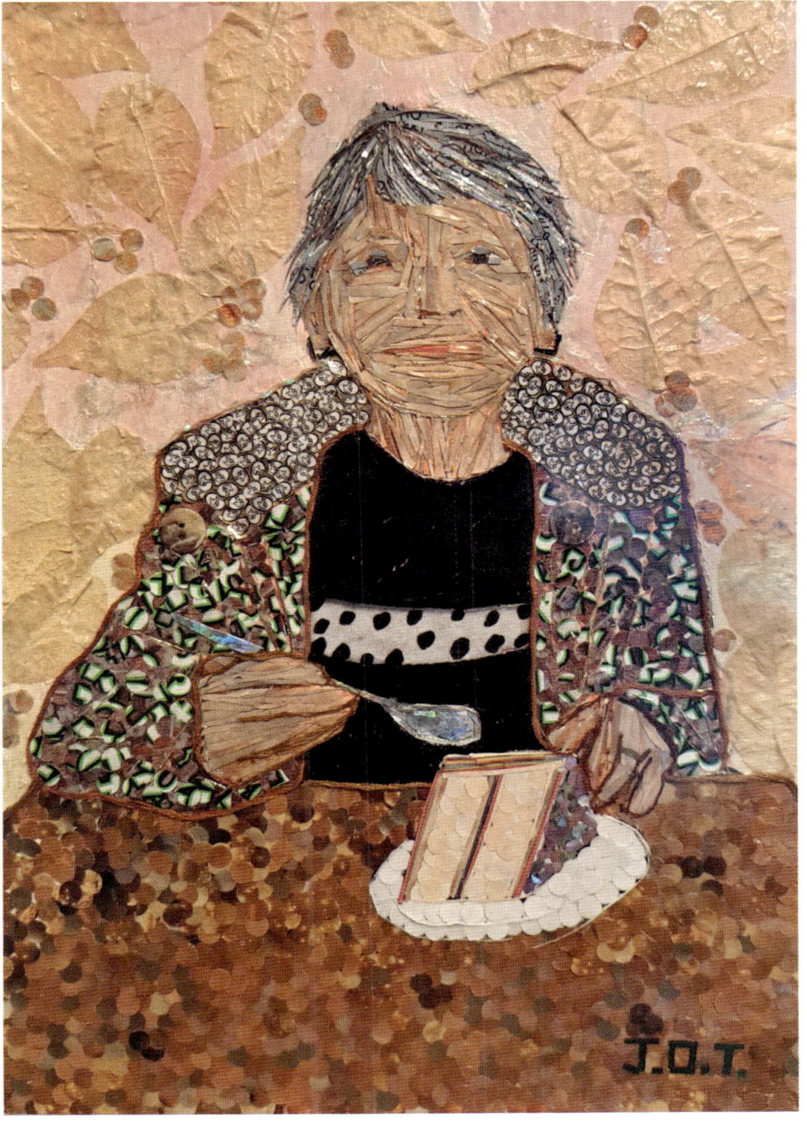

▲ *Marlene.*

VINCENT VAN GOGH

Even prior to James' time at Bradford School of Art, where he was taught about many renowned artists, he had admired Van Gogh's paintings and his dedication to art despite the difficulties he faced. James can suffer from low mood and anxiety but his own art is characterised by the use of bright colours. In that way there is a link to Van Gogh's vibrant palette. Vivid colours possess an energy and potency that can bring an artwork to life. Van Gogh's thick impasto brushwork has a similarity to the tactile quality of collage; his belief that 'Great things are done by a series of small things brought together' can perhaps be compared to James' method of collage-making. Each piece of torn-up or hole-punched scratch-card is sorted into colours like oil paint on a palette and can be meticulously applied to a canvas to build up a powerful portrait.

People have often commented that the cut strips that James uses in his collages remind them of Vincent van Gogh's brush strokes. So he was very proud when a visitor to the gallery commissioned a large-scale copy of one of the artists he regards as a hero (see page 33 for the portrait itself and a description of the technique).

BY MOONLIGHT

This collage of a man and a woman embracing included recycled pieces of T-shirt material for the background, a second-hand dress for the woman's clothing, donated fabrics for the man's clothing and the tree and tea-stained shredded paper for the path. He added locks of real hair given to him by a lady he knew and used his own dark hair for the man.

This piece was exhibited for two months in the summer of 2022 at Art In The Mill in

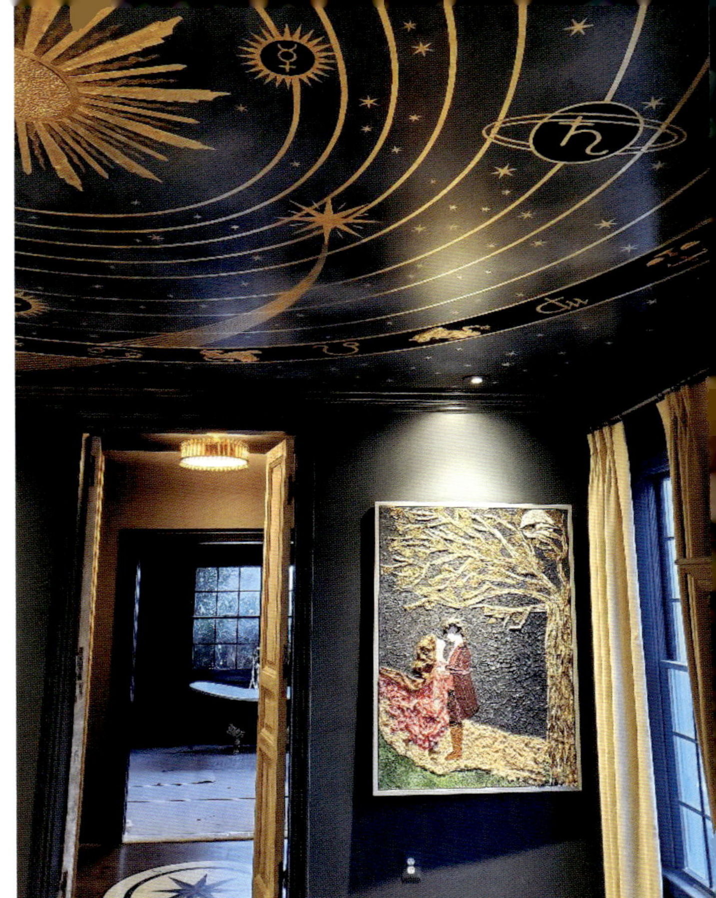

▲ **By Moonlight** *in its romantic domestic setting.*
(Photograph © Jim Knowles)

▶ **By Moonlight.**

Knaresborough, a gallery where James had previously exhibited his art. Many visitors asked him about his relationship with colour and he replied that the colours he uses affect or reflect his mood, even though he is not always aware of it. *By Moonlight* is an unusual artwork for him, as its colours are more subdued than the tones he normally uses. He hopes that it reflects a romantic mood created by the moonlight as the couple come close to each other.

The collage was bought by a customer in the USA as a wedding present for his wife. James is proud that it hangs in such a prominent position against the dark 'night-time' walls and the solar system and stars shining brightly in gold above.

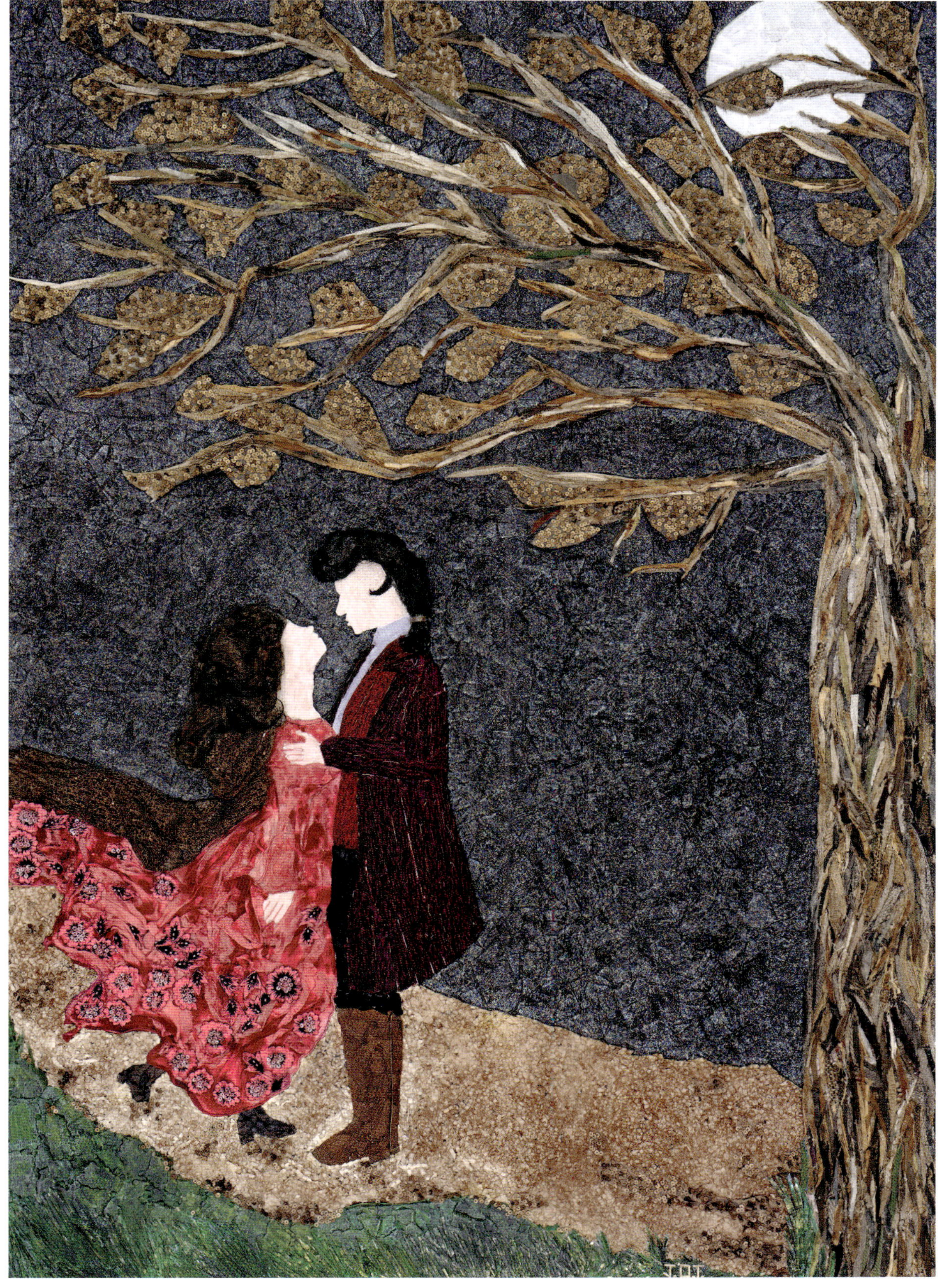

TREES

Trees are a wonderful presence on the planet. Not only are they beautiful but they also play their part as the 'lungs' of the world. Unfortunately, we often take them for granted. They have captivated James, even from early childhood, and still inspire him to make artworks conveying a sense of their beauty and enchantment. His fascination with trees is never passive. He actively seeks them out and takes countless photographs of them. These photographs serve a dual purpose: he not only enjoys looking at them but also uses many of them as reference points for his artworks.

THE 'VAN GOGH TREE'

Among the trees James cherishes, one local example stands out – a favourite of his in Nidderdale. The tree has become a personal landmark for him as he takes a weekly walk along the quiet country lane where it grows. It is such an isolated place that he hardly sees anyone on his walks there. Strolling along this lane relaxes James and gives him time and space to think.

James calls this tree the 'Van Gogh tree', as he thinks it looks as if it were painted onto the landscape by Vincent himself. In summer, it is cloaked in luscious green leaves. In winter, when all its leaves have dropped, not only can its branches be clearly seen, but also the massive burr around its trunk. Burrs are more common than most people think. This mass of tree tissue tends to grow over wounds in the trunk and protects the tree from further damage.

James collaged the 'Van Gogh Tree' over a photograph taken during the winter. Using the stylus from his encaustic wax kit, he dabbed spots and squiggles of different shades of green and silver natural waxes onto the photograph. The thickness of the encaustic wax echoed the style of Van Gogh. James loved experimenting with the wax, taking great care to ensure that he did not burn the photographic paper.

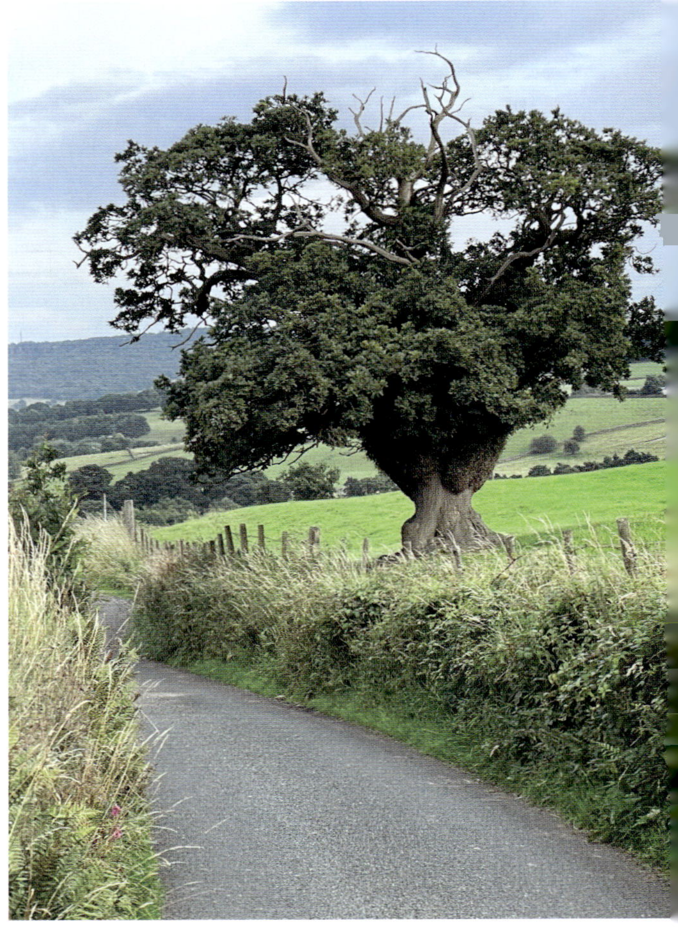

▲ *The 'Van Gogh Tree'.*

▶ *The **'Van Gogh Tree'** photograph with silver and green encaustic wax.*

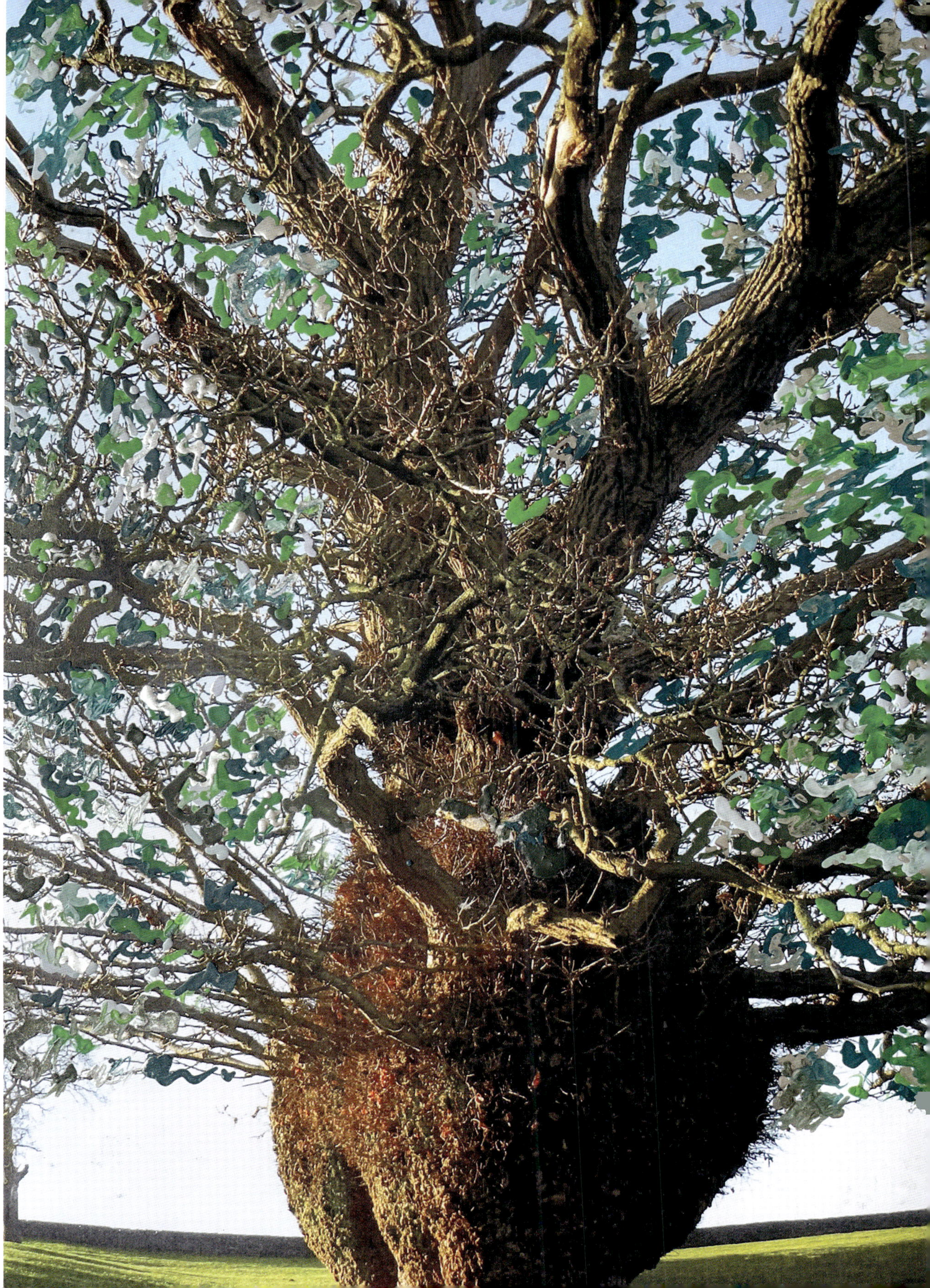

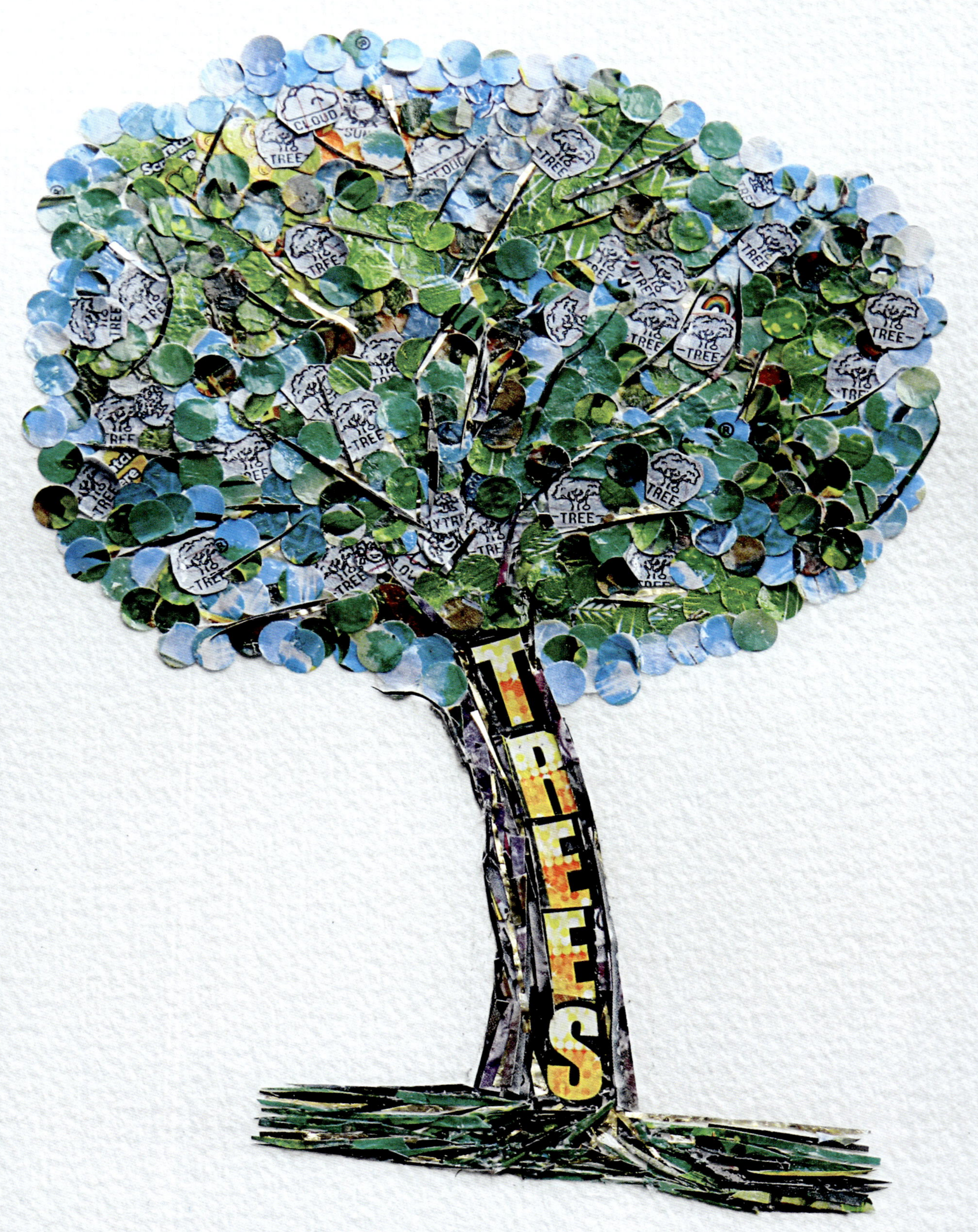

TREES

CHERRY TREE

A simple cherry tree that James collaged for The Tree Council demonstrates his love of symbolism. As well as the cherry n his garden being his favourite tree of all, in Japan the cherry is a symbol for a fresh start. James felt that, as with the cherry tree, he too had been given the chance to have a new beginning. Trees were one of the symbols he used on his PECS cards and now, in his own art, to communicate environmental aspects of being able to turn unwanted material into something creative.

UNDER A SPELL

◀ *Cherry tree collage for The Tree Council.*

▼ *One of James' reference photos for* **Under a Spell.**

James regularly takes walks in Fishpond Wood in Bewerley during different seasons. Some of his best tree photographs have been taken there and he has been filmed twice at Fishpond Wood talking about the therapeutic benefits of being out in nature (BBC *Gardeners' World* and also a short video clip for NHS Cumbria).

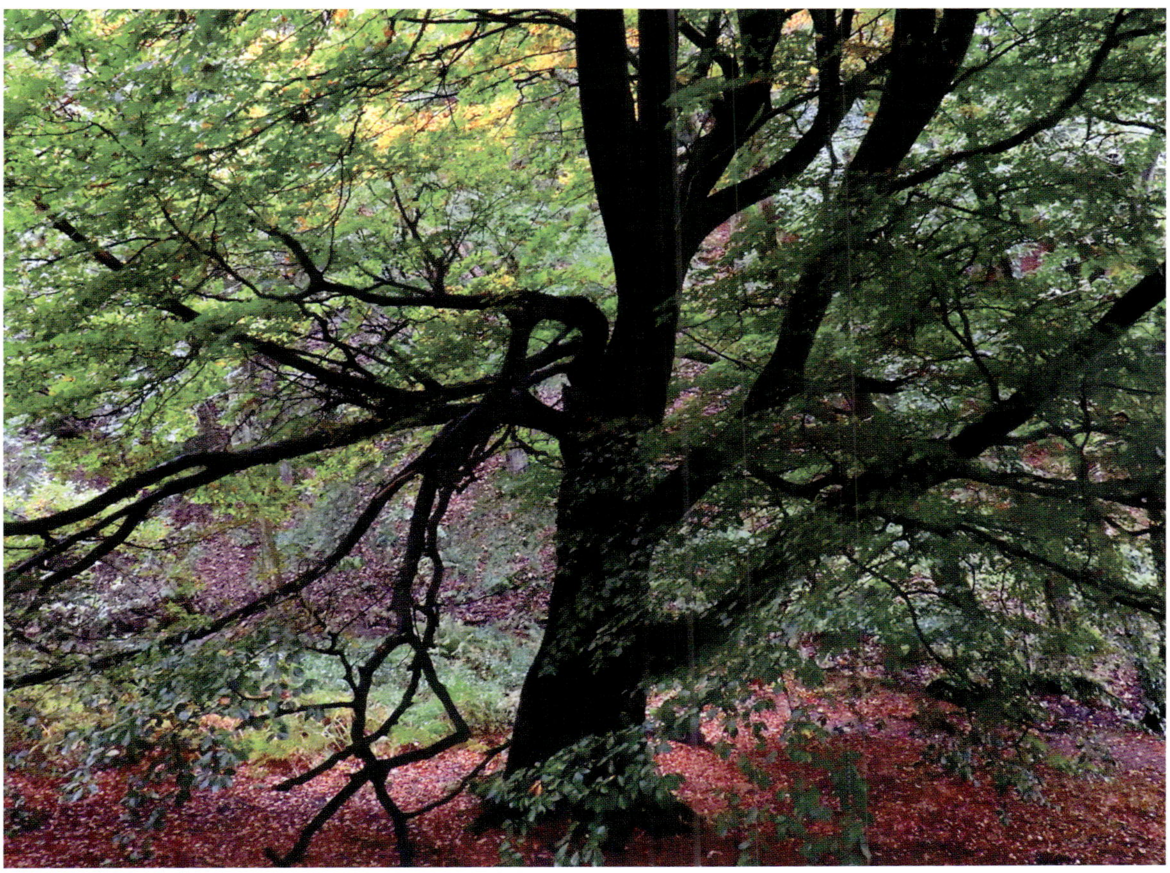

Dr Peter Brambleby, owner of Fishpond Wood, commissioned James to create a large collage based on one of the trees there. The one that James chose is an enormous sprawling tree and he called the collage *Under a Spell*. The collage is a mass of intertwining branches and he created it after looking at the many forms and shapes in the woodland of twisted, gnarled roots and round-shaped fungi clinging onto branches.

The process of recreating the autumn colours was not as straightforward as James had hoped with his selection of recycled materials. He found there was too

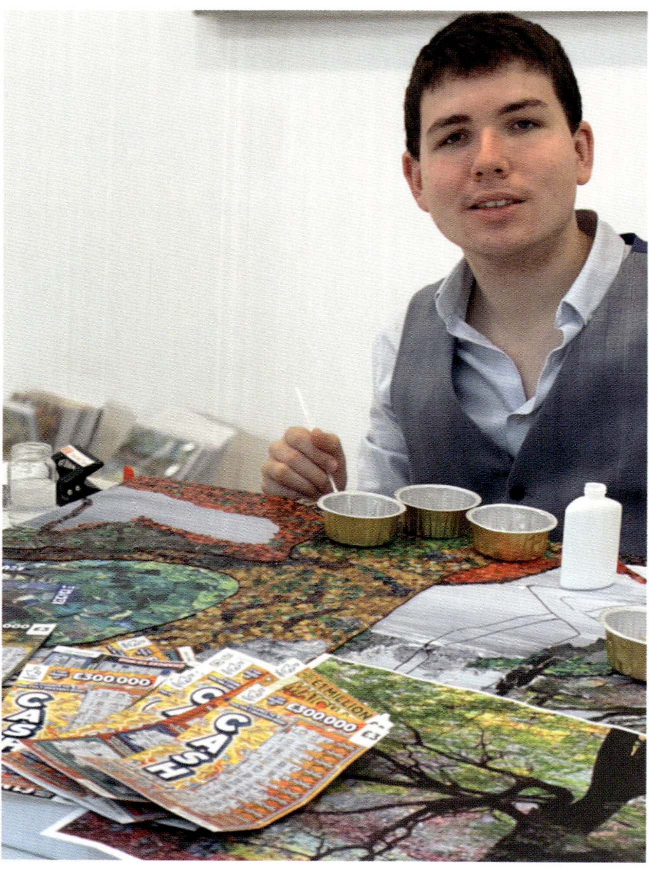

▲ *During a 'Meet the Artist' event at his exhibition in Leith, Edinburgh, James showed visitors how he was layering pieces of recycled fabric, string, magazine paper, old leaflets and used scratchcards into **Under a Spell**.*

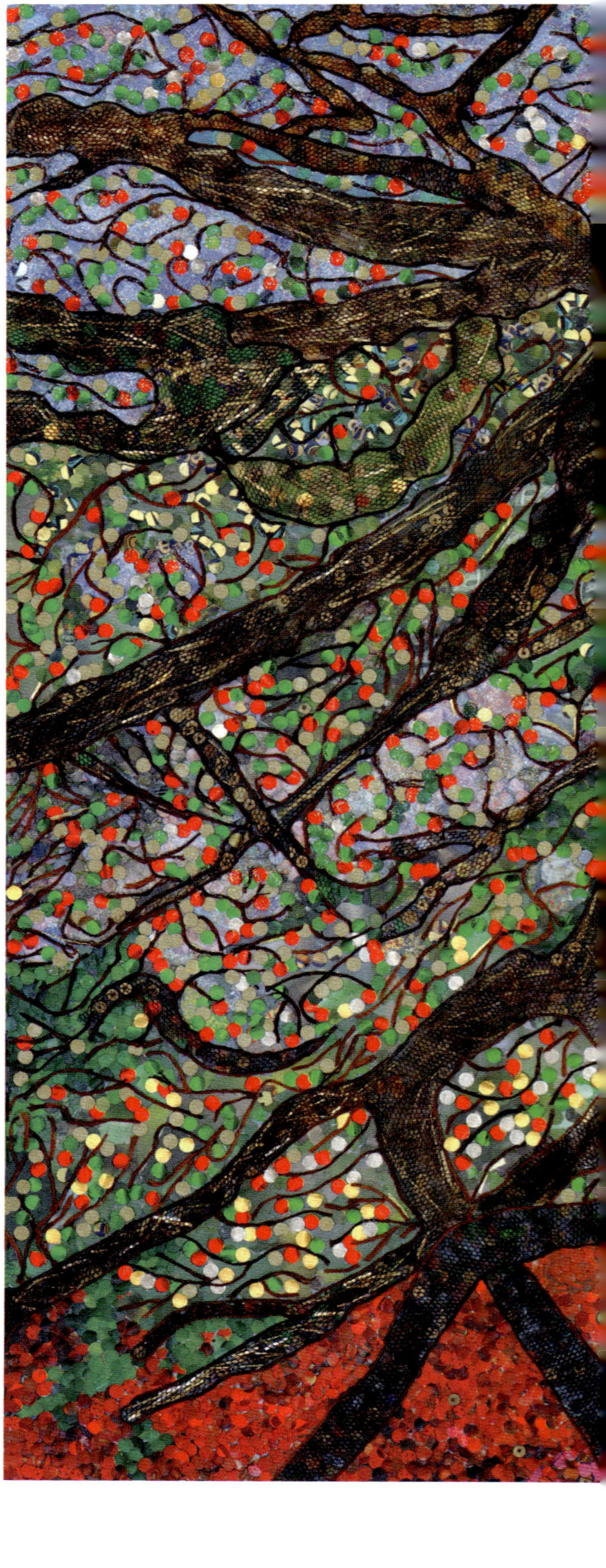

▶ **Under a Spell.**

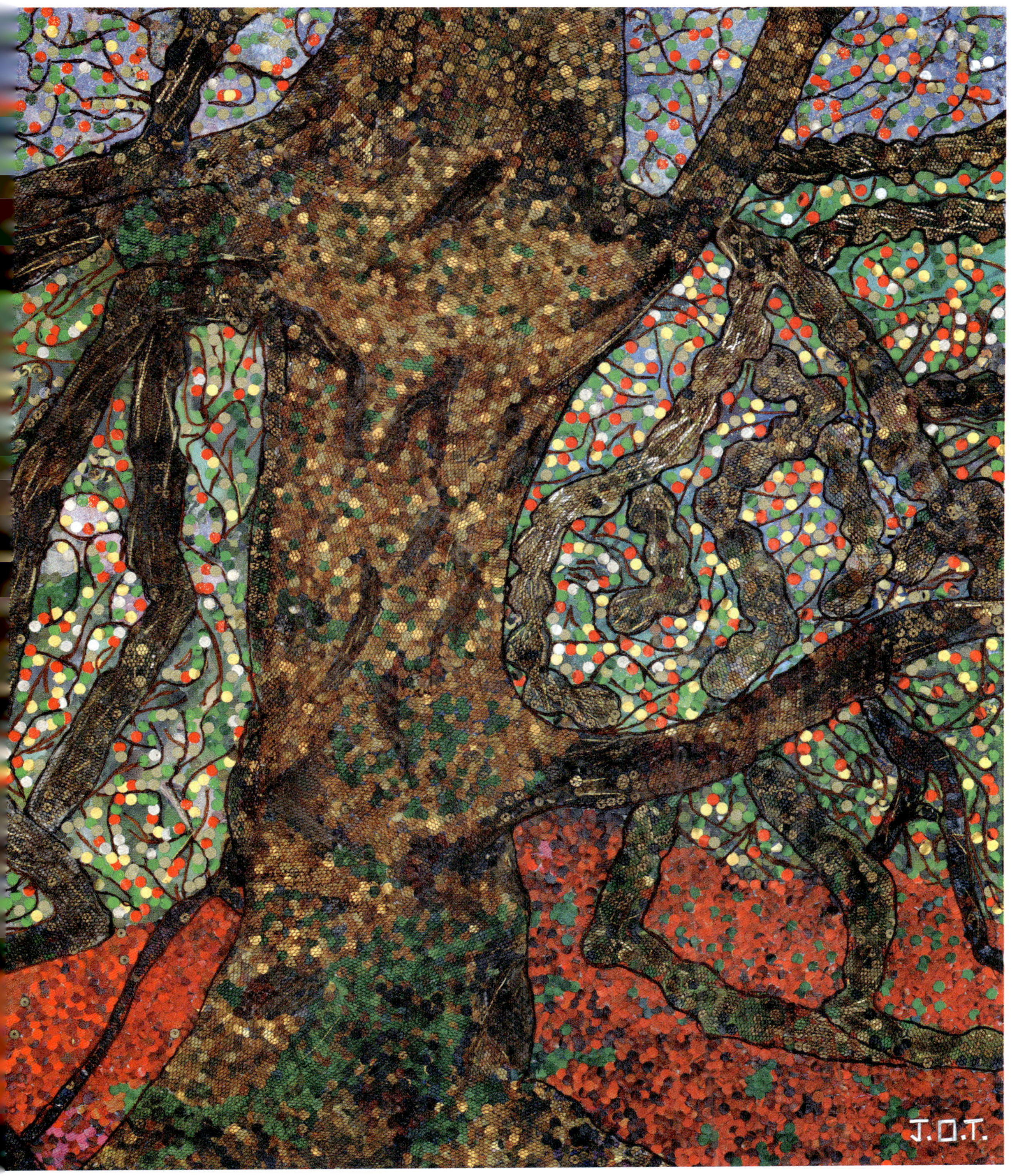

much red at first in the collage so had to try to find a way of toning it down. Firstly, he pulled off bronze-coloured sequins from fabric purchased in a charity shop, which was time-consuming but made the collage glisten. However, it still wasn't enough so James went into a remnants shop when he couldn't find what he needed at home. Luckily, there was some left-over brown netting that enabled him to create the right finish for the tree trunk. The netting captured the roughness of the bark and pulled together the green areas of moss, the paler rounded formations of lichen and the growths on the tree. It sealed everything together well and still allowed the colours beneath to show through the netting.

FORCE FOR NATURE

Representatives from The Tree Council visited JOT's Gallery in January 2023 and told James all about their plans for an immersive Force for Nature exhibition at Birmingham Botanical Gardens, featuring the voices of children from across Britain expressing their hopes for a greener future.

In their brief, The Tree Council had an image in mind of children interacting with a willow tree, and asked that golden orbs be included. They also asked that James incorporate words relevant to the preservation of trees and some lines from a poem written by a young Tree Council Ambassador.

For inspiration, James took some photographs of willow trees in North Yorkshire, and set to work

▲ *The Force for Nature piece starts to take shape.*

▼ *Bark under the microscope.* (Photograph © The Tree Council)

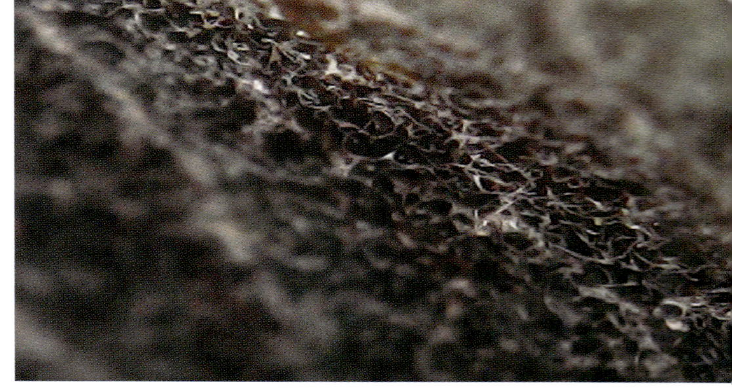

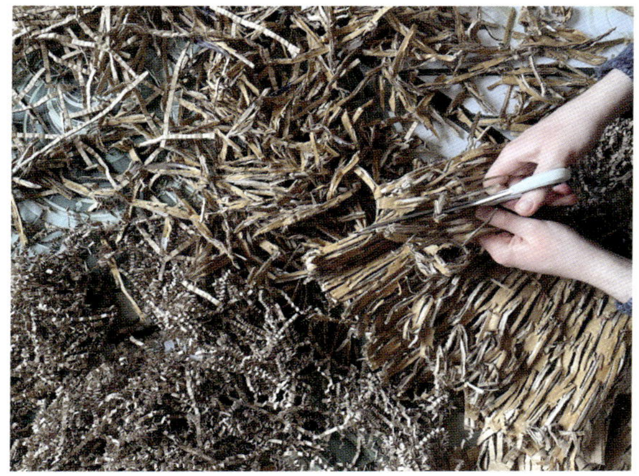

▲ *Strips of packing material for use as bark.*

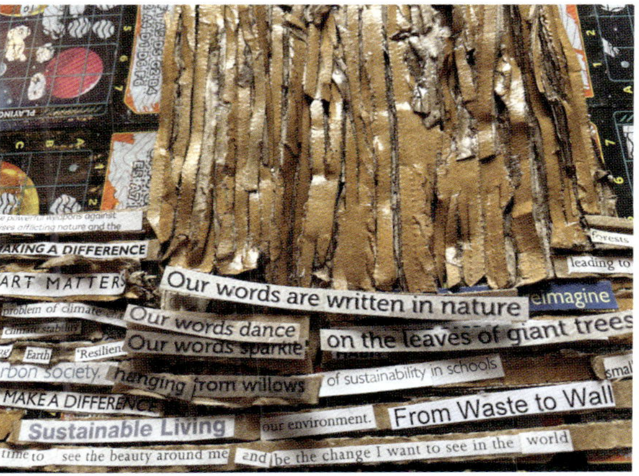

▲ *Incorporating words into the ground beneath the willow.*

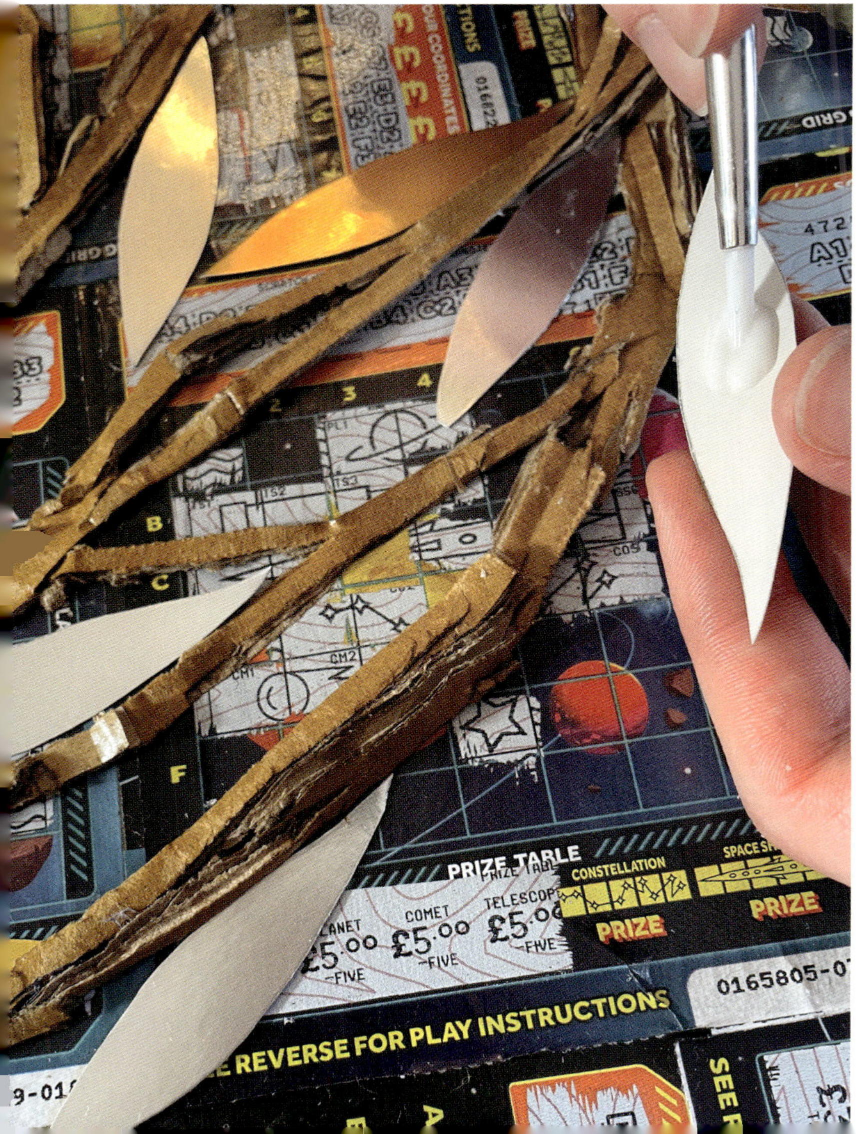

▲ *Collaging one of the four children in gold.*

◀ *Sticking down leaves made from recycled gold and silver card.*

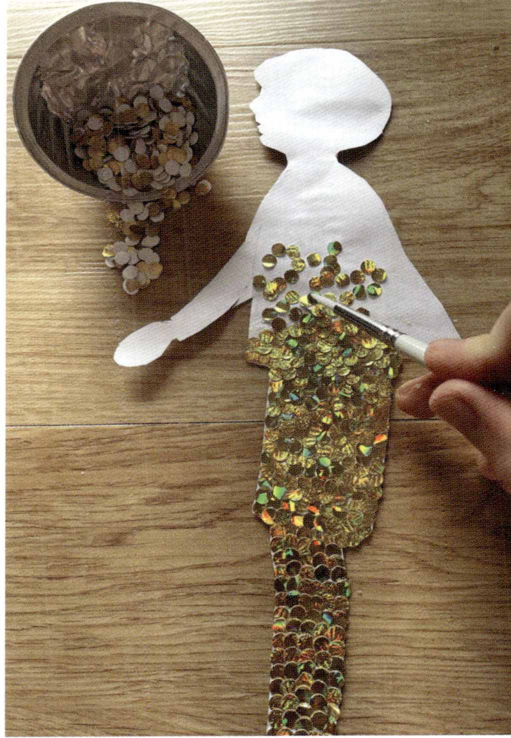

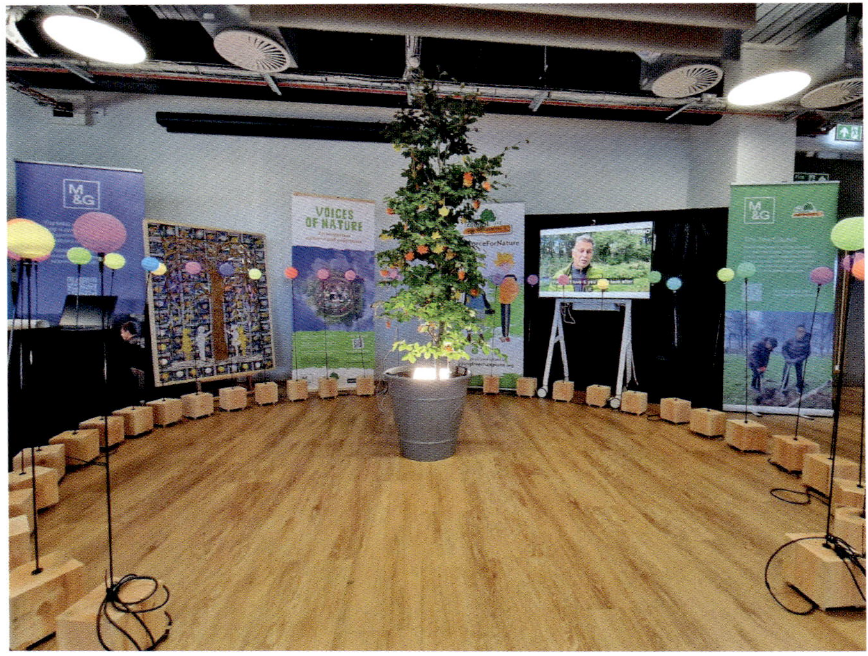

▶ *The finished **Force for Nature** collage.*

◀ *The collage in situ at the Force for Nature exhibition – the orbs used in the collage tie in with the glowing orbs used as part of the installation, which were linked to music and the voices of children concerned about the future of nature.*
(Photograph © The Tree Council)

finding a used canvas that was large enough to convey the importance of the special tree. He then covered its entire surface with whole scratchcards, choosing ones with a beautiful deep-blue, black, silver and orange colour, reminiscent of a night sky.

Next, James started to depict the trunk of the tree, cutting and separating long strips of cardboard packing material for the bark. The Tree Council had sent him fascinating images of tree bark taken through a microscope, which James used as a point of reference.

James used the same packing material to act as the ground in which the tree was rooted and included some phrases from the poem and other meaningful words along these cardboard strips. He arranged more of the strands of packing cardboard into the curved branches and cut out many leaves. He imagined the children he wanted to depict, glowing as if touched by the wonder of the tree, so he hole-punched some gold and silver cards and placed them over paper images of the children.

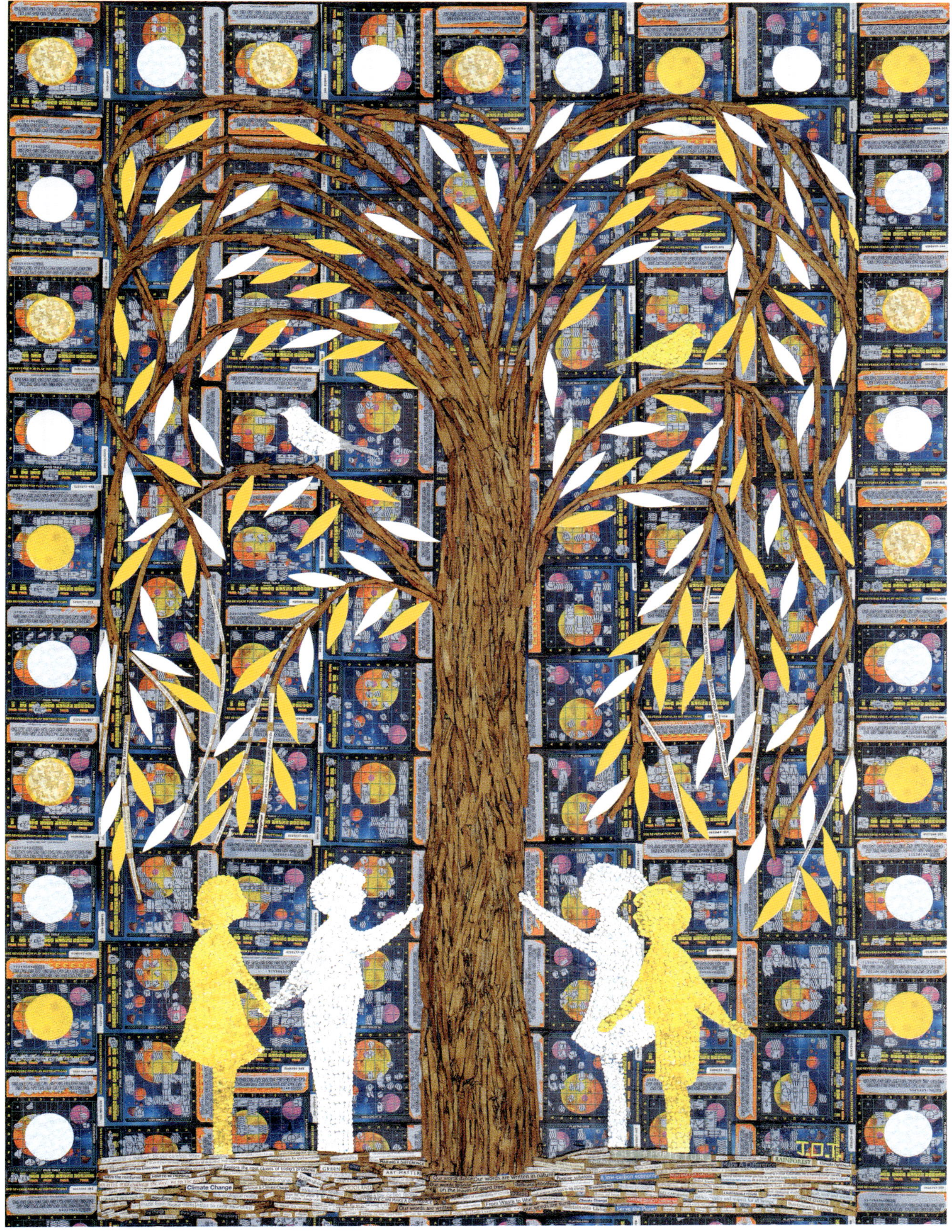

ARCHITECTURE

James' world as a young child was one of great stress and confusion and he liked the routine of returning to familiar places when he lived in East Sussex. In Yorkshire, he became more accustomed to visiting new places. His enjoyment grew in the huge variety of buildings he saw, including ancient abbeys and castles, cathedrals and churches, industrial mills, workhouses, country houses, museums, galleries, farms and field barns and all the modern architecture in cities. The world was opening up to him.

SALTS MILL

Salts Mill, a former textile mill in Bradford, West Yorkshire, is a real-life demonstration of a single person improving the working conditions for the poor labourers in the area during the Victorian era. The mill, and even the surrounding village, were financed by visionary industrialist Sir Titus Salt. He built what was, at the time, the largest mill in the world, and made sure that the working conditions for his employees were much better than elsewhere, including building decent homes for them to live nearby.

This collage shows a row of cottages leading to the mill, which James often visits as it is now an art gallery containing shops and restaurants. He finds great inspiration from David Hockney's art displayed there, as well as from the way the former mill sits within the landscape. He loves the way the row of workers' cottages leads up to the large mill building and the tall chimney rising high into the sky.

James has used scratchcards for this whole artwork. The horizontal strips for the background contrast with the vertical ones of the high chimney. Sir Titus Salt had moved his workers away from the city to the more rural area where the mill was situated. This is reflected in the green and trees in the distance.

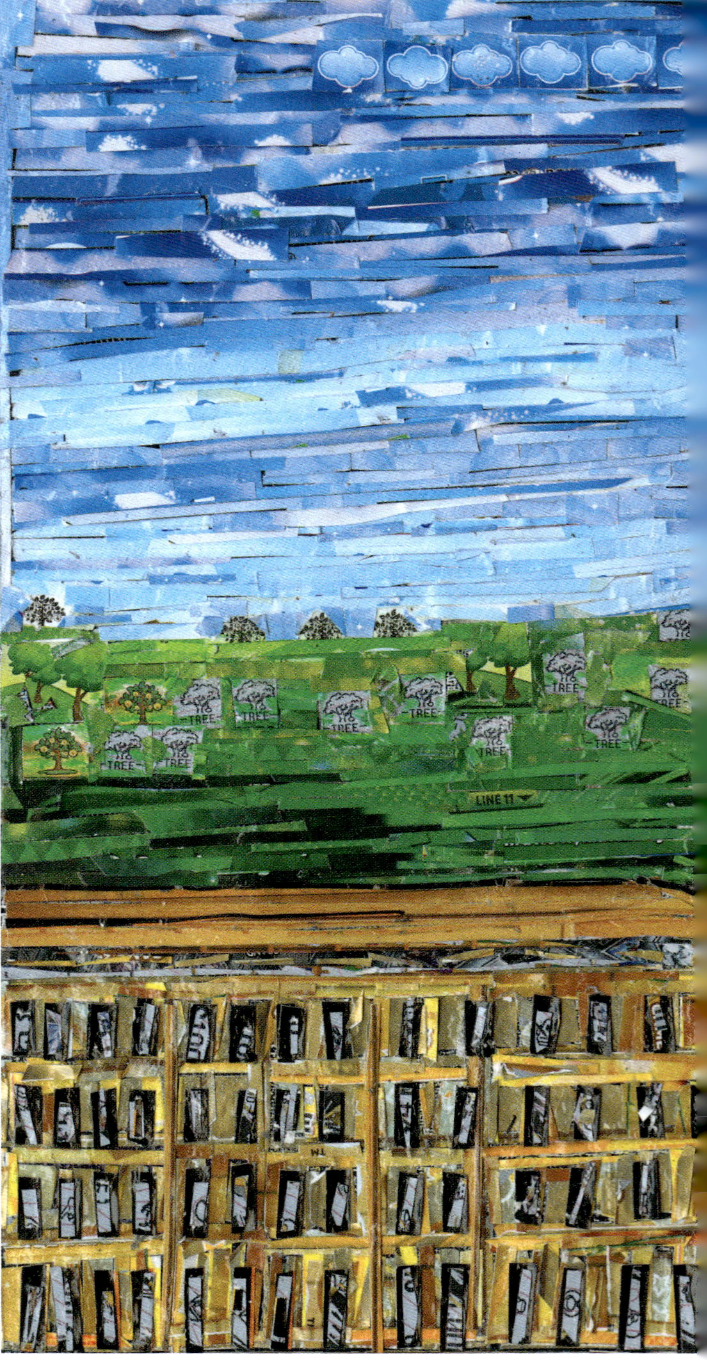

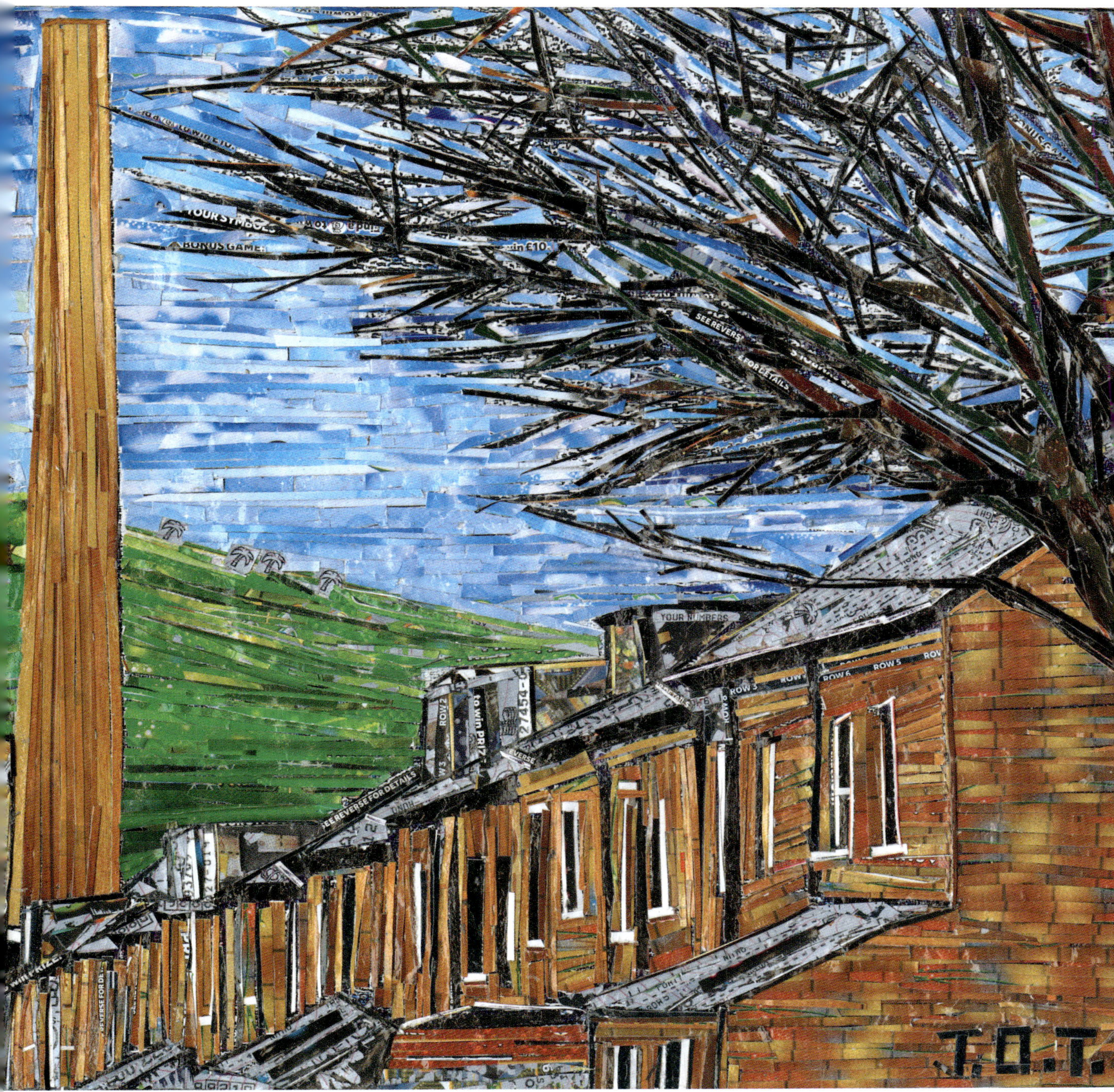

▲ *Salts Mill.* *This image and many other of James'
designs were chosen in 2024 for display as greetings cards
in Salts Mill's 1853 Gallery.*

KNARESBOROUGH VIADUCT

The viaduct at Knaresborough crosses over the River Nidd and, while trains cross from one side to the other, people can be seen walking or rowing boats far below, another example of how architecture can complement the surrounding natural landscape. James has always enjoyed visiting Knaresborough with its impressive view of the viaduct from the castle ruins. He once entered a photography competition and won first prize with a photograph of this viaduct.

James started this collage by measuring the proportions of the viaduct from the photograph. Next, he sketched the outline of the viaduct and its surroundings. Collaging was an extremely long process as he used a pointillist effect by hole-punching the paper. Measuring 90x44cm, it was the largest collage he had done and it took well over 100 hours to complete. He used a large variety of scratchcards for the different shades of colour. He hole-punched small words and symbols to provide pattern in the sky and trees. The viaduct itself was created from £50 note symbols from scratchcards, lined with thin slivers of gold foil. The purple train achieved its bright appearance from patterned scratch-cards. As always, no paint was added to the collage, just a coating of varnish.

Black hole-punched scratchcards were cut with nail scissors into tiny quarters to produce the chequered house in the scene. This Old Manor House has this design as one of the owners in the 1800s was reportedly a chess fanatic. Since then, other buildings and shops nearby have copied this style.

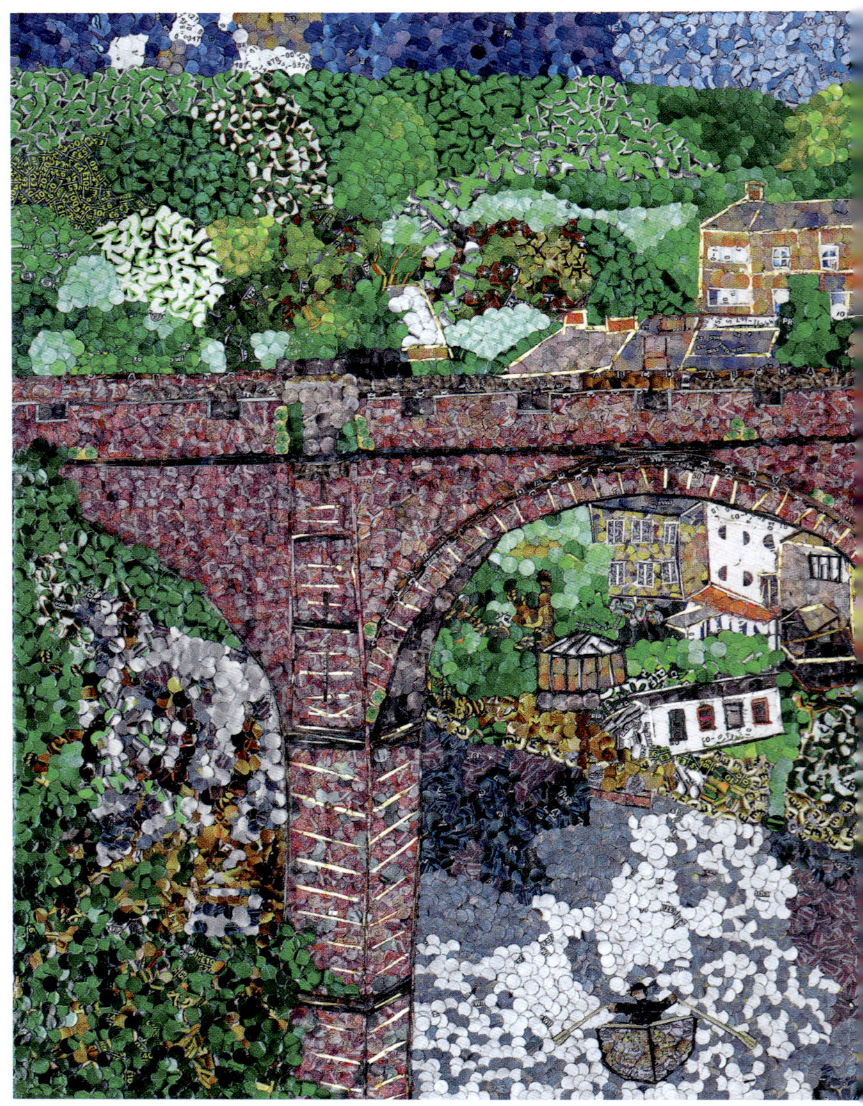

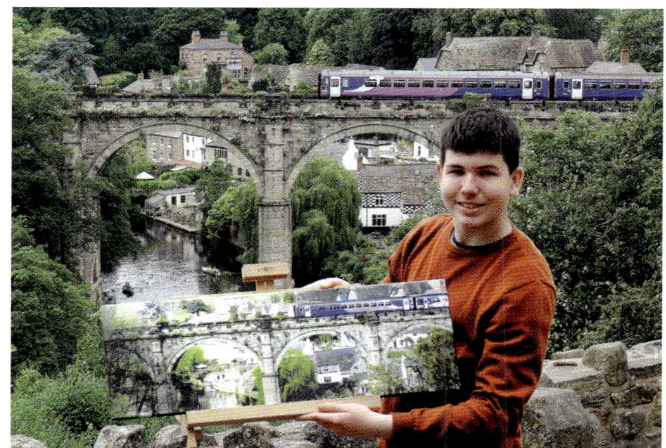

▶ *James with his prize-winning photograph of Knaresborough Viaduct.*

▼ *Knaresborough Viaduct.*

*OVERLEAF: A detail of **Knaresborough Viaduct**, showing some of the finer details, including those on the Old Manor House.*

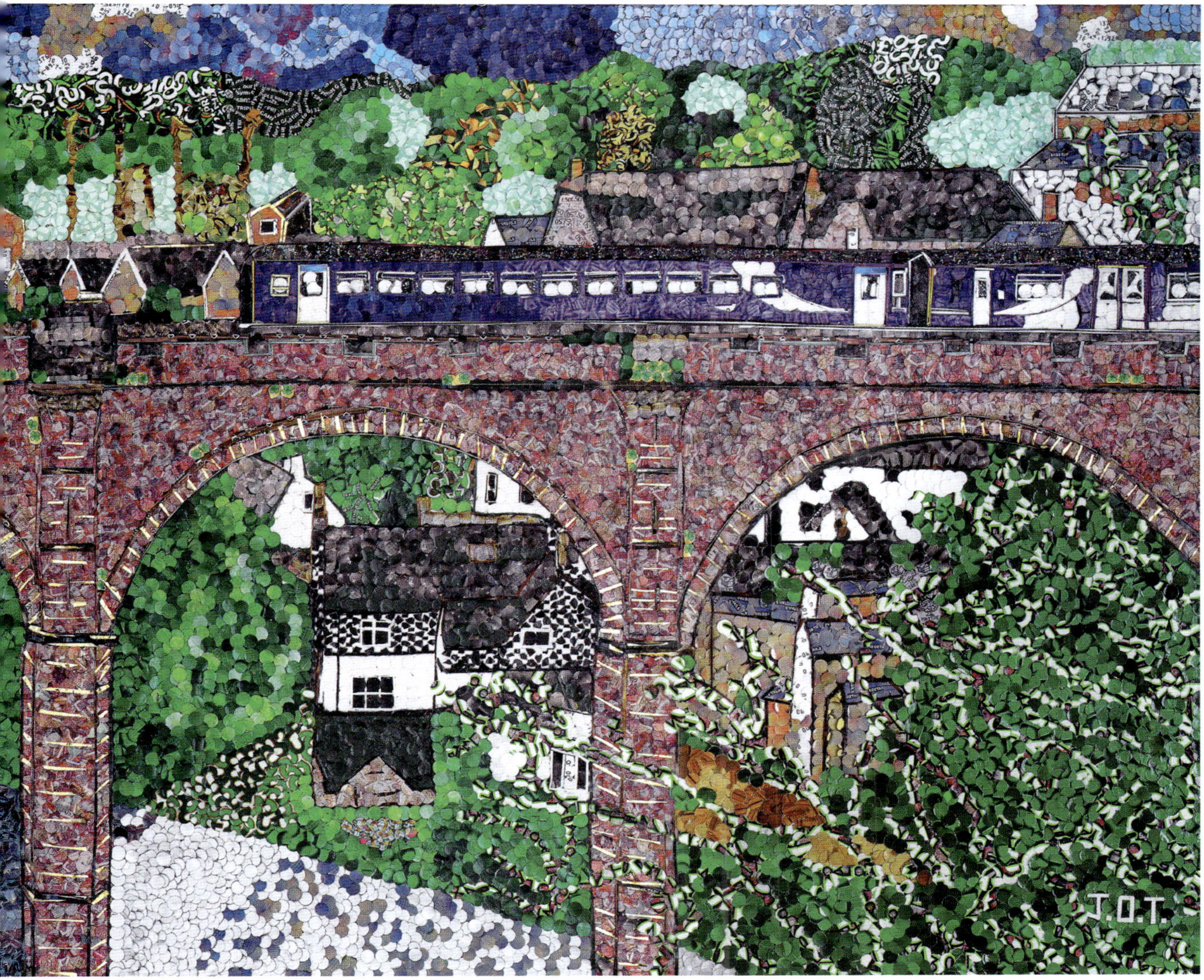

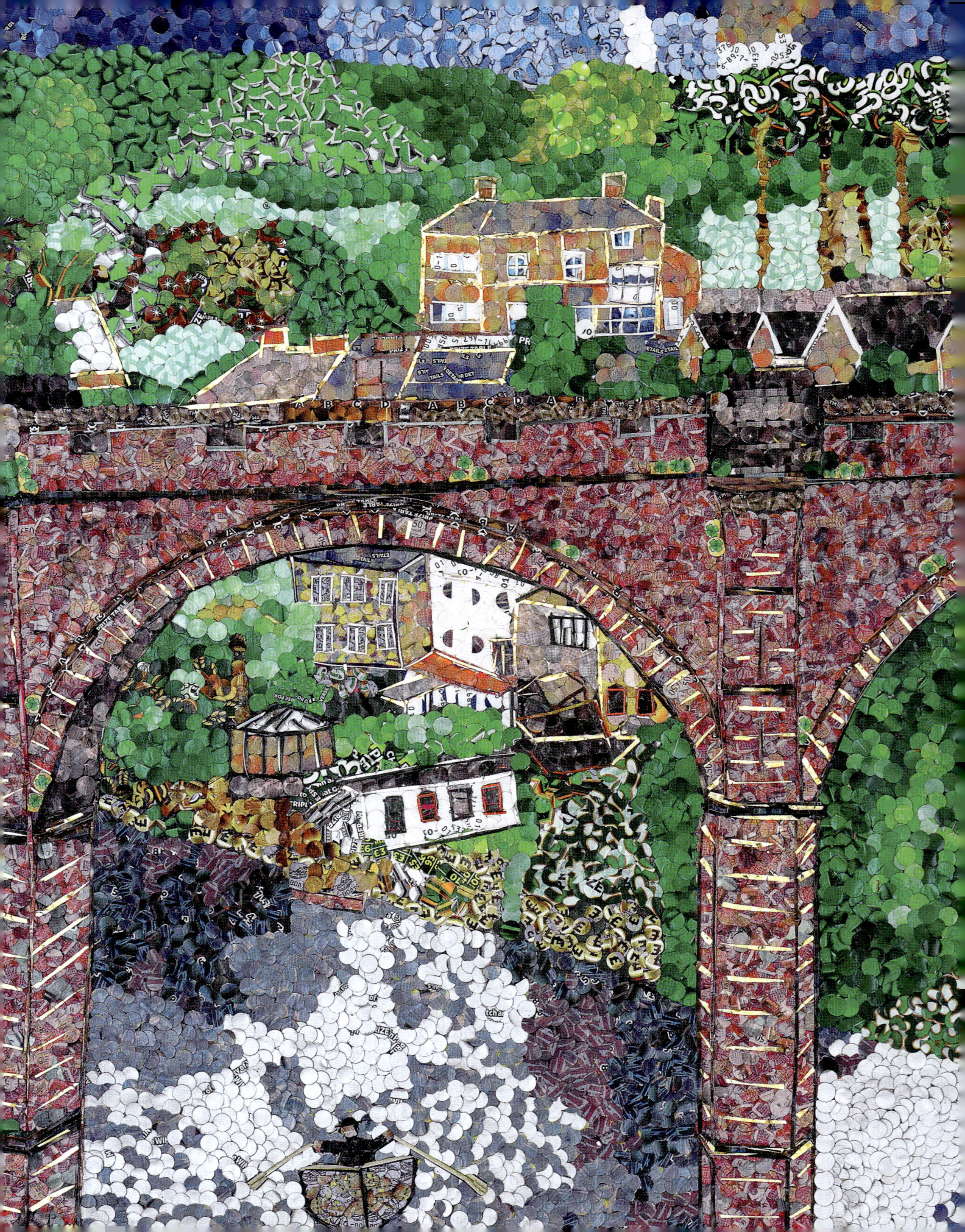

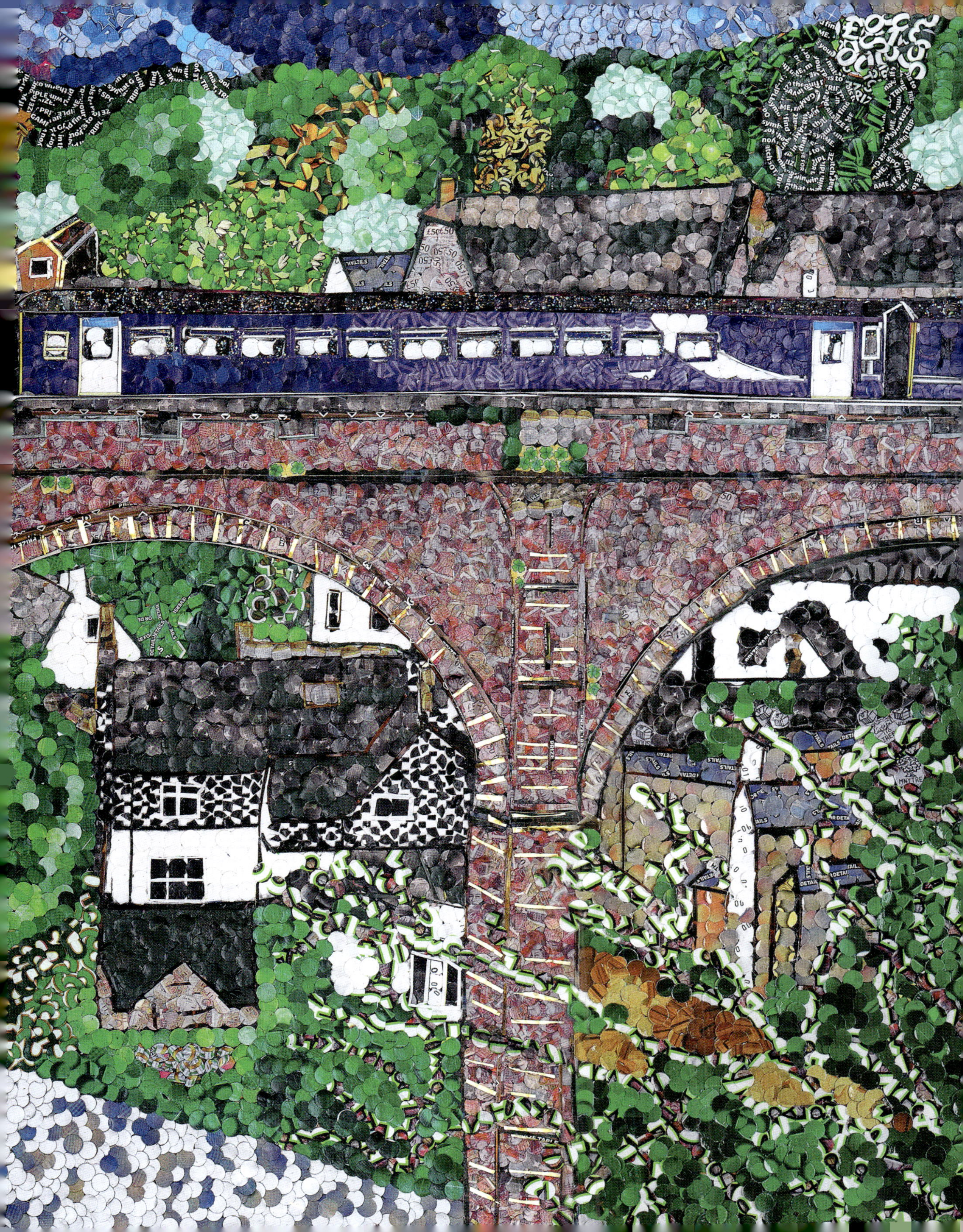

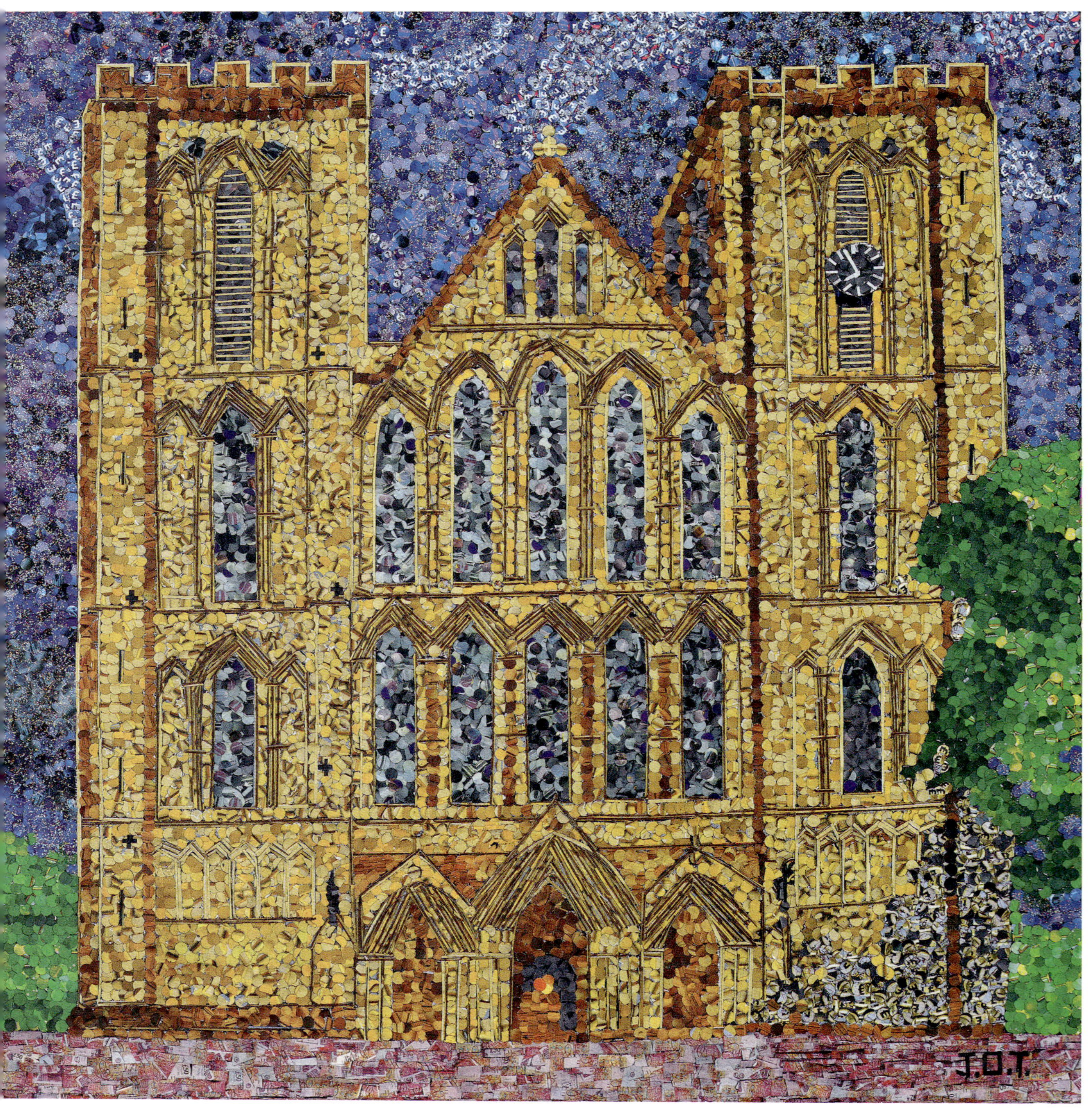

The collage of Ripon Cathedral, which prompted a commission of Fountains Abbey.

▶ *Fountains Hall.*

FOUNTAINS HALL

While volunteering for the National Trust at Fountains Abbey, James created a collage of Fountains Hall, which was used by the abbey to encourage visitors to take a look at the country house. This is one of James' most noted pieces, with the stone walls of the hall represented by symbols of bank notes, highlighting the wealth of the abbey and its estate.

FOUNTAINS ABBEY

Fountains Abbey sits in the English countryside, near the town of Ripon in North Yorkshire. Though it is a ruin, it is considered to be a very well-pre-served Cistercian monastery and is incredibly beautiful. It is now owned and looked after by the National Trust and English Heritage.

James began his collage of the abbey after a client, who had bought a collage of Ripon Cathedral, commissioned one of Fountains Abbey to match. The customer expressly asked for the sky to be collaged in a similar way to the Ripon collage, in deep shades of blue and using symbols.

James took reference photographs at the site, one of which inspired him to use intense shades of blue for the sky, deep greens and brown for the trees and a sandy-pink path area.

James started by collaging some of the trees in the background, but later decided to make a small

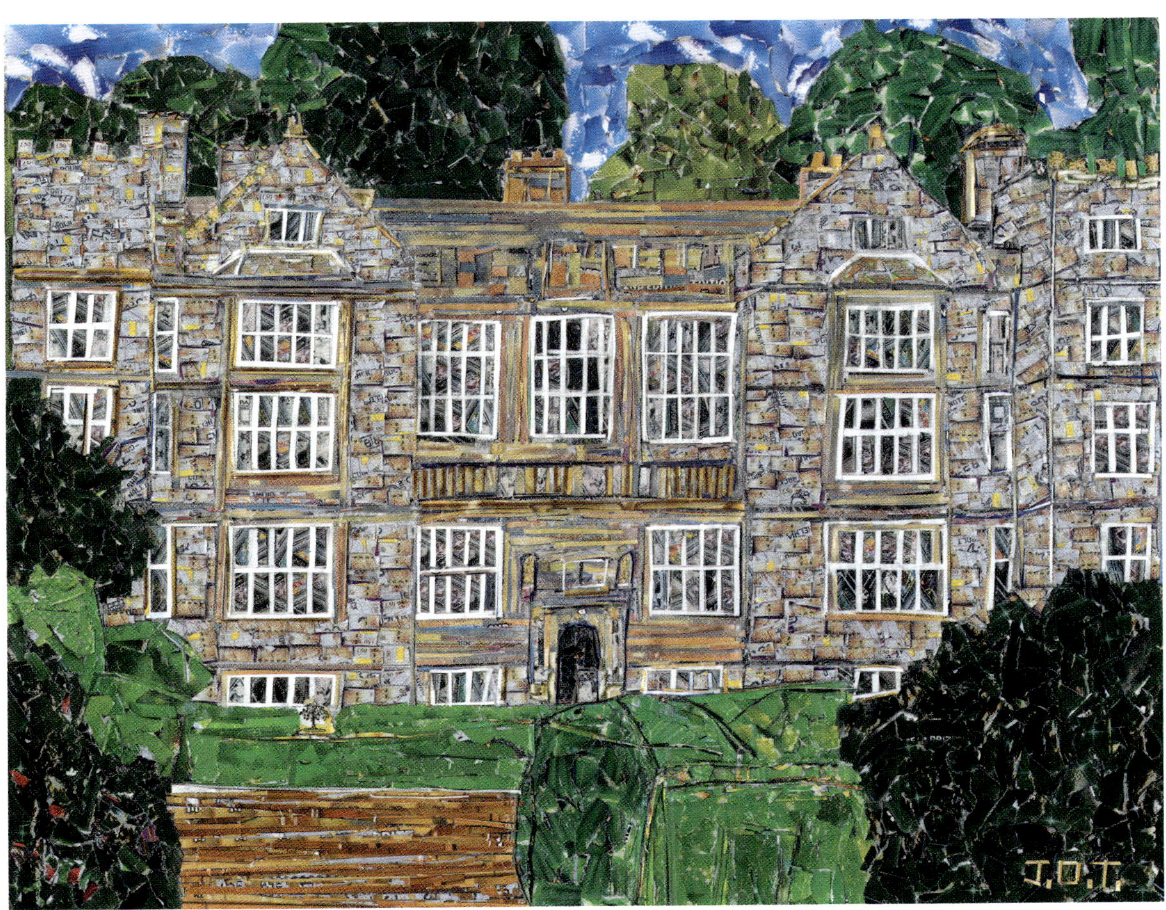

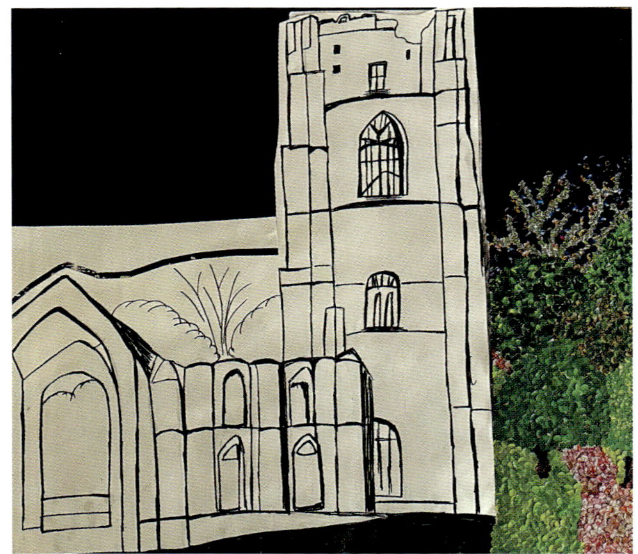

▶ *Sticking sketches on white paper over the black canvas*

▼ *Detail of the trees.*

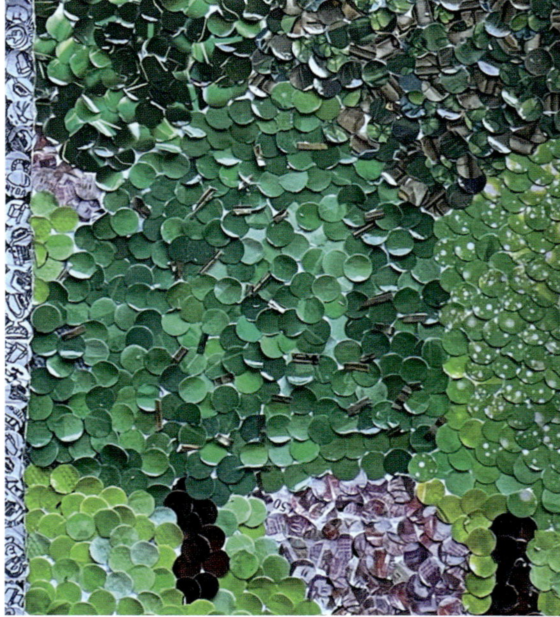

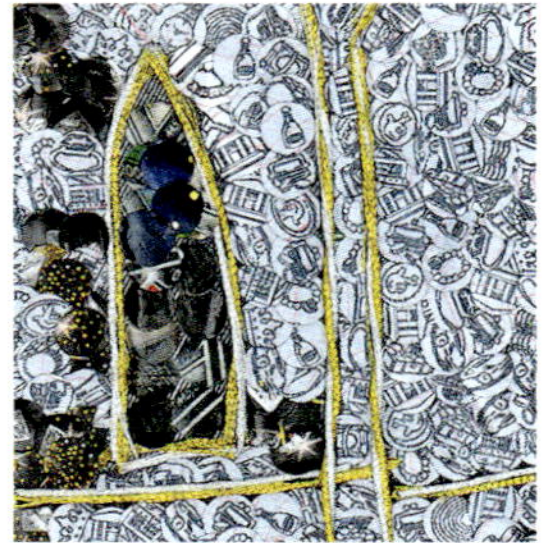

▲ *Some of the symbols James used to represent the wealth of the abbey.*

▶ *The completed collage of Fountains Abbey.*

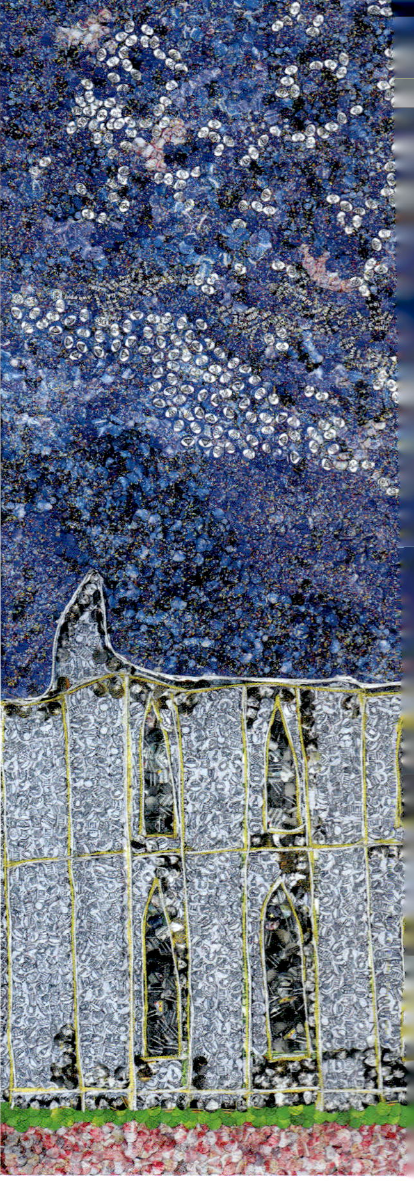

sketch to stick over the black canvas, which was so dark that he could not draw on it. The whole collage was put together in this way, in sections.

The path was created from hole-punched pieces of bank notes found on scratchcards. James spent some hours hole-punching the colours he needed in advance, then applied them to the canvas in layers until he was happy with the colour mix.

James used money symbols for the abbey's stonework as he thought this would be appropriate, taking into account that, until its dissolution in the 1500s, the abbey had been very wealthy. The pointillist style he used here was a reference to images of gold and silver coins, money bags, jewels, vaults

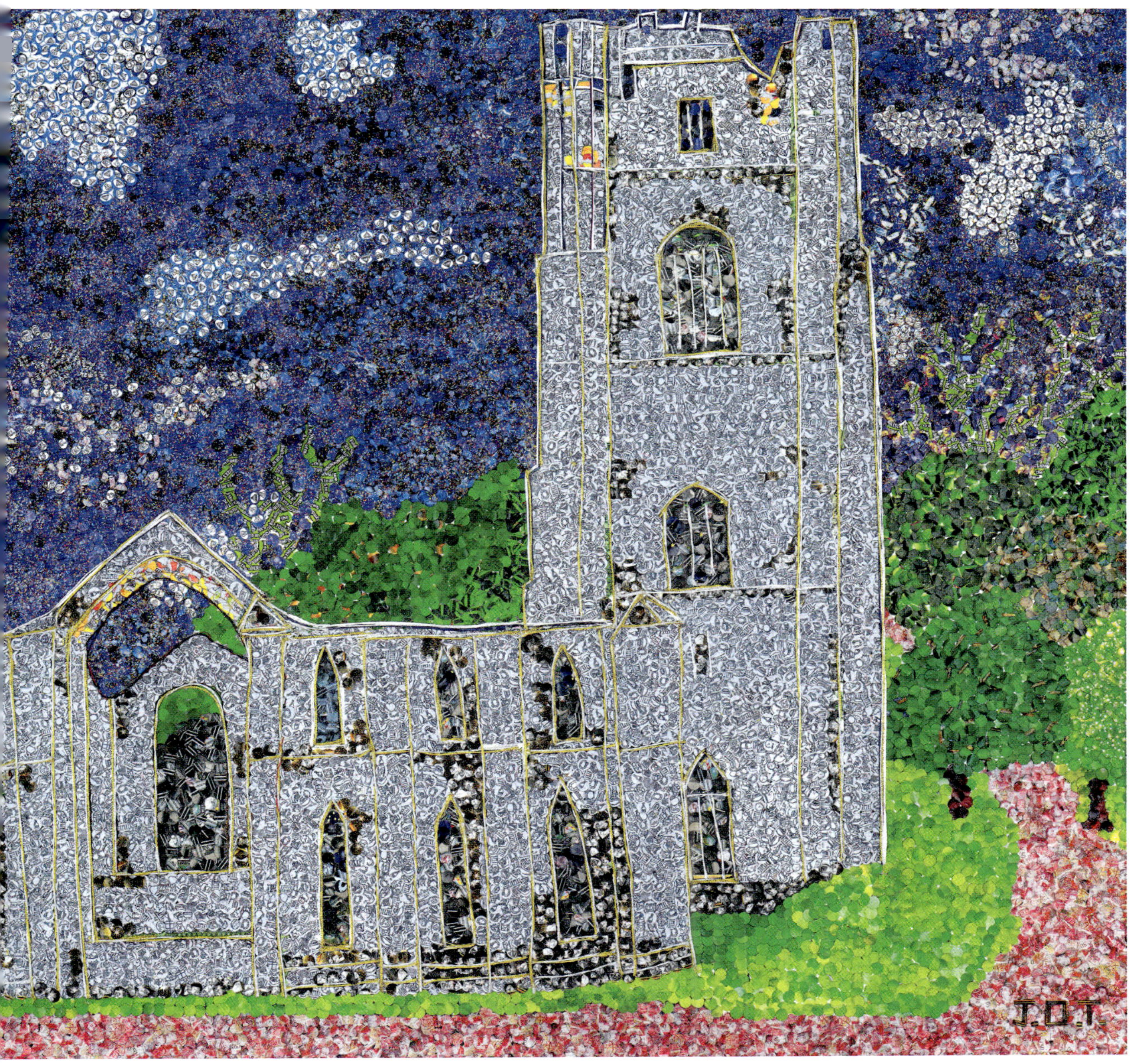

and chests of treasure and wealth; even bottles to reference the ale or wine the monks were drinking at the time. The juxtaposition of items from our modern lifestyles being used as stonework on an ancient abbey interested him as he combined the present day with ancient times. He used a combination of gold and silver strands of metallic thread to add definition in this quite complex piece.

While he prefers to complete collages indoors, James spent one day working in the abbey's grounds, to take photographs for social media for the customer who commissioned the work, but also to absorb some of the atmosphere! These were not ideal conditions for collaging as it was freezing cold, with pieces of paper blowing about.

BUSES AND TRAINS

At a playgroup that James attended, the last activity of the day was singing the nursery rhyme, 'The Wheels on The Bus Go Round and Round'. Children would sit on the floor and sing but James refused to take part and preferred to stay on the bouncy castle. He didn't dislike the song itself, as he would sometimes hear the tune at home on children's television; rather, he could not sing or even say the words at the time. He also used to watch 'Transporters' on the television, a series of programmes with cartoon vehicles moving on tracks, which helped children with autism to recognise certain emotions. Seeing the vehicles move along a repetitive track was just as calming to James as the physical motion of travelling on a bus.

As he got older, James' special interest in buses developed to such an extent that he was able to remember bus numbers and routes. He wanted to collect timetables and had them stored in a box that had been converted into his own little bus. He would feel calm and relaxed if he found his favourite seat upstairs at the front of a double decker, sometimes resting the side of his face against the cool glass of the window.

On his 9th birthday, James had a personal tour of the Eastbourne bus depot. It had taken quite some planning to ensure that the bus depot staff were aware of his special interest and how he loved to travel everywhere by bus. He was even allowed to sit in the driver's seat and was shown the controls. What appealed to him most was switching the different lights on and off, as well as being able to sound the horn! He was delighted with his time at the depot and was given a selection of books about the buses from the bus company.

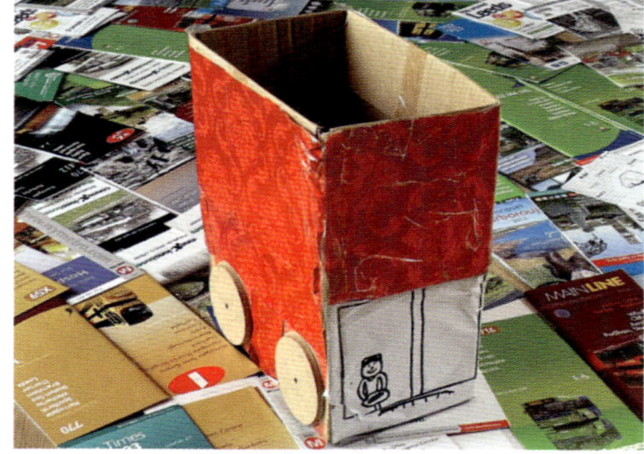

▲ *The bus box in which James kept bus timetables.*

▼ *James on his visit to the bus depot.*

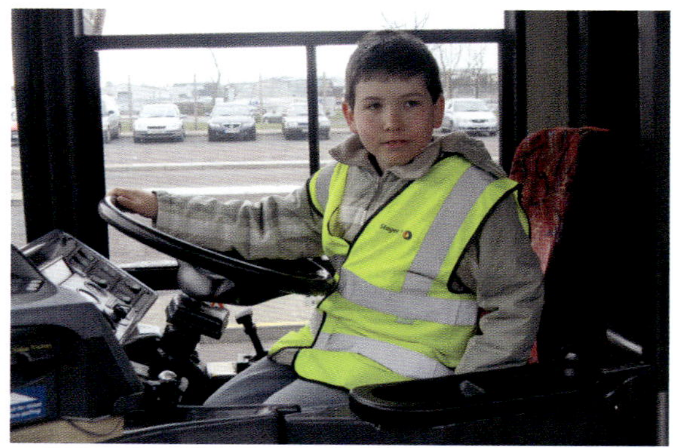

CHRISTMAS SPECIAL

Inspired by memories of these bus journeys, James designed this Christmas Special in 2023 to be used on a card. It was made from many torn pictures of buses from magazines. The artwork became a photo collage using a green bus from a magazine and red pieces of scratchcards to make a Christmas scene. It was glazed with glittering varnish to give a Christmas look. The sky is a blur of cut-outs of white/grey buses to give a cold, wintry feel. There is just one person seated on the bus in this collage (back seat, lower deck), who represents James with all his thoughts about how bus journeys have influenced his life.

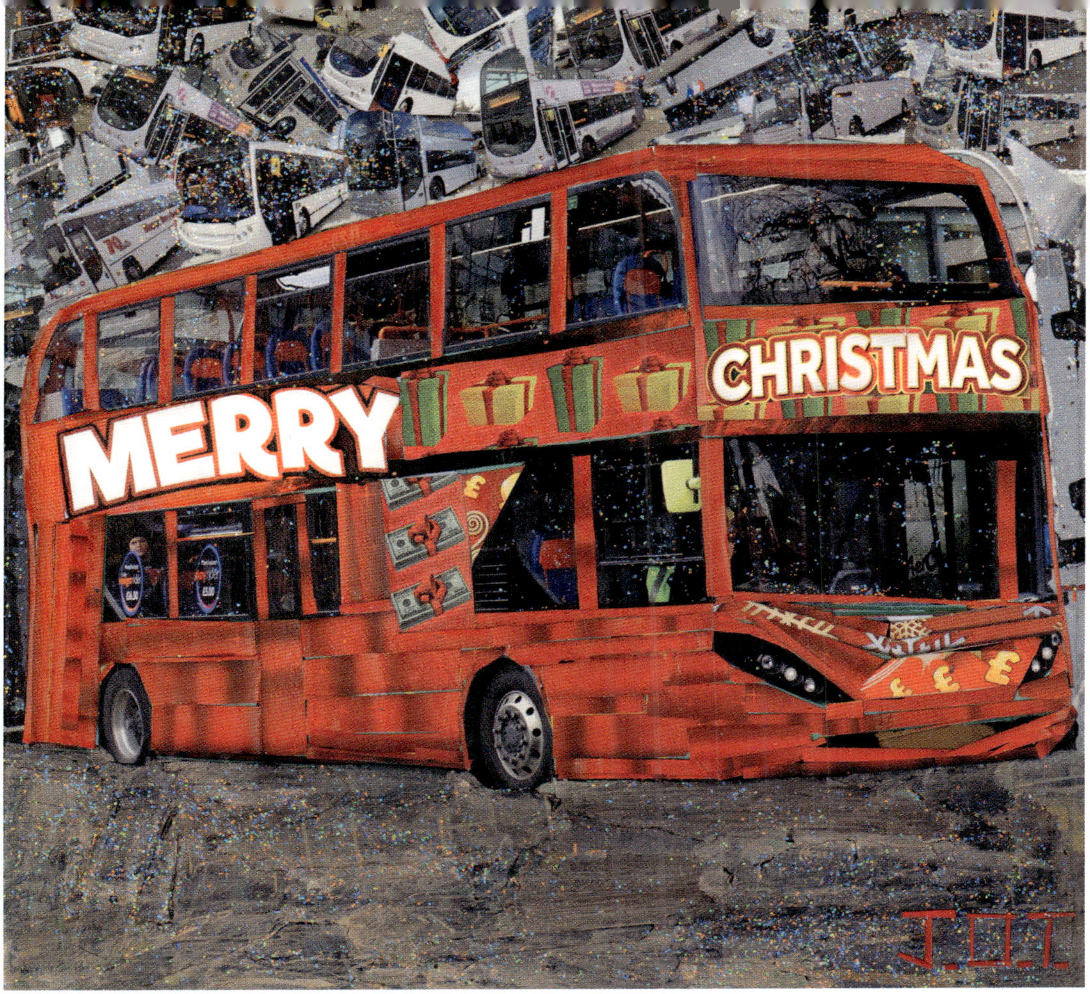

TRAINS

As James began to travel more to London by train, his interests turned to collecting train tickets. At Victoria Station, he once noticed a long line of blank rail tickets hanging out of a self-service machine and asked if he could take these home. They became part of his GCSE art and photography project, when he carefully stuck miniature photos he had taken of trains onto the tickets and decorated them to create viaducts and colourful skies. These tickets later became part of some of his exhibitions, for example at The Station Gallery at Richmond, North Yorkshire.

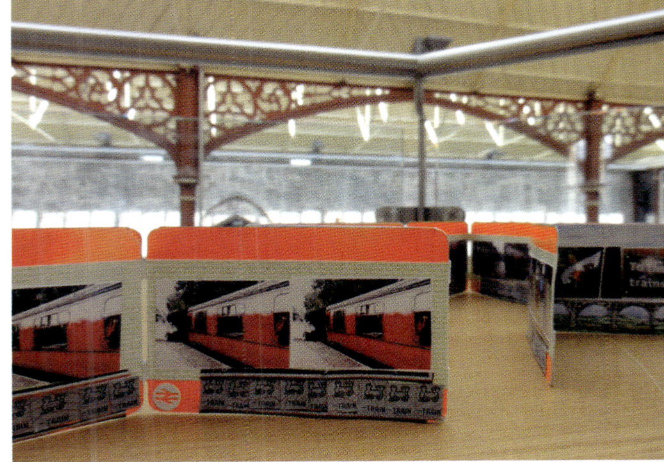

▲▲ *Christmas bus collage.*

▲ *A close-up picture of James' collaged train tickets on display at The Station Gallery.*

SURREALISM AND 3-D ART

Surrealist art is renowned for often incorporating strange juxtapositions and images that reflect aspects of our subconscious. From fragmentation and distortion to bizarre configurations of everyday objects, these images can shock or disturb us. They can seem like dream states or contain symbols that might unlock repressed thoughts, make us think about things in ways we are not used to and make the everyday come to life.

ST CUTHBERT

James once took some prize-winning photographs of a wooden Fenwick Lawson sculpture in the garden of St Mary-le-Bow church in Durham. He gave it a surreal look by adding cut pieces of photographs and scratchcards, experimented by applying shards of other photographs over the main picture and included some pink scratchcard fragments to represent the brick wall in the background.

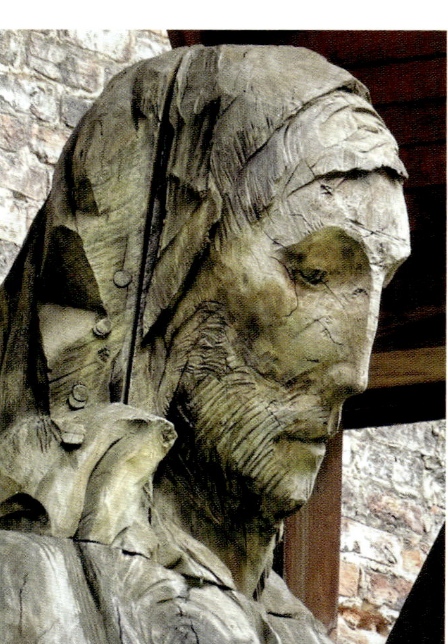

▲ *St Cuthbert photograph prior to being collaged over.*

▶ *The collaged version of St Cuthbert.*

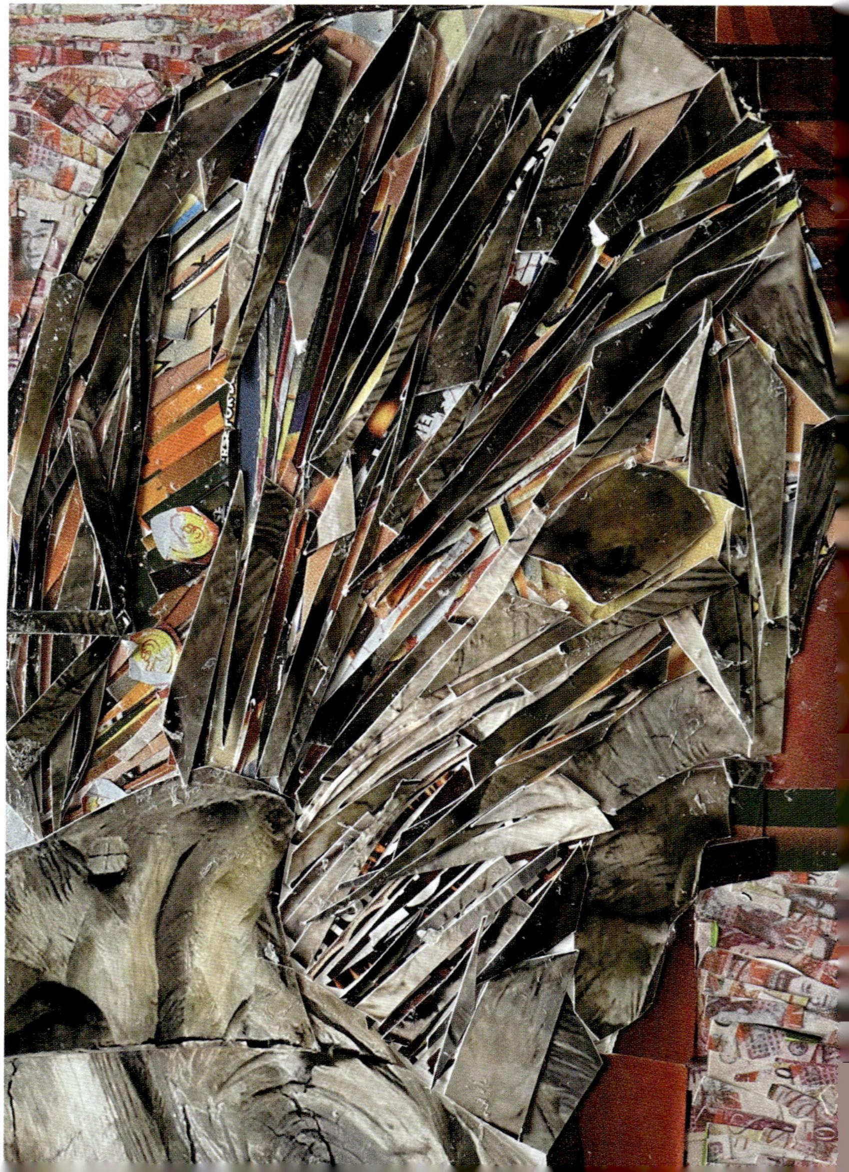

ÁRBOL DE LA VIDA (TREE OF LIFE)

Over the years, James has visited Farleys House & Gallery, a former hub of the Surrealists in East Sussex, and has enjoyed seeing the variety of artwork and photography on display.

He even had the opportunity to exhibit his own art at Farleys in the spring of 2021, in his *From Waste To Wall* exhibition. The oak tree in his *Árbol de la Vida* (*Tree of Life*) collage was represented in the exhibition.

James was given Spanish scratch-cards by a friend from the Basque Country, Marisa Muelas, who collected them for him and told him about the town of Guernica. James went on to research an oak tree that stands in front of the council building there. It replaced a 146-year-old oak tree that died during a particularly hot summer in 2004 and that had survived the city's 1937 bombing during the Spanish Civil War – the bombing that Picasso portrayed in his 'Guernica' painting. Here, James' *Árbol de la Vida* might be seen to represent the enduring life force contained in nature.

When James created the *Árbol de la Vida* collage, he also had Picasso's depictions of birds in mind. The birds that James particularly liked in Picasso's art were *The Pigeons* (1957) and he sketched birds with a deliberately chunky appearance before adding collage, using them as symbols of peace and freedom and highlighting their innate beauty.

The background layers of turquoise and blue tissue paper were already stuck on the surface when James was given this second-hand canvas

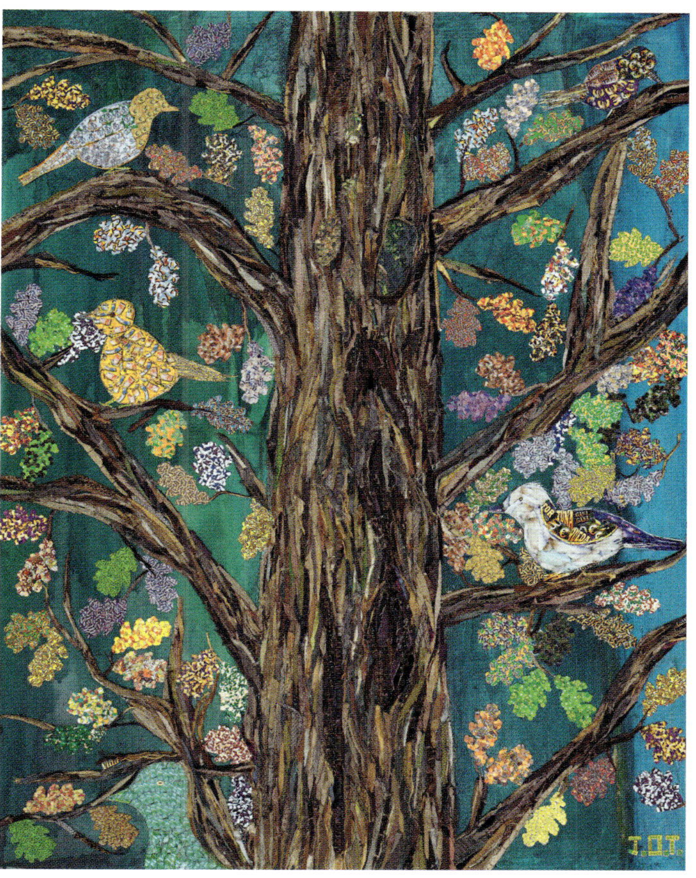

▲ *Árbol de la Vida* (*Tree of Life*).

by a friend to use for his art. He then sketched the tree outline over the top. The bark of the tree was made from many pieces of roughly cut fabric in shades of brown, green, grey, purple and black, blended together but with pieces of cotton coming away from the edges to create a very rough surface for the oak tree.

The leaves were shaped from circular pieces hole-punched from Spanish-language scratch-cards. Parts of Spanish words can be seen on the leaves and the birds themselves: Fortuna (luck) and Gana (win). Some dark staining in the background came from the application of glue followed by varnish.

SO SURREAL

Another of James' pieces, *So Surreal*, was inspired by the photograph *Meret Oppenheim Arm With Ink*, taken by the famous American Surrealist photographer and painter Man Ray in 1933.

It inspired James to think about how he might create his own Surrealist-style collage of a lady's arm. He decided to link the idea to his special interest in trees.

Farleys sent James some old leaflets to use creatively. He arranged some discarded scratchcards with colours that would complement those on the donated leaflets. They had ancient Egyptian symbols printed on them, which added an unusual effect to the background of the collage. These symbols had a distant connection to Farleys as

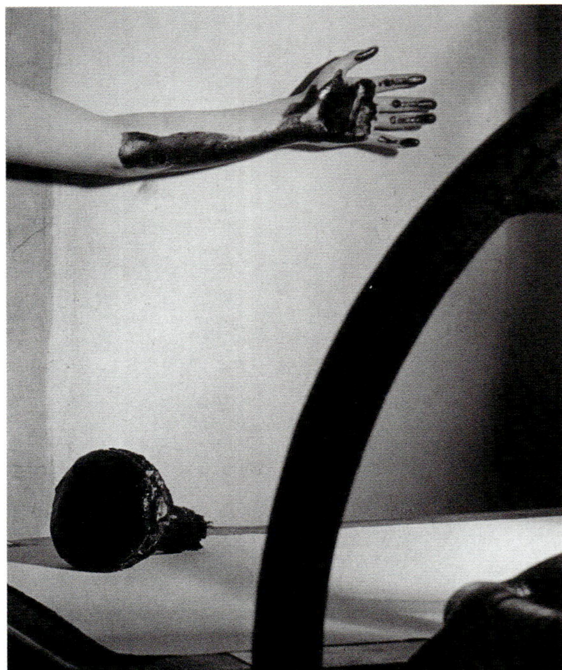

▲ *Meret Oppenheim Arm With Ink by Man Ray.* (© *Man Ray 2015 Trust / Adagp, Paris, 2025: Telimage / Adagp Images*)

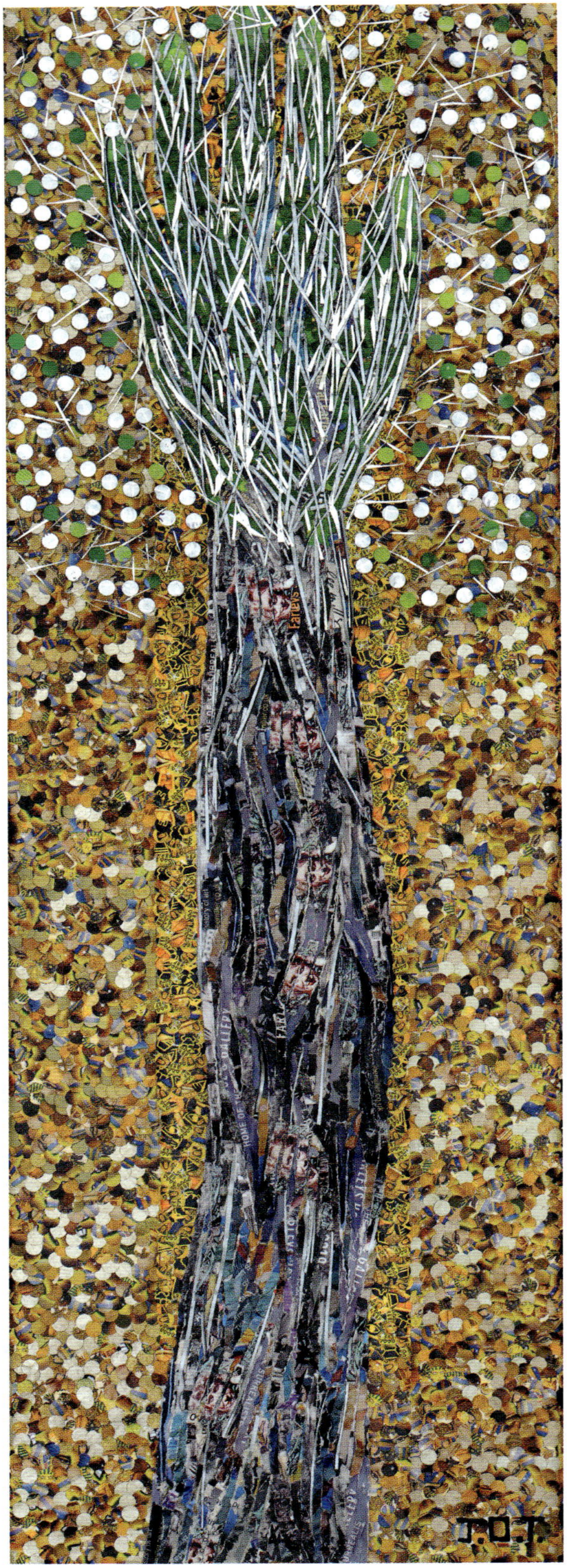

▶ *So Surreal.*

the famous photographer Lee Miller had moved to Farleys from Cairo in 1949 and James used the scratchcard symbols of a miniature Pharaoh, Ankh, Scarab and Horus in reference to this. The arm was made from shredded pieces of the Farleys leaflets and torn pieces showing the face of Lee Miller.

In *So Surreal*, the outstretched arm, inspired by Man Ray's photograph, shows veins in the hand-like branches spreading out in a tree. The dark collage of the tree-arm echoes the ink-covered arm in Man Ray's photograph.

FRIDA KAHLO

James has also enjoyed looking at other artists' work, including Frida Kahlo's brightly coloured Surrealist paintings that represent people and important events in her life. She even managed to capture in her art the pain she felt after being involved in a terrible accident. He admires all the detail and vibrant colours in her work.

James once depicted Frida in one of his sketchbooks, again using discarded scratchcards.

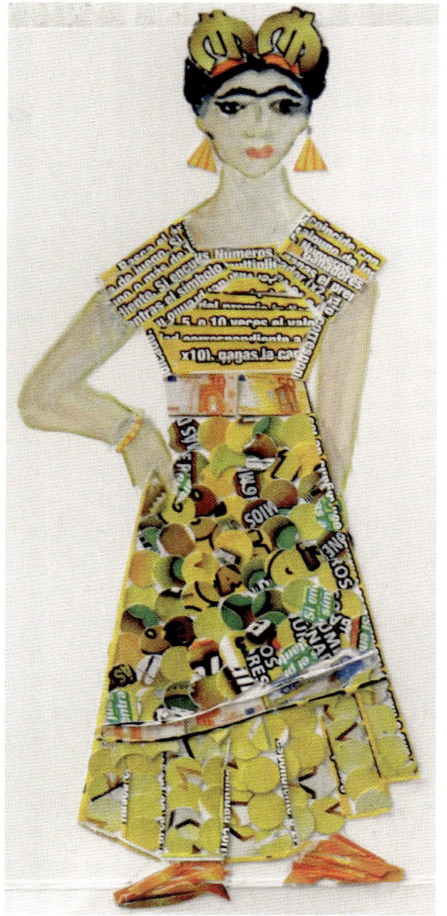

▶ *Frida Kahlo.*

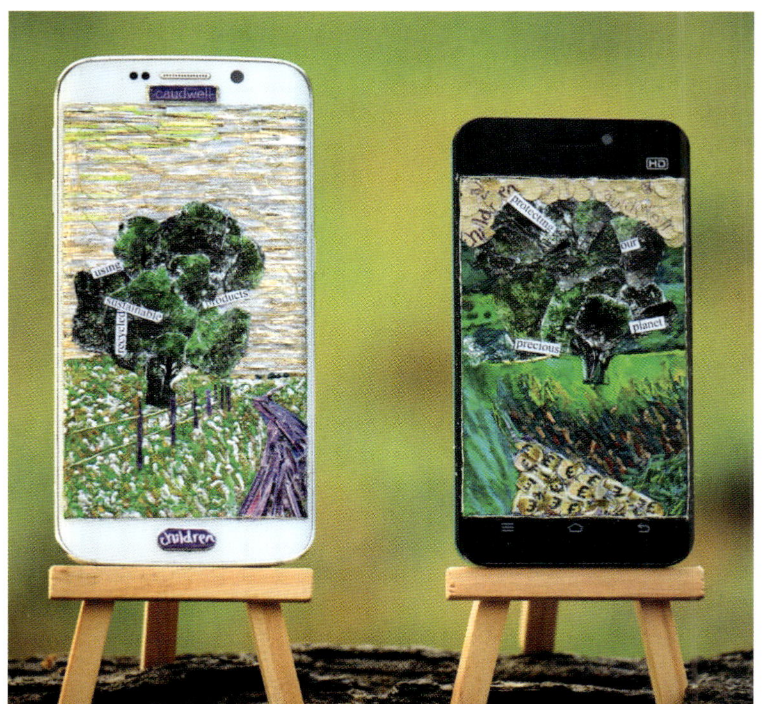

MOBILE PHONES

James has also collaged scenes directly onto old mobile phones, from which the recyclable components have been removed. Since the collaging pieces are tiny, the method is painstaking but he finds the process appealing and therapeutic.

◀ *Collages on retired mobile phones.* (*Photograph © Paul Howell*)

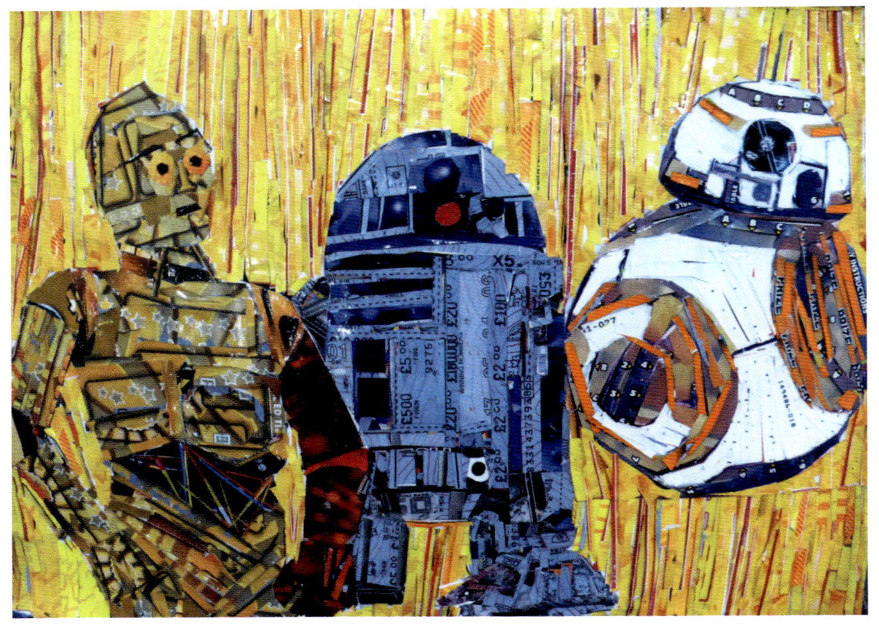

◀ ▼ Star Wars collage on an old TV, and a found chair, collaged.
(MK Calling 2020 installation view; MK Gallery, Milton Keynes; chair and TV photograph Andy Keate)

STAR WARS TV SET

Some of James' earliest collage artwork was created using three-dimensional objects, using recycled materials including an old television set.

James was (and still is) very keen on Star Wars. He represented three of the Star Wars droids as if they were being broadcast on the screen of the small TV set. This was put on display at several of his art exhibitions, including the *MK Calling* event at Milton Keynes in 2019–20. It was part of a series where he had also collaged a Star Wars scene on canvas.

Also on display at the Milton Keynes exhibition was an abandoned chair that James had collaged with discarded scratchcards. It had originally been fly-tipped in a Sussex woodland. With its new seat cover and a glossy coating on its wooden surface, it was given a new lease of life and rescued from pointless decay.

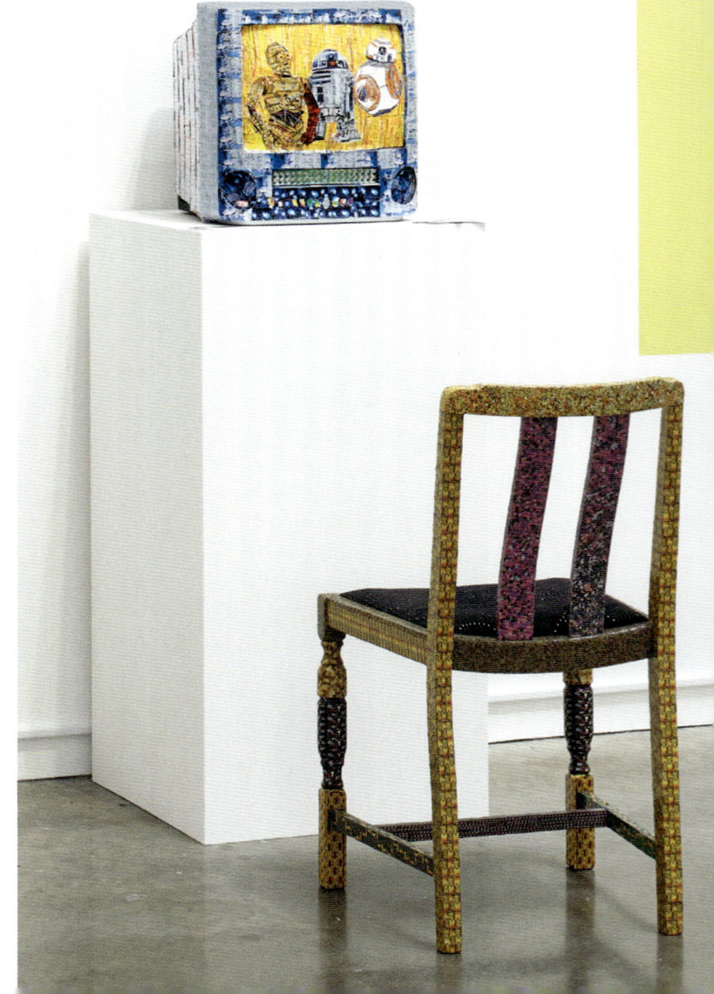

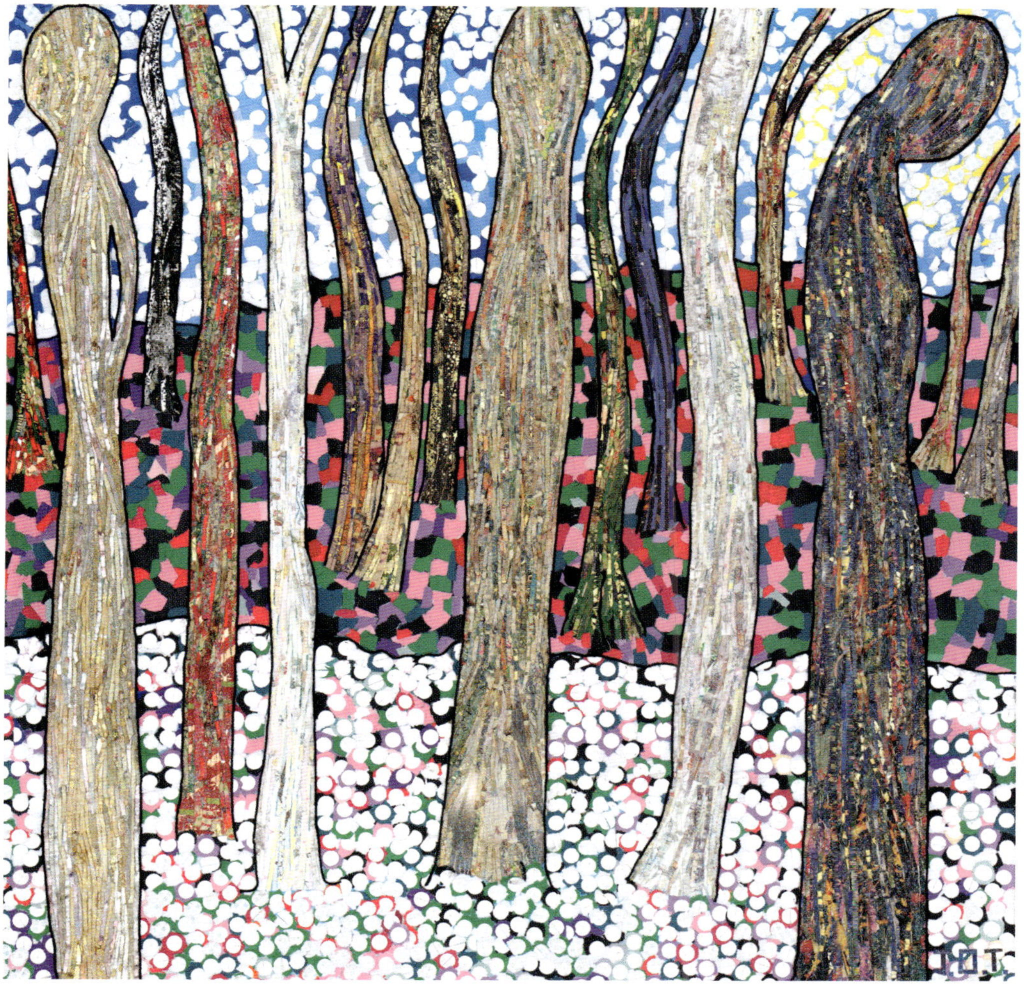

THREE WOODLAND FIGURES

One of James' best surreal pieces is *Three Woodland Figures*. It links in with his woodland series but with three figures becoming part of nature. He was thinking of three members of his family (his mother and her siblings). There is also a message about being out in nature and the hope it can bring, in terms of better health and wellbeing.

The figures are made from shredded pieces of old Christmas cards, most of which were soaked in tea-stained water (apart from the two white-coloured trees where the Christmas cards were shredded but not stained). The background is made entirely from the left-over tickets given to him by Pontefract Races. All of them have now been used. He roughly tore around the holographic circle on the tickets so that the blue, yellow, black, pink, purple and green edges would show. James said it gave the artwork the colours of Liquorice Allsorts!

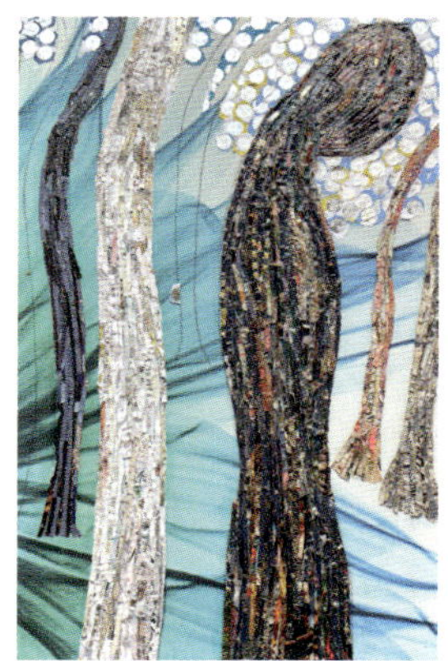

▲ *Working over an old canvas to create* **Three Woodland Figures.**

▲▲ **Three Woodland Figures.**

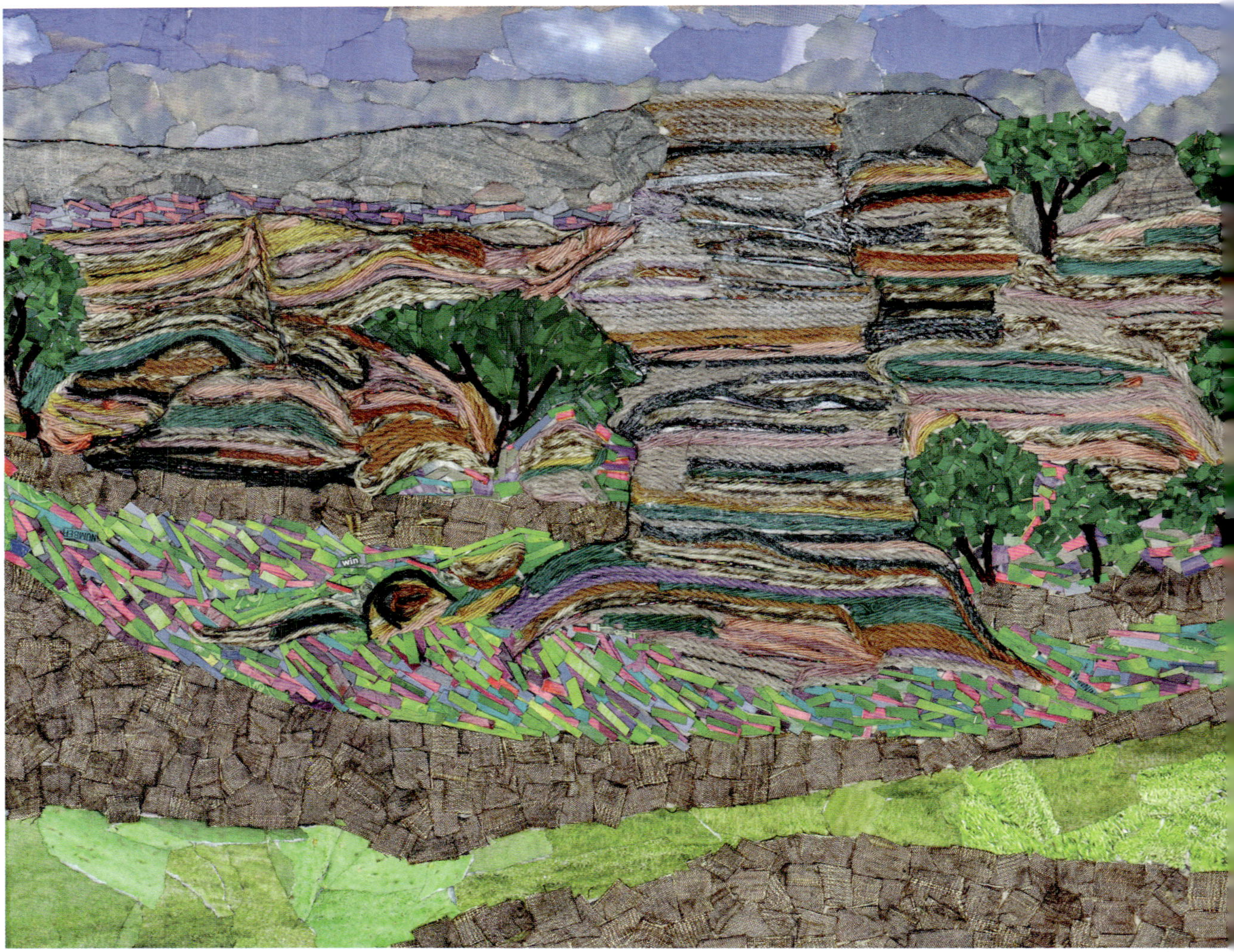

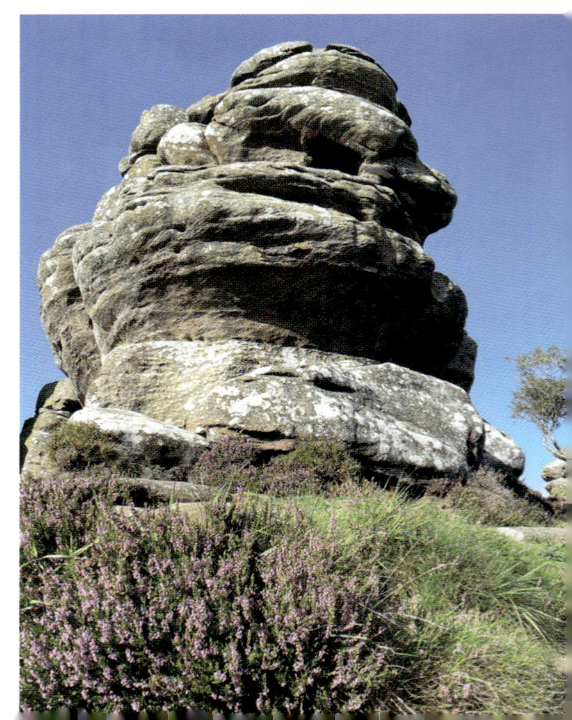

BRIMHAM ROCKS

Not far from James' home is the unusual landscape of Brimham Rocks. These high-standing rocks, many of which look precariously balanced, have been shaped into fantastical forms by wind and water over millions of years.

James has enjoyed collaging the rocks since he was an art student. He experimented with recreating their texture using old scratchcards over a drawn and lightly painted surface. He has donated one to his old school, where it remains on display with some information about him and his work.

▲ *One of James' two large Brimham Rocks canvases.*

▶ *One of the formations at Brimham Rocks.*

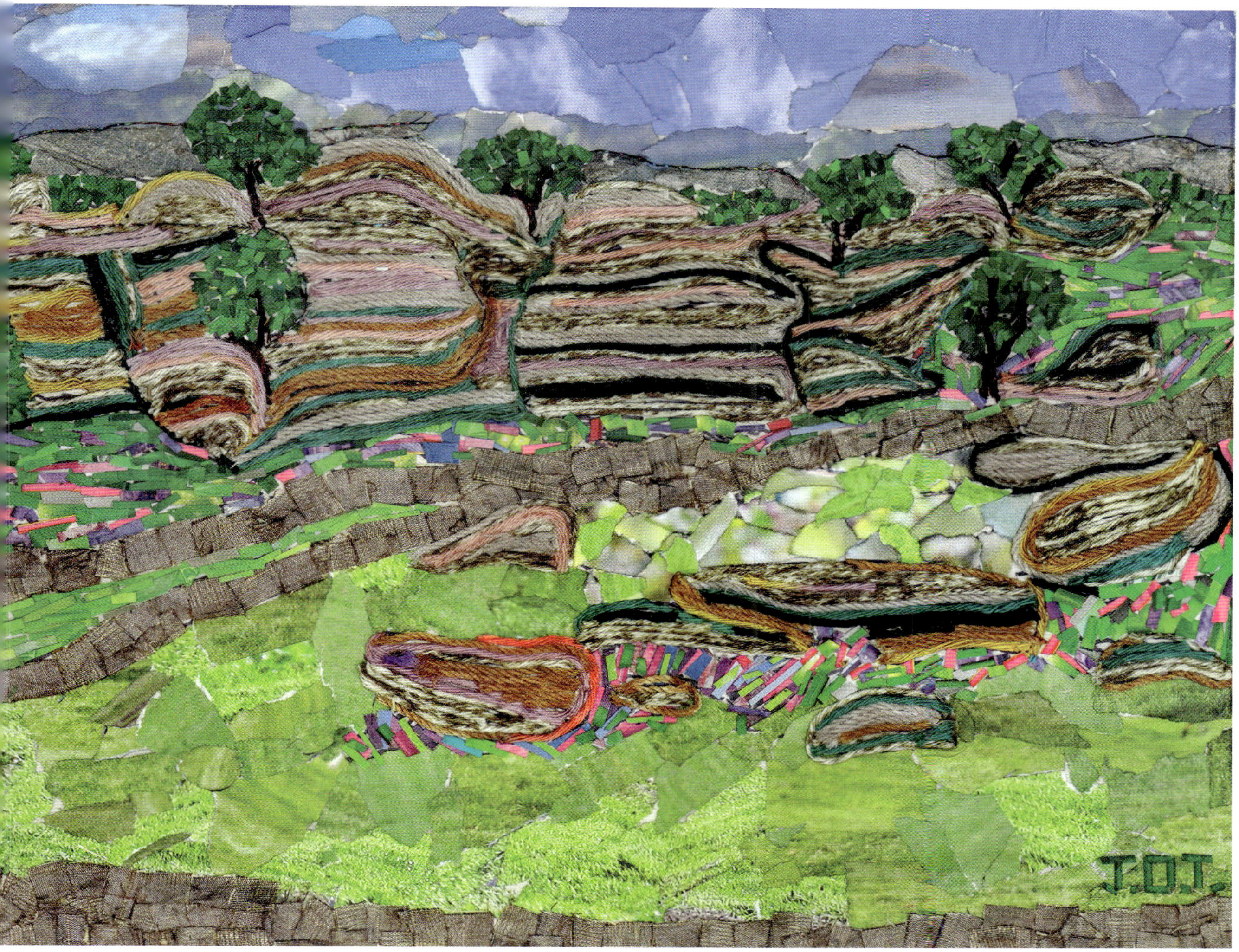

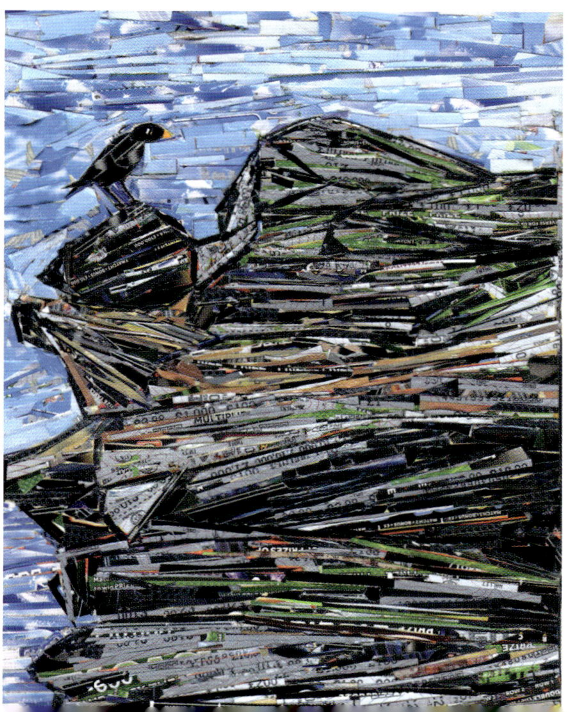

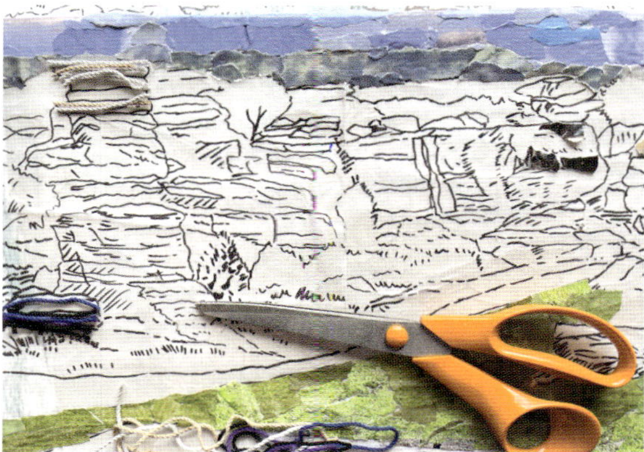

▲ *Preparing to apply string to a Brimham Rocks collage, to add texture and a surreal colour.*

◀ *A crow on Brimham Rocks, now donated to James' old school.*

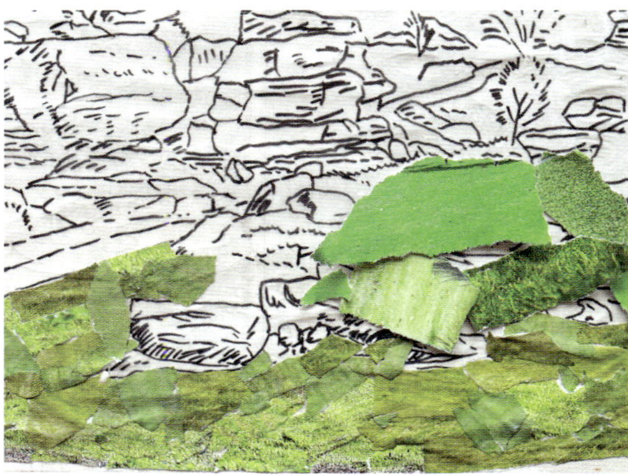

▲ *For the grassy areas, James used brightly coloured torn-up pieces of green and images of grass sourced from old magazines.*

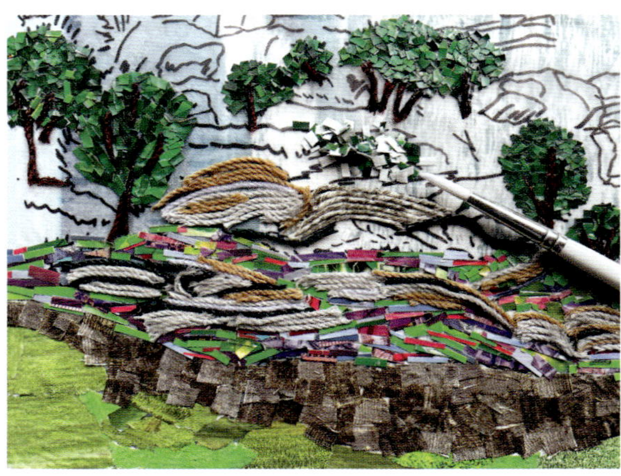

▲ *Short lengths of coloured string and thread were combined with cut strips, small squares of scratchcards and other recycled papers to represent the different facets of the rocks and the intervening land and trees.*

◄ *James used larger golden-brown squares of fabric (from the Pontefract Races cushion fabric) for the path. Strips of coloured paper depict the heather and other wild flowers growing among the grass. For the sky, torn magazine paper was used in shades of blue, white and grey, then glossed using water-based sealer.*

Several years later, James decided to create a larger artwork to showcase the weird and wonderful rock formations using different techniques. His first step was to sketch out the rocks and paths. Then he used various materials to give a surreal look and a variety of textures.

The overall landscape came together as each component of the collage filled the scene. At the final stage, he used water-based sealer to better secure the strings and fabrics to the canvas.

James completed two similar long canvases to showcase the stunning Brimham Rocks landscape.

ARMCHAIR TRAVELLER

James has never previously wanted to travel overseas and cannot remember a journey made to America for medical advice when he was very young. However, he considers himself very fortunate to have friends and contacts from countries all over the world. He has found it interesting to hear about these new places and thanks everyone who has sent him used scratchcards from abroad. He always feels inspired when he receives them and sets about creating artwork that reflects something about each country.

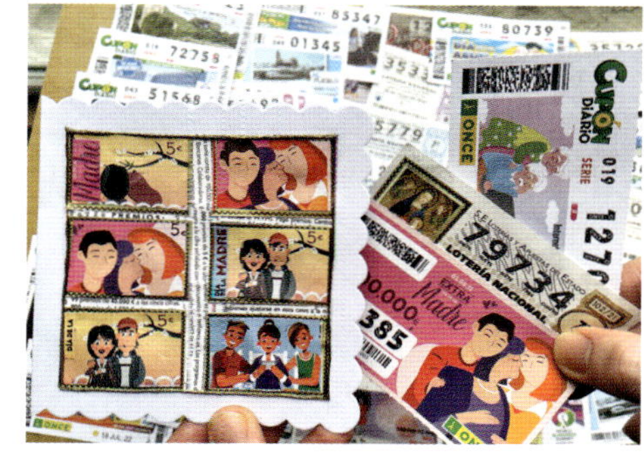

▲ *Some of the ONCE cards that James was sent, along with a collaged Mother's Day card.*

▼ *Collage of the forest using fabric and Spanish scratchcards.*

SPAIN

James' Spanish friend Marisa sent him some used Spanish scratchcards that a kind attendant at a kiosk for the Organización Nacional de Ciegos Españoles (ONCE) had been collecting for him. The ONCE organisation sell the scratchcards to help people who are blind or visually impaired. When Marisa also included paper lottery tickets, James decided to make some special Mother's Day greeting cards for the attendant at the kiosk, which Marisa took back during her next visit to Spain.

Marisa also sent James some beautiful photographs that a friend had taken of trees in a forest shrouded in an atmospheric mist. Immediately inspired by these scenes, James lightly collaged one of the images. Using thin strips of Spanish scratchcards and twisted threads to form more texture on the bark and by pulling apart some green fabric for the foliage until only the bare fibres were left, he was able to create a very fluffy effect. It was finally smoothed out with PVA glue.

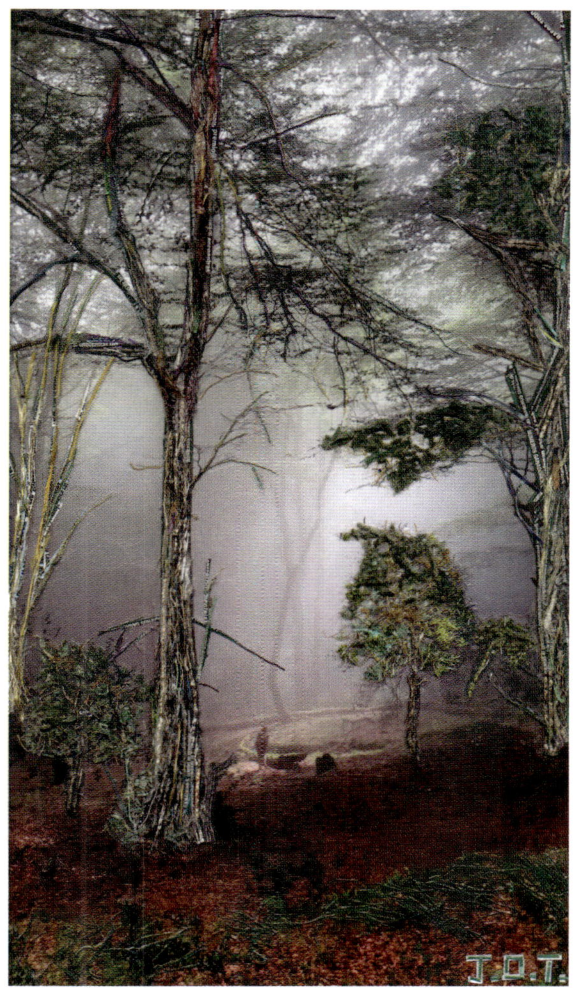

PORTUGAL

This photo collage of Porto uses small pieces of blue fabric for the River Douro, squares of green and yellow recycled magazine paper for leaves and smaller rectangles of recycled scratchcards and magazines (sent by a Portuguese acquaintance) for the bushes. The use of Portuguese symbols and words adds shape, texture and detail to the artwork, as well as meaning and context.

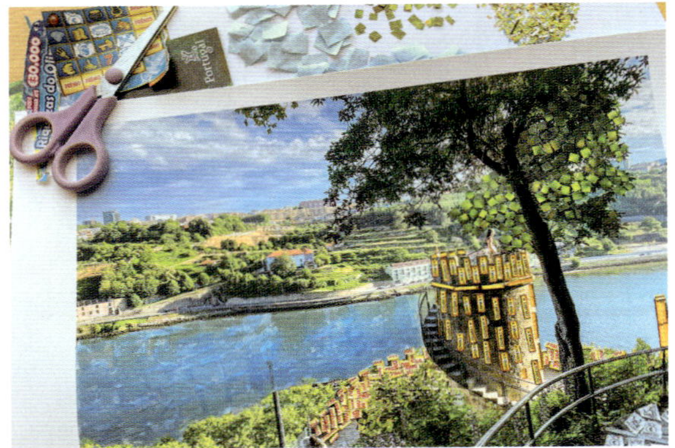

▲ *The Porto collage in progress.*

NEW ZEALAND

A contact from New Zealand sent James some of their national scratchcards and a photograph of a park in Auckland. James selected the best colours, symbols and words for the photo collage, cut them out and laid them in place. In this way, he could move the pieces around until the positioning was right. Then he attached the kiwi birds before building colour into the branches on the left-hand side as he felt they looked dull and lacking in life. When collaging on photos, James often looks for areas he feels need improvement, adding in texture and tone to give a three-dimensional appearance.

UNITED STATES OF AMERICA

Several of James' pieces have links to the USA – for example *In Unison* (see pages 86–7) and *By Moonlight* (see page 118–19). He also created a heavily collaged photograph of *An American Home* using scratchcards collected from Maryland and Tennessee. There are dollar signs on the trunk and branches of the tree and James cut up green magazine paper with pinking shears to give an effective impression of oak leaves.

▶ *Collage using scratchcards from New Zealand.*

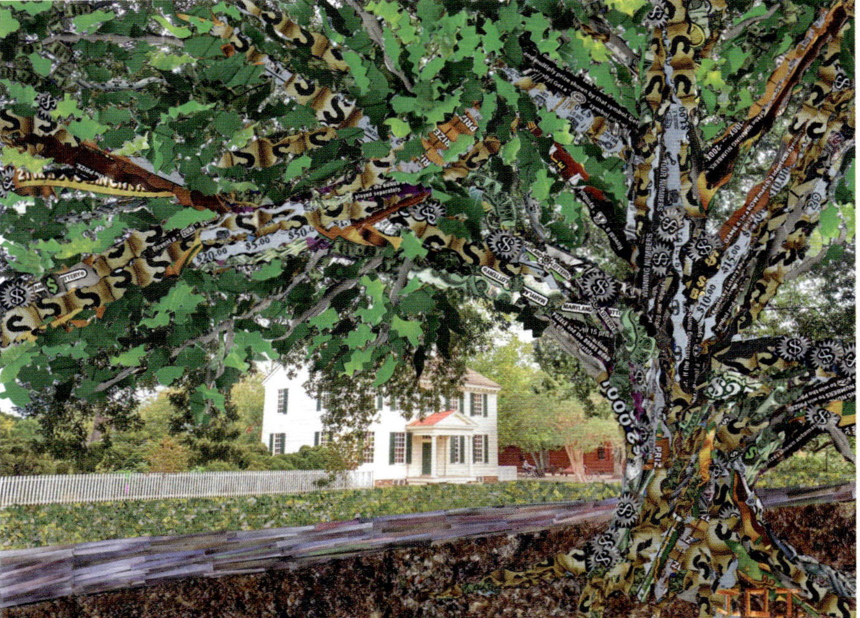

◀ *An American Home.*

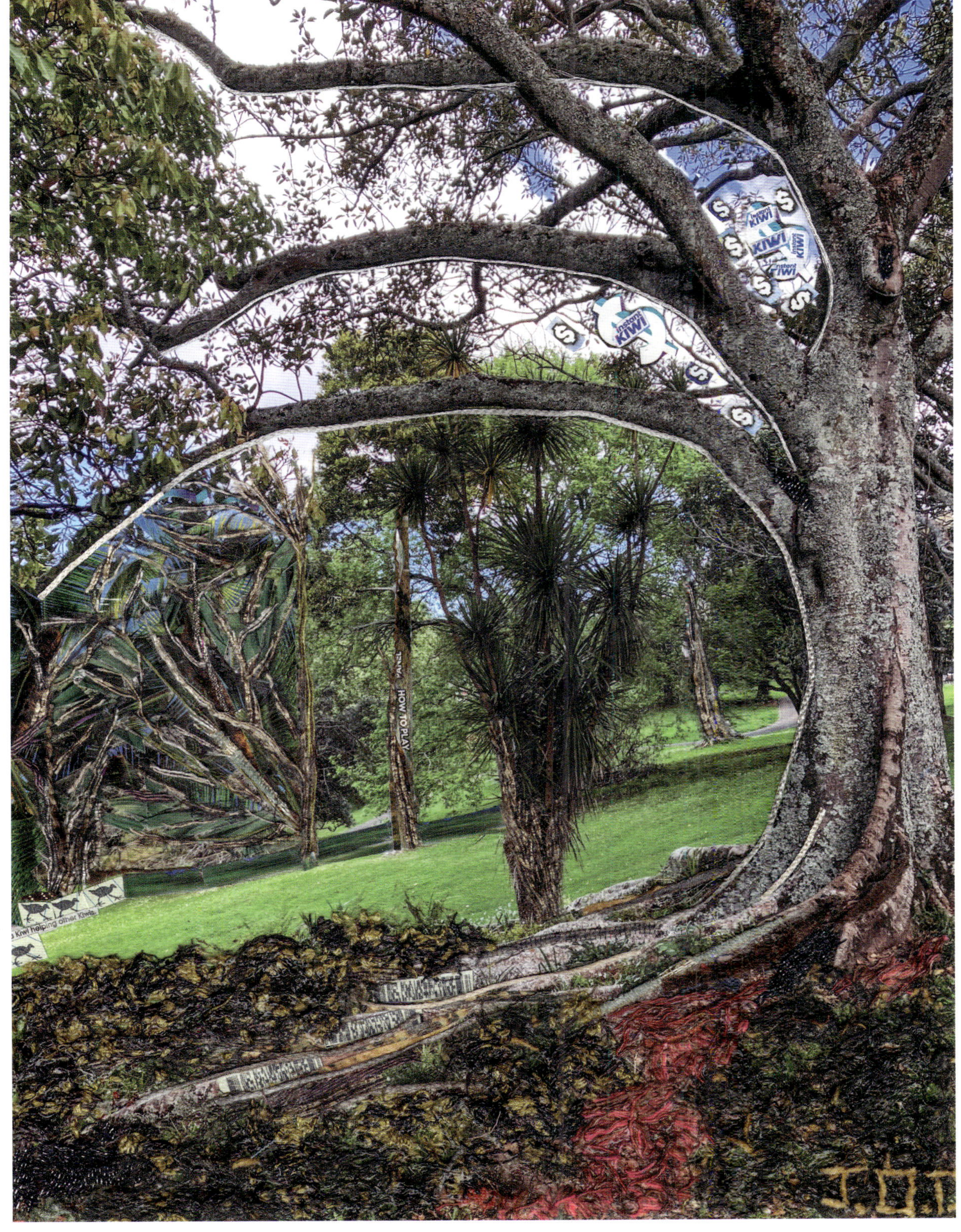

FRANCE

James bought a second-hand A3 mounted photograph of a rustic French house and bicycle at a car boot sale and collaged it to make *Chez l'Artiste*. Unfortunately, he didn't have any French scratchcards but he did have an old French art magazine. James tore out relevant words about galleries, art exhibitions, studios and even collage, while tiny pieces of green magazine created a border of grass.

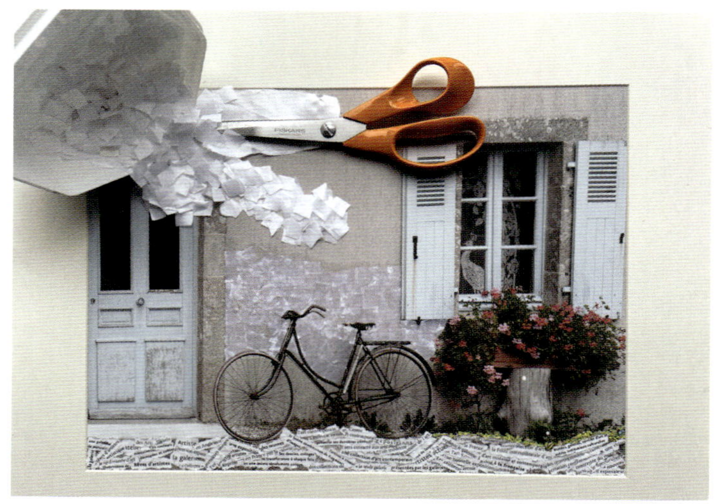

▲ *French-inspired collage in progress.*

▼ *Chez l'Artiste.*

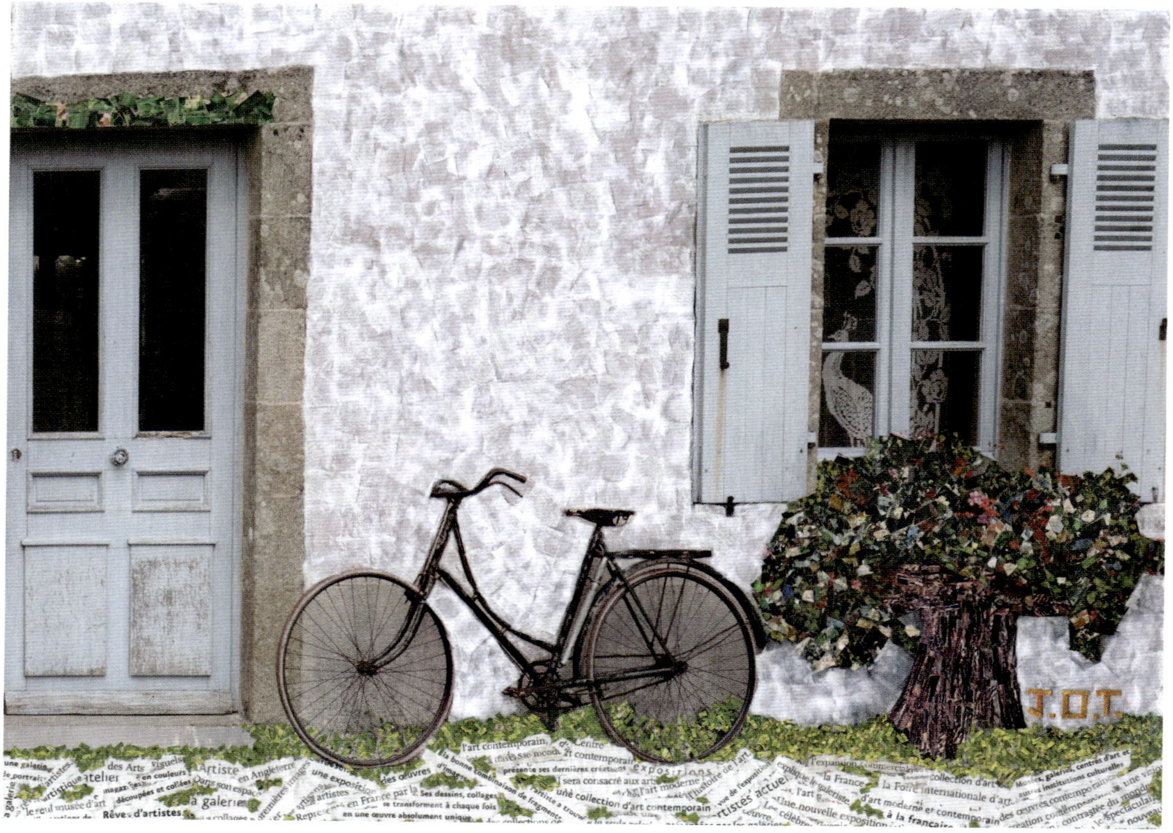

ITALY

One of the places most vulnerable to global warming is the fragile Italian island of Venice, 'floating' precariously in the lagoon on the north-east coast. When James' friends visited the city, he asked them to take a photograph of one of the few gardens on the island. This beautiful shot was taken from a small bridge in the San Marco district.

James used some Italian scratchcards his friends had obtained and sorted them into a palette of colours and styles. He also prepared lengths of thread that he could use to highlight certain aspects of the photograph. As his mother had also visited Venice some years before, he was able to add a personal touch by using some of her old photographs. From these, he cut up sections of blue and grey sky to stick over the canal water and photos of old buildings from other parts of the city to apply over the bare plaster of the apartments on the right. The very convincing canal water is a mix of blues and greys taken from the skies in the small photographs.

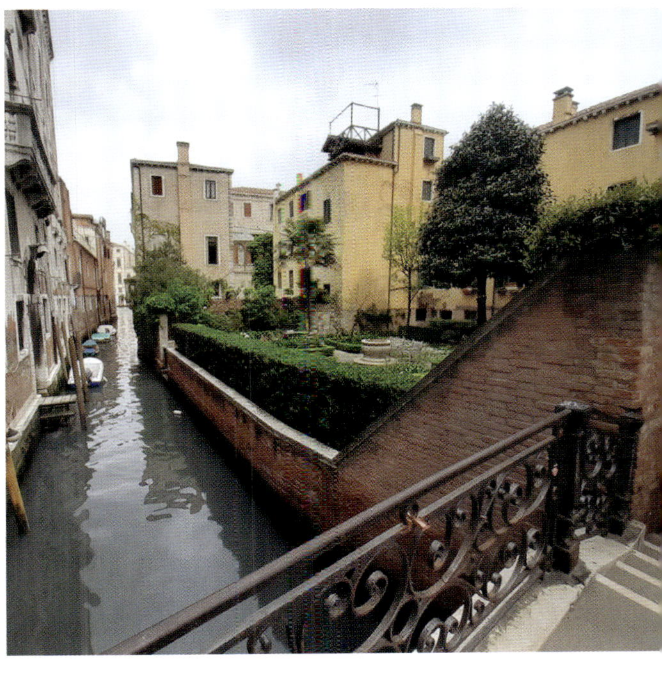

▲ *The original picture of Venice.*

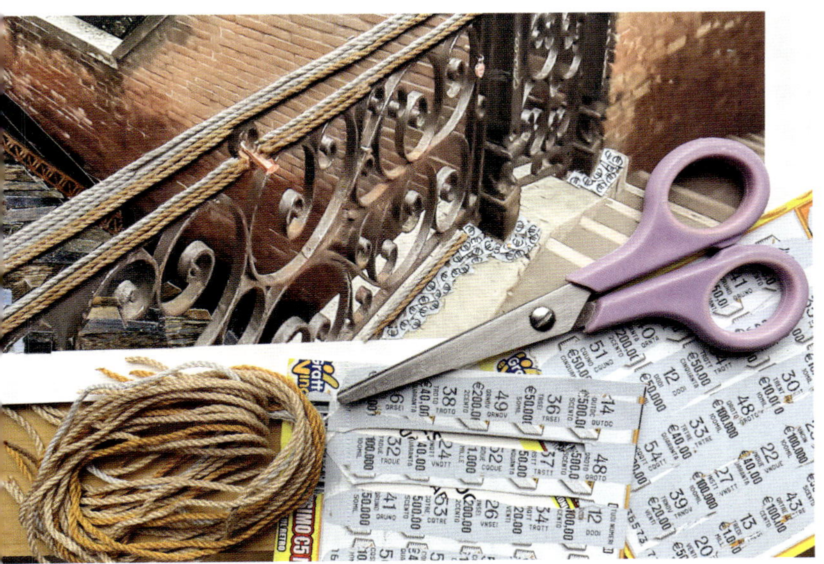

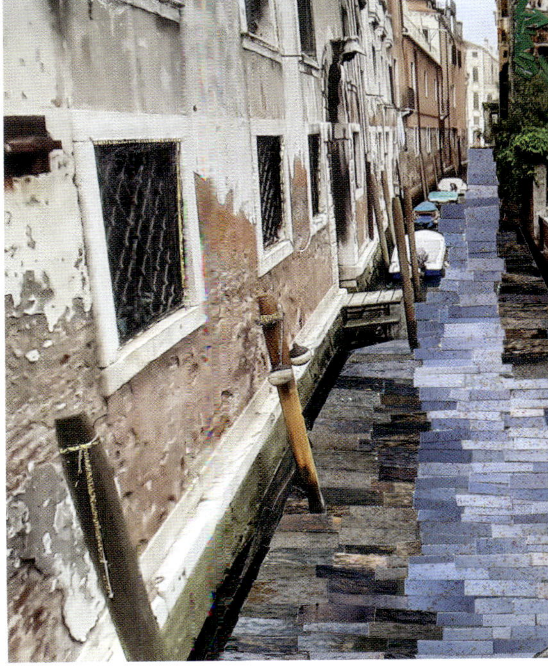

▲ ▶ *Details of **A Garden in Venice** in progress, showing how the threads were used on the railing and the effective use of cut-up photographs for the water.*

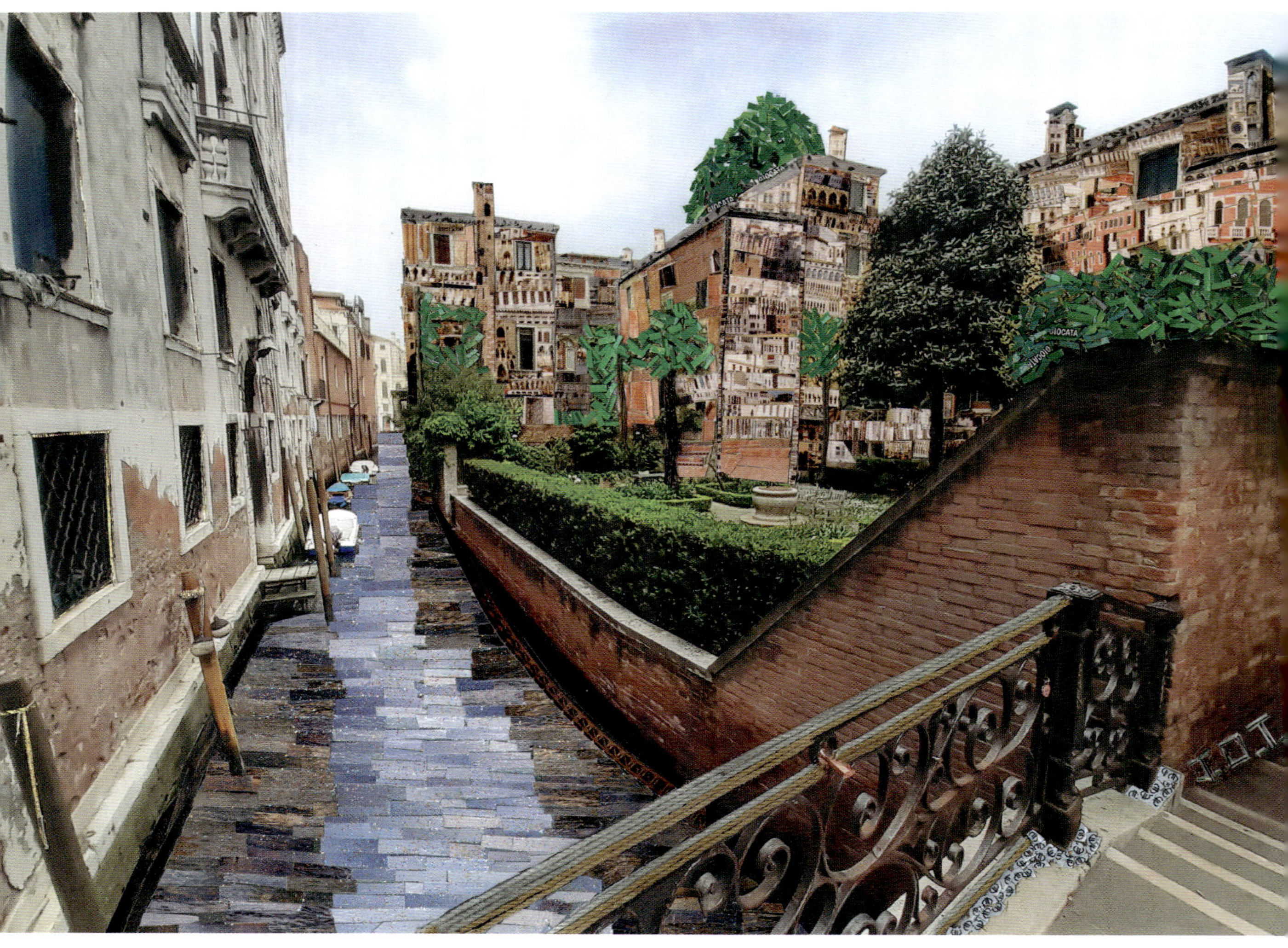

He also added some gold threads on the left-hand side as highlights for the windows and mooring posts.

    James is extremely grateful to the various friends and acquaintances who have given him scratchcards, tickets and leaflets from overseas for his art. He enjoys explaining to visitors at his exhibitions that these pieces have come about thanks to his contacts who travel abroad. He hopes that when people look at them, they can share in his sense of wonder in the places beyond our doorsteps.

▲ *A Garden in Venice.*

Conclusion

When James was a child, his mother was informed that he was always likely to remain 'low functioning', language that is often considered stigmatising today. She refused to listen and with the positive influences of professionals and organisations involved with James' therapy and education, as well as friends and family encouraging his special interests, he has grown to be an incredibly talented young man. This is actually a story of someone on a pathway to success, and it demonstrates that autistic people should never give up, or be given up on.

There were many difficulties for James at school and college, pointing to a need for greater understanding about autism and better training. Now, James has the opportunity to make a difference and speak up for disabled and neurodivergent children through the Council for Disabled Children and SENDIASS, the Special Educational Needs and Disability Information Advice and Support Service, where young people's views are welcomed.

Encouraging an interest in nature for children is important, and a series of positive people and experiences helped James to flourish. He developed his interests further when offered voluntary work with the National Trust and other outdoor settings; a family friend bought James his first I-Spy Birds book; having a supportive, encouraging art teacher boosted James' confidence to feel able to display some of his artwork in the school hall, leading to his first exhibition at the age of 15. Significant encouragements such as these have all helped him progress, as one thing leads to another.

The natural world is also an extension of the idea of a sensory room for someone with autism. Noticing smells, listening to birdsong and crunching leaves, feeling the bark of trees and looking at all the sights and colours are important sensory experiences. James likes to have his mobile phone switched off during these times so he isn't disturbed by phone calls and text messages. Everyone is in a rush nowadays and time disappears so quickly.

We should all really take a leaf out of James' book by spending more time out in nature for walks or to sit and enjoy time in woodland areas. There is such significance to looking after the environment and looking for the things it can give us in return.

Organisations mentioned in the text:

Alzheimer's Society (www.alzheimers.org.uk)

Beamish: The Living Museum of the North (www.beamish.org.uk)

Bradford Industrial Museum (www.bradfordmuseums.org/bradford-industrial-museum)

Bradford School of Art (www.bradfordcollege.ac.uk/bradford-school-of-art)

Caudwell Children (www.caudwellchildren.com)

COP26 One Step Greener initiative – https://webarchive.nationalarchives.gov.uk/ukgwa/20230312075614/https://together-for-our-planet.ukcop26.org/onestepgreener-ambassadors/)

Corn Close Care Farm (www.cornclosecarefarm.com)

The Donkey Sanctuary (www.thedonkeysanctuary.org.uk)

Drusillas Park Zoo (www.drusillas.co.uk)

Encaustic Art UK (www.encausticart.co.uk)

Farleys House and Gallery (www.farleyshouseandgallery.co.uk)

Fishpond Wood (www.whitewoodswellbeing.co.uk)

Great British Racing (www.greatbritishracing.com)

Hesketh Farm Park at Bolton Abbey (www.heskethfarmpark.co.uk)

Horticap (www.horticap.org)

Level Centre (www.levelcentre.com)

National Coal Mining Museum for England (www.ncm.org.uk)

National Park Authority (www.nationalparks.uk)

National Trust (search for Fountains Abbey, Fountains Hall or Brimham Rocks at www.nationaltrust.org.uk)

ONCE (www.once.es)

Paradise Park and Gardens (www.paradisepark.co.uk)

Pontefract Races (www.pontefract-races.co.uk)

Project Art Works (www.projectartworks.org)

Pyramid Educational Consultants (www.pecs-unitedkingdom.com)

SJ Equestrian Centre (www.sjequestrian.co.uk)

Raystede Centre for Animal Welfare, Lewes (www.raystede.org)

Saltaire World Heritage Site (www.saltairevillage.info)

The Station Gallery (www.thestation.co.uk)

The Tree Council (https://treecouncil.org.uk/)

Thirsk Racecourse (www.thirskracecourse.net)

Thorp Perrow Arboretum (www.thorpperrow.com)

Towner Eastbourne (https://townereastbourne.org.uk) (Formerly Towner Art Gallery)

Yorkshire Arboretum (https://www.yorkshirearboretum.org/)

Yorkshire Contemporary (www.yorkshirecontemporary.org) (Formerly The Tetley Gallery, Leeds)

York Theatre Royal (www.yorktheatreroyal.co.uk)

Zen Sensory (www.zensbsensory.co.uk)

Other helpful organisations:

Ambitious About Autism (www.ambitiousaboutautism.org.uk): UK charity that strives to improve opportunities for children and young people on the autistic spectrum.

ASLTIP (www.asltip.com): The Association of Speech and Language Therapists in Independent Practice provides information and a contact point for members of the public searching for a private speech and language therapist.

Autism Eye (www.autismeye.com): Magazine giving useful autism information and advice.

Autism in Racing (www.racingtogether.co.uk/autism-in-racing): The

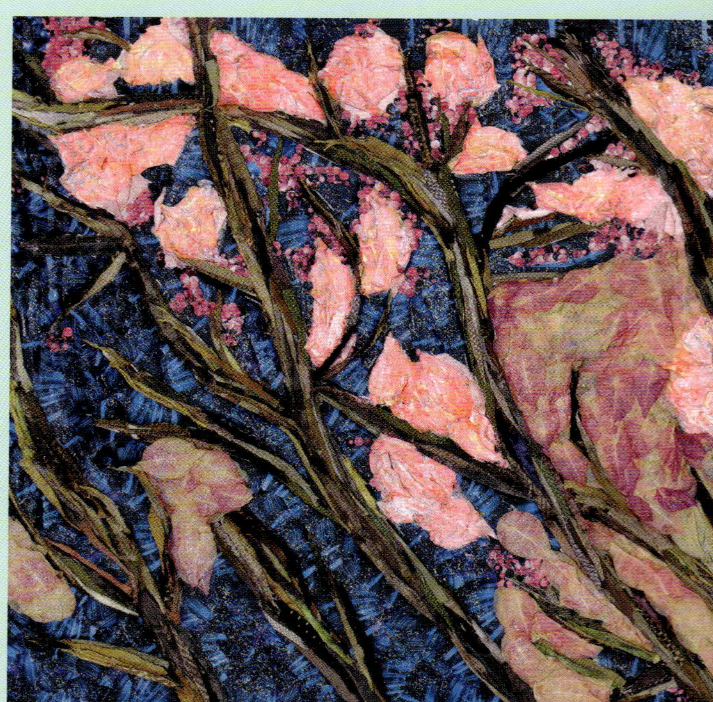

▶ *The upper canvas of the cherry tree in blossom composite artwork (see pages 36–7), produced for the Caudwell Children charity.*

idea of racing broadcaster Bobby Beevers, which was brought to life in 2021 as a collaboration between Bobby, Racing Together and the RCA. It works to increase autism awareness and has installed sensory rooms at racecourses such as at Aintree, Ascot, Cheltenham and Pontefract.

Autism Society, USA (www.autismsociety.org): Connects people to the resources they need through education, advocacy, support, information and referral, and community programming.

The Autism Trust (www.theautismtrust.org.uk): Provides employment training opportunities that allow people on the autistic spectrum to lead fulfilling lives and make a positive contribution to society.

Autistic Minds (www.autisticminds.org.uk): Empowers and equips autistic adults to advocate for themselves, by improving access to support, education, employment and social opportunities.

Council for Disabled Children (www.councilfordisabledchildren. org.uk): Provides the Information, Advice and Support Services Network (IASSN) to ensure that disabled and SEND children and young people can get impartial information, advice and support.

HANDLE (www.handle.org): The Holistic Approach to NeuroDevelopment and Learning Efficiency looks beyond limiting labels and provides tools that can enable and empower every human being to live the most stress-free life possible.

MENCAP (www.mencap.org.uk/learning-disability-explained/ conditions-linked-learning-disability/autism-and-aspergers-syndrome): Charity that offers assistance to people with learning disabilities.

Mental Health Awareness Week (www.mind.org.uk/get-involved/mental-health-awareness-week): Promotes awareness and understanding of mental health and various conditions that affect the mind and behaviour.

National Autistic Society (www.autism.org.uk): Provides support, guidance and advice, as well as campaigning for improved rights, services and opportunities to help create a society that works for autistic people.

Royal College of Occupational Therapists (www.rcot.co.uk): Occupational therapy helps people make adjustments to their lives to help deal with the challenges of daily activities and environment.

Scope (www.scope.org.uk): Information and emotional support for disabled people, campaigning to create a fairer society.

SENDIASS (www.kids.org.uk/sendiass-home): SENDIASS stands for Special Educational Needs and Disabilities Information Advice and Support Service. A free, impartial, and confidential service offering information to young people with special educational needs and disabilities (SEND) and to their parents and carers.

World Autism Awareness Day (www.un.org/en/observances/ autism-day): Early each April, this United Nations enterprise promotes the affirmation and promotion of consolidation of all human rights and fundamental freedoms for autistic people on an equal basis with others.

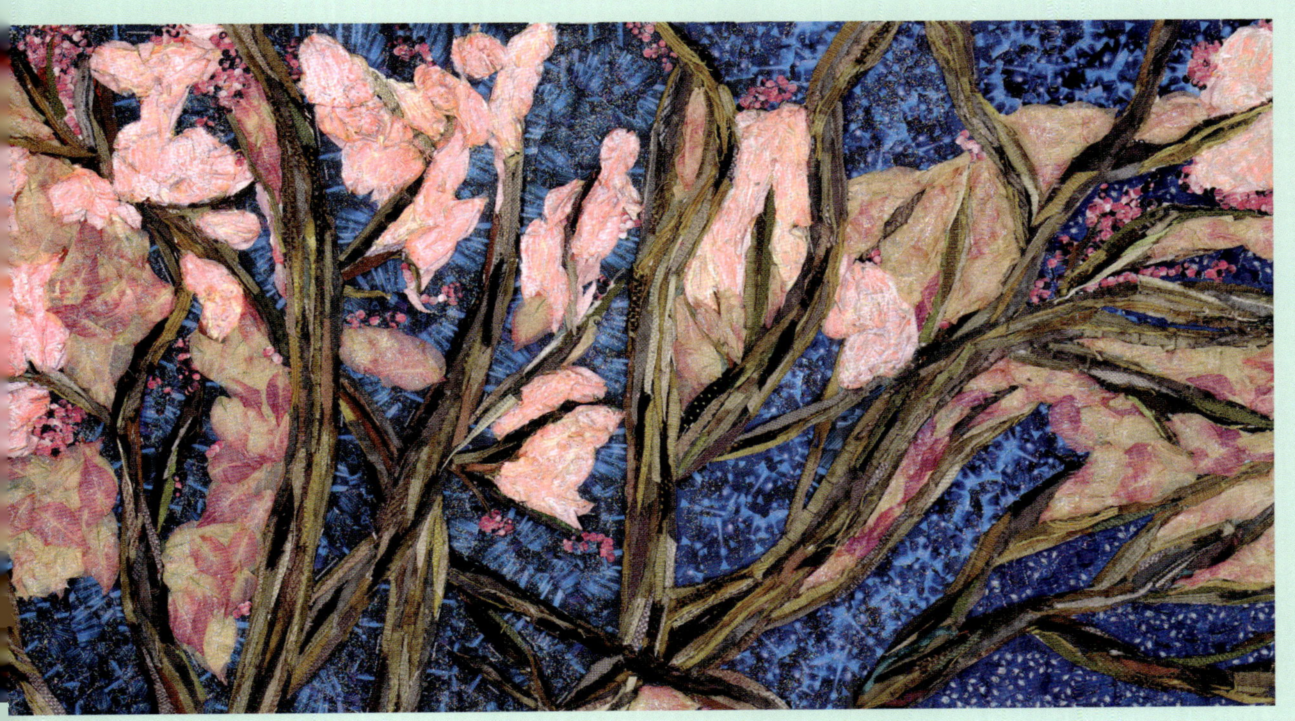

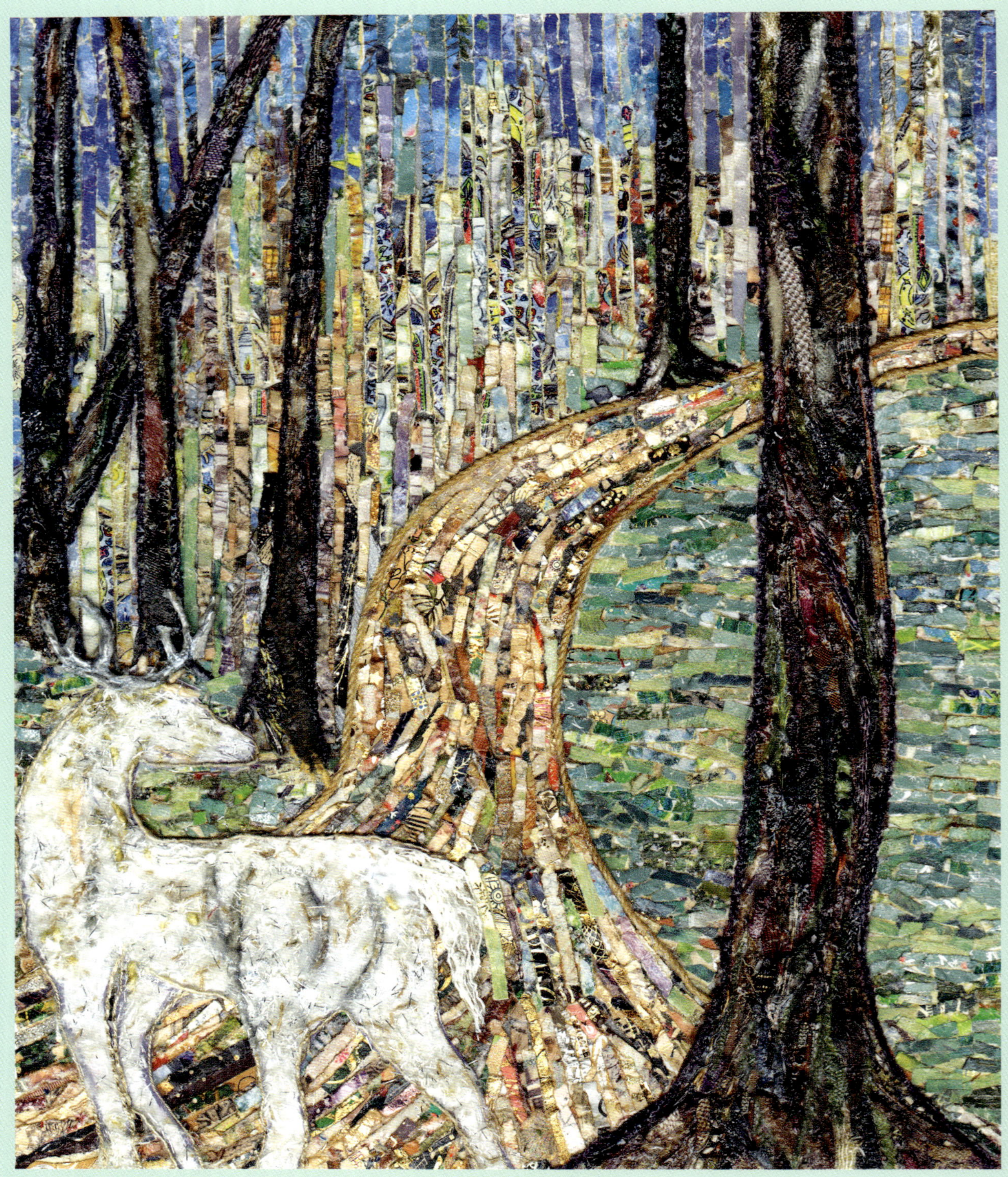

Memories of White Hart Lane. *Created for mum's brother, David Thomas (1959–2024). He was a keen supporter of Tottenham Hotspur F.C.*